THE OTHER
JAPAN

An East Gate Book

THE OTHER

JAPAN

POSTWAR REALITIES

Edited with an introduction by
E. Patricia Tsurumi for the
Bulletin of Concerned Asian Scholars

M. E. Sharpe, Inc.
Armonk, New York
London, England

An East Gate Book

Copyright © 1988 by the *Bulletin of Concerned Asian Scholars*

First published in the United States in 1988 by M. E. Sharpe, Inc.
80 Business Park Drive, Armonk, New York 10504

Available in the United Kingdom and Europe from
M. E. Sharpe, Publishers, 3 Henrietta Street, London WC2E 8LU.

Library of Congress Cataloging-in-Publication Data

The Other Japan.

    1. Japan—Social conditions—1945–   . 2. Japan—
Economic conditions—1945–   . I. Tsurumi,
E. Patricia, 1938–   . II. Bulletin of concerned
Asian scholars.
HN723.5.086   1988   306′.0952   87-23365
ISBN 0-87332-450-1
ISBN 0-87332-451-X (pbk.)

Printed in the United States of America

Contents

THE OTHER JAPAN

Introduction

The Other Japan: Postwar Realities

E. Patricia Tsurumi

The North American public has been offered a steady stream of seemingly endless scholarly and nonscholarly books, articles, and productions in both print and electronic media about "the Japanese challenge" to Western industrialized countries in the post-World War II era. Although these accounts have sometimes touched upon disadvantages of doing things "the Japanese way," on the whole, whether serious or as entertainment—from Ezra Vogel's *Japan as Number One* to Paramount Pictures' *Gung Ho*—the message has been overwhelmingly positive. Such attractive portrayals of how Japan supposedly functions as a polity, economy, and society, as Herbert P. Bix pointed out in an incisive review of Vogel's book, are amazingly one-sided.[1] Without the other side of postwar Japan's remarkable story, half-truths and distortions in the highly affirmative reports breed misconception and misunderstanding.

This book is about the other side of the story. In Western and Japanese voices, all the selections in it lay bare the prices paid for the road modern Japan has taken. Some of them offer hints regarding different routes that are not yet blocked.

Analyses and literary portraits in this volume concentrate more on existing realities then they do on potentials for yet-to-be-explored developments in Japan's postwar history. Basically they draw the reader's attention to the unresolved conflicts beneath the smooth surface of managed capitalism in Japan today. Yet, as they fill in awkward gaps in our understanding of contemporary Japan, they underline the urgency of discovering alternatives. Some of the articles do deal with experience that contains seeds for alternative development. Joe Moore's study of labor struggles immediately after the war, when wage workers took control of production in their work places to gain security and dignity, describes a vastly different situation from that of the enterprise-based unions of today's corporate giants. But those struggles are every bit as much a part of Japan's history as the latter. Daizen Victoria shows us that the Zen Buddhism used by large companies to enforce conformity, much as feudal lords and prewar militarists once used Zen, has also begun to produce some individuals who will "work toward the ultimate demise of state power and the emergence of a communal society free of the capitalist mode of private property."

To the casual observer, a demand that highly industrialized Japan drastically restructure itself may sound wildly utopian. In their history, however, the Japanese people have demonstrated an extraordinary capacity for changing course. There was that momentous decision to discard feudal politics of the Tokugawa regime (usually symbolized by the Meiji Restoration of 1868) long before the defeat by foreign powers in 1945 swept away political, economic, and social edifices.

In 1945 the first reaction of most of the populace to the emperor's public announcement that the war was over was shock. Susan Phillips' essay introduces us to Miyamoto Yuriko's autobiographical documentation of ordinary people struggling to come out of that shock. Stripped down to their basic humanity, the resilient women in Miyamoto's novel draw upon long-dormant strengths to reorient themselves to the beginnings of a new society. The industrial workers Moore writes about take vigorous action to shape the direction that society will take. Their drive for democratization of enterprises and for participation in management was ultimately halted by the American occupation forces that ruled Japan immediately after the war and by the comeback of the Japanese right wing which the occupation facilitated, but it refused to disappear. Driven underground and often invisible, it has continued to surface as a minority trait: in the 1970s militant metalworkers in South Osaka took over a number of small factories and ran them under workers' management, and in 1985 dissident auto workers at huge Nissan withdrew from their company's union to form a Nissan local of a maverick union in order to fight Nissan management's labor "rationalization" programs, which had the cooperation of the company union.[2]

The shadow of the atomic bomb, which devastated Nagasaki and Hiroshima, is another legacy of the end of the war that, although it may have grown less conspicuous, refuses to fade. Memoirs of children who endured the bombing remind us how very young some of the victims were. Hayashi Kyoko's autobiographical "Two Grave Markers" sensitively explores the tragic terrain familiar to so many young victims and their families. John Dower's article is about artists who creatively use their personal encounters with the atomic horror to remind Japanese children and adults what nuclear war means. The contributions of Janet Bruin, Kamata Sadao, and Stephen Salaff relate how survivors of Nagasaki and Hiroshima have also dedicated themselves to anti-nuclear activism. The Nagasaki Association of Young Hibakusha Women and the Osaka *hibakusha* women demonstrate again the determined strength of postwar Japanese women.[3]

Before the Land Reform of 1946–47 ended the landlord-tenant class relationships that had dominated the countryside since premodern times, Japan was largely a country of peasant farmers. Since the reform, agriculture and rural life have changed drastically. Bernard Bernier reminds us that the agricultural population, more than 48 percent of the total population in 1950, was reduced to less than 20 percent of the total population by 1977. As giant food combines took over agriculture, production became organized on an industrial scale, and formerly independent cultivators became wage workers in large food factories using chemical feeds for animals and other substances that are poisoning consumers. Since Bernier wrote his article, a "clean food movement" has sparked some consumer resistance and health food stores and cooperatives can now be found throughout Japan, but the dominant trends he describes have grown stronger.

Rob Steven's analysis of the Japanese working class goes far beyond the clichés in the Western press about extreme diligence and loyalty to employers. He shows us how rankings by sex, age, and education are used to channel Japanese workers into classes and factions within the working class. In addition to estimating some of the costs of this system—especially to those workers who are not members of the labor aristocracy—Steven outlines possible strategies for changing the situation. Strategies must involve a united attack upon sexism and elitism because women, who have been replacing the men who move out of the bottom layers of the working class, fill most of the ranks of Japan's industrial reserve army, laboring for low pay with little job security, few benefits, and poor working conditions. Despite the tremendous power of elitism and sexism, Steven is not unhopeful: he sees a potential for revolutionary change in both the activities and organizational structures of Japanese women's organizations and in minority developments within the Japanese labor movement.[4]

The sad laborers of Tokyo's Sanya flophouse district about whom Brett de Bary writes have much in common with the unloved, aimless bank teller in Shimizu Ikkō's short business novel: both represent sordid little side streets, essential to but unseen from the great intersections of the brightly lit Japanese business world. That world proves itself able to bend even the free spirit of Zen Buddhism, but, as Daizen Victoria points out, Japanese capitalism's contemporary manipulation of Zen follows a pattern begun by medival feudal lords and carried on by militarist governments before and during World War II.

As Ishimure Michiko tells us about the boy Yamanaka Kuhei and others with Minamata disease, industrial progress becomes a deadly nightmare, ravaging the innocent in natural and human worlds alike. The nightmare grows completely out of control when the high-tech road stops abruptly at the nuclear power plants Yuki Tanaka describes. In these plants are the nuclear power plant gypsies who wander from plant to plant, pariahs to their fellow citizens because they do the frighteningly dirty work of the nuclear power industry that is the logical outcome of the gargantuan appetites of Japanese capitalism. The economic miracles can be kept going—but only by a bitter sea of poison, capable of destroying land, air, and water as well as generations of human beings.

Notes

1. Herbert P. Bix, "Japan at the End of the Seventies; The Treatment of the Political in Recent Japanology," *Bulletin of Concerned Asian Scholars* 12:1 (Jan.-Mar. 1980), pp. 53–60.

2. See Sasahara Kyoko, "Labor Unity and Militancy in South Osaka," *AMPO* 13:4 (1981), pp. 2–7, and Kayama Masao, "Nissan: Maverick Union Takes on Management over Plant Closure," *AMPO* 18:1 (1986), pp. 69–70.

3. See Arata Osada, compl., *Children of the A-Bomb* (New York: G. P. Putnam's, 1959); Iri and Toshi Maruki, *The Hiroshima Panels* (Saitama, Japan: Maruki Gallery for the Hiroshima Panels Foundation, 1984); (Toshi Maruki, *Hiroshima no Pika* (New York: Lothrop, Lee and Shepard Books, 1980); Keiji Nakazawa, *Barefoot Gen*, vols. 1 and 2 (Tokyo: Project Gen, 1979).

4. He has argued this at greater length elsewhere. See Rob Steven, *Classes in Contemporary Japan* (Cambridge, England: Cambridge University Press, 1983), esp. pp. 217–329.

Beyond Borders: Class Struggle and Feminist Humanism in *Banshū heiya*

by Susan Phillips

Introduction

Miyamoto Yuriko was born in Tokyo as Chūjō Yuri on 13 February 1899. Her father, Seiichirō, a graduate of Tokyo Imperial University, became one of Japan's leading modern architects; her mother, Yoshie, was the daughter of the famous moral philosopher Nishimura Shigeki, and a graduate of the aristocratic Gakushūin school. During Yuriko's early childhood, especially during the years when her father was away in England studying at Cambridge University, the Chūjō family income was modest. But after Japan's victory in the Russo-Japanese War and the stimulus it contributed to Japan's modernization, her family attained upper-middle-class affluence.

Yuriko excelled in Japanese literature and composition at what later became the middle school attached to Ochanomizu Women's University. Brought up in a supportive liberal home, she was somewhat unhappy with the restrictions that were imposed on her at this prestigious but conservative institution. Very interested in literature herself, Yuriko's mother encouraged her daughter's creative aptitudes. The Chūjō library was well stocked with the Japanese classics as well as the books of European art and literature that her father had brought home from England. What Yuriko could not find at home was available in the Ueno Library where she frequently went when she played truant from high school. Wide-ranging literary discussions and artistic endeavors were encouraged at home, reinforcing her sense of alienation from authoritarian educational and social institutions.

In 1916 Yuriko began studying English literature at Japan Women's University. But after the publication of her first novel, *Mazushiki hitobito no mure* (A group of poor people), the seventeen-year-old girl left school during her first term. The overnight success of this novel, thoughts of embarking on a serious literary career, and her deep sense of malaise with the school environment probably helped bring her to this decision.

Although she was brought up amid few material discomforts, Miyamoto Yuriko's early works deal with the poverty-stricken lives of the lower classes, landless peasants, and the vanishing race of aboriginal Ainu.[1] *Mazushiki hitobito no mure* is set in a Tohoku farming village where her paternal grandmother was a landowner and where Yuriko spent her summers as a child. The story of the Ainu, *Kaze ni notte kuru koropokkuru* (Koropokkuru riding the wind), was written after several months of research in Hokkaido where she had spent the first three years of her life. Both the White Birch Society (*Shirakabaha*), which gained prominence after 1910 with Mushanokōji Saneatsu at its head, and its offshoot, the Blue Stockings Association (*Seitosha*), in which Nogami Yaeko was active, influenced the humanistic concerns of these early works.

In the fall of 1918 Yuriko accompanied her father to New York, where she studied for a time at Columbia University. There she met Araki Shigeru, fifteen years her senior, who was a scholar of ancient Persian languages. Shortly after they married the following year, Yuriko returned to Japan to be with her mother who had fallen ill. Araki joined her in Japan six months later. This marriage—which ended in divorce five years afterwards—became the subject of her second major work, *Nobuko*, published in 1926. Yuriko's life with Araki proved a disappointment, since in temperament and outlook they were fundamentally incompatible. Romantic love, which she had hoped would provide the emotional and economic stability for her literary career, proved an illusion. Eventually she concluded that middle class marriage crippled rather than encouraged women's intellectual and spiritual growth.

In terms of her career, marriage to Araki was detrimental, and her five marriage years were one of her most unproductive periods. Instead of writing, Yuriko became involved in philanthropic efforts, including relief work for victims of the Russian famine of 1922 and the Kanto earthquake the following year. Though politically uncommitted, she did make the acquaintance of a number of key people in the Japanese intelligentsia of the day who influenced her future political interests and writing career. One of these was the established writer Nogami

Yaeko, who introduced her to Yuasa Yoshiko, a well-known scholar and translator of Russian literature. Following her divorce, Yuriko lived with Yoshiko, and during this period she completed *Nobuko*.

To mark the tenth anniversary of the Russian Revolution in 1927, scholars and artists from around the world were invited to the USSR. Yuasa Yoshiko was among them and Yuriko decided to accompany her there, using the next three years to search for new directions. Embarking on an intensive study of Soviet society, the Marxist classics, and the new socialist literature, Yuriko was greatly influenced by her sojourn there. She was particularly impressed with the new role of women in the Soviet Union as it initiated its first Five-Year Plan. Equal rights, the protection of motherhood and children, the enthusiastic acceptance of women in the workforce, and the positive role of the state in universal education all became topics for her later essays on women's issues in Japan. Not only did the two women travel extensively throughout the USSR during their stay, but they also met Yuriko's family in Europe in 1929 where they visited the major urban centers. Firsthand exposure to the poverty of Europe's working class, the social unrest there on the eve of the great stock market crash, and the rise of fascism hastened Yuriko's acceptance of socialism and her commitment to political activism.

Two additional unrelated incidents strongly influenced her. Shortly before her departure for the Soviet Union, the novelist Akutagawa Ryūnosuke shocked Japan's intelligentsia by committing suicide. And before Yuriko joined her family in Europe, her younger brother, to whom she was very close, also committed suicide.[2] In these two deaths she saw the impasse of modern intellectualism and its defeat in the face of emerging historical currents. As she saw it, the solution lay in political action. In his last letter to her, Yuriko's brother wrote: "Feel no hatred toward anything." In her personal journal, Yuriko responded:

> On the one hand, this unforeseen death—symbolizing the bankruptcy of the age—and on the other, the new Soviet society that I observed ablaze and advancing day and night, opened my eyes. I discovered a meaning, a shape and a direction which I could link to the struggle I had previously waged alone. In political action, I attained a completely different perspective. As an artist, I will never abandon my uncompromising stance toward the present social system. I will never abandon my ability to hate.[3]

Thus resolved, Yuriko returned to Japan in late 1930 to participate in the ongoing workers' movement.

By 1930 the proletarian literary movement was reaching its peak, and the All Japan Federation of Proletarian Arts (NAPF)[4] had just been organized. The economic depression following the 1927 Japanese stock market crash caused a sharp increase in urban unemployment and the bankruptcy of the farming population. As elsewhere, the spread of Japanese worker-peasant movements was greatly influenced by the Russian Revolution. The proletarian literary movement was also radicalized by the periodic arrest and detention, under the infamous Peace Preservation Law, of communists and political activists after 1928, and it evolved from a broad united front into a highly politicized organization directly controlled by Moscow and the outlawed Japanese Communist party.

After joining NAPF in 1931, Yuriko began to write articles and essays introducing the new Soviet society to Japan. She was elected to the standing committee of NAPF and put in charge of the Women's Bureau of the Writers' League. In

*Miyamoto Yuriko when she was a sixth grader.**

October of that year NAPF was reorganized as KOPF (Japan Proletarian Cultural Federation),[5] and Yuriko joined both its central committee and its women's committee. She also became the editor of the new publication, *Hataraku fujin* (Working women) and joined the illegal Communist party, keeping her membership secret until after the Pacific War. As various organizational activities continued to occupy much of her time, her literary output remained relatively low.

After joining the movement Yuriko met Miyamoto Kenji, whom she married in 1932. Yuriko was thirty-three years old at the time, and Kenji was a brilliant twenty-four-year-old economics graduate of Tokyo Imperial University. Yuriko, Kenji, and the proletarian writer Kobayashi Takiji became central figures in KOPF. But with the Manchurian Incident in the fall of 1931 and Japan's accelerated preparations for war, the government began vigorously suppressing political dissidents. In March 1932, a police roundup of leftists and social activists made life increasingly difficult for people connected with the worker and peasant causes. In April, Yuriko's activities in the proletarian literary movement led to her arrest and imprisonment for three months, and two months after their marriage, Kenji was forced underground. Attempting to destroy the proletarian literary movement and the Communist party which controlled it, the government initiated intensive anti-dissident measures. Yuriko was arrested again and Kobayashi Takiji was interrogated and murdered by the police. Kenji, a Communist party member, was sentenced to life

*The three photos in this article are courtesy of Susan Phillips and are from Setouchi Harumi, ed., *Hi to moeta joryū bungaku*, vol. 1 of *Onna no isshō jinbutsu kindai josei shi* (Tokyo: Kōdansha, 1980), pp. 147, 175, and 178.

imprisonment and remained incarcerated until the end of the Pacific War twelve years later.

Yuriko was never free from the threat of imprisonment. During her third detention in 1933, her mother fell seriously ill, and Yuriko was released to be at her deathbed. In 1935, she spent another seven months in jail, during which time her father died. Eventually she was tried for violations of the Peace Preservation Law but received only a four-year suspended sentence. This was probably because her Communist party membership remained a secret and also because her own health had so seriously deteriorated as a result of repeated internments that the government grew nervous about her possible death and martyrdom.

After the commencement of Sino-Japanese hostilities in 1937, members of the popular front were censored, and following the start of the Pacific War in 1941, freedom of speech for opponents of government policy was completely suspended. Yuriko therefore lost the right to publish until the end of the war. Imprisoned again in late 1941, she fell into a coma from extreme heat prostration the following summer, and given up for dead, she was released to her brother's home. She gradually improved, although her eyesight remained impaired for more than a year and by then her heart and liver were permanently damaged. Until her death in 1951, she never fully regained her health, and under such conditions writing became a perilous task.

Between 1932 and 1945 there were less than four years during which Yuriko was allowed to publish. Nevertheless, she continued to write. Her prison experiences were recorded in the novels *Senkyūhyaku sanjūninen no haru* (The spring of 1932) in 1933, and *Kokkoku* (Moment by moment) which was published posthumously. She also completed *Kowai no ikka* (The Kowai family) in 1934, and *Chibusa* (Breast) in 1935. In addition, she spent a great deal of time writing essays and articles on culture and society, writers and their works, women's issues, and literary criticism. Thousands of letters to her imprisoned husband also gave her an outlet for pent-up creative energies. A selection of these were published in 1949-50 under the title *Jūninen no tegami* (Twelve years of letters) and were considered by some critics to be literary works of merit.[6]

Unlike many communist writers of the period who recanted under government pressure or retreated into silence, Miyamoto Yuriko never succumbed to despair, nor did she abandon her "uncompromising stance toward the present social system." Her essay published in 1934, *Fuyu o kosu tsubomi* (The bud which survives winter), typifies her dogged attitude during the war years. Yuriko believed that like all winters this one would also eventually melt into a new spring, when the fragile buds of peace would blossom once again.[7]

The end of the Pacific War in August 1945 marked the beginning of the final stage in Miyamoto Yuriko's career. Political prisoners like Miyamoto Kenji were released and censorship was lifted. In a burst of energy Yuriko began working on *Banshū heiya* (The Banshu Plains), which appeared in August the following year, and *Fūchisō*, which was published that September. She also resumed her activities as an outspoken social critic and promoter of constitutional reforms and equal rights for women.

Yuriko's works were generally ignored before the war, both by the mainstream and by left-wing critics who considered her pre-KOPF novels to be petite bourgeois in nature.[8] After 1946, however, her anti-militarist activities during the 1930s and 1940s made her an instant heroine, and *Banshū heiya* and *Fūchisō* won the first postwar Mainichi Cultural Award.

Her high-profile role in a number of new postwar political and cultural organizations and her continuing literary activities played havoc with the fragile state of Yuriko's health. Dangerously high blood pressure and deteriorating eyesight forced her to retire from public life in 1947 to devote herself to writing. *Futatsu no niwa* (The two gardens) was completed in January 1947, and *Dōhyō* (Roadsign), her last novel completed one month before her death, was written between October 1947 and December 1950. During this time she also wrote some two thousand pages of essays on culture, society, and women's issues. A pioneer in the field of women's issues, her *Watakushitachi no kensetsu* (Our foundation) is her most representative work on the subject in the postwar period. On 21 January 1951, the eve of her fifty-second birthday, Miyamoto Yuriko died suddenly of cerebrospinal meningitis.

Japanese literary criticism tends to place a disproportionate weight on autobiographical influence in an author's work, especially in the case of Miyamoto Yuriko where the autobiographical element is pronounced. Active in the major social and political movements of her day, Miyamoto's life was greatly changed and in many ways typified the challenges facing modern intellectuals. These concerns prompted most modern Japanese critics to look to her personal life for clues to explain her literary development. Although relatively ignored by literary critics before the war, Miyamoto's progressive anti-government activities made her the darling of postwar literary circles, particularly the left wing which made a strong comeback during the early years of the American occupation. Consequently, the novels which expressed the strongest opposition to the militarist regime and which were written during the years when intellectuals suffered the most oppression became the primary focus of critical attention. As a result, the novels written between 1934 and 1945 are given a disproportionate amount of importance in her total career, resulting in her being pigeonholed as a proletarian writer.

Miyamoto Yuriko did play an important role in the Japanese proletarian literary movement, but her involvement was not the result of a radical political or artistic departure from her earlier so-called humanist period. Her early childhood was influenced by the enlightened Meiji environment in which she grew up, and her formative years were influenced by the beginnings of Taishō democracy. Her attraction to the radical politics of the thirties and forties was a gradual process and, seen within the context of her earlier works, was a smooth transition from a generalized humanism to feminism and class struggle. Miyamoto Yuriko neither made a sharp turn toward the proletarian literary movement, nor did she drift away from it once it had disbanded. Her early literary development carried the seeds for future points of contact with this movement, and while her writing was influenced by it, her works reveal a consistent direction which challenges the label of "proletarian writer," a label which restricts and diminishes the scope of her creative development and achievement. In my view, her feminist-humanist vision—passionate concern for the human potential in all people but particularly sensitive regarding women's problems—is as important as her support of collective social action.

One can see the cumulation of this development and achievement clearly in her important post–Pacific War novel, *Banshū heiya*. Since Miyamoto's novels are rarely analyzed from the standpoint of plot, characterization, or use of imagery, this paper will attempt to discuss these elements as they appear in *Banshū heiya*. *Banshū heiya* will be dealt with within the context of her total body of works.

Banshū heiya

Banshū heiya was the first novel Miyamoto Yuriko published after the Pacific War.[9] Despite her politicization in the proletarian literary movement during the 1930s and her subsequent distancing from the humanistic and feminist concerns expressed in such earlier works as *Nobuko*, Miyamoto never abandoned her commitment to women's issues. In *Banshū heiya*, feminist issues reemerge in altered form. This does not mean that the bitter experiences of the war years forced a rejection of earlier political and historical perspectives. Rather, in *Banshū heiya* one finds the merging of themes and concerns found scattered throughout her earlier works, creating a new sense of balance and maturity. Miyamoto's somewhat strident treatment of class issues during the war years gives way to individual character development and a sensitive portrayal of women's issues. And a concern for technical complexity is revealed in her use of imagery.

Banshū heiya opens on 15 August 1945, the day of Japan's unconditional surrender. Evacuated to the countryside during the fire bombing of Tokyo, Hiroko, the heroine, is living with her married brother in Fukushima. With the announcement of the war's end, Hiroko initially decides to visit her husband, Jukichi, who has been a political prisoner for the past twelve years. But on learning that her husband's younger brother is missing following the atomic bombing of Hiroshima, she instead joins her grieving mother-in-law and sister-in-law in Yamaguchi Prefecture. When the occupation forces announce the release of political prisoners, she returns to her home in Tokyo to await Jukichi's homecoming. The novel ends during this final journey.

Imagery in *Banshū heiya* makes three major shifts: from darkness to light, from silence to sound, and from paralysis to movement. Unlike Miyamoto's earlier novels where characters display inflexible social and political attitudes, characters in *Banshū heiya* vacillate between inactivity and action, negativity and positivity, and silence and communication. During the final pages of the novel, action, optimism, and communication become the dominant motifs.

In the first scene in *Banshū heiya*, when Japan's unconditional surrender is declared, silence dominates:

> Hiroko was alarmed by the desolation of her surroundings at that moment. The intense heat that August afternoon made the air burn and the fields and mountains were enveloped by the endless heat. There was not a sound in the village. Not even the sound of coughing. Hiroko sensed this with her whole being. From noon until one o'clock on August 15, the entire Japanese nation held back its hushed voices as an enormous page of history was turned without a sound.[10]

Moved at first by the silence, Hiroko gradually becomes critical of this seeming passivity, epitomized by her brother, Yukio, who throughout the war maintained that, " 'For people like me who, ultimately, have no power to do anything, it's better to listen to what they tell us.' As the war progressed this side of Yukio's character became even stronger."[11] Yukio, however, is not the only person to have hidden behind silence. Travelling to her mother-in-law's, Hiroko notices how quiet the overcrowded train is, as if the nation had been rendered mute and insensitive by Japan's

Miyamoto Yuriko at work on her book Dōhyō *in her study in 1949.*

defeat. In contrast, her friends, the Ayusawas, with whom she stays in Tokyo en route, display rare signs of vitality. And in the evening, when she hears the sound of wooden sandals and bicycle bells as people make their way to a summer festival, Hiroko realizes how long it has been since she has heard these once normal sounds of city life.

During the next leg of her journey to Yamaguchi, Hiroko observes more socializing among the train's passengers than previously. But when damaged rail lines temporarily halt the train's progress, her fellow passengers retreat once again into gloomy silence. Only the Koreans in the adjoining car continue to talk and laugh among themselves. And the sound of a lone Korean woman, singing the song of Ariran, indicates to Hiroko that these Koreans, at least, have not lost hope.[12]

Hiroko arrives in Yamaguchi to find her sister-in-law, Tsuyako, changed by the news of her missing husband. She is sullen and quiet except when addressing other household members, when her voice takes on a bitter edge: "Instead of warmth which could move the heart of the person she addressed, her voice rang with a forced harshness."[13] When Hiroko leaves for Hiroshima to enquire after the missing brother-in-law's whereabouts, Tsuyako neglects to discharge her duty as his wife by seeing Hiroko off. Nevertheless, as the days pass and life returns to normal, Tsuyako's attitude gradually softens so that by the time Jukichi's release from prison is announced she is able to acknowledge Hiroko's good fortune.

During the final journey home to Tokyo, Hiroko's train passes many towns and villages ravaged by floods: "Not a sound could be heard. Flooded by an expanse of muddy water, the deserted scene spoke of the extent of the inhabitants' despair.''[14] Throughout *Banshū heiya*, silence is evocative of Japan's despair and its sense of helplessness in defeat. Gradually, however, this silence is broken: by the sounds of children at play, by the singing of Koreans returning home, and by individuals who are eventually able to face the future. By the novel's end travellers talk unreservedly with their neighbors, Koreans whistle and sing, and even the grinding noises from the wheels of the horse-drawn carts hitting the ruts in the road create a sense of rhythm and harmony which was absent at the beginning of the story.

Images of light and darkness are used in a similar way in character development. *Banshū heiya* begins in the evening. Despite the end of the wartime blackout, Hiroko's brother and sister-in-law are reluctant to turn on the electric lights. But when they finally overcome their initial hesitation, ''the brightness after so long made the worn corners of the house come alive again . . .''[15] This scene is later contrasted with the Ayusawas' decisiveness, reflecting Hiroko's critical attitude toward her brother's family.

When it became permissible to brighten the lights at her younger brother's house where Hiroko was staying, Yukio, as the head of the household, haltingly brought out only as many white ceramic light shades as were absolutely necessary. After Sae dusted them off, Yukio replaced the old ones with them. The blackout shades were tossed down by the packing crates in the storage room. And that was that. The Ayusawas had not dealt with the light shades in their living room in this way. Husband and wife together remodelled the shades originally designed to obstruct light to give off more light. It was a trivial thing, but Hiroko, who had seen virtually everything in her environment changed by external forces, either unknowingly or mechanically, found it refreshing that the Ayusawas, who could see changes coming, had decided to make new light shades of their own design.[16]

The movement from darkness to light is repeated in other scenes as well. During Hiroko's first trip by train to her mother-in-law's, the gloomy carriage in which she is riding is contrasted with the brightness and vitality of the next car from which the sounds of Koreans' laughing and singing can be heard: ''There was an inexpressible sense of life's richness in their joyful spirit which filled the darkness.''[17]

Later, Hiroko arrives at her mother-in-law's home to find it dark and gloomy. But when she leaves to return to Tokyo, she notices a small new window in the front door. The light trickling in from it suggests the beginning of new hope in their lives. On her final journey back to Tokyo, the train is forced to stop in the dark and rain because of extensive flooding. But after it leaves Himeiji the weather improves and warm autumn sunshine continues until the novel's end. The final scene is set on the Banshū Plains bathed in sunlight where the cheerful songs and energetic footsteps of the returning travellers echo hope and optimism.

During her involvement in the proletarian literary movement, Miyamoto Yuriko's characters were divided into well defined opposing groups whose political stances and attitudes were relatively inflexible. Passive characters, usually those portrayed as politically unaware, remained inactive, while workers and political prisoners representing the proletarian vanguard remained steadfast under pressure, their sense of commitment to the cause never shaken. In *Banshū heiya*, however, characters from a variety of political and socioeconomic backgrounds are given the opportunity to change their outlooks. Perhaps because of the personal trauma she experienced during the war years, Miyamoto Yuriko realized that

weakness and hesitation exist in everyone—regardless of social class or gender. Moreover, realizing the price the Japanese nation had paid for its passivity, she is restrained in her criticism, preferring to portray people as capable of effective social transformation. While characters in *Banshū heiya* are initially passive and despairing, they eventually embrace hope and change, a shift in attitude reflected in the movement of imagery from silence and darkness to light and sound.

Paralysis and movement are used in a similar way to develop thematic elements. On the day of Japan's surrender, the Tohoku village where Hiroko is living is described in the following way: ''From noon until evening on August 15th, and even after darkness had finally fallen, the paralyzed stillness of the entire village remained unchanged.''[18] Only after two or three days does the village begin to show signs of stirring:

On the night of the 15th when Hiroko went for a bath, Jinsuke and his son, clad only in loincloths, sat by the summer hearth where the stumps were burning low. His wife, Otome, wore only a skirt after the bath. Their heads hung down in fatigue. But recently their appearance had changed. They seemed more alert, they moved with agility, and when night fell father and son could be seen pulling their heavy wagon into the darkness of the cedar trees.[19]

While she prepares to leave Tohoku for Yamaguchi, even Hiroko's brother and his wife become more physically active. But it is the children who have changed the most. Throughout the war, normal childhood activities had been severely disrupted by the tyranny of the constant air raid sirens. With the arrival of peace, days of uninterrupted enjoyment stretch before them.

Crowded with demobilized soldiers and passengers who appear to be in a state of shock following Japan's defeat, the Tokyo-bound train is described by Hiroko as a ''rout train.'' But after changing trains in Tokyo for Hiroshima, she notices changes in the attitudes of the occupants:

Although it had only been three days since the surrender, this train which had passed through the capital and was heading along the Tokkaido road was no rout train. The aftermath of August 15th had entered a second phase and travellers appeared to be moving again. This time they were not abandoning their homes, making off with anything that could be carried. The feeling was that these people had tasks to perform at the journey's end which were in keeping with Japan's new circumstances.[20]

But not all Japan is on the move. Arriving at her mother-in-law's in Yamaguchi, Hiroki finds the village still in a state of shock. No vehicles or pedestrians are to be seen on the streets and no one greets her at the door. When the village is hit by a flood, the inhabitants mobilize to save their belongings. But Hiroko finds the most dramatic change in people during her return trip to Tokyo. Until this point in the novel, movement is only sporadic, typified during the first stretch of her journey by the train's lurching progress as it limps along the damaged rail lines. Like the train, Hiroko and many fellow passengers are not in perfect physical shape. Hiroko has weak legs and her companion has glaucoma, but somehow they manage to help each other walk through the evening rain to the next town where another train awaits them. Gradually ''they overcome each succeeding obstacle and head for Tokyo, getting nearer with every step.''[21] By the end of *Banshū heiya*, the entire nation appears to be moving: ''The horse-drawn carts rumbled along the straight line of the national highway toward their destination . . . All of Japan was moving like this.''[22]

Although passivity and action had been used to define the political stance and attitudes of characters as far back as

Miyamoto Yuriko's first novel, *Mazushiki hitobito no mure*, usually only the central character tries to effect changes in an environment of passive resistance or outright opposition. In her fiction done during the proletarian literary movement, the number of characters committed to political and social change increases, although they are usually restricted to members of the working class. In *Banshū heiya*, however, virtually all characters are portrayed as capable of change—albeit in varying degrees. By the end of the war, Miyamoto Yuriko realizes that all people, regardless of class background, have the potential to change, and that they must also bear the responsibility for making their world a better place.

In her earlier novels, Miyamoto Yuriko attempts to portray human behavior in terms of its relationship to the sociopolitical environment. But *Banshū heiya* marks a high point in this development because for the first time historical events are an integral part of the novel's internal structure. Characters are portrayed within a historical context and are forced to react and come to terms with the major events of their times. In previous novels, events like the Kanto earthquake do not directly influence characters' lives but, rather, mark the abstract passage of time. In contrast, *Banshū heiya* is structured around Hiroko's journeys across the country. The trains and roads on which she travels are symbolic of life and Japan's past and present movement through history. Travelling to her mother-in-law's home in western Japan, Hiroko observes the nation coming to terms with the path on which it had travelled so far. And during her return journey to Tokyo, she notes new developments as people advance along another, and as yet incomplete, route which leads them from the present into the future.

In the opening scene of *Banshū heiya*, the Japanese nation is portrayed as silently watching as an "enormous page of history turns."[23] Hiroko describes the unconditional surrender as "the moment history convulsed,"[24] as if Japan had been brought to its knees by the quakes and tremors of some uncontrollable external force. In her earlier novels dating from the proletarian literary movement, protagonists try to expose the irrational and arbitrary ideological premises of the Japanese military state. In *Banshū heiya*, a state gone mad has been smashed, not by a united working class as she had hoped, but by Japan's enemies.

Past events in *Banshū heiya* are revealed through a series of flashbacks: "During the past fourteen years the Nazi prison system had been incorporated into Japan's Peace Preservation Law and one wasn't allowed to even breathe."[25] Hiroko depicts this period in her life as "a heavy weight." Before her departure from Tokyo, she recalls her visits to her imprisoned husband where the doors and walls of the compound reflect the power of the state:

> The heavy revolving door opened slowly from the inside. The door was several times the height of any human and while Hiroko stood waiting by the small window she felt as powerless and small as the weeds which grew at the base of the high outside wall. The height of this wall was not the only daunting thing. Unless the revolving door was opened from the inside Hiroko's strength was not enough to budge it one inch, even if she was to faint against it.[26]

When Hiroko first arrives at her mother-in-law's, she reflects on how the village had been changed during the war:

> Since then the war, which brought the invasion of Manchuria and China, had escalated and life had changed remarkably. Business became difficult to conduct due to the controls which were imposed. Situated on a large river with fields scattered between low mountain peaks and woods, the village had been divided into

so-called upper and lower sections. In addition, it was incorporated as a town with Tawara which faced the sea three kilometers away. The village had not become a town through any development from its earlier rural form. Rather, the fields and rice paddies had been transformed into a town for purely military objectives. Subsequently, a new military road had penetrated the eight kilometer stretch between Tokuyama City and the newly constructed town. This road was to be used exclusively by military trucks ... The bus, truck and Datsun traffic which hurried over the narrow highway day and night shook the loose joists of Jukichi's poor house from morning until late at night. From the second-story window, one could see train loads of soldiers waiting for long periods of time on the railroad tracks where women from the town's Women's Committee served them tea and rice balls. The heart of this new military town became an enormous arsenal which mobilized the young men and women from the neighbouring villages. At set times in the morning and evening, the road before Jukichi's home was filled with people riding bicycles to and from their villages. . . . [27]

In this way the traditional rural economy is destroyed to meet the needs of the military machine. But Jukichi's village is not the only place where such changes have occurred. Throughout the novel, Hiroko also sees numerous other villages similarly afflicted, including the village in Fukushima where she first stays with her brother. After Japan's surrender, however, only the ruins of these military installations remain. And like the inhabitants, they are described in terms of paralysis and silence: "Only yesterday, military trucks and motorcycles had dashed along the needlessly wide road. Today, nothing passed by. The road was white and dusty, silent and deserted. . . . "[28]

The influence of the past on the present does not stop with the signing of the peace treaty. Towns like Jukichi's, where the local economy has been warped to meet military objectives, face total collapse with the war's end. As entire industries cease to exist, the youth who had been mobilized to work them retreat to their native villages, leaving the new towns to deteriorate into *goke no machi*, or widows' towns. In addition, construction of these military roads ignored the ecological balance of the surrounding terrain, resulting in poor soil drainage and severe flooding during the autumn rains. During her stay in Yamaguchi, Hiroko helps her in-laws fight flood waters, and when she makes her final journey to Tokyo she witnesses other towns that have suffered a similar fate.

One of the most brutal aspects of Japan's wartime militarization is that many of these villages' sons and husbands who had left for combat duty never returned home on these unnecessary networks of roads. Within these past and present movements of Japan's history along the web of roads and railways, the characters of *Banshū heiya* act out their lives, vacillating between silence and sound, darkness and light, and paralysis and movement.

Scenes of wartime ruin and destruction gradually give way to descriptions of renewal, which first appear in terms of natural imagery after the flood when Hiroko surveys the gutted remains of the arsenal:

> The people who had triumphed in greed in these various structures had disappeared since the 15th of August. Where Hiroko walked, the windows of the building were now boarded up and some buildings still sporting signs had become empty. Perhaps because of the pelting rains of four or five days before, or because of earlier air bombardments, a stand of sycamore trees was uprooted and had toppled onto the sidewalk for several blocks. Though soiled by

mud, the foliage of these fallen sycamores was luxuriant with new green leaves.[29]

The theme of new life rising from destruction is repeated shortly afterward as Hiroko regards Nuiko's sister's room: "There was an elegance surrounding Sawako's desk like a dandelion blooming amid a pile of ruins. A small and innocent thing, the perfection of this purity nevertheless moved Hiroko who had just witnessed desolation as far as the eye could see. It revived her faith in living things."[30]

Like other characters, Hiroko looks to a better future, realizing that it must be built on the ruins of the past. Looking at Sawako's room she muses: "Today is born from yesterday, tomorrow breaks away from today and then continues on. . . ."[31] The final description of the Banshū Plains further develops this theme:

> The autumn sunshine turned the Banshū mountains, the fields, small hamlets and trees a golden colour in the breeze. The horse-drawn carts rumbled along the straight line of the national highway toward their destination. The noise from the ruts in the road harmonized strangely with the cheerfulness of the young people and blended with the many emotions that filled Hiroko's heart. This advance along the national highway would not happen twice in their lifetime. The hedges of the small hamlets they passed, the ruins of the large factories, rusted red and standing in the distance of the Akashi pine forest . . .: All of Japan was moving like this. Hiroko felt it keenly.[32]

In her first novel, *Mazushiki hitobito no mure*, Miyamoto Yuriko attempts to explain her characters' behavior in terms of their relationship to the social environment in which they live. *Nobuko* further develops this, and in *Kokkoku* politics and history are given a larger role. However, although the protagonist in *Kokkoku* states that "history inevitably advances,"[33] the historical process is not part of the novel's overall structure and the reader must accept the character's statement as fact. But in *Banshū heiya*, history and characterization are interconnected and developed through imagery and symbolism.

While natural imagery is also present in Miyamoto's earlier works, it is not central to the development of thematic elements. In *Kokkoku*, for example, the protagonist often views the sky, flowers, and trees from her squalid prison cell. While this juxtaposition does produce a sense of irony, it does not develop the role of the working class in the historical process.

The theme of love also reappears in *Banshū heiya*, and through it Hiroko's world view is revealed. Hiroko's relationship with her husband is different from the type of male-female relationships found in earlier works. In *Nobuko*, the heroine views romantic love as the basis for a relationship enabling both parties to attain emotional and intellectual growth. Nevertheless, she realizes that the existing marriage system makes both of these impossible, especially for women intent on pursuing independent careers. In the novels written during her involvement in the proletarian literary movement, romantic love is conspicuously absent, as if it is a bourgeois preoccupation irrelevant to class struggle. In *Banshū heiya*, Hiroko does not regard herself as the free individual Nobuko did and is very conscious of her role as Jukichi's wife and of her relationship and responsibilities to his family.

Hiroko compares the relationship to a ship: "Their life together did not resemble ocean waves that moved aimlessly back and forth. Rather, their relationship was like an advanc-

ing ship. And together they viewed the movement of history and the passage of time which would not be repeated."[34] This connection between their relationship and history implies a type of political partnership. The younger Nobuko believed that she could only realize her potential alone. The mature Hiroko believes that women alone are incomplete:

> Looking back over the past ten years or so it became obvious to her. It was impossible for Hiroko to think of her life during that time without Jukichi. For example, seven years before Hiroko had been indicted because of her participation in the proletarian literary movement. She was sentenced to three years in jail with a five-year suspended sentence. Even then she had continued to emphasize the class nature of literature. During the preparations for her trial, Jukichi read through the relevant documents and, although restricted by having to do so through letters, wrote often criticizing the material on the basis of whether she had heroically defended reason or compromised too much. Hiroko learned a great deal from this. For her the compromises were small, but for Jukichi they represented the limit of what he would tolerate in his wife.[35]

The sharing of ideologies became the basis for a lasting relationship capable of surviving twelve years of separation and persecution.

For the heroine of *Nobuko*, the roles of daughter, wife, and daughter-in-law represent petty concerns for social position and economic security, and she tries to eliminate them from her life. Although not abandoning her critical stance towards the family system she once abhorred, in *Banshū heiya* Miyamoto expresses sympathy for female characters and relatives who bear the dual burdens of gender and social class. Like Hiroko, thousands of women are deprived of their sons and husbands during the war. But Hiroko has been fortunate because she has known that her husband, although imprisoned, is alive. Many other women have had to face the future alone. Hiroko criticizes her sister-in-law's coldness toward her husband's family but sympathizes with her plight:

> "The Japanese are bankrupt." This short phrase uttered by foreigners pierced her to the heart . . . The misfortune of losing Naoki—the centre of their lives—had prevented these lone women from succumbing to even feelings of grief. This is what real misfortune is, Hiroko thought. This is how emotions become bankrupt.[36]

At the end of the war, Japanese women are left to contend with both the physical scars left on their environment and deep emotional wounds. During the war, women shouldered the greatest burden to ensure the survival of their families. With the war's end, their efforts to raise their children and rebuild the country continue, often without the aid of their men who have been maimed or killed. Discipline and perseverance have seen them through the difficult years. But, like Hiroko's sister-in-law, the times have made them hard and bitter. "Where was the real bitterness of the war to be found in people's lives? . . . It was found daily in the silent ruins of the tens of thousands of 'widows' towns' created throughout Japan."[37]

Conclusion

Miyamoto Yuriko's novels reveal both a consistency and development of form and content throughout the more than thirty years of her career. The subject matter of her novels concerns the plight of oppressed people, although the nature and definition of this changes with each of her major literary periods. In *Mazushiki hitobito no mure*, her first novel, the

Miyamoto Yuriko with her husband Miyamoto Kenji at their home in Hayashi-machi (1950).

unhappy lives of rural sharecroppers are the focus. Later, with *Nobuko*, the emphasis shifts to the personal sphere of the author as she analyzes the situation of women within the restrictions of family and marriage. During her association with the proletarian literary movement, Miyamoto Yuriko deals with the urban proletariat struggling against police oppression. Thus, in novels such as *Kokkoku*, we see a serious attempt to universalize the individual experience in terms of the social and political system.

From the beginning of her writing career, Miyamoto Yuriko was concerned with the effect of the sociopolitical environment on the quality of human life. She looked for the causes of negative behavior in existing social structures rather than individual personality. Even in her first novel, characters are shown in conflict with society, and they are forced to engage in some kind of activity to alter their situation. However, action is restricted to the personal level. During the proletarian literary movement, her characters for the first time embrace change through collective action. And with *Banshū heiya* collective action merges with the theme of collective responsibility, reflecting the gradual broadening of her historical perspective.

Throughout her career, Miyamoto Yuriko consistently developed characters who reject passivity and struggle for change. In her earlier works, the central characters are generally alone in their battles against injustice, but they nevertheless represent that optimistic view of humanity that dominates her later works. Rather than representing the period in which Miyamoto first embraced political action to achieve social change, the proletarian literary movement was a transitional period when humanist issues evolved from the personal center to a larger group with shared ideologies and aims. By the end of the war when she wrote *Banshū heiya* she was able to view not just those committed to a specific political ideology but all humanity as capable of effecting significant social transition through collective effort. Emerging at the time of Japan's surrender, her optimism and ability to combine the desire for

personal inner growth with a commitment to political action and fundamental social change enabled her to avoid the nihilism and sense of defeat that was so widespread in Japan at that time.

Miyamoto Yuriko's novels portray humanity as rejecting obstacles to growth and advancement; her characters strive to break the fetters that bind them—be they family, marriage, the state, or destruction and despair. Her heroines refuse to admit defeat in the face of adversity and possess an unflagging optimism that a better world is within their grasp. Reaching beyond the negative aspects of present society, novels like *Banshū heiya* anticipate a better world. The vitality and integrity of Miyamoto's novels emerge from within this movement as well as from the defiant stance taken by her protagonists against unjust situations.

Banshū heiya is one of Miyamoto Yuriko's most artistically successful novels. Sophisticated use of imagery and stylistic devices to develop thematic elements creates a sense of depth and maturity not found in her pre-1945 novels, with the possible exception of *Nobuko*. In addition, *Banshū heiya* marks a return to humanistic issues and the progressive middle-class female character found in such early works as *Mazushiki hitobito no mure* and *Nobuko*, indicating that ultimately she felt more comfortable with protagonists who mirrored her own life experiences than she did with the somewhat politically strident working class characters who appeared during the time of her involvement in the proletarian literary movement. However, during the postwar period, Miyamoto Yuriko's heroines develop into a harmonious blend of both these character types, suggesting both personal, artistic, and political growth.

Despite the emphasis on female characters whose experiences echo her own, Miyamoto Yuriko does not indulge in the gloomy introversion of the *shi-shosetsu*, or "I" novel. Her sense of social change within history, and her belief in social responsibility and political commitment raise the stature of her characters from isolated individuals to universal modern heroines. In addition, her return to feminist issues in the postwar period reveals the lasting effects of the enlightened humanist environment in which she grew up, even as her belief in the need for a more radical social and political revolution continues to make its presence felt. Looking at social and political contradictions within the framework of feminist issues, Miyamoto Yuriko was able to create a unique form of popular literature which transcends the boundaries of both cultural difference and time.

Notes

1. See *Miyamoto Yuriko senshū* (Tokyo: Shin nihon shuppansha, 1968), 12 vols. for early works. See also Noriko Mizuta Lippit, "Literature, Ideology and Women's Happiness: The Autobiographical Novels of Miyamoto Yuriko," *BCAS* Vol. 10, No. 2 (April-June, 1978); and Brett de Bary, "After the War: Translations from Miyamoto Yuriko," *BCAS* Vol. 16, No. 2 (April-June, 1984).

2. As he stated in his suicide note, Akutagawa's reason for suicide was a vague feeling of unease about the future, aggravated by his own deteriorating emotional state. Yuriko's brother, Hideo, was still a student at the time of his death, but it is suggested in *Futatsu no niwa* that this sensitive and introverted young man was deeply disturbed by the increasing radicalization and polarization of society and, like Akutagawa, was overcome by intense feelings of unease about the future.

3. Miyamoto Yuriko, *Jihitsu nempu*, as quoted in Nakamura Tomoko, *Miyamoto Yuriko* (Tokyo: Chikuma shobō, 1973), p. 114. This and all subsequent quotations are my own translations.

4. NAPF is abbreviated from the Esperanto translation Nippona Proleta Artista Federacio of *Zennihon musansha geijutsu renmei* as cited in George T. Shea, *Leftwing Literature in Japan* (Tokyo: Hōsei Daigaku, 1964), p. 200.

5. KOPF is abbreviated from the Esperanto translation Federacio de Proletaj Kultur-organizoj Japanaj of *Nihon puroretaria bunka renmei*, cited in Shea, *Leftwing*, p. 205.

6. Notable among these critics are Nakamura Tomoko and Honda Shūgo. See Nakamura, *Miyamoto*, p. 242 and Honda Shūgo, *Senji sengo no senkō-sha tachi* (Tokyo: Keisō shobō, 1971).

7. Nakamura, *Miyamoto*, p. 170.

8. See Honda, *Senji sengo*, pp. 134–140, and Kurahara Korehito, *Kobayashi Takiji to Miyamoto Yuriko* (Tokyo: Tofusha, 1966), p. 121.

9. *Miyamoto Yuriko senshū*, IV, pp. 3-136.

10. Ibid., p. 10.

11. Ibid., p. 11.

12. Nym Wales and Kim San, *Song of Ariran* (San Francisco: Ramparts Press, 1941). See p. 56 for an English translation of the text of this song. Also "Prologue," pp. 57–61 for a discussion of the significance that this song has held for Koreans for more than three hundred years.

13. *Senshū*, IV, p. 60.

14. Ibid., p. 116.

15. Ibid., p. 16.

16. Ibid., p. 32.

17. Ibid., p. 46.

18. Ibid., p. 11.

19. Ibid., pp. 18–19.

20. Ibid., pp. 39–40.

21. Ibid., p. 120.

22. Ibid., p. 136.

23. Ibid., p. 10.

24. Ibid., p. 10.

25. Ibid., p. 12.

26. Ibid., pp. 34–35.

27. Ibid., p. 56.

28. Ibid., p. 15.

29. Ibid., p. 86.

30. Ibid., pp. 88–89.

31. Ibid., p. 88.

32. Ibid., p. 136.

33. *Senshū*, III, p. 66.

34. *Senshū*, IV, p. 100.

35. Ibid., pp. 123–124.

36. Ibid., p. 54.

37. Ibid., p. 60.

Production Control: Workers' Control in Early Postwar Japan

by Joe Moore*

Introduction

When the Allied Occupation of Japan began in September 1945 neither the Japanese nor the Americans knew for certain what the eventual outcome would be for Japanese society. It might seem in retrospect that the only real possibility was the type of liberal reform of Japanese society that actually took place. Yet, at that time there were many in both countries who feared an early return to fascist repression, while others were equally alarmed about a communist revolution.

The American scholars who have long dominated the study of the Occupation in the West have not taken such concerns seriously. Virtually transfixed by the Japanese 'economic miracle,' they have concentrated singlemindedly on finding the secret ingredients in the modernization of Japanese capitalism that took place during the decade and a half following World War II. Indeed, they scoff at the suggestion that there might have been some other outcome. Others, following the lead of E.O. Reischauer, have carefully constructed a chain of causality linking the democratic trends of the twenties with the supposed postwar political and economic democratization of Japan under American tutelage, all but ignoring the legacy of the period of fascism and the postwar reaction of the Japanese people to the long years of oppression. The natural consequence of this selective approach has been the loss of the sensitivity the scholar ought to have to paths not taken and possibilities unfulfilled. Instead, what eventually did happen in Japan has come to be regarded as what had to happen, a way of looking at things that is both convenient and satisfying for the American purveyors of this brand of establishment orthodoxy.

The charge of writing history without people has been

made in other contexts, but has truly been the case here. The flesh and blood of mass firings and joblessness, destitution and hunger, bitter strikes and union busting, political struggle and government repression has been submerged in dry statistics and abstract theory. The revolutionary ferment of the times has not come through, and the depth of the postwar crisis of capitalism in Japan has not yet been appreciated.

It takes only the briefest consideration of the vast differences separating Japanese society as it was before the war from what it came to be after the Occupation to see what a wrench was needed to 'modernize' the country. The liberal reform of Japanese capitalism was in no sense automatic and only became possible at all through the combination of a catastrophic war and a foreign occupation. There was no preordained course toward liberal capitalism before Japan in late 1945, but a number of alternatives, the likely realization of which changed in response to changes in the strength and immediate interests of the three major participants in the battle to control the course of Japan's reconstruction: the Supreme Command for the Allied Powers (SCAP), the conservative economic and political establishment, and the working class.

Insofar as war and occupation had created a situation of flux by breaking the hold of the established elites in the economy and politics of Japan, thereby granting the working class increased freedom of action, it became an open question which road to reconstruction Japan would eventually follow. As the Japanese recognized at the time, the confrontation of labor and capital did indeed admit of a number of different resolutions, ranging from a straightforward restoration of the prewar economic and political order to the establishment of a democratic people's republic.

Labor and capital fought it out, socialism versus capitalism, during the first nine months of reconstruction. The most outstanding characteristic of this period from August 1945 through May 1946 was that the working class went on the

* I would like to gratefully acknowledge the help of a number of people who read this article in its various forms—Helen Chauncey, Bill Doub, John Dower, Ben Kerkvliet, Bob Marks, and Rob Steven—but I bear the sole responsibility for its faults.

offensive while capital lost its nerve and sought refuge in a wait-and-see policy of economic retrenchment and political passive resistance. By May 1946 SCAP felt compelled to make common cause with the Japanese government in turning back the working-class challenge.

The impulse toward change from below was expressed most clearly in the early postwar attempts of wage workers to gain control over the workplace and to realize security and dignity in their personal lives through production control *(seisan kanri)*—the seizure and operation of a workplace by its employees for their own interests. This became both symbol and means for the broader social movement in 1945–1946, just as unionization assumed the central place for the working class thereafter. The society toward which Japanese workers were moving in the spring of 1946, when production control was spreading rapidly, cannot be fully known, however, for the simple reason that this drive for radical change was turned back. The workers' movement developed within a capitalist, occupied Japan and thus can give only a partial indication of what promised to become an alternative form of social organization. Nevertheless, such an indication can be seen.

The orthodox interpretation ignores this first phase in the postwar history of the working class, concentrating instead on the 1 February, 1947 General Strike. Here Western scholars often have depicted the General Strike as the peak of a narrowly based revolutionary movement, the frustration of which by SCAP turned the tide back toward the essential moderation and conservatism of both the Japanese populace and their leaders. This shift has been viewed as marking the beginning of a policy transition within SCAP from democratization to economic reconstruction. In 1947–1948 conservatism and retrenchment became bywords following the initial period of quasi-revolutionary reforms inspired by the New Deal legacy in America. In this interpretation, the US government and SCAP were clearly the active elements, defining not only the conditions for the conservative resurgence but also the conditions for the leftist challenge by extending to the Japanese an unaccustomed freedom of action which was used irresponsibly. Accordingly, the SCAP ban on the 1 February General Strike has been treated by many establishment authors as a legitimate action against leftist excesses.

It should be noted that the shift toward reconstruction has not been viewed as a rolling back of democratic reforms already implemented. Rather, it has been argued that the reforms had already provided the essential preconditions for the orderly development of American-style political and economic pluralism in Japan. In effect, all that remained to do from 1947 to ensure the institutionalization of the reforms was to put the economy back on its feet, as was supposedly done over the next few years.

One does not have to be Japanese to wonder if the Japanese people were truly as passive or malleable as this interpretation implies. That Japanese appear to come onstage and retreat to the wings in response to SCAP initiatives says less about Japanese 'docility' than it does about the inadequacies of a problem consciousness and periodization that consistently place SCAP's activities and US interests center stage. To mention but two groups, both the *zaibatsu* leaders and the workers showed themselves to be determined from the outset to gain the upper hand in defining the course reconstruction would take. They engaged in a long series of bitter conflicts outside of SCAP control, though not immune to SCAP

interference. Needless to say, this ill accords with the prevailing American interpretation of Occupation history.

The usual two-stage, America-centric interpretation that has dominated the field distorts the meaning of events even during the first phase of the Occupation, when the majority of the reforms were enacted. Accordingly, it will be abandoned here, and the following periodization used, one focusing on the working class as it experienced the broad economic and social changes taking place within Japanese society. Although this paper deals with only the first of the three periods, it may be helpful to present an overview in order to give a sense of the general context within which the argument is posed.

Workers' Control

The early months after surrender (August 1945–May 1946) brought widespread popular revolutionary challenge to the old order by industrial workers, peasants, and impoverished city people. This period extended from surrender through the mass demonstrations in May against Premier-to-be Yoshida Shigeru. The first half of the period (August through January) began quietly but saw increasingly open expression of popular discontent practically everywhere and the first faltering steps toward organization. Workers on the shop floor sounded the keynote by spontaneously turning from ineffective strikes to production control *(seisan kanri)*. A major part of their intent was to carve out a substantial degree of workers' control within the enterprises, but within the bounds of legality as defined by the liberal reforms being implemented by SCAP.

The second half of the period (February through May) was characterized by explosive growth in workers' organizations and the imminent transformation of production control into a revolutionary movement acting in disregard of capitalist legality. The situation was the more volatile because of the tentative coalescence of a broad popular movement around the industrial workers. By May 1946 the wider movement was gathering momentum. Goaded beyond endurance, urban and rural people were taking direct action at the point of production and distribution. Their immediate aims were worker control over industry in order to bring about the resumption of production in the face of a capitalist sit-down, peasant control over the compulsory delivery of staple foods to the state for rationing, and popular control over the rationing system itself.

The popular challenge to a capitalist reconstruction reached its peak in the mass actions of April and May, but it was burdened by a vacillating and footdragging national leadership which fell to pieces when confronted by SCAP opposition on 20 May. On that day, General MacArthur publicly threatened the suppression of the popular movement in a strong statement on mass demonstrations. The reinvigorated Japanese business and government elite, now assured of SCAP support for its continuation in power, went on the counter-attack. With SCAP's backing they turned back the movement for workers' control. Thus, the real beginnings of what has come to be called the 'reverse course'—the halting or rolling back of democratic reforms proclaimed at the outset of the occupation—occurred in May 1946 and not February 1947.

Industrial Unionism

From Spring 1946 to Spring 1947 the working class and small farmers, foregoing their previous anti-capitalist demands for popular control over vital areas of the economy, turned toward defending and extending their own particular interests within the capitalist economic reconstruction that was now seen as inescapable. A decent job, an adequate food ration, and a share in the distribution of land became central concerns. Workers turned toward the union as the means for securing their rights and their livelihood within the capitalist order. But not all wage workers succeeded in unionizing, and not all unions were militant. The turn to trade unionism, therefore, meant a narrowing of the inclusive scope of the working-class movement of the spring. Organized labor hereafter avoided anti-capitalist direct action such as had typified production control and instead pressed conventional economic demands for union contracts, better wages, and job security, using the strike as the prime means of persuasion.

Big-business and government leaders had already shown their determination not to knuckle under to the national federations of the unions, but to make the enterprise the fundamental unit for bargaining with organized labor. In order to counter this effort the leftist majority in the labor movement consolidated behind Sambetsu (Zen Nihon Sangyōbetsu Rōdō Kumiai Kaigi, Congress of Industrial Unions), and mounted an offensive in the second half of 1946 to establish the power of national union federations built upon a federation of subordinate enterprise locals. When the struggle escalated into an attempt to topple the vehemently anti-labor Yoshida government, SCAP once again stepped in. SCAP's prohibition of the 1 February 1947 General Strike was a major defeat that destroyed the chance for a unification of Sambetsu and Sōdōmei (Nihon Rōdō Kumiai Sōdōmei, Japan Federation of Labor) into one national organization for labor—a unification that had seemed within reach in mid-winter. By preventing the unification of the unions, the SCAP doomed as well the fight to make industrial unions the basic means for worker organization in Japan. Although the national federations affiliated with Sambetsu held their own for a time after the failure of the General Strike, no doubt because a socialist premier had succeeded Yoshida, big business had in fact regained the initiative. This would become clear in early 1948.

Enterprise Unionism

Finally, during the period from Spring 1947 to Summer 1950, Sambetsu was broken and the enterprise union, Japan's contribution to industrial relations, was created. From 1947, the leftist labor unions had come under attack from within by so-called democratization leagues which claimed to represent rank-and-file discontent with the policies of left-wing leaders. There undoubtedly was dissatisfaction with the left, and resentment over communist influence, but the splits and bitterness resulting from the democratization movement served the employers' interests far more than the interests of any other group, except, perhaps, labor's right wing. These internal difficulties were compounded in 1948 by anti-labor legislation designed to cripple the strong public-employee unions that were the mainstay of the left and to permit big-business and government employers to make mass dismissals as part of a program of economic retrenchment considered to be essential before recovery could begin.

The leftist labor federations proved unable to overcome internal disunity and fend off the damaging changes in labor laws and mass firings of union members that followed. The disarray the big-business and government attack produced in the labor movement abetted the splitting of leftist unions by the democratization leagues working in close cooperation with management. This frequently resulted in the setting up of rival, "second" unions at the enterprise level to which management at once granted sole recognition. This period closes with an open red purge that put out of action those leftist party and labor leaders who had been putting up the greatest resistance to the reverse course in labor reform. Thus the attempt to establish industrial unionism went to defeat, and Japanese workers were driven back into the framework of weak and isolated enterprise unions.

The Old Order in Disarray

Yoshida Shigeru, who became prime minister in May 1946, characterized the period in which he came to power as revolutionary. In so doing, he had several things in mind— among them the resurgent Communist party and the massive street demonstrations—but the main object of his concern was the phenomenon of worker seizure and operation of mines, factories, and offices, and production control. This situation was not at all unique to post-surrender Japan. Rather, those developments were of much the same nature as the factory occupations in Leningrad, Berlin, and Turin of some twenty-five years before. As European workers had done after World War I in Europe, large numbers of Japanese workers after World War II stood up to protest their situation, to make the radical demand for workers' control, and to take over and run their enterprises through their own system of councils.

The crisis of the old order was played out in circumstances of seemingly bewildering complexity. Big business was internally divided into conflicting liberal and conservative camps, and the governing bureaucracy was similarly split. Communists and socialists fought among themselves while battling the resurrected conservative parties for control of the government. The US occupation headquarters loosed a flood of directives for democratizing Japanese society. Workers, farmers, and city people sought their own answers to the desperate times, organizing in unions and councils, and groping toward a new, populist order. Yet, one question cut through the complexity and provided a shared point of reference for coalitions forming on left and right: how to deal with economic chaos.

Foremost in actual power at the time was the old elite of big-businessmen and government officials (from which military elements were now excluded) who were seeking through often contradictory policies a revival of the capitalist economy. Their rivals were party and union leaders advocating competing versions of socialist reconstruction, and a popular movement at the grass roots that the left hoped to lead. The nexus of their conflict was what form economic revival would take—socialist or capitalist. No one could avoid taking sides for long, and because the stakes over whose vision of economic reconstruction was to prevail were high, the fight was bitter.

When the Occupation began in August 1945, the labor front was peaceful. Measures for control of labor dating back to the Meiji perod, and periodically extended as new crises called forth sterner measures, were still in effect in the immediate post-surrender weeks. The fact that surrender took place before war had destroyed the basis of the established social order had far-reaching effects. The old elite, even without the military, retained its grip on power and saw to it that the police continued to be active in enforcing repressive political and economic controls until the fall of the Higashikuni Cabinet in early October. With few exceptions the surrender did not bring early actions by workers, for the long decades of oppression had succeeded in uprooting workers' organizations and in undermining the will to resist.[1] Surrender had not brought home to the working class that a new dispensation was at hand. That understanding dawned only in the closing months of 1945, after workers realized just how vulnerable the old political and business leaders were and how greatly the old social order had been undermined by the disastrous war. In October 1945, SCAP made its contribution to kicking the props out from under the old regime by abolishing many repressive laws and organizations,[2] thereby clearing the way for the long-pending confrontation between capital and labor.

It has become a truism that business circles during the early occupation were demoralized, "lost the will to produce," and were unable to act in overcoming Japan's economic problems in the face of shattering defeat and uncertainty over Allied policy for Japan. Big business began a general retrenchment as a hedge against the troubled days ahead. They shut down production and dismissed many workers, while simultaneously trying to corner the remaining supply of essential commodities. These efforts went hand in hand with a looting of the government treasury and the wartime stockpiles of crucial materials, ranging all the way from food and medicine to machinery and precious metals.[3] The refusal by big businesses to produce and invest during the first few years of the occupation was directly related to their having amassed the wherewithal to wait out an extended period of inactivity and uncertainty. Statistics for the period are poor, but industrial activity in the winter of 1945–1946 may have amounted to as little as 10 percent of the 1935–1937 average (see table 1). The stoppage caused severe shortages of all kinds, giving rise to a major inflation that cut deeply into wages which were for the most part already below subsistence.

Conditions for blue- and white-collar workers alike were desperate at the time of surrender and steadily worsened with the onset of the first winter of occupation. Wholesale closures of factories resulted in mass dismissals, the effects of which were compounded by the return of several million servicemen and overseas residents. Unemployment soared to a staggering 10–12 million during the winter of 1945–1946, this at a time when Japan's non-agricultural labor force was approximately 18 million out of a total work force of roughly 32 million. Unemployment and shortages made the cities all but uninhabitable, and those who could returned to their family villages. The population of Tokyo alone had declined some 4 million by November 1945 to 2.8 million people. Even so, mass starvation loomed in Japan's urban areas as the first winter ended, and was narrowly averted by America's grudging importation of foodstuffs in the spring and summer.[4]

In midwinter all wage workers were driven to protect their jobs against the wave of dismissals and to increase production, but neither could be done by tactics like strikes or slow-downs when there was widespread retrenchment and mass unemployment. Employers were more than ready to meet the workers' challenge in that case simply by locking out strikers or closing down altogether. A strike could hurt only in the most essential industries and services like fuel or transportation, but here the real victims would not be the employers, but the public. Striking could only worsen the general economic situation and earn public hostility. Outside of big business and government

circles the need for production suffused the very atmosphere, and workers knew their personal survival was intimately tied to economic revival. In sum the sit-down by the *zaibatsu* had created conditions which required worker occupation and operation of factories if their twin demands for jobs and production were to be met. Japan's workers did not arrive at their solution of production control overnight; instead they began their efforts in the more orthodox vein of trade unionism.[5]

Business Unionism and Workers' Control

The response of workers and labor organizers to the new conditions began in October when the first postwar unions were formed and disputes began to break out widely (see tables 2 and 3). From the outset workers displayed various and often contradictory tendencies regarding the structure of worker organizations and the nature of demands. Postwar worker organizations originated in one of two ways: from spontaneous, shop-floor efforts, and from the efforts of outside organizers representing one of the three basic camps of the prewar union movement.[6]

The second category, unions set up by outside organizers, included on the one extreme an orthodox 'business-union' approach epitomized by right-wing social democrats like Matsuoka Komakichi and Nishio Suehiro, who in most cases sought to reimpose prewar-style hierarchical and conservative unions in close coordination with the old elites.[7] On the other extreme, such JCP (Japan Communist Party) leaders as Tokuda Kyūichi and Shiga Yoshio were constructing 'red' unions which would take an active political and economic role, if not always a revolutionary one.[8] In between (and largely ineffectual) were those sympathetic with the position of the left wing of the JSP (Japan Socialist Party), who worked to erect a progressive union movement dedicated to a political and economic transformation of Japan within the framework of parliamentary democracy.[9]

An examination of the initial demands of the unions organized from below shows a basic congruence with the immediate (i.e. non-revolutionary) goals set forth by the socialist left as a whole, which may be summed up in the catch-phrases of industrial democracy in the workplace and political democracy for the nation. The workers' organizations originating on the shop floor made demands which usually came strikingly close to those already set forth by SCAP, including the right to organize, strike, and negotiate a union contract.[10]

In essence, these were demands for the extension to Japanese workers of basic economic rights possessed by labor in the democratic West. Broad support existed for a minimalist catch-up program for reforming Japan's labor relations establishing the basic conditions for the growth of unions. Indeed, the need was universally recognized in Japan except among conservatives.

Preeminent among conservative elite interests had been *zaibatsu* owners and top executives who pursued a corporate version of laissez-faire through powerful big-business associations. Instinctively hostile to labor, but hostile also to any government interference in economic planning and to bureaucratic controls over business activity, these groups advocated self-regulation through a structure of monopolies and cartels. Their viewpoint dominated Japanese policy throughout most of the period considered here.[11]

The conservative mainstream was therefore responsible for the earliest and most reactionary approach to economic

Table 1

Index of Economic Indicators, 1945–46

Year	Month	Bank of Japan Note Issue (million ¥)[a]	Tokyo Black Market Price (Consumer Goods) Index (9/45 = 100)[b]	Average Multiple of Official Price Level	Industrial Production (1935–37 = 100)[c]	Wage Index	Cost of Living Index (1937 = 100)[d]	Real Wage Index
1945	Jun	26,181	–	–	18.1	–	–	–
	Jul	28,456	–	–	12.8	–	–	–
	Aug	42,300	–	–	8.5	–	–	–
	Sep	41,426	100	–	9.0	229	2,540	9
	Oct	43,188	92	28.7	13.0	218	2,330	9
	Nov	47,749	112	31.8	13.6	231	2,740	8
	Dec	55,441	128	29.7	13.4	313	3,080	10
1946	Jan	58,566	170	40.1	13.4	452	4,000	11
	Feb	54,342	200	39.8	15.6	606	4,470	14
	Mar	23,323[e]	196	23.7	18.8	740	4,790	15
	Apr	28,173	187	21.3	21.8	827	4,510	18
	May	36,316	191	15.1	25.2	888	4,820	18
	Jun	42,759	201	20.6	25.7	986	5,310	19
	Jul	49,731	200	14.7	27.6	1,060	5,330	20

a. Japan Prime Minister's Office, Cabinet Bureau of Statistics, *Japan Statistical Year-book* (Tokyo: Cabinet Bureau of Statistics, 1949), p. 528.
b. Bank of Japan, Statistics Department, *Economic Statistics of Japan (Annual), 1948* (Tokyo: Bank of Japan), p. 134.
c. Japan Ministry of Finance and Bank of Japan, *Statistical Year-Book of Finance and Economy of Japan, 1948* (Tokyo: Ministry of Finance Printing Office), p. 558.
d. Ohara Shakai Mondai Kenkyūjo, *Saitei Chinginsei no Igi*, Tokyo: Daiichi Pub., 1949), p. 37.
e. Currency conversion.

reconstruction. They sought to recreate the prewar laissez-faire era, when *zaibatsu* activity was unfettered by government regulations, and labor was docile, hard working, and cheap. As before, cheap labor was considered a prerequisite for the Japanese economy for two interrelated reasons. Externally, resource-poor Japan desperately needed commodities for export to finance necessary imports of raw materials and technology, and in the past cheap labor had provided the margin for successful competition as an exporter of textiles. Internally, cheap labor had permitted the rapid accumulation of capital necessary to finance industrial expansion and would be even more important to rehabilitate war-devastated industry.[12] To the controlling elite that meant strong labor organizations could not be tolerated, not even business unions.

This attempt by conservatives to recreate prewar labor relations was likely to fail since the political conditions for keeping labor as cheap and docile as it had been in the past no longer existed. SCAP directives ordering the dismantling of the old curbs on civil rights had undermined the legal structure and police apparatus that had served in the past to keep labor under control in the face of harsh exploitation. Furthermore, the US was actively pursuing its stated policy of encouraging a strong labor movement. Insofar as formation of strong unions guaranteed future demands for higher wages, a re-thinking of the overall problem of economic reconsruction was in order, but that was yet to come. When it did it would be undertaken by the more progressive stratum of managers

who felt the old-line conservatives were leading Japan to ruin by seeking a confrontation with labor. It would be better to recognize business unionism as a fact of postwar life and plan accordingly.

The Emergence of Production Control

The Japanese workers' advance bears witness to a tremendous desire and capacity to organize. Examples abound of workers spontaneously organizing unions far more quickly than SCAP had intended and striving to end the employers' 'divine right' to rule the work force. One of the most original and effective of the tactics workers used to obtain their rights and their demands was production control, a form of struggle that the employees of the *Yomiuri* newspaper originated in late 1945 as part of their fight to democratize their paper.

The link between the official ideology of the state and the point of view of the leading newspapers had been drawn closer than ever once war broke out in China. The defense of Japan's national interest soon seemed to require omission of certain kinds of news and eventually the printing of outright falsehoods about Japan's situation at home and abroad. The *Yomiuri* stood in the forefront of the controlled press, under the enthusiastic lead of its president, Shōriki Matsutarō.[13]

In the early 1920s Shōriki had been Director of the Secretariat of the Metropolitan Police Board of Tokyo and a key figure in the surveillance and suppression not only of the activities of the Communist party in particular, but also of other leftist groups, labor, and Koreans. In 1924 he used contact with influential people in business, government, and politics to buy control of the faltering *Yomiuri*. By tightening control over employees to cut labor costs and raise productivity, and by adopting a policy of sensational yellow journalism, Shōriki made the *Yomiuri* into one of the three largest newspapers in Japan by the late 1930s. He was an ultra-nationalist who showed a preference for former police or intelligence figures who were staunch anti-communists like himself.[14]

During the war, newspapermen were among the few to have both the intellectual training and the access to hard news that would enable them to pass judgement on their company's activities. The newspaper employees bitterly resented Shōriki's policies for two reasons in particular: the reactionary editorial policy that subordinated news reporting to state propaganda, and the highly authoritarian system of personnel management which was designed to extract maximum work from each employee for minimum pay. When the war ended, both aspects of Shōriki's leadership came under sharp attack, and the *Yomiuri* employees put forward demands for pursuit of war responsibility and internal democratization of the paper, regarding them as at least as important as economic demands for better pay and benefits.[15]

The *Yomiuri* dispute broke out in mid-October 1945 when a group of employees presented Shōriki with demands for the democratization of the company's organization, a shakeup of personnel, acceptance of war responsibility by company officials, and better pay for employees. Shōriki angrily rejected the demands and on the next day called together all officials from the assistant department chiefs up to say:

> I will not permit employees selfseekingly to set up an organization within the company. If you set one up against my will, I will compel your resignations. It is outrageous that some wrong-headed employees are using democracy as an excuse for conspiring something else. This company is mine, and I am utterly determined to stop you.[16]

A few days later, in response, over 1,000 out of a total of 1,875 *Yomiuri* employees turned out en masse to demand the formation of an employees' union, a thoroughgoing democratization of the company's organization, better pay, respect for the employees as human beings, and the collective resignation of all bureau chiefs and higher executives (including Shōriki) on grounds of war responsibility.[17] Shōriki had no intention of giving in and was determined to break through and establish a pattern at the *Yomiuri* for the settlement of future dispute throughout Japan. For him the *Yomiuri* was in the front line battling against a communist conspiracy to take over Japanese industry.[18]

Shōriki typified the conservative majority among business leaders which detested unions almost as much as they did communists and had feared the resurgence of both after the end of the war. Their ideal of proper labor relations was that of prewar Japan when government oppression kept labor fragmented and weak, and therefore cheap. Such men were unwilling or unable to distinguish militant unionism from communism, and insisted that any erosion of the rights of private property would contribute to the communist goal of destroying the whole capitalist system. Thus Shōriki insisted that his authority must be absolute within the *Yomiuri*, and that the workers' organization being set up was nothing but a front for a communist conspiracy.[19] Shōriki notwithstanding, the Communist party had nothing to do with the origins of the

Table 2
Rate of Unionization
(cumulative end-of-month totals)[a]

Year	Month	Unions	Membership
1945	Aug	–	–
	Sep	2	1,177
	Oct	9	5,072
	Nov	75	68,530
	Dec	509	380,677
1946	Jan	1,517	902,751
	Feb	3,243	1,537,606
	Mar	6,538	2,568,513
	Apr	8,531	3,023,979
	May	10,541	3,414,699
	Jun	12,007	3,681,017
	Jul	12,923	3,814,711
	Aug	13,341	3,875,272
	Sep	14,697	4,122,209
	Oct	15,172	4,168,305
	Nov	16,171	4,296,589
	Dec	17,265	4,849,329
1947	Jan	17,972	4,922,918
	Feb	18,929	5,030,574[b]

a. Japan Prime Minister's Office, Cabinet Bureau of Statistics, *Japan Statistical Year-book*, (Tokyo: Cabinet Bureau of Statistics, 1949), p. 717.
b. Membership only exceeds 6 million in December 1947.

Yomiuri dispute, which arose out of the unique situation of the Japanese press during the early occupation.

In the fall of 1945 SCAP was promoting the democratization of the press at the same time that it was insisting that production of newspapers must continue because they were an essential vehicle for Allied policy in general.[20] When SCAP on the one hand said workers must not strike, especially newspaper workers, and Shōriki on the other categorically rejected all demands for reform, the *Yomiuri* workers were placed in a difficult spot. To strike invited trouble, since both the government and SCAP would oppose it, but far worse, a strike could end in the closure of the paper entirely, which Shōriki considered more desirable than handing the company over to the employees.[21]

What could be done? The answer came out of an informal gathering of *Yomiuri* workers at a restaurant on the evening of that day in late October when the mass meeting of employees had served far-reaching demands on Shōriki. One of those present proposed that, if it was no good to strike, then:

> . . . why don't we put out the paper ourselves? If we do that we don't have to worry about bankrupting the company. And if we gain the support of the readers by putting out an excellent newspaper, then we can reconstruct the *Yomiuri* as a democratic paper . . .[22]

At that a lively discussion ensued that touched on such things as the prewar Italian and French examples of factory occupation and control. The result was that the editorial staff resolved, if need be, to take control over the editing, printing, shipping, and distribution of the *Yomiuri*.

The next day, Shōriki summarily rejected the demands and ordered the resignation of Suzuki and four others whom he considered to be ringleaders.[23] Suzuki and the others went back to the editorial office to report to the workers. On the spot a second employees' meeting was convened. Suzuki reported and ended by saying, "We are entering a state of dispute in order to achieve our demands. And from the newspaper for the 25th, we are going to put out the paper independently by ourselves." In order to carry this out, the

Newspaper and communications workers supporting the Yomiuri strikers. In front of the Yomiuri offices, 24 June 1946.

meeting elected a supreme struggle committee with Suzuki as chairman, and decided that supporting struggle committees would be elected in every department. When the meeting ended, the workers, raising shouts of victory, occupied the editorial office and evicted the bureau chiefs. With this the *Yomiuri* newspaper production-control struggle began, the first in postwar Japan.[24]

The day after production control began, 25 October, a meeting of workers set up the *Yomiuri* Newspaper Employees' Union and elected Suzuki chairman, but in the struggle that followed the union did not play an active role. From the outset, real authority lay in the system of struggle committees through which production control was being carried out. The union members and executive committee acted merely as one of the constituent parts of the struggle committee, and the union chairman and standing executive committee had no function. As the production-control struggle progressed, decision-making and executive functions in the struggle-committee system were merged. Whenever a problem came up requiring some kind of action, the struggle committee would call together as many of the workers concerned as it could to discuss the matter. The mass meeting would make a collective decision, and collectively carry it out. In short, the struggle-committee system operated on the basis of direct, participatory democracy.[25]

Under production control the *Yomiuri* took a progressive editorial stance and overnight became the most left-leaning and outspoken of Japan's major newspapers. The new policy gained public approval, and circulation shot up to nearly 1,700,000 copies.[26] Many outside organizations, such as the other newspaper unions, the JSP, and the JCP, rallied to the side of the *Yomiuri* workers.

At first Shōriki was not to be moved, but in December he was finally forced into arbitration. The agreement arrived at on 11 December provided (1) Shōriki would resign and sell all shares he owned in excess of 30 percent of the total stock of the *Yomiuri*; (2) the company would be reorganized as a corporation, allowing a wider distribution of shares; (3) Baba Tsunego (a former editor of the *Yomiuri* Sunday Review who was a right-wing socialist) was to be the new manager as Shōriki had urged; (4) a management council (*keiei kyōgikai*) on which management and employees were represented equally would be set up to consult on important matters concerning editing and business operations. Other items dealt with such specifics as further consideration of pay raises, withdrawal of dismissals for being active in the struggle, union recognition, collective bargaining, and conclusion of a contract.[27]

An editorial in the *Yomiuri* on 12 December 1945—the day after Shōriki had signed the arbitration agreement—celebrated the "Settlement of the *Yomiuri* dispute" and proclaimed a new policy:

> Heretofore the newspaper has been the organ of capitalists, it has oppressed the people, it has published articles that deceived and has suffocated the voice of the people. Now the *Yomiuri Shimbun* has been freed from this yoke of capital . . . . We proclaim that from this day the *Yomiuri Shimbun* will become truly a friend to the people and an organ of the people for eternity.[28]

The editorial argued that political democratization was meaningless in the absence of economic reform. An economic liberation from below, given impetus by the struggles of the people to stabilize their livelihood, was essential for the realization of a true democratic revolution. The *Yomiuri* now stood ready to support the people in their fight for economic sovereignty. The editorial cited the success of the *Yomiuri* workers in running the paper on their own, despite having to overcome 'sabotage' by the company.

After the arbitrated settlement, the members of the supreme struggle committee disbanded the production-control committees and in their place established a similar system based on the management councils for which the agreement had provided. The company was democratized and the employees gained unprecedented rights over what was to go into the paper and how the actual process of production was to be conducted. In effect, the reporters and writers were turned loose to dig up their own stories, regardless of how derogatory they were to the government and big business. Typesetters and printers threw out the oppressive system of top-down labor control that Shōriki had introduced in the twenties and took direct control over the printing of the paper. Thus, workers' control became a practical reality at the *Yomiuri*, with the enthusiastic participation of the mass of the employees,[29] who used the 'democratic' *Yomiuri* to champion the radical, populist reconstruction of Japan.

The first *Yomiuri* struggle is significant in two ways. First, it shows the importance of the workers' fight in postwar Japan for greater control over the work process at the point of production. The *Yomiuri* employees had asked for the right of

Table 3

Types of Dispute Actions and Workers Involved[a]

Year Month		Total		Strikes		Slowdowns		Production Control		Production Control as % of Total	
		Actions	Workers	Actions	Workers	Actions	Workers	Actions	Workers	Actions	Workers
1945	Aug	–	b	–		–		–		–	
	Sep	2		2		–		–		–	
	Oct	20		16		3		1		5%	
	Nov	27		21		2		4		15	
	Dec	39		33		3		3		9	
1946	Jan	49	37,720	27	6,142	9	2,549	13	29,029	26	77%
	Feb	53	29,176	23	6,532	10	6,847	20	15,806	38	54
	Mar	80	79,950	32	48,527	9	10,722	39	20,651	50	26
	Apr	89	50,417	30	14,726	6	840	53	34,815	60	69
	May	106	51,295	42	9,047	8	3,401	56	38,847	53	76
	Jun	80	26,707	29	6,735	7	1,916	44	18,056	55	70
	Jul	90	27,346	48	14,721	17	10,147	25	2,478	28	9
	Aug	107	52,282	61	24,054	18	4,983	28	23,245	26	44
	Sep	124	118,242	59	81,368	28	14,484	37	22,390	30	19
	Oct	156	200,729	104	188,958	17	2,633	35	9,138	22	5
	Nov	127	87,488	89	76,563	14	3,262	24	7,663	19	9
	Dec	108	93,496	65	61,361	17	23,569	26	8,566	24	9
1947	Jan	65	26,050	30	17,491	9	2,316	26	6,243	40	24
	Feb	90	34,600	52	28,101	14	1,462	24	5,037	27	14

a. Japan Prime Minister's Office, Cabinet Bureau of Statistics, *Japan Statistical Year-book* (Tokyo: Cabinet Bureau of Statistics, 1949), p. 730–731; SCAP, ESS, Advisory Committee on Labor, *Final Report: Labor Policies and Programs in Japan* (Tokyo: 1946), p. 35; Miriam S. Farley, *Aspects of Japan's Labor Problems* (New York: The John Day Company, 1950), pp. 83–84.

b. Figures not available for 1945.

participation in management, but their own actions belied those moderate-sounding words both during and after production control. Spearheaded by the editorial bureau, their struggle committees had simply taken over production and distribution at the outset, and after the settlement the employees continued to dominate the paper, this time through the union and the management council.

Second, the widespread societal influence of production control was extraordinary. Even while the dispute was going on, workers and organizers streamed to Tokyo *Yomiuri* headquarters from all parts of Japan to learn at first hand how to organize themselves and take action. And of course the *Yomiuri* newspaper, with its wide national circulation, carried the message to uncounted others unable to make the pilgrimage to Tokyo. The *Yomiuri* employees had won their dispute, without going out on strike and without interrupting production, by the novel step of dispossessing the owners and managers. The lesson seemed clear. Production was critically needed but so was radical social and economic change. If employers resisted worker demands, victory could still be had by seizing and operating the enterprise.

The Lines of Confrontation

The spread of production control throughout all sectors of Japanese industry contributed greatly to a sharpening of the lines of confrontation between the workers' movement and big business, and between the political extremes of left and right. On the one side was the conservative mainstream of business supported by established politicians and bureaucrats, on the other the radical shop-floor workers' organizations supported by the JCP taking up production control as their primary means of struggle. By mid-winter all parts of Japanese society were coming to realize that what was being called into question by the growing economic and political crisis was capitalism itself; the government seemed unable to act even though the economy continued its plunge and threatened to bring on a collapse of tremendous proportions. Reconstruction had to begin, but who was to do it and how? Under what conditions and limits? To many Japanese there seemed only two alternatives: a capitalist reconstruction by the holdover conservative establishment, seeking what was in essence a return to the laissez-faire twenties, or a socialist reconstruction with the JCP playing a leading part.[30] The polarization was symbolized by two important events in early 1946: the production control and people's court incident of January and February at the Mitsubishi Bibai Coal Mine, and the government's Four Ministry Declaration denying the legality of production control that was issued on 1 February.

The Mitsubishi Bibai situation was relatively straightforward.[31] The coal miners had set up a union in early November covering all of the 5,000 or so workers of the Mitsubishi mines. Within a week the union sent a package of largely economic demands to the company to which the company replied unsatisfactorily. In mid-November the miners struck and gained a very substantial increase in total pay, in the form of a basic wage plus allowances. Then in mid-December, when the government published its new, upwardly-revised standards for total pay per worker recommended by the coal industry, the company discovered that it had been paying the miners a rate higher than the new standard, whereupon the company unilaterally deducted the 'overpayment' from the workers' December pay and on the same grounds also abolished the special allowance for daily attendance at the mines.

Since the company's action threatened the miners' livelihood, the union hardened its position and submitted a list of eight demands in early January. The most important of these were (1) maintenance of the wage standard previously negotiated; (2) abolition of the contract system (a type of piecework, under which the productivity requirement was high); (3) continuation of the attendance allowance separately from the standard wage; and (4) opposition to the transfer to Tokyo of the refining-section head, who had been popular among the production and staff workers and had aided their efforts to organize unions.

A compromise agreement, negotiated in Sapporo by Assistant General Manager Noda Tōichi and union chairman Mizutani Takashi, conceded a great deal to the company. When the news reached the union, the miners' union repudiated the agreement on the grounds that Mizutani had conducted the negotiations on his own and did not have the authority to make an agreement in the first place. The company took an unbending stand on the wage issue, arguing that the matter had been settled and that in any case it could not exceed the new standard for coal-mine wages since this would cause difficulties at its other mines. Union members then not only reaffirmed their demands but added three more, including one about participation in management. No progress was made and a confrontation became unavoidable.

The union called an extraordinary meeting for 7 February at which the miners voted a list of three key demands: (1) abolition of the contract system for surface and pit workers; (2) inclusion of all existing allowances in the basic wage; and (3) continuation of the attendance allowance in goods 'to the bitter end.' After the company categorically rejected these demands, union members reconvened and voted to begin production control on the eighth if their demands were not met. The company in turn dismissed that decision as illegal and vowed to defend its management rights 'to the bitter end.'

The miners next set up a dispute organ (sōgi dan), and the four union executives who had been acting as the miners' negotiating committee became the leaders of the dispute organ. They were, by occupation, an outside-the-pit railway worker, a clerk-in-charge in the labor section, a construction-section assistant, and a coal miner. On the eighth the union entered production control at 7:00 AM and dispatched a control committee to the offices and to every workplace. For about ten days all went on much as before, with the staff still accepting instructions from the company and the workers digging coal under the supervision of the staff. Labor productivity and total output increased dramatically.

Due to the company's intransigence, negotiations had been discontinued completely since the workers' takeover, so on 17 February the union called a meeting to discuss the situation. The meeting ended with a resolution to push onward to victory. Afterwards a group of several hundred union members sought out and forcibly seized both General Manager Gōtō Tarō and Assistant General Manager Noda at an executives' clubhouse where the two were in conference with other high officials of Mitsubishi's enterprises in Hokkaidō. The union members forcibly marched the two through the snow to a meeting hall nearly two kilometers away, where the miners sat them down on the stage across the table from the union officials. The workers and their families jammed into the hall and with that began thirty-six hours of nonstop mass negotiations, the famous "people's court" incident.

Soon after the mass negotiations began, the union officials persistently questioned the managers, asking why the company could not pay the workers' wage demands. Noda was backed into a corner from which he tried to extricate himself by an evasive and flippant, "Anyhow, we can't pay it," provoking a torrent of abuse from the workers' assembly. This account of the beginning stages of the people's court by one of the main participants, Nishimura Takeo, catches some of the flavor of the anger of the miners and their families:

> "What's this, you can't pay [the demanded wages]?"
> "We workers are never going to be silenced!"
> "Hey! You managers, you came here to cheat us, didn't you? What about it? Answer!"
> General Manager: "That is not the case."
> "Liar! What about today's tempura?"
> "You feed your dogs on white rice; where did you get that rice?"
> "You are always cheating us of our sake and drinking it, aren't you? Just look at those red noses!"
> In the midst of this twenty-some police poured into the hall with their boots on.
> "What's this? Get those cops out of here. They're the capitalists' watchdogs!"
> "What kind of thing is this, coming into our hall with your shoes on? Take them off!"
> "Take off your hats!"
> The crowd of people knew the ugly side of the police, who were in collusion with the capitalists.[32]

SCAP took a hands-off attitude even during the people's court, and the Japanese authorities were unable to take action on their own. Nearly thirty police had come out to the mine at the outset of the incident, but were uncertain what to do and asked their superiors for instructions. They were simply told to "take appropriate measures." The continuing abuse was too much for the police in the hall to take for long, and they left in pairs without doing anything. The company's appeal to SCAP was equally fruitless since the local occupation authorities who came to see what was going on were not inclined to intervene, merely giving the company the indifferent reply: "Should it lead to acts of violence inform us immediately."

The company officials were forced to listen to the bitter personal attacks of the miners and their wives for treating the workers brutally in the mines, and for callously feeding pet animals good food from their own excess stocks while the workers and their families ate scraps little better than garbage in order to survive at all. At one point, according to Nishimura's account:

> A lone woman stood and rushed up onto the stage. Composing her white face, she took a handful of something from her pocket. Wanting to say something, lip quivering, boiling with agitation, she began to cry in mortification.
>
> "Managers, please look at this. It's the guts of a pumpkin. While you were eating rice every day and drinking sake, there was no rice ration for us. We were told it was in order to win the war. The sweet potatoes ran out, and we came to the point of eating this, every day, every day (choking sob). Our family was patient with this, even though I couldn't even give my husband something to take when he went to work (cries). And what of the feelings of a mother when her child says again and again, 'Rice, I want to eat rice' (voice rising and crying) If you are human, you ought to understand a parent's feelings. And recently, when we thought that thanks to the union, wages had been raised a little, now they say that you will take back the sardines that we have been living on. After all that, are you human? If that were all, it might be endured, but what kind of a thing is it that you are snatching away the things we eat, that you are raising pet horses and dogs and letting them eat white rice? The coal-mine pitworkers are leading more miserable lives than dogs. We worry about something to eat every day, every day, and it feels like we will go crazy over getting something to eat. While I'm standing here right now I'm thinking about what we will eat this evening."
>
> Unable to go on she broke down in tears. Her heaving shoulders touched the hearts of those present. It was probably the first time in her life she had spoken in front of people. Deeply moved by her own words, she finally broke down completely on the stage. The women in the hall raised their voices in a wail at the sad memories she had called up.[33]

The attitude of the gathered workers and their families was menacing as the pent-up hatreds bred of years, even decades, burst out in words such as these.

The Mitsubishi Bibai miners were, nonetheless, several steps away from conscious, anti-capitalist solidarity. A large step closer would be taken by subsequent production-control struggles when, in complete disregard of legality, the struggle committees would reach out to other organizations to make a breakthrough into a more self-sustaining form of production control. The Mitsubishi workers foreshadowed this when their struggle committee made an unsuccessful appeal to the Hokkaidō farmers' unions for a joint struggle to secure food for the miners, but the conscious intent to break with the capitalist order was yet to come.[34] When the company officials finally broke under the pressure and gave in to the union demands, the result was the same type of settlement that had come at the conclusion of most previous production-control struggles: large pay hikes, democratic reforms of the enterprise, recognition of labor rights, and formation of a management council.

Even before the people's court incident, the violence attending the main-office demonstration that had ended the production-control struggle at Japan Steel Tube had made Japan's leaders disturbingly aware of the social consequences of a continuing stagnation of production.[35] The workers' defiance of authority and the connections being forged with the JCP shocked them into action against what they saw as a communist-directed attack against the rights of private property.[36] The government responded on 1 February 1946 when the Home, Justice, Commerce and Industry, and Welfare Ministries in response to a request from the president of Japan Steel Tube[37] issued a joint policy declaration which branded production control an illegal act in violation of property rights.[38]

The intent of the Declaration could not have been clearer. Henceforth the government would regard production control as an illegal act to be dealt with summarily by the police. The government in principle acknowledged labor's right to engage in acts of struggle like strikes, but in reality the Declaration was a fundamental negation of that right, for it prohibited the sole effective means of dispute available at the time—production control—as "illegal and excessive actions," a phrase flexible enough to permit application of the Declaration much more broadly should the necessity arise.[39]

The increased resistance by business and government did not prevail for the time being, however, since SCAP would not countenance the Shidehara Cabinet's unilateral proscription of production control and the projected use of the police to combat it, maintaining instead that the issue must be resolved through legislation or the courts.[40] Without the SCAP support and faced by a storm of protest, the government backtracked a week later and the question of legality remained unresolved.[41] But in effect, since the practice spread ever more widely over the next months (see table 3) in spite of concerted government and business opposition, the radical workers' organizations on the shop floor carried the day.

The workers' careful attention to keeping production control legal as a dispute tactic eroded as the employers dug in their heels and labor disputes became increasingly bitter. At this juncture, the anti-capitalist implications of production control surfaced in two ways: the workers' committees began to assume sweeping rights to use company assets and facilities during the dispute for whatever purposes they deemed fit, and demands for permanent extension of workers' control to matters of policy-making and organization began to displace strictly economic demands as the crucial issue. Stiffening government and business resistance was being countered by a growing worker radicalization in practice, and the smell of revolt in the factories began to permeate the air.

The JCP and Production Control

One of the more difficult theoretical questions for the Japan Communist Party after the war was the proper characterization of Japan's postwar stage of development. If Japan was still to a significant degree feudal, then the proper policy would be completion of the bourgeois-democratic revolution. If Japan was now on balance a mature capitalist society—not to mention monopoly capitalist—then a socialist revolution was the objective.

Some fifteen years earlier, the 1932 Theses of the JCP had resolved this debate by positing a rapid transformation of the bourgeois-democratic revolution into a socialist one through a two-stage revolution to be carried out by a soviet government of workers, peasants, and soldiers under the hegemony of the proletariat. The early formation of soviets and the rapid transition from the bourgeois-democratic to the socialist revolution could take place because "objective conditions for socialism exist and the necessity for the destruction of the capitalist system of exploitation has become fully developed."[42]

In fact, the two-stage revolution in the 1932 Theses was telescoped to the extreme, coming down to a rapid and violent seizure of power by soviets under the leadership of the JCP.[43]

The thirteen years since 1932 had seen great economic and social change. The war had forced the pace of industrialization, and heavy industry displaced light to become the overwhelmingly dominant sector of the economy. By 1945 the now numerically larger non-agricultural work force could justifiably be characterized by its largest component as an industrial working class. Although 'feudal remnants' did still exist, like the landlord and labor-boss systems, in Marxist terms Japan was indisputably a thoroughly capitalist society at the war's end[44] giving Tokuda and the other JCP leaders all the more reason for building upon the revolutionary positions in the 1932 Theses. Yet, even while tacitly acknowledging Japan's capitalist maturity in Party policies and pronouncements, the party leaders also pointed to the facts of defeat and foreign occupation as preventing the use of tactics appropriate to normal times. That is, they did not believe it possible to take the theoretically logical next step of dedicating the Party to leading the socialist revolution openly and at once. Now at a point when capitalist maturity had largely been reached, the JCP still felt it necessary to fall back on a variant of the old two-stage line.

The two-stage line created a series of contradictions that would plague the JCP for some time to come, and were to prove especially costly during the first nine months when the revolutionary tide was rising. This compromise formulation avoided the necessity of a direct confrontation with SCAP, but it created an ambiguity in Party policies and formulations that led to confusion among party ranks and softened the Party's Leninist resolve to mobilize the working class for the cause of the revolution.

A prime example of the ambiguous analysis was the concept of the "people's republic" (jinmin kyōwa seifu).[45] The 1932 Theses had not used this term, but had spoken of a soviet government to be followed by the dictatorship of the proletariat. Party policy called for the establishment of a people's republic, but this was not to be one composed of workers' and peasants' soviets. Rather, the term signified a parliamentary form of government in which a broad united front of democratic forces would hold power,[46] a progressive bourgeois democracy in which the unions and parties of the workers and peasants would not only sharply circumscribe the powers of the big bourgeoisie and their feudalistic allies, but would also outweigh and increasingly dominate other bourgeois elements that SCAP favored.[47]

It is clear that the strategic line of establishing a people's republic and completing the bourgeois-democratic revolution was an exceedingly elastic concept which could be used equally well to justify either an early drive onward to socialism or an extended democratic transition. The people's republic was an uneasy way station between the liberal capitalist order and socialism. Intentionally or not, these early Tokuda-Shiga formulations masked considerable theoretical vacillation about the speed with which the JCP could proceed to the main task of social revolution. It was one thing to talk about the character of the present revolution being bourgeois-democratic with a strong tendency towards progression into the socialist one—as did the 1932 Theses and postwar Party policy less precisely—but it was quite another to put practical content into that ambiguous phrase. A people's republic worthy of the program enunciated in the 1932 Theses would have to be built on soviets, not parties and unions, the very existence of which would compromise the viability of Japanese capitalism and arouse the wrath of SCAP.

The JCP did not have a well-worked-out policy on production control, however, nor was it promoting it solely to hasten the socialist revolution. This can be seen in JCP documents and publications from the period, but more convincingly in the actions of JCP organizers in mines and factories. In both writings and behavior, party theorists and organizers like Tokuda Kyūichi lumped together reform tactics with revolutionary strategy, just as had been done in the 1932 Theses.

The documents issued at the Fourth Party Congress in December 1945 (written under Tokuda's direction), for example, set out a policy of promoting unions and workers' control simultaneously. This was to be done by having the unions undertake two tasks: (1) bargaining with employers over narrow economic issues like wages and hours; and (2) taking basic *control over production* (this phase would be downgraded at the 5th Congress in February to *participation in management*) in order first, to overcome the economic breakdown, and second, to pave the way for socialist revolution.[48] Production control was facilely regarded as a workers' action appropriate for either end. In retrospect this was a blunder. Based as it was on worker direct action, posing a fundamental challenge to the rights of private property, production control pointed toward a worker-soviet or council type of factory organization, not the union. And in fact production control was usually carried out by production-control struggle committees, organizationally distinct from ·and superior to the usual union structure.[49]

Tokuda for one seemed to think that production control could coexist in the interim with unions using the more conventional labor tactics of strikes and collective bargaining, perhaps thereby preserving within the capitalist order the germ of the revolutionary factory society, much as was argued in the 1932 Theses of the JCP.[50] He apparently believed the progression from bourgeois democracy to socialism would be relatively rapid and peaceful, arising out of Japan's new democratic society in a matter of a few years or even months. The rapid progression would presumably make it possible for the nucleus of the production-control struggles to evolve into permanent soviet-style workplace councils.[51] However, at least this much is clear in retrospect: production control contradicted not only the capitalist organization of Japanese industry and society, but also the authority of conventional unions within the enterprise. Ultimately production control could no more coexist with business unions bent upon exercising maximum authority over labor's rank-and-file than it could with owners and managers determined to safeguard property rights.[52]

The councils in such a conception would not so much coexist with unions as gradually usurp their functions and engulf them. The continuing enlargement of the revolutionary role of the councils at the union's expense would presumably solve the theoretical and practical problems resulting from the confusion of production control as a dispute tactic with production control as a revolutionary act. To the extent that the progression from bourgeois democracy to socialism proved long and difficult, however, business and government resistance to the councils was bound to increase in intensity and effectiveness, thus making the survival of production control increasingly difficult. Tokuda did not face this problem squarely, and by and large it seems the enemies of production control saw the fundamental contradiction of preserving it under a revivified capitalism more clearly than its supporters did. Production control—just as conservative business and government leaders, right-wing socialists, and labor leaders realized—even when carried out strictly as a dispute tactic, amounted to using revolutionary means for non-revolutionary ends. Moreover, it threatened to become the central strategy in a popular movement developing in a revolutionary direction.

The JCP Changes Its Policy

The ambivalence with which the JCP had approached production control, simultaneously as dispute tactic and revolutionary strategy, ended abruptly when Nosaka returned to take over an important role in Party leadership and institute the so-called "loveable JCP" line of revolution through the ballot box.[53] If Japan was expected to follow the parliamentary road to socialism, rather than see the early establishment of a people's republic, then neither extra-legal revolutionary bodies like soviets nor illegal worker takeovers of enterprises through production control could have a role.[54]

At the Fifth Party Congress of the JCP from 24–26 February, the policy on labor was rewritten to emphasize unions and their role as the proper vehicle for worker participation in management, and to delete earlier demands for worker control over essential enterprises as a basic precondition for Japan's reconstruction.[55] Tokuda, too, endorsed the policy change, though unwillingly. Consequently production-control struggles on the shop floor aiming at a radical rearrangement of authority in the enterprise were on their own, essentially without any national political organization interested in or capable of coordinating their individual struggles nationwide.[56]

This is not to say that the JCP had rejected what is sometimes ambiguously referred to as political unionism. That was hardly the case considering the unions' later political confrontations with the Yoshida Cabinet, culminating in the 1 February 1947 General Strike movement. What was being rejected in theory and practice was that part of the strategy laid down in the 1932 Theses calling for the organization of powerful workers', soldiers', and peasants' soviets for the purpose of enforcing the "transformation of the bourgeois-democratic revolution into a socialist revolution."[57]

Under Nosaka's lead, the Party defined the postwar changes Japan was undergoing as completion of the bourgeois-democratic revolution. It was argued that an immediate and possibly violent socialist revolution to establish a people's republic could not succeed since Japan was occupied, but that a gradual and peaceful socialist revolution through the ballot box could.[58] The question of whether Nosaka's appraisal was correct is important, for if correct, then Tokuda's projected development of production control from dispute tactic to revolutionary soviet was doomed to failure. No categorical answer is possible, but Tokuda at least had been prepared to take the gamble and try to bring on the socialist revolution through adapting to Japanese conditions the Leninist program of all power to the soviets, and seizing upon the production control struggle organization as the Japanese equivalent of the Russian soviet. Certainly Nosaka was wrong in thinking that the US would ever stand by and watch even a loveable JCP be voted into power, as would become increasingly clear after the SCAP suppression of the 1 February 1947 General Strike

which had been called to force the replacement of the Yoshida government with a leftist coalition cabinet.

At any rate, the economic corollary of the political recognition of parliamentary democracy by the JCP was acceptance of a capitalist reconstruction and by extension recognition of the rights of private ownership of the means of production. Workers' councils, such as those struggle committees engaged in production control, challenged property rights and were accordingly downgraded, while unions which eschewed such challenges were emphasized as the correct workers' organizations under existing conditions. From there it was but a short step to call, as the Declaration of the Fifth Party Congress (24–26 February 1946) did, for joint labor-management bodies whose role was to put the economy back upon its feet, but, it must be noted, upon capitalist feet. The JCP now conceived the role of production control to be solely that of a dispute tactic of industrial unions and a means of bringing about labor participation in management concurrently with continuing production for reconstruction.[59]

The relegation of production control to the role of a dispute tactic of labor unions or labor-capital cooperation in the form of the enterprise-level council blinded the Party to the meaning of the quickening of the workers' movement in the spring of 1946. Just when the production-control struggles were moving in a militantly anti-capitalist direction and beginning to reach out and forge alliances with the city poor and needy farmers, the JCP fell behind the popular movement. As the Party became ever more deeply involved in parliamentary politics and the formation of popular electoral fronts, a gap opened between the JCP national leadership and the workers' movement.[60]

Business and Government Leaders Try Co-optation

The Shidehara Cabinet quickly took steps toward formulating a new, more moderate strategy after the failure of its outright proscription of production control in the Four Ministry Declaration of February 1946. These government efforts were complemented by conciliatory measures within that part of the business world that was dissatisfied with the confrontationist tactics of the advocates of laissez-faire.[61]

Aware of their weakness vis-a-vis the popular movement and the organized left, the more progressive members of the elite began to seek grounds for accommodation. The leaders of Keizai Dōyūkai (the Japan Committee for Economic Development), which was formed in April 1946, were representative of this tendency, which they proposed to implement through imposition of economic controls and planning by a stratum of enlightened managers and technocrats freed from the domination of enterprise owners and government bureaucrats alike.[62]

The immediate object of these progressives was an increase in the supply of consumer goods in order to remove one of the basic causes of social unrest. Over the longer term they could envision a significant upgrading in technical skill and standard of living for the hitherto submerged workers and farmers. By treating labor less as an enemy and more as a junior partner, so to speak, they hoped labor could be brought closer to management, and cooperation, not conflict, could become the new keynote for labor relations. The cost would be unions strong enough to gain real benefits for their members. Hence, big business had to try to upgrade labor skills and productivity, because the financial impact of the increased-wage bill could only be ameliorated by encouraging increased

A demonstration raising the demand "Give us rice" advances on the Sakashita Gate of the Imperial Palace in Tokyo, 5 May 1946.

productivity from these workers.[63] There was also some willingness to extend limited recognition to production control as a dispute tactic of labor unions, insofar as it was carried out on a 'production' basis, meaning continuation of production by the employees in strict adherence with the pre-existing plans of the rightful owners and managers.[64]

In early February the Shidehara Cabinet had already put together a new policy for reconstruction on the basis of light industry. The key aspects of the policy were (1) economic controls and priority planning stressing coal—coal because it was a crucial raw material for the chemical industry, rail transportation, and power generation—and chemical fertilizers as the essential ingredients for increasing the supply of consumer goods and foodstuffs; and (2) a plan to mobilize labor behind this end by encouraging healthy business unions and setting up joint labor-management factory councils in priority industries. These two items stand in sharp contrast to the government's prior laissez-faire approach to the economic crisis.[65]

Although SCAP had provided the basis for unionization, and had begun to press the Shidehara government to devise a plan for taking effective steps towards economic reconstruction, this attempt to formulate a new and more progressive economic policy in early 1946 was primarily in reaction to the workers' movement. The rapid spread of worker organization and radicalization of production control seemingly gave substance to the fears of social revolution haunting every faction of the political and business elites in the winter of 1945–1946, however liberal or conservative.[66] The new policies were intended to neutralize the anti-capitalist inspiration behind production control in two important ways: on the one hand by drawing organized labor into the system, and thereby splitting the working class, and on the other by overcoming the deepening food crisis and general economic collapse that were generating serious social unrest. The enterprise-council structure of the production control struggle committee was vulnerable to cooptation by the kind of labor-management councils envisaged by both the Shidehara Cabinet and the more liberal representatives of the business world, the more so since

the left parties also endorsed participation in the councils.

The outcome of the above shifts in policy, understandably, was eventually to be a convergence in the direction of accepting and institutionalizing a denatured form of production control within a reconstructed capitalist order through extending to legally recognized organizations of labor certain narrow rights of participation in management, but no rights of control over management.[67] It could hardly have been otherwise, given the mutual acceptance by the JCP and the progressive elite of the necessity for an immediate capitalist reconstruction of Japan.

Radicalization of Production Control

Meanwhile, since February 1946 the production control struggles had been rapidly moving to the left, toward illegal factory seizure and operation, regardless of the various grand strategies for bringing them into line with one policy or another. On top of this, they also greatly increased in number, becoming the major form of labor dispute in April and May with 110 production control struggles recorded and nearly 75,000 workers involved (see table 3). A pair of examples may help to show the strength of the workers' movement centering around production control.

At the Takahagi coal mines north of Tokyo, a dispute broke out in March which resulted in the implementation of production control from 6 April to 14 June. Once the dispute began, the issue boiled down to the question of whether payment for coal produced and sold by the miners should be made to the Takahagi union or the mineowners. Coordinated worker demonstrations, mass negotiations in Tokyo, and threats by the national union federation, to which the Takahagi union belonged, to institute production control at coal mines all over Japan soon forced the government to back down from its position that the payments must be made to the mineowners. It now took a hands-off position, declaring that until the legality of production control was decided the parties involved would be allowed to settle the dispute among themselves. Thereupon the national allocation and distribution agency for all coal, the Japan Coal Company, directed that payment be made to the mineowners. At this the employees' union of the Japan Coal Company itself instituted production control and arranged for payment to be made to the Takahagi union, and that settled the matter for the time being.[68]

The union and miners had won a clear victory over the government and the mineowners, but the payment of the fee to the union did not mean a return to routine operations pending settlement of the miners' demands. Instead the Takahagi workers went on to extend their support to the series of popular demonstrations against the Shidehara Cabinet in April and May that led up to Food May Day and General MacArthur's subsequent "Warning against Mob Disorder or Violence." Beyond the highly significant victory over the payment of the coal fee, other gains were made: first, extension of the scope of the production control struggle beyond enterprise lines; second, attainment of coordinated broad support through the national union federation; and third, projection of workers' participation in production control onto the national political scene.

These gains pointed toward the acquisition by workers of the ability to conduct production control on a more or less long-term basis despite government and business opposition. A second struggle illustrates this theme even better, and also demonstrates the effective cooperation of workers and peasants with a common interest in increasing production of coal, fertilizer, and food. It shows in striking fashion that workers and peasants were capable of responding to the economic crisis by working out their own practical solutions independently of both government and business.

What the Takahagi workers had the consciousness and will, but not the means, to accomplish (i.e., establishment of nation-wide production control of their own industry), the chemical workers, coal miners, and farmers in the Tōyō Gōsei production-control struggle from 13 March to 27 August did accomplish. Tōyō Gōsei was a small chemical factory in Niigata City that was part of the Mitsui combine. Mitsui ordered the factory to be closed around the end of January, but the employees defied the order, publicly declaring: "Despite the closure order of the authorities, we will not close." Mitsui caused production to be suspended anyway on 19 February by cutting off materials. The next day the employees gathered to organize a union of 190 members. Besides presenting the usual demands for union rights, the employees expressed their total opposition to dismissals and demanded a guarantee of a reasonable minimum wage as well as the setting up of a labor-management council. The union also denounced and called for the ejection of the two top officials at the factory.[69]

In reply the company called in all the white-collar staff workers separately from the more radical production workers and put pressure on them. One company official said he was determined to either dismiss the union executives and close the factory or resign himself. The union held a third mass meeting on 27 February at which the production workers, over the objections of the staff, rejected the company's stand. Thirty-one staff workers reacted by withdrawing from the union. The company dealt the union another blow two days later when the two company officials put out a directive which said that the factory would be closed no later than the 28th, 108 people would be retained as interim employees for winding up business, and there would be a 10:00 A.M. deadline on the 28th for those who wanted to accept a dismissal allowance. Fifty-three workers immediately left the union to accept the offer of temporary employment.

On the day set for closure, the remaining union members convened a meeting which demanded that those who had left the union for temporary employment be discharged, that the factory not be closed, and that all union members be retained as employees. The company agreed to the discharges, but rejected the rest. The situation remained in limbo until 13 March when a company official visited the factory and declared that it was closed and that the company would not retract the dismissal of all employees.

Once again the union convened a general meeting, at which the workers decided to reopen the factory that very day by instituting production control. The workers at Tōyō Gōsei completely severed contact with the Mitsui combine leaders and unhesitatingly took whatever steps they deemed necessary to keep the factory in operation. They abolished the old hierarchy of managers and department and section chiefs and shouldered the burdens of management collectively, since most of the white-collar staff had already deserted the struggle.

The production workers took a long-range view and methodically set about reconverting the plant to the production of chemical fertilizer with the aim of attaining full operations on 16 June. The biggest hurdle was capital, and the first attempts to secure working funds failed. Then the Tōyō Gōsei

workers learned about a Tokyo chemical factory, Edogawa Manufacturing, that was in the midst of implementing production control and had solved its cash problem by selling formalin (a 40 percent solution of formaldehyde in water) in the union's name. The Tōyō Gōsei union decided to sell methanol (used in the manufacture of formaldehyde) to Edogawa and thereby obtained ¥300,000 in cash.

In a related step, the Tōyō Gōsei workers worked out a mutually beneficial barter arrangement with the 15,000-member Niigata farmers' association whereby the factory got the coal and coke, and the farmers the fertilizer. The farmers' association organized among its members a special cooperative to which the farmers subscribed for ¥100 apiece. The association used the proceeds to buy coal and coke from coal mine workers, and bartered this in turn to Tōyō Gōsei for the fertilizer ammonium sulphate.

The hardheaded realism of this arrangement, by means of which production of industrial goods and foodstuffs both rose, illustrates the capacity of ordinary working-class people to manage their own interests. The Tōyō Gōsei workers acquitted themselves well. They installed complicated equipment, changed over from one product to another, expanded the work force, increased wages, and raised production using machinery that the company said was so antiquated and out of repair as to be nearly useless. They did all this in cool disregard for property rights and capitalist managerial prerogatives. What is more, the company and the government seemed powerless to resist.

Equally significant was the struggle at Edogawa Manufacturing, a small Mitsubishi company of about 500 employees. The employees had organized a union in January encompassing both the staff and production workers and simultaneously set up a three-tiered system of elective workers' councils organized functionally according to the company's operating structure. The main decision-making body was the employees' general meeting, but there were also an elected central executive committee of twelve members, a small number of workshop committees, and a larger number of departmental committees staffed by workers which took over the formulation and implementation of a production plan.[70]

The Edogawa union presented demands on 12 February, but company officials arrogantly rejected them, the business manager going so far as to say, "I don't care if you employees die; I don't have to guarantee your right to live."[71] Until 1 March, when the workers instituted production control, the company and the union fought over which side was to receive payment for a large order of formalin that the national agricultural association had placed much earlier. The business manager, who controlled official allocations through his power over the chemical control association, had been quietly sabotaging the formalin shipment by obstructing the arrival of railroad cars. This he did because the price of methanol was rising at a dizzy rate, from ¥1,800 per ton in January, to ¥8,600 in February, and ¥13,500 in March, and he hoped to reap a speculator's profit. Now he suddenly rushed to complete the transaction with the national agricultural association in order to cripple the workers' position before production control commenced.

The Edogawa union frustrated his plans by itself negotiating with the agricultural association and obtaining a promise to pay the union. The shortage of formalin needed in the manufacture of fertilizers for use in the fields of Tōhoku

Chart 1

Expanded Production Control at Tōyō Gōsei and Edogawa Manufacturing[a]

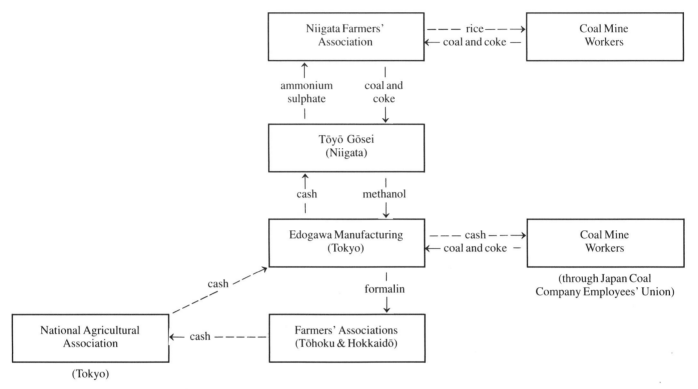

a. Yamamoto Kiyoshi, *Sengo Kiki ni okeru Rōdō Undō*, vol. I. of *Sengo Rōdō Undō Shi Ron*, (Tokyo: O-Cha no Mizu Shobo, 1977), pp. 147–150.

and Hokkaidō was becoming critical at this time, and each day that passed without delivery would result in lower yields. The Edogawa workers' success was directly related to their ability to make early delivery, which it could do because of the support of the railroad workers' unions.

At this juncture the Edogawa workers received another hard-line rejection of their demands and decided in a general meeting on 1 March to begin production control. The employees organized for this by tight coordination of the union central executive committee vested with the highest authority and a production-control committee to administer operations. Overall they made few changes and ran the plant much as before, though entirely without the old managers.

The Edogawa workers immediately sent off the available railroad cars for Tōhoku and Hokkaidō loaded with formalin and, in spite of opposition from the Ministry of Transportation, managed within nine days to transport the whole amount that had been on order for two months. The cooperation of the transportation workers and their unions was important, as was the dispatching of two of their own union members to Hokkaidō for liaison work. Mitsubishi and the government tried to obstruct payment, too, by tying up funds through litigation. But the employees' union of the national agricultural association made common cause with the Edogawa workers

and saw to it that payment was made.

Acquiring the raw materials for production posed a greater problem, one not entirely solved. To a small extent the Edogawa workers were able to circumvent the monopoly control of the *zaibatsu* and the government over coal supplies by establishing a tight liaison with the employees' union of the Japan Coal Board. Absolute shortages of coal and coke brought about the suspension of production of methanol in April, but, as related above, they managed to get it from Tōyō Gōsei. In this instance, the Edogawa and Tōyō Gōsei workers, by maintaining their internal solidarity and uniting in joint struggles with sympathetic outside organizations, overcame the limitations of workers' control conducted in a hostile, capitalist environment. The relationships they developed are presented schematically in Chart 1.

Workers might have embarked on production control in these coal mines and chemical companies and elsewhere at the outset in order to achieve a set of concrete and not very radical goals having to do with wages and job security. But as their struggles lengthened and became more difficult, they tended to escalate to a new phase. This new phase was marked by a more or less conscious decision to seek outside cooperation in producing essential commodities in critically short supply, commodities that were vital to improving the living conditions

Chart 2

Evolution of Production Control

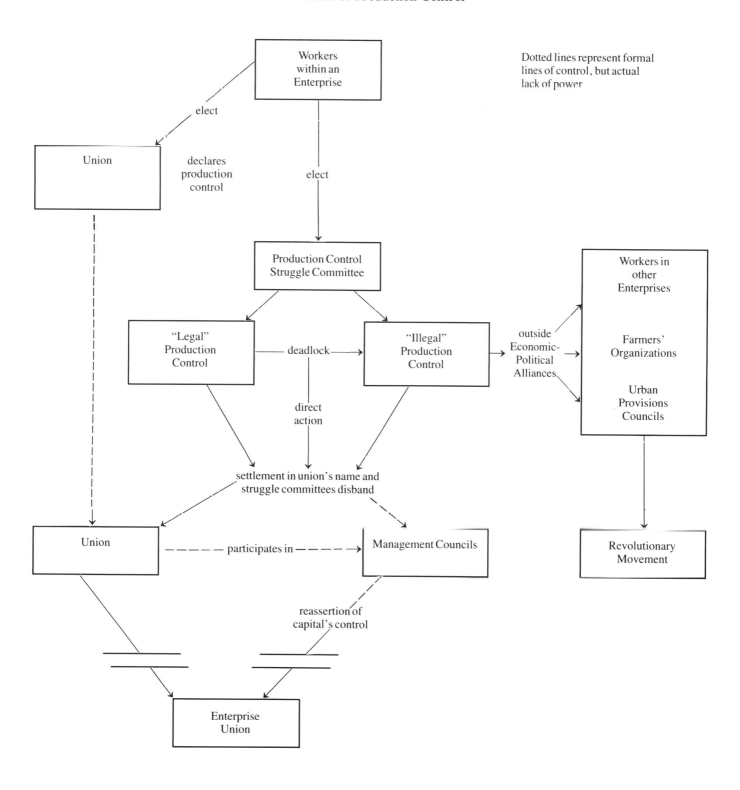

Schoolchildren participating in Food May Day by carrying banners for the revival of school lunches. The plaza in front of the Imperial Palace in Tokyo, 19 May 1946.*

of the people. Altruism was a factor, but what counted most was that during the economic revival different sectors of the working class were able to advance their mutual interests outside capitalist relations of production. In short, profits and wages ceased to be the sole object of operations, and social needs assumed first place.

Several things are especially noteworthy about this struggle. The union took over and operated the company in its own name, completely excluding the company executives. They installed equipment, changed over from making one product to another, expanded the work force, increased wages, and took whatever steps they saw fit without concern for property rights or employer prerogatives. In addition to this, very large numbers of workers and farmers were drawn into the expanded struggle, the farmers' association alone having 15,000 members.

The taking of control over enterprise operations for the long term by a production control struggle committee, as had

*All three photos in this article are courtesy of Herbert P. Bix and Mary Anne Oliver. They are from *Senryō to Minshū Undō* (Tokyo: Sanseidō, 1975), vol. 10 of *Nihon Minshū no Rekishi*, pp. 90, 59, and 144.

happened at Tōyō Gōsei, assumed even greater significance in the light of the upswelling of popular protest movements—notably the Tokyo city dwellers' efforts to assert control over food supplies through provisions councils and peasant efforts to assert their interests through leftist tenant unions.[72] The potential for an alliance between these movements and industrial workers carrying out production control certainly existed during the first half of 1946 (see Chart 2). The goals of all three were complementary in much the same way the various participants' goals in the Tōyō Gōsei were. For example, as at Tōyō Gōsei, chemical fertilizer or agricultural implements could have been exchanged for food, thereby breaking through the "scissors crisis"—low official prices for foodstuffs in conjunction with soaring prices for manufactured goods, causing the withholding of food in the countryside for increased personal consumption, black-market sale, or speculation—that had led to a government policy of forced requisitions of food from the countryside.

Production Control and Parliamentary Politics

All of the above suggests that the time was ripe for a national movement prepared to challenge the conservatives for control of the government and the economy. The Democratic People's League which was organized in March 1946 by Yamakawa Hitoshi, was intended to do just that. The League's activities, however, were somewhat removed from the popular currents which were gathering strength. The D.P.L. sought to act as an umbrella organization for those who wished to topple the Shidehara Cabinet and install a center-left coalition cabinet under a socialist premier. As such, the League reflected the interests of reform-minded leaders of formal organizations like trade and tenant unions and the left-wing parties much more than it did the attempts by shop-floor workers to implement workers' control. Its main reason for existence was to take part in the parliamentary struggle for power attendant upon the April elections to the Diet, not to encourage and lead radical popular actions.[73]

The leftist national leadership associated with the League was eager to mobilize the already existing popular movement behind its electioneering efforts to bring a center-left coalition cabinet to power. Despite the moderation of the national political movement against Shidehara and then Yoshida in spring 1946, more than once the mass political demonstrations and rallies called to exert extra-parliamentary pressure on the government exhibited a spontaneous radicalism alarming to SCAP and the US government.[74] Strong public denunciations soon came from George Atcheson, the American Chairman of the Allied Council, and from General MacArthur who made a threatening speech on May 20 in reaction to the mass demonstrations on 19 May, Food May Day, which had been called to prevent Yoshida from forming a cabinet as well as to demand an immediate solution of the food crisis by putting the mechanism of distribution under popular control.[75]

MacArthur's speech had the immediate result of propelling Yoshida into power even though he had just given up the attempt to form a right-wing cabinet because of the widespread and vehement popular opposition to the kind of business-as-usual approach that he symbolized.[76] SCAP's blasts against communists and mob violence also served to reinforce the right-wing socialists' hold over the JSP and the conservative labor unions. The left-socialist and JCP consternation at seeing SCAP openly repudiate the left and give open support for a most conservative cabinet—indeed reactionary in respect to labor—produced consternation among the left-wing socialists and the JCP. Divisions on the left were thus intensified, and the effort to form a parliamentary socialist opposition that would be nationally organized and unified quickly faded with the disintegration of the Democratic People's League.

The grass-roots mass movements which had rallied to the call on May Day, Food May Day, and other occasions and had shown themselves prepared to stand up against the old order were now set completely adrift without any organizational focus capable of helping them transcend their own individual interests—be it land distribution, food distribution, or factory control—in a comprehensive, nationwide solution of Japan's political and economic crisis. Thrust back upon their own resources it was hardly surprising that peasants, city dwellers, and workers alike turned to particular solutions to the urgent problems confronting them. For employed workers, obviously the best vehicle for overcoming the economic problems at hand was a strong union capable of gaining recognition, wage increases, job security, and so forth. Unfortunately, this kind of solution did nothing for the unemployed, the female worker, or those in small and medium businesses, and thus did not address the most pressing problem, that of resuming production on a new and more equitable basis for all working people.

SCAP had already been moving with its own solution to the demands for food distribution and land reform and had preempted both of these as issues for popular mobilization well before the next upsurge in the workers' movement in the winter of 1946–1947. Large-scale distribution of food imported from the US began almost immediately after the May upheavals. The land reform program was passed by the Diet in October 1946. With both of these issues defused and the Japanese government moving against production control with SCAP backing, there was little likelihood of another opportunity of the kind that had surfaced in the spring of 1946. If Tokuda's program of Leninist revolutionary action had ever had a chance, that chance was now past.[77]

Conclusion

In brief, the period under review here witnessed the following progression in the deepening of Japan's postwar crisis. Economic breakdown attendant upon the lost war and a business sit-down combined to make production control the most effective dispute action for desperate blue- and white-collar workers. The severity of the economic crisis and the stubborn but not very effective resistance of business and government to workers engaging in production control stimulated a radicalization that was leading in the spring of 1946 to illegal anti-capitalist takeovers of enterprises by workers' councils.

By the time of the one-month socialist cabinet interregnum (April-May 1946) it had become apparent that despite the moderate parliamentarism adopted by the leftist party and union leaders, the possibility of a socialist reconstruction for Japan was being raised anyway by a popular movement attempting to solve the economic crisis by taking matters into its own hands at the point of production. It is problematical whether a further development of the radical production control struggles of the time in intimate cooperation with the popular movement could have succeeded in pushing a reluctant JCP leadership into the revolutionary vanguard role it claimed for itself. JCP reluctance was matched by a pragmatic readiness on the part of many conservative political and economic leaders to make tactical concessions and resume production on the basis of a reformed capitalism.

In any event SCAP's intervention stiffened the resolve of the conservatives, who counterattacked against the left. The disarray within the leftist leadership ensured that the popular movement would be left to its own devices. The participants in the struggles in the villages, on factory floors, and in local neighborhoods drew the conclusion that operating under continued conservative control required caution. Whether caution was dictated by a fear of retaliation or by the necessity of simply surviving while the old order still controlled the distribution of food and other necessities of life, there was a general turn away from radical answers toward making the best accommodation possible within the existing order. This rejection of radicalism became increasingly evident among the blue- and white-collar workers, who eventually abandoned their production control committees for a more orthodox trade-union movement.

Production control as an anti-capitalist act or as a dispute tactic was on the wane by June when SCAP sanctioned a government crackdown on its use, and strikes re-emerged as the major form of dispute action. A minimal resumption of economic activity at about this time also had enhanced the effectiveness of strikes as a means to gain concessions for industrial workers, at least in key sectors of the economy like transportation, power, and coal. And from that point on it was the unions which became the main arena for the conflict with big business since the right to organize and to bargain collectively over wages and working conditions had become the central issue.

Since the advent of Taylorism[78] and scientific techniques of production and personnel management, capitalists have striven to extend their control over the processes of production down to the most minute level. They have pursued their quest for maximizing labor productivity by an ever-increasing curtailment of worker autonomy in organizing the actual work to be done. They have withdrawn matters of choice or of decision-making from the work process and made them the exclusive property of management. Harry Braverman has described how the consequent degradation of work has built the problem of overcoming worker resistance into the very tissue of modern capitalism.

> The apparent acclimatization of the worker to the new modes of production grows out of the destruction of all other ways of living, the striking of wage bargains that permit a certain enlargement of the customary bounds of subsistence for the working class, the weaving of the net of modern capitalist life that finally makes all other modes of living impossible. But beneath this apparent habituation, the hostility of workers to the degenerated forms of work which are forced upon them continues as a subterranean stream that makes its way to the surface when employment conditions permit, or when the capitalist drive for a greater intensity of labor overstrips the bounds of physical and mental capacity.[79]

Japan has not escaped the inevitable destruction of worker autonomy which Braverman cites as being characteristic of capitalist development. The subterranean drive for workers' control—understood here in the commonsense meaning of control over policymaking as well as the processes of production—surfaced after the war in the form of demands for the democratization of the enterprise and for participation in management. It gained added strength from the workers' pressing need to revive production in the face of capitalist sabotage. Workers did not arrive at their solution of production control overnight; instead they set out in the more orthodox vein of trade unionism.[80] As they organized, workers put forth three basic types of demands: for recognition of their economic interest, for democratization of personal relationships in the work place, and for democratization of the processes of production.[81]

The economic demands usually constituted a package calling for recognition of the workers' right to organize, strike, and bargain collectively over wages, hours, and working conditions. Goals like those pointed at particular solutions, at an attempt to overcome personal catastrophe by collective action within the framework given by the capitalist enterprise. Even if granted in full, they could not provide a means for surmounting the economic crisis, nor did they pose a radical challenge to employers.

Demands for democratization within the workplace focused primarily on putting an end to cruel and dictatorial treatment by employers and supervisors, and the abolition of the status system in the plant, which discriminated sharply between white-collar staff and production workers. They also encompassed attacks on those employers and managers who had been supporters of Japan's imperialist policies. Important as they were, such demands were not in themselves much more radical than economic demands centered on wages; they could be met by more employer attention to human relations in industry.

Workers' demands for democratization of the processes of production were most often summed up in the general demand for participation in management.[82] This could not be satisfied so easily. Whether it concerned the setting of company goals, organizing production or personnel policies, demands of this type impinged on the rights of private property, and no employer was ready to concede more than symbolic worker participation in management.

These demands, which correspond to those of workers in all industrialized societies, took on a heightened meaning in a country on the edge of economic chaos. Japan's working class somehow had to protect itself against a wave of dismissals and to increase production of essentials, but neither could be achieved by tactics like strikes or slowdowns during the immediate postwar period when there was widespread business retrenchment and mass unemployment. Employers could defeat a strike simply by locking out strikers, hiring strike breakers, or closing down altogether. A strike could hurt employers only in certain essential industries and services like fuel and transportation where employers had some stake in continued operation, but even here striking could only worsen the economic situation, victimize the public, and earn SCAP's displeasure. Thus capitalist sabotage had created conditions under which worker occupation of enterprises was the sole means available for attaining the mutually supportive goals of jobs and production.

Had economic goals, even the key ones of saving jobs and resuming production, been all that there was to production control, it might well be dismissed as nothing more than a dispute tactic of unions, one suited to exceptional times when strikes did not work. Many have argued in this way, discounting the seizure and operation of factories as the excesses of an immature union movement. Once production resumed, accord-ing to this view, there was no further use for such tactics and they faded away, to be replaced by collective bargaining as unions assumed their rightful place as the protectors of the economic interests of the working class.

As for this assumption that the basic demands of workers after the war were economic in detail and reformist in intent, the evolution of production control presents quite the contrary picture. Indeed, the congruence in early 1946 of a seemingly unresolvable economic crisis, the desperate needs of workers and their families, and a fundamental drive towards workers' control guaranteed that production control would not remain a mere dispute tactic of unions aiming at a better contractual bargain for labor.

The business union and its leaders ultimately recognize only the workers' right to withdraw labor, to strike; they seldom support the workers' right to seize control over and operate the enterprise in their own best interest. Union leaders pursue their ends through a process of collective bargaining which takes as given the legitimacy of the division between mental and physical labor, between managers and workers. Accordingly, they restrict themselves to but one aspect of the total organization of production within the capitalist enterprise, labor supply, and see their first order of business as the striking of the best economic bargain for the membership. The business union, dedicated to securing the privileged economic position of a relatively small aristocracy of labor, is opposed to mass organization and sees little to gain in acting as the spearhead of broader working-class interests. In this respect, it is the vehicle of a co-opted labor movement.

C. Wright Mills has described the leader of the American business union as a jobber and dealer who bargains and sells labor to the employer, who controls conflict and keeps worker discontent from erupting and spoiling the bargain once made. Even so, the labor leader must in part be a rebel against the capitalist system, for his power does not derive from property. His is an accumulation of power deriving from the organiza-tional solidarity of discontented workers, themselves opposed to the undisputed dominion of capital. Paradoxically, the labor leader strives to gain acceptance into the existing capitalist system by mobilizing discontent against it.[83] Nevertheless, the labor leader's rebellion must always be partial, aimed at maximizing the union's power within the existing order:

> Yet even as the labor leader rebels, he holds back rebellion. He organizes discontent and then he sits on it, exploiting it in order to maintain a continuous organization; the labor leader is a manager of discontent. He makes regular what might otherwise be disruptive, both within the industrial routine and within the union which he seeks to establish and maintain . . . the labor union is a regulator of disgruntlement and ebullience, and the labor leader, an agent in the institutional channeling of animosity.[84]

Unions are drawn into a defence of capitalist institutions as part of the bargain for economic concessions, but as pointed out by Braverman, conflict does not arise from economic deprivation alone. More is at stake—the loss of control over the work process. Herein lies the root problem of unions as organizations of the working class. The union must deny the workers' attempts to regain control at the point of production, or lose its legitimacy in the eyes of the employer and the state and its ability to secure economic concessions through collective bargaining.

Placed in the difficult position of having to cooperate with the employer even while standing up for the membership, the union leader must minimize rank-and-file participation in union affairs. The independence of the union leadership is vital to the union's ability to enforce its side of the contract because in addition to the guarantees of the workers' economic rights, the contract commits the union to enforcing unpopular prohibitions on the workers' rights in most other areas such as discipline on the job. That is the trade-off that the employer demands for extending recognition.

In the end, unions are not particularly democratic organizations, much less revolutionary bodies. They are an integral part of the system of industrial relations of advanced capitalism and cannot advocate radical goals like workers' control without undermining their own legitimacy and existence as unions. This applies with equal force to socialist or communist unions, which succeed in a capitalist society only to the extent that they in reality give up goals that cannot be achieved and are in contradiction with the capitalist system of production. Nor can a union long tolerate the existence of a rival body in the enterprise having workers' control as its aim, for dual organization in the workplace undermines the only power base that the union has, worker solidarity.

In times of chaos or revolutionary flux, however, the union may suddenly find it must respond to demands for workers' control. Two possibilities then face the union: either being remade internally in the image of the workers' council which is structured for operating the enterprise, or being thrust aside by the workers' own council arising from the struggle on the shop floor.

At the beginning the Japanese workers did view production control as an effective if unorthodox dispute tactic of labor unions, not as a revolutionary act. Participants in the early production-control struggles took care to stay within the law by keeping the locked-out management informed and by adhering to the existing production plan, often allowing company officials to continue making policy and operating decisions subject to worker review. Since they conceded the fundamental legitimacy of managerial prerogatives based on the rights of private property and kept accurate records in anticipation of turning things back over to the employer, the settling of a dispute made it easy for the temporarily dispossessed managers to resume control over the enterprise.

Even legal production control struggle of this sort was indisputably an anti-capitalist act, because the workers, against the will of owners and managers, in fact were denying the rights of private property in the means of production. They had to. Once embarked on production control, the workers in the enterprise found it immediately necessary to set up machinery accountable to themselves in order to continue production. This commonly took the form of the struggle committee (tōsō iinkai).

The struggle-committee system echoed the enterprise organization, but differed in that at the workshop, section, or department level the workers elected committees which became the building blocks for a three- or four-tiered pyramid culminatng in an executive committee at the top. The committees might assume control over production by taking on the tasks of management directly, by election of responsible supervisors, or by holding existing supervisors accountable. The highest authority resided in the general enterprise conference (taikai) which often played an extraordinarily active role, making decisions as the need arose and implementing

them at once through collective action. There was, consequently, no sharp organizational separation of policymaking and execution. The workers ran their own enterprise through the production-control struggle committee. Furthermore, the struggle committee either hollowed out or displaced the union, because it provided a more effective means for realizing the workers' interests than the union with its narrow bureaucratic channels designed for gaining economic rewards for its members.

Without doubt, big business and government opposition to production control from January 1946 onward can be accounted one of the major factors conducive to its radicalization. Unable to prohibit production control by law and suppress it with the police due to SCAP opposition, Japan's leaders sought to confine the duration and scope of production control by denying the participants access to funds, supplies, and markets, hoping thus to bring the workers to terms. This policy of containment generated intense pressures on workers engaged in production control as they ran out of money and materials, operations ground to a halt, and the possibility of achieving concessions on their demands steadily receded. Such stonewalling by management did not necessarily force the workers to a settlement. Instead it often precipitated rapid radicalization of the workers' struggle and their repudiation of the framework of legalism that had constrained the workers heretofore. (See Chart 2 for a schematic presentation.)

Two characteristics distinguished 'illegal' from 'legal' production control: a conscious denial of the legitimacy of capitalist legal limitations and other obligations that the workers had previously accepted in disputes between capital and labor, and the workers' impelling need to reach outside the enterprise for allies and resources to continue the fight. Once having taken the step into illegality, it was but a short step further to the position that the enterprise need not ever be returned to the control of the owners. Workers who crossed this line were tying their own fate to the fate of their collectively-operated enterprise. The cost of failure would be high, certainly the loss of their livelihood and perhaps worse, and men with families did not undertake such an effort lightly. Behind their decision lay a basic confidence that they as workers could not only run an enterprise successfully, but also do it better than the capitalist owners.

Workers came by that confidence both by the example of others and by their own experience. For example, the workers at the *Yomiuri* newspaper gained tremendously in self-confidence as their struggle developed. Furthermore, their successful operation of the paper provided daily proof for all to see of the ability of employees to operate a business. Nonetheless, production control was bound to fail if confined by business and government opposition within the narrow legal bounds of a dispute tactic of labor within the capitalist order. Not the least of these restrictions was the workers' inability to secure supplies of raw materials for production at the same time that they found it difficult to sell the finished commodities.

In sum, the central issue of the workers' movement in Japan at the outset of the Occupation, when two central demands were for democratization and participation, was not unionization. Rather it was workers' control which involved mounting an attack on the prerogatives of employers, prerogatives which had long been virtually absolute. Production control called into question the most fundamental aspect of the capitalist system, private property. It pointed toward a sweeping reorganization of the internal order of business enterprise and a rapid erosion of the rights of management in hiring and firing, in supervision of the work force, even in making policy decisions on what to produce, to whom to sell, and where to allocate the firm's resources.

Production control was a manifestation of the disintegration, not the amelioration, of capitalist production in Japan, and business and government leaders could not afford to tolerate it any longer than they had to. In constant contradiction of the imperative of modern capitalism to appropriate all decision making as the exclusive preserve of management, production control could end in only two ways: in soviets and an unremitting revolutionary struggle for power, or in the total defeat of workers' control and the aggressive reimposition of unquestioned employer authority over the process of production.

Notes

1. Jerome B. Cohen, *Japan's Economy in War and Reconstruction* (Minneapolis: University of Minnesota Press, 1949), pp. 59f, 75f, 272–293, 318; Suehiro Izutarō, *Japanese Trade Unionism: Past and Present* (Tokyo: Mimeographed, 1950), chapter 3, section 5; Tōyama Shigeki, "Sengo Nijū Nen no Gaikan," *Shiryō Sengo Nijū Nen Shi*, Vol. 6, *Nempyō*, ed. Tōyama Shigeki (Tokyo: Nihon Hyōronsha, 1967), p. 3; U.S., Department of State, Interim Foreign Economic and Liquidation Service, *Labor Developments in Japan Since Surrender: August 15–November 15, 1945* (Record Group No. 226, Office of Strategic Services, XL 37772, Nov. 30, 1945), pp. 8–10; Yamamoto Kiyoshi, "Sengo Kiki no Tenkai Katei," *Sengo Kaikaku*, Vol. 5: *Rōdō Kaikaku* (Tokyo: Tōkyō Daigaku Shakai Kagaku Kenkyū-jo, 1974), p. 84.

2. Supreme Commander for the Allied Powers, General Headquarters, *History of the Non-military Activities of the Occupation of Japan*, Monograph 28, *Development of the Trade Union Movement: 1945 through June 1951*, pp. 10–14, appendix pp. 16–19.

3. Japan, House of Representatives Special Committee for the Investigation of Concealed and Hoarded Goods, *Supplementary Report* (Tokyo: December, 1947), in SCAP, GHQ, *Summation: Non-Military Activities in Japan*, No. 27, pp. 25–29; SCAP, Government Section, *Political Reorientation of Japan: September 1945 to September 1948* (Washington, D.C.: U.S. Government Printing Office, 1949), pp. 307–313; Ōuchi Hyōe, "Keizai," *Sengo Nihon Shōshi*, Vol. 1: ed. Yanaihara Tadao (Tokyo: Tōkyō Daigaku Shuppan-kai, 1958), p. 82; Thomas A. Bisson, *Prospects for Democracy in Japan* (New York: The MacMillan Co., 1949), pp. 14, 98, 117.

4. Cohen, pp. 407–408; Japan Ministry of Finance and Bank of Japan, *Statistical Year-Book of Finance and Economy of Japan, 1948* (Tokyo: Ministry of Finance Printing Office, 1948), p. 670; Keizai Dōyūkai, *Keizai Dōyūkai Jūnen Shi* (Tokyo Keizai Dōyūkai, 1956), p. 14; Ōkōchi Kazuo and Matsuo Hiroshi, *Nihon Rōdō Kumiai Monogatari*, Vol. 1: *Sengo* (Chikuma Shobō, 1969), p. 63.

5. SCAP, Economic and Scientific Section, Advisory Committee on Labor, *Final Report: Labor Policies and Programs in Japan* (Tokyo: 1946), p. 36; Rōdō Sōgi Chōsa Kai, *Tekkō Sōgi*, Vol. 7: *Sengo Rōdō Sōgi Jittai Chōsa* (Tokyo: Chūō Kōron Sha, 1958), pp. 89–90.

6. Nihon Tankō Rōdō Kumiai, *Tanrō Jūnen Shi* (Tokyo: Rōdō Jumpō Sha, 1964), pp. 43–60; Rōdō Sōgi Chōsa Kai, *Sekitan Sōgi*, Vol. 1: *Sengo Rōdō Sōgi Jittai Chōsa* (Tokyo: Chūō Kōron Sha, 1957), pp. 49–59; Ōkōchi and Matsuo, p. 98.

7. Takano Minoru, *Nihon no Rōdō Undō* (Tokyo: Iwanami Shoten, 1958), p. 11; Shioda Shōbei, "Zen Sen'i Sangyō Rōdō Kumiai Dōmei," *Nihon Rōdō Kumiai Ron*, ed. Ōkōchi Kazuo (Tokyo: Yūhikaku, 1954), pp. 288–289; Watanabe Tōru, *Gendai Rōnō Undōshi Nempyō* (Tokyo: San'ichi Shobō, 1961), p. 157; Ōkōchi and Matsuo, p. 82.

8. Nihon Kyōsantō Chūō Iinkai, ed. *Nihon Kyōsantō Kōryōshū* (Tokyo: Nihon Kyōsantō Chūō Iinkai Shuppan Kyoku, 1962), pp. 100–104; Shakai Undō Shiryō Kankōkai, ed. *Nihon Kyōsantō Shiryō Taisei* (Tokyo: Ōdosha Shoten, 1951), pp. 23–25.

9. Arahata Kanson, *Kanson Jiden* (Tokyo: Ronsōsha, 1960), p. 530; Shinobu

Seizaburō, *Sengo Nihon Seiji Shi* (Tokyo: Keisō Shobō, 1965), Vol. 1, pp. 178–179; Tagawa Kazuo, *Sengo Kakumei no Haiboku*, Vol. 1: *Sengo Nihon Kakumei Undō Shi* (Tokyo: Gendai Shichōsha, 1970), p. 3.

10. SCAP, ESS. Advisory Committee on Labor, Appendix A.

11. Horikoshi Teizō, ed. *Keizai Dantai Rengōkai Jūnen Shi* (Tokyo: Keizai Dantai Rengōkai, 1962), Vol. 1, pp. 4–10, 25–26; Vol. 2, pp. 490–496; Vol. 3, pp. 304–307, 547–548.

12. *Ibid.*; Miwa Yoshikazu, "Keisai Dantai Ron," *Dokusen Keitai*, Imai Noriyoshi, ed. Vol. 1: *Gendai Nihon no Dokusen Shihon*, (Tokyo: Shiseidō, 1964), pp. 215–216; Noda Kazuo, ed. *Sengo Keiei Shi*, Vol. 1: *Nihon Keiei Shi*, Nihon Seisansei Honbu (Tokyo: Nihon Seisansei Honbu, 1965), p. 51.

13. U.S. Department of State, Division of Research for Far East, Office of Intelligence Research, "The Yomiuri Shimbun Case: A Significant Development in the Post-surrender Japanese Press" (OIR Report No. 4247, March 19, 1947), pp. 5–6, (RG 331, box 8499, folder: Labor Rels: Disputes—Newspapers, Yomiuri Case [Confidential]).

14. Tōkyō Daigaku Shakai Kagaku Kenkyū-jo, ed., *Sengo Kiki ni okeru Rōdō Sōgi: Yomiuri Shimbun Sōgi (1945–1946)*, part 1, Vol. 6 of *Shiryō* (Tokyo: Tōkyō Daigaku Shakai Kagaku Kenkyū-jo, 1973), pp. 9–11, 26–27, 75; Edward Uhlan and Dana L. Thomas, *Shoriki, Miracle Man of Japan: A Biography* (New York: Exposition Press, 1957), pp. 61–67; Tōkyō Daigaku Shakai Kagaku Kenkyū-jo, ed., *Sengo Kiki ni okeru Rōdō Sōgi: Yomiuri Shimbun Sōgi (1945–1946)*, part 2, Vol. 7 of *Shiryō* (Tokyo: Tōkyō Daigaku Shakai Kagaku Kenkyū-jo, 1974), pp. 18–20.

15. Tōkyō Daigaku, *Yomiuri Shimbun Sōgi*, part 1, pp. 19, 23–25; Takano, pp. 30–31.

16. Masuyama Tasuke, "Dai Ichiji Yomiuri Sōgi Shi," *Rōdō Undō Shi Kenkyū Kai*, ed., *Sambetsu Kaigi: Sono Seiritsu to Undō no Tenkai*, Vol. 53 of *Rōdō Undō Shi Kenkyū* (Tokyo: Rōdō Jumpō Sha, 1970), p. 22; Rōdō Sōgi Chōsa Kai, ed., *Rōdō Sōgi ni okeru Tokushu Kēsu*, Vol. 6: *Sengo Rōdō Sōgi Jittai Chōsa* (Tokyo: Chūō Kōron Sha, 1957), pp. 13–14; Uhlan, p. 169.

17. Tōkyō Daigaku, *Yomiuri Shimbun Sōgi*, part 1, pp. 9–10, 22.

18. Rōdō Sōgi Chōsa Kai, *Tokushu Kēsu*, p. 16; Tōkyō Daigaku, *Yomiuri Shimbun Sōgi*, part 1, pp. 9–10.

19. Rōdō Sōgi Chōsa Kai, *Tokushu Kēsu*, p. 27; Uhlan, pp. 170, 172; Tōkyō Daigaku, *Yomiuri Shimbun Sōgi*, part 1, pp. 9–10.

20. Tōkyō Daigaku, *Yomiuri Shimbun Sōgi*, part 1, pp. 5–6.

21. Masuyama, "Dai Ichiji Yomiuri Sōgi," p. 28.

22. *Ibid.*, p. 29.

23. Rōdō Sōgi Chōsa Kai, *Tokushu Kēsu*, pp. 15–16.

24. *Ibid.*, pp. 21–22; Masuyama, "Dai Ichiji Yomiuri Sōgi," pp. 27, 29; U.S. Department of State, "The Yomiuri Shimbun Case," pp. 73–78.

25. Tōkyō Daigaku, *Yomiuri Shimbun Sōgi*, part 1, pp. 33–35, 38–39; Yamamoto Kiyoshi, *Sengo Kiki ni okeru Rōdō Undō*, Vol. 1: *Sengo Rōdō Undō Shi Ron* (Tokyo: O-Cha no Mizu Shobō, 1977), pp. 262–265.

26. Mark Gayn, *Japan Diary* (New York: William Sloane Associates, Inc., 1948), p. 23.

27. Rōdōshō, pp. 7–8; Rōdō Sōgi Chōsa Kai, *Tokushu Kēsu*, pp. 29–33; U.S. Department of State, "The Yomiuri Shimbun Case," pp. 17–18.

28. Tōkyō Daigaku, *Yomiuri Shimbun Sōgi*, part 1, p. 80.

29. *Ibid.*, p. 81.

30. Sumiya Mikio, "Mitsubishi Bibai Sōgi," Tōkyō Daigaku Kagaku Kenkyū-jo, ed. *Sengo Shoki Rōdō Sōgi Chōsa*, Vol. 13 of *Chōsa Hōkoku* (Tokyo: Tōkyō Daigaku Kagaku Kenkyū-jo, 1971), p. 25; William J. Sebald, memorandum of conversation with leading Japanese businessmen (February 12–1946), pp. 1, 3, enclosure to Dispatch No. 258, Max Bishop, Office of the Political Adviser (Record Group 59: 740.00119/2-1546).

31. The following discussion is based on: Rōdōshō, *Shiryō 20–21-nen*, pp. 44–58; Sumiya, "Mitsubishi Bibai," pp. 22–30; Nihon Tankō Rōdō Kumiai, pp. 68–69; Rōdō Sōgi Chōsa Kai, *Sekitan* pp. 66–69.

32. Nishimura Takeo, *Jinmin Saiban no Shinsō*, (April 15, 1946), p. 33. I am very much indebted to Professor Yamamoto Kiyoshi for making this document available to me.

33. *Ibid.*, pp. 43–44.

34. Sengo Kakumei Shiryō Hensan Iinkai, ed. *Seisan Kanri Tōsō: Shiryō Sengo Kakumei* Rinji Zōkan: Jōkyō (Tokyo: Jōkyō Shuppan, October 1, 1974), p. 184.

35. Nikkeiren Sōritsu Shūnen Kinen Jigyō Iinkai, ed. *Jūnen no Ayumi* (Tokyo: Nikkeiren Sōritsu Shūnen Kinen Jigyō Iinkai, 1958), pp. 100–102; Horikoshi, Vol. 1, p. 38; Vol. 2, pp. 498–499; Vol. 3, p. 689; Keizai Dōyūkai, *Jūnen Shi*, pp. 34–36.

36. Asahi Shimbun Sha, ed., *Shōdo ni Kizuku Minshushugi*, Vol. 1: *Asahi Shimbun ni Miru Nihon no Ayumi* (Tokyo: Asahi Shimbun Sha, 1973), p. 153; Noda, p. 243; Horikoshi, Vol. 3, p. 689.

37. Yamamoto, *Sengo Kiki*, p. 168.

38. Ōkōchi Kazuo, ed. *Rōdō*, Vol. 4: *Shiryō Sengo Nijū Nen Shi* (Tokyo: Nihon Hyōronsha, 1966), p. 8.

39. Chūō Rōdō Gakuen, ed., *Rōdō Nenkan: Shōwa 22* (Tokyo: Chūō Rōdō Gakuen, 1947), pp. 292–293; Max Bishop, Office of the Political Adviser to the Supreme Commander for the Allied Powers, Despatch No. 250: "Political Parties in Japan: Developments During the Week Ending February 9, 1946," (R.G. 59: 740.00119/2-1346), pp. 3–4. Noda, pp. 242–243; Horikoshi, Vol. 1, Appendix, p. 136.

40. Theodore Cohen, Chief, Labor Division, ESS, SCAP, conference with Mr. Iguchi, Chief, General Affairs Bureau, Central Liaison Office, in regard to issuance of government statement on legality of production control, (Record Group 331, box 8481, folder: Production Control); Rōdōshō, pp. 33–34; Keizai Dōyūkai, *Jūnen Shi*, p. 32.

41. SCAP, GHQ, *Summation*, No. 5, p. 194.

42. George M. Beckmann and Genji Okūbo, *The Japanese Communist Party: 1922–1945* (Stanford: Stanford University Press, 1969), p. 341.

43. *Ibid.* pp. 336–41, 343, 346.

44. Sumiya Mikio, *Social Impact of Industrialization in Japan* (Japan: Government Printing Bureau, Ministry of Finance, 1963), Chapters 4 & 5 *passim;* Shinobu, p. 188.

45. Shakai Undō Shiryō Kankō Kai, pp. 3–4; Tokuda Kyūichi, Shiga Yoshio, *et al*, "An Appeal to the People," Appendix 2, Despatch No. 31 of October 27, 1945 from George Atcheson, Acting Political Adviser to the Supreme Commander for Allied Powers, "Periodic Report: Developments of Political Parties and Movements for the Week Ending October 26, 1945," (General Records of the Department of State, National Archives, R.G. 59: 894.00/10-2745.

46. Nihon Kyōsantō Chūō Iinkai, ed., *Nihon Kyōsantō no Gojū Nen, Zenei*, Rinji Zōkan, No. 342 (August, 1972), p. 114–116.

47. Tokuda Kyuichi, E. Herbert Norman, John K. Emmerson, "Communist Party Policy and Current Japanese Problems," Memorandum of Conversation, Despatch No. 51 of November 13, 1945 from Atcheson to the Secretary of State, "Political and Economic Policies of the Japanese Communist Party," (R.G. 59: 894.00/11-1345). Saitō Ichirō, *Sengo Rōdō Undō Shi*, (Tokyo: Shakai Hyōron Sha, 1974), p. 31.

48. Nihon Kyōsantō Chūō Iinkai, ed. *Kōryōshu*, pp. 99–111.

49. Tōkyō Daigaku, *Yomiuri Shimbun Sōgi*, part 1, pp. 33–39.

50. Beckmann and Okubo, pp. 341–346.

51. Shakai Undō Shiryō Undō Kankōkai, pp. 3–7, 23–25, 36–37; Nihon Kyōsantō Chūō Iinkai, ed. *Kōryōshū*, pp. 100–104; Tsukahira Toshio, *The Postwar Evolution of Communist Strategy in Japan* (Cambridge: Center for International Studies, Massachusetts Institute of Technology, 1954), pp. 8–9.

52. Yamamoto Kiyoshi, "'Sangyō Saiken' to Shoseiji Shutai," *Sengo Kaikaku*, Vol. 5: *Rōdō Kaikaku* (Tokyo: Tōkyō Daigaku Shakai Kagaku Kenkyū-jo, 1974), pp. 208–209.

53. Shakai Undō Shiryō Kankōkai, p. 53.

54. Yamamoto, "'Sangyō Saiken,'" pp. 212–215.

55. Nihon Kyōsantō Chūō Iinkai, *Kōryōshū*, pp. 105–107.

56. SCAP, Gov. Sec., Harry E. Wildes, *et al.*, report of interview with Nosaka Sanzō, (February 19, 1946), pp. 2–3 enclosure to Dispatch No. 265, Max Bishop, Office of the Political Adviser, (Record Group 59: 740.00119/2-1946).

57. Beckmann and Okubo, p. 338.

58. Shakai Undō Shiryō Kankōkai, pp. 53–56; U.S. Army Forces, Pacific, GHQ, Office of the Chief of Counter-Intelligence, Research and Analysis, "Strategy of the KYOSANTO (Community Party)," memorandum of interrogation of Nosaka Sanzō, (January 31, 1946), p. 2, enclosure to Dispatch No. 243, Max Bishop, Office of the Political Adviser, (Record Group 59: 740.00119/2-1946).

59. Nihon Kyōsantō Chūō Iinkai, Kōryōshū, pp. 106–107.

60. Yamamoto, "'Sangyō Saiken,'" pp. 215, 219–220.

61. Horikoshi, Vol. 3, p. 309.

62. Arisawa Hiromi and Inaba Hidezo, eds. *Keizai*, Vol. 2: *Shiryō Sengo Nijū-nen Shi* (Tokyo: Nihon Hyōronsha, 1966), p. 116; Miwa, p. 223; Horikoshi, Vol. 3, pp. 309–310; Keizai Dōyūkai, *Jūnen Shi*, p. 3, 32–36.

63. Keizai Dōyūkai, *Jūnen Shi*, pp. 3, 32–36.

64. Gōshi Kōhei, "Seisan Kanri no Keizaiteki Seiyaku," *Keiei Hyōron*, Vol. 1, No. 2 (May, 1946), pp. 6–9; Takano, p. 32; Keizai Dōyūkai, *Jūnen Shi*, pp. 3, 32–36.

65. Keizai Kikaku Chō, Sengo Keizai Shi Hensanshitsu, ed. *Sengo Keizai Shi: Keizai Seisaku Hen* (Tokyo: Ōkurashō Insatsukyoku, 1955), pp. 66–68; Ouchi Hyoe, *Financial and Monetary Situation in Postwar Japan* (Tokyo: Japan Institute of Pacific Studies, International Publishing Co. Ltd., 1948), pp. 22–24; SCAP, GHQ, *Summation*, No. 5, pp. 203–223, 225–226.

66. Keizai Dōyūkai, *Keizai Dōyūkai Gonen Shi* (Tokyo: Keizai Dōyūkai, 1951), p. 2; Keizai Dōyūkai, *Jūnen Shi*, p. 27.

67. Yamamoto, "'Sangyō Saiken'", pp. 229f.

68. Rōdōshō, pp. 90–99; Nihon Tankō Rōdō Kumiai, pp. 63–66; Rōdō Sōgi Chōsa Kai, *Sekitan*, pp. 71–75; Sengo Kakumei Shiryō Hensan Iinkai, pp. 184–186.

69. The following discussion is based on: Rōdōshō, pp. 83–84; Yamamoto, *Sengo Kiki*, pp. 147–150.

70. Nihon Sangyō Rōdō Chōsa-kyoku, "Sōgi Shudan Toshite no Seisan Kanri," Tokyo Daigaku Kagaku Kenkyu-jo, ed., *Sengo Shoki Rōdō Sōgi Chōsa*, Vol. 13 of *Chōsa Hōkoku* (Tokyo Daigaku Kagaku Kenyu-jo, 1971), pp. 286–287; Yamamoto, *Sengo Kiki*, pp. 147–150.

71. Nihon Sangyō Rōdō Chōsa-kyoku, p. 287; The following discussion is based on: Ibid., pp. 286–291, Yamamoto, *Sengo Kiki*, pp. 147–150.

72. Rōdōshō, pp. 920-921; Unno Yukitaka, Kobayashi Hideo, Shiba Kiyoshi, eds. *Sengo Nihon Rōdō Undō Shi*, Vol. 1 (Tokyo: San'ichi Shobō, 1961), p. 92; Yamamoto, *Sengo Kiki*, pp. 154–190 *passim*.

73. Ōkōchi Kazuo and Ōtomo Fukuo, "Sengo Rōdō Undō Shi," *Rōdōsha to Nōmin*, Vol. 7 of *Nihon Shihoinshugi Kōza: Sengo Nihon no Seiji to Keizai* (Tokyo: Iwanami Shoten, 1954), pp. 36–37; Bishop, Dispatch No. 250, p. 2; Bishop, Dispatch No. 314: "Political Parties in Japan: Developments During the Week Ending March 16, 1946," (Record Group 59: 740.00119/3-1946), p. 2.

74. Gayn, pp. 164–171.

75. SCAP, Gov. Sec., "Counter-Measures Against the Subversive Potential in Japan—1946 to 1951 Inclusive," Tabs A and B, (Record Group 331, box 8497, folder: Communism: Miscellaneous Data on Communist Counter-Measures Committee); Allied Council for Japan, Meeting 4, Verbatim Minutes, (May 15, 1946, Afternoon session), pp. 10–12, (Far Eastern Commission, National Archives, Record Group 43, Allied Council Japan, Box 70), pp. 13–16.

76. George Atcheson, U.S. Political Adviser to the Supreme Commander for the Allied Powers, Dispatch No. 453: "Demonstrations and Growing Tendency towards Violence in Japan," Enclosure 4: "Summaries of 20 incidents in Japan involving violence or threatened violence (September 12, 1945 to May 19, 1946)," (Record Group 59: 740.00119/6-1946). Ōkōchi and Matsuo, pp. 144–147.

77. SCAP, GHQ, *Summation*, No. 10, pp. 183–190; No. 11, pp. 181–186; SCAP, Gov. Sec., "Counter-Measures," Tabs A, B, and C; Ronald P. Dore, *Land Reform in Japan* (London: Oxford University Press, 1959), Chap. VI, *passim*; Andrew J. Grad, *Land and Peasant in Japan: An Introductory Survey* (New York: Institute of Pacific Relations, 1952), Chap. IV, *passim*; Ōkōchi, Rōdō, p. 8–9.

78. Taylorism is a system of scientific management aimed at raising production through rationalization of the means of production and the installation of piecework and incentive systems for workers. See F.W. Taylor, *Scientific Management* (New York: Harper & Bros., 1947).

79. Harry Braverman, *Labor and Monopoly Capital: The Degradation of Work in the Twentieth Century* (New York: Monthly Review Press, 1974), p. 151.

80. SCAP, ESS, LAC, *Final Report*, p. 36; Rōdō Sōgi Chōse Kai, Tekkō Sōgi, Vol. 7: *Sengo Rōdō Sōgi Jittai Chōsa* (Tokyo: Chūō Kōron Sha, 1958), pp. 89–90.

81. Japan Prime Minister's Office, Cabinet Bureau of Statistics, *Japan Statistical Year-book* (Tokyo: Cabinet Bureau of Statistics, 1949), pp. 734–735; for examples see Rōdōshō, pp. 7, 14, 23, 44, 82–83.

82. Suehiro Izutarō, "The State's Policy in Respect to Production Management [Control]," *Mainichi*, April 15, 1946, translation in Supreme Commander for the Allied Powers, Economic and Scientific Section, Labor Division, National Archives, Suitland Record Center, (R.G. 331, box 8481, folder: Production Control).

83. C. Wright Mills, *The New Men of Power: America's Labor Leaders* (New York: Harcourt, Brace and Co., 1948), pp. 6–7.

84. *Ibid.*, pp. 8–9.

Children of the A-Bomb: I

by Tomoyuki Satoh

a boy in 4th grade
4 years old in 1945.

On that sixth of August I wasn't going to school yet. At the time, I was playing in front of the public bath near home. Then Sei-chan said, "Please go to the garden and pick some flowers." So I was on my way to get them. All of a sudden there was a big flash and I was scared and tried to go back to the house. And all of a sudden a lot of needles got in my eyes. I couldn't tell where anything was. When I tried to go toward the house I bumped into the front door. When I opened my eyes everything was darkish. Then Grandma rushed out with Keika-chan on her back. I followed Grandma. We went toward our bomb shelter.

My younger big sister was already inside the shelter so the four of us huddled together. Then my older big sister came running in and we huddled together again. That older big sister was old enough so that she had already gone to work at a bakery; our mother had already died from illness.

Father, who had been working with the Volunteer Labor Group, came back and was looking to find where we were. When she heard him, my big sister went out and took Father's hand and led him to the shelter. Father was burned all over above his hips. When Sister and the other people saw it they were all scared. A stranger spread some oil on his body for him.

In my heart I thought, "Thank you."

After that we went away to Fuchu in the hills. In a broken temple we put up a mosquito net and we lay down there. We stayed here for a long time. After a while other people began to go back to their homes so we went home too. When we got back we found that the glass was all broken, the chests were all toppled over, the family altar was tipped over, the *shoji* were torn, the roof tiles were broken and the plaster had fallen off the walls. We all helped to clear it away and laid Father there. After about sixty days, in the middle of the night, Father called to Grandma and said he wanted to eat a sweet potato. Grandma said, "All right," and cooked the sweet potato.

"Father, the potato is ready," she said and looked at him, but he didn't answer. I touched his body and it was cold, and he was already dead. Dear Father, dear Mother, good-bye.

Children of the
A-Bomb: II

Ikuko Wakasa

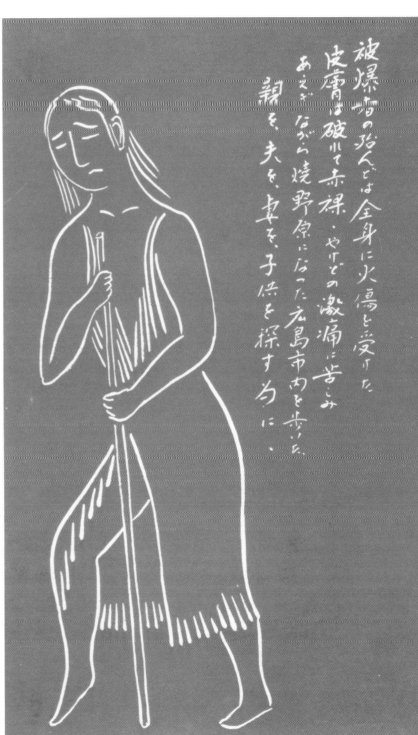

a girl in 5th grade
5 years old in 1945

I really hate to think about war and I hate to remember the day when the atom bomb fell. Even when I read books I skip the parts about war. And I shiver at the newsreels in the movies when the scenes of the war in Korea appear. Since I was assigned this for homework, and even though I don't want to do it, I am making myself remember that awful time.

That morning of the sixth of August my brother's friend who was in second grade then, came calling him to go to school in the temple. At that time I was five and my little sister was two. My little sister and I were playing house in the garden.

Father, although he always left for work at eight o'clock, happened on that day to say, "I'm not going until eight-thirty today."

He was facing the north windows and practicing brush-writing. Mother, in front of the south windows, was clearing up after breakfast and from the kitchen I could hear the noise of dishes being washed.

Just about then I could hear the sound of an aeroplane flying very high, and thinking it was a Japanese plane I shouted, "Oh, there's an aeroplane!"

Just as I looked at the sky there was a flash of white light and the green in the plants looked in that light like the color of dry leaves.

I cried, "Daddy!" and just as I jumped into the house there was a tremendous noise and at the same time a bookcase and chest of drawers fell over and broken glass came flying past grazing my face. I dashed back into the garden scared to death.

Mother called, "Ikuko, I'm over here."

I went blindly in the direction of Mother's voice and I dived into the shelter. After a little while a lot of blood came out of my ears and it didn't stop for a long time. Even when we put cotton and gauze in, the blood came pouring out between my fingers holding the cotton and gauze in place. My father and mother were frightened and they bandaged my ears for me. Father had his little finger cut with glass—it was almost off. And below his eye there was a big cut from glass. When I looked at Mother she was all bloody below the hips. It must have been from the glass that came flying from the north windows. A big piece of glass was still sticking in Mother's back. The cut was about six inches long and two inches deep and the blood was pouring out. The edges of the cut were sort of swollen out like the lips of a savage. As Mother cried out with the pain, Father pulled out the glass and poured a whole bottle of iodine on the place to sterilize it. When my older brother dived under the table he hit his head and he got a big bump on it. My little sister who had been outside, even though she only had on a pair of pants, wasn't hurt because she had crawled under the porch.

After they finished bandaging me, a pain stabbed me so I lay down. When I woke up I was lying in a funny little shed. When I tried to lift my head it was stuck to the mattress by the blood that had seeped out and I couldn't lift it.

Father said, "We don't want this to get any worse, so let's go to the hospital." So he carried me on his back to a military hospital nearby. The hospital was full of people who were groaning and people who were naked. I was scared to death. Finally I said to Father, "I'm too scared; let's go home." Since there were so many people that we didn't know when our turn would come—and besides that, there were so many people who were hurt worse than I was—Father said All right, let's go back, and we did.

We had a good view from the fields and we could see that it wasn't only the part where we lived but the whole city that was burning. Black smoke was billowing up and we could hear the sound of big things exploding. Since a north wind was blowing and the fire was gradually coming closer and closer to the place where I was standing, I didn't know what to do and I was scared to death. About noon the wind changed to the south and our house was saved from being burned.

Mother's younger brother was a high school student but since he was seventeen he had gone to be a soldier. He was a big strong man and he belonged to the Second Army. He was stationed at the Nobori-cho School. Since he didn't come home on the night of the sixth, Father and Mother and all of us went searching for him until late at night in those dreadful streets. The fires were burning. There was a strange smell all over. Blue-green balls of fire were drifting around. I had a terrible lonely feeling that everybody else in the world was dead and only we were still alive. Ever since that time I haven't liked to go outside. A soldier friend of my Uncle Wakasa said that my Uncle Wakasa had finished his night duty and was sleeping at a place at the school that was next to the rice storehouse.

Father and Mother went right away to the school. Next to the rice storehouse among the ashes there were lots of bones scattered around. Since they didn't know which were my uncle's they picked up a lot of them and put them in a funeral urn. Also among the ashes they found his schoolcap insignia and his aluminum lunch box. Even now we are making ourselves think that my uncle was killed instantly by the blast and we are not letting ourselves think that he was burned or pinned under a house and burned while he was still alive.

A man who was so badly burned that you couldn't tell whether he was a young man or an old man was lying in front of Grandpa's house which is right next to ours. Poor thing, we laid him on the floor in our hall. Then we put a blanket down for him and gave him a pillow; while we were looking at him he swelled up to about three times his size and his whole body turned the color of dirt and got soft. Flies came all over him and he was moaning in a faint voice and an awful smell was coming from him.

He kept saying, "Water! Water!"

Father and Mother and Grandpa, although they were wounded, picked up broken glass because the house was badly damaged and since it was wartime they were taking important things to the little shack in the country and they were so busy they couldn't take care of that sick man. I went and looked at him every now and then and gave him water but when I had to pass the place where he was I closed my eyes and held my breath and ran past. Soldiers came and took him to the hospital; we gave him the blanket and pillow.

The house was squeezed sideways three feet, the floor was fallen in, the bookcase and chest of drawers had fallen on top of each other, and the ceiling and roof had fallen on top of all that, and you could see the blue sky.

I thought, "We can never live in this house again."

There were ten eggs in a basket on the table in the north room. Strangely enough they were plastered around the farther, south side of the sliding doors of that room. Mother said, "What sort of a wind could have carried those eggs there? The blast must have come first from the north and then turned around and come from the south to have soiled the south side of the doors that way."

Father said that ten of the tiles from the roof were piled up in one place in a spiral. Since the foundation stones of the house had moved we imagine that the whole house must have been lifted into the air at some time. From about then on Mother began to be sort of sick. The doctor said, "It's probably because she breathed poison while she was walking around looking for her brother."

A half year ago a ten-year-old girl suddenly developed radiation sickness. All her hair fell out and she became entirely bald and the doctor at the Japan Red Cross Hospital frantically did everything he could for her but she vomited blood and died after twenty days. I shudder when I think that even though it is already six years after the end of the war, still people are dying in a way that reminds us of that day. I can't think that those people who died are different people from us. What would I do if such a thing happened in my house? When I only hear about the suffering of people who have that radiation sickness, it makes me so frightened that I wish I could think of some way to forget about it.

The grandma of some of our relatives was made lame. Every time I see her I remember the sixth of August and I feel miserable. Sometimes when I ride on the streetcar I see people with their ear burned so that it's just a little bump of flesh, not even an inch, stuck on their head. The father of the Sarada family also lost his ear.

Even though the atom bomb was so terrible and hateful, they're saying in the news broadcasts on the radio that a bomb ten times more dreadful than the Hiroshima bomb has been made and they are discussing whether or not to use it in Korea.

This is a dreadful thing.

I think that everybody who was in Hiroshima on the sixth of August hates war. Our grammar school still hasn't been fixed where it was damaged during the war. The reason my family became poor is because all the houses that we were renting out fell down or were burned. This sixth of August is the seventh anniversary of my uncle's death. When that day comes around, everybody will be reminded of that terrible time; this makes me feel very bad.

Art, Children, and the Bomb

by John W. Dower

Among the various arguments which were advanced by Americans in the summer of 1945 in support of using the atomic bombs against Japan, there is one that has been generally neglected. We might call it the concept of idealistic genocide.

This line of reasoning, endorsed by a spectrum of eminent men associated with the Manhattan Project, held that the world at large would never be able to imagine the awesome destructiveness of the new weapon unless it was actually demonstrated in combat for all to see. To convey the urgency of arms control in the future, it was necessary to first create an unforgettable atomic wasteland in the present.

This chilling line of thought has proven to be both naive and prescient. The arms race occurred despite the immediate shock of the bombs, but the memory of Hiroshima and Nagasaki remains absolutely central to peace movements throughout the world. No slogan is more graphic than "No More Hiroshimas." No voices are more eloquent than the cries for peace of the *hibakusha* atomic bomb victims).

At least two strong forces work against the perpetuation of these memories of August 1945, however. One is the technocratic jargon of the managers of the arms race, whose language is often deliberately meant to confuse the public and place the human and moral aspects of nuclear confrontation beyond the pale of "realistic" discourse. The other counterforce is the simple passage of time itself. Memories fade and die if special efforts are not made to preserve them for succeeding generations.

Not surprisingly, it is the Japanese who have done the most to preserve the memory of Hiroshima and Nagasaki. Their anniversary observances serve this purpose, and the memories have been recreated over and over again in prose, poetry, and the graphic arts. It is noteworthy, moreover, that Japanese children share in these expressions, and much of the work on the bomb is specifically directed to them.

By contrast to the Japanese, youngsters elsewhere in the world generally have been shielded from exposure to intimate and graphic depictions of the atomic-bomb experience. In the United States, this was readily apparent prior to the television showing of "The Day After" late in 1983, when self-styled experts of every stripe debated how old one should be before being allowed to watch this film about the nuclear destruction of a Midwestern city. In 1982, a team of American educators repsonsible for preparing a teaching unit on nuclear issues for middle-school students actually adopted a policy of using no graphics whatsoever, on the grounds that young people could not cope with their traumatic impact.

These are serious, legitimate concerns, and in Japan too, more cautious and conservative voices have argued that graphic depictions of Hiroshima and Nagasaki are "too blunt" or "too cruel" for children. These were, in fact, the very phrases used

All cartoons from *Barefoot Gen* are reprinted by permission of New Society Publishers, Philadelphia.

when (in the first instance) the serialization of Japan's most famous cartoon-style depiction of Hiroshima, *Barefoot Gen,* was terminated by its original publisher in 1974. And the phrase used was "too cruel" in a case of textbook censorship in 1982, when the Ministry of Education refused to recertify a text that included among its illustrations a detail from one of the famous "Atomic Bomb Panels" (Genbaku no Zu) painted by the husband-and-wife team Iri and Toshi Maruki.

In Japan, however, the political significance of the debate over exposing children to depictions of nuclear destruction is clearer than in other countries, for it is transparently tied up with the issue of accelerating remilitarization and more active Japanese support of American global anti-communist policies. Japanese educators, politicians, and parents alike are acutely sensitive to the importance of historical consciousness in shaping the political inclinations of the young; and the treatment of World War Two in the schools and mass media now plays a central role in the struggle to control this critical aspect of education and socialization. For the large number of Japanese who are too young to remember the war, the atomic bomb is the single most unforgettable symbol of a dark recent past.

In Japan, for adults and children alike, recollection of the atomic-bomb experience thus leads inexorably to a host of intertangled non-nuclear issues. The bomb is placed in a context of militarism and imperialism, for example, and eventually racism and prejudice enter the picture and even the identity of "victim" and "victimizer" begins to blur. Thus, we soon learn that tens of thousands of Koreans were in Hiroshima when the bomb fell, and the Japanese *hibakusha* continued to discriminate against their Korean fellow sufferers in medical treatment and even disposal of the dead. Afterwards, the Japanese *hibakusha* themselves were forced to endure discrimination at the hands of other Japanese.

Both the Marukis and Nakazawa Keiji, the author of *Barefoot Gen,* have introduced such themes in their atomic-bomb art, and have gone on to address other non-nuclear aspects of the war and postwar period as well. After completing their fourteenth major panel on the Hiroshima motif in 1972, the Marukis turned their extraordinary talents to depictions of the Rape of Nanking, Auschwitz, and the victims of the Minamata mercury poisoning. Nakazawa's cartoon books, which have been assembled in a 19-volume "peace comics" collection in Japanese, include such subjects as the Japanese invasion of Manchuria. He and the Marukis have also used their art to record the exploitation of the people of Okinawa under both Japanese and U.S. rule.

The Japanese art of the atomic-bomb experience also leads, at least potentially, in another direction: to skepticism toward authority. It is not anti-American per se, but rather a stark reminder of what was done by both the Japanese and American sides four decades ago in the name of patriotism and high ideals. This is not conducive to seeing current global conflicts in black-and-white terms. And in contemporary Japan, where the ruling groups are deeply concerned with reinstilling "love of country" and consolidating a highly paternalistic democracy, any such encouragement of skepticism toward authority is extremely discomforting to the elites. It is, in fact, all the more unsettling because, by all available evidence, young people as a whole respond positively and maturely to these materials. *Barefoot Gen,* which has now been expanded into a 7-volume paperback edition in Japanese (each volume is over 250 pages), continues to enjoy immense popularity ten

Copyright © 1978 by Keiji Nakazawa

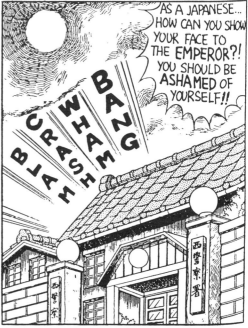

Mii and her mother and father continued their escape and crossed another river. When they reached the far bank, Mii's mother put her husband down and collapsed on the ground beside him.

years after the original serialization was terminated. The museum in Saitama (the Maruki Bijitsukan) in which the Marukis' "Atomic-Bomb Panels" are displayed is visited by thousands of school-children annually (I myself have watched them become absorbed in these masterworks of high art). And in 1980, Toshi Maruki, herself one of Japan's best-known illustrators of children's books, published a picture book for very young readers titled *Hiroshima no Pika* which quickly became well known.

Western artists and illustrators have not ventured to engage the atomic-bomb experience at these levels of sustained intimacy, but several of the Japanese works, including the best ones for children, are available in translation. Toshi Maruki's *Hiroshima no Pika*, published under the same title in English, won several prestigious American prizes in 1982. The first volume of the lengthy *Barefoot Gen* series, based on Nakazawa's own experiences as a boy of six living in Hiroshima when the bomb fell, can be obtained in an excellent

Mii felt something moving past her feet. Hop...hop....
It was a swallow. Its wings were burned, and it couldn't
fly. Hop...hop...
  She saw a man floating slowly down the river.
Floating behind him was the body of a cat.

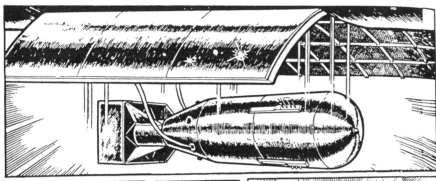

...THERE'S SOMETHING **WHITE** FALLING...

43 SECONDS LATER, 1800 FEET OVER HIROSHIMA, THE ATOMIC BOMB NAMED "THIN BOY" EXPLODED WITH A WHITE-HOT LIGHT —
IT WAS AS IF A MILLION FLASHBULBS HAD GONE OFF AT ONCE...

FLASH

black-and-white English version; for young readers, it is hard to imagine a more vivid and engrossing introduction to life in wartime Japan, the bomb experience itself, and the ordeals of the survivors. This famous *Gen* series was inspired by a short version of his experiences done by Nakazawa in 1972, and in 1982 this was made available in a standard colored comic-book format in English under the title *I Was There*.

Gen can be read as meaning "root" or "source" in Japanese, and in the introduction to the first English volume of his famous series, Nakazawa explains how he came to call his semi-autobiographical protagonist Barefoot Gen:

I named my main character Gen in the hope that he would become a root or source of strength for a generation of mankind that can tread the charred soil of Hiroshima barefoot and feel the earth beneath their feet, that will have the strength to say "no" to war and nuclear weapons. . . . I myself would like to live with Gen's strength—that is my ideal, and I will continue pursuing it through my work.

Out of the terrible destruction has thus emerged a heightened commitment to creativity. Adults may ponder this. Children seem to appreciate it intuitively. For them, art may be the most constructive medium through which they can begin to come to grips with the nuclear world they have inherited.

Hayashi Kyoko's "Two Grave Markers" (Futari no bohyō)

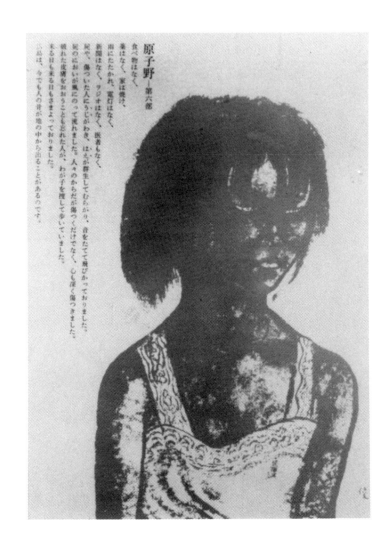

translated and introduced by Kyoko Selden

Introduction

Hayashi Kyoko was born in Nagasaki in 1930 and spent most of her childhood in Shanghai. She returned to Nagasaki in March 1945 and enrolled in Nagasaki Girls' High School. At that time students were mobilized for factory work, and Hayashi was among those sent to work at a munitions plant in Nagasaki. She was at work there when the atomic bomb hit the city on 9 August, three days after the first explosion at Hiroshima and six days before Japan's surrender. She was seriously ill for two months, and suffered thereafter from fragile health. Hayashi attended the nursing section of the Welfare Faculty for Women attached to Nagasaki Medical School, but left before graduation. She started to write in 1962.

Hayashi first drew attention in 1975 with an autobiographical story about her experience of the bombing, "Ritual of

Death" (Matsuri no ba, June issue of *Gunzō;* trans. Selden, *Japan Interpreter*, 1978; *Nuke Rebuke*, 1984). It received the *Bungei Shunjū's* Akutagawa Prize. This was immediately followed by "Two Grave Markers" (Futari no bohyō, *Bungei Shunjū*, August 1975), an account of a mobilized girl student who, like the first-person narrator of "Ritual of Death," helped herself out of an instantly shattered factory building, but who had the added pain of having failed to stay with a dying friend. These two stories were published in book form in the same year along with "March on a Cloudy Day" (Kumoribi no kōshin, *Bungei Shuto,* 1967), which focuses on the author's reaction to the anti–atomic bomb movement.

Prior to "Ritual of Death" and "Two Grave Markers," the atomic bomb experience had already been a theme of stories and novels such as Agawa Hiroyuki's "Year by Year" (1946) and "August 6th" (1947), Hara Tamiki's "Summer Flower" (1947, tr. George Saito, 1969, 1985), Ota Yoko's *Human Tatters* (1951) and *Half Human* (1954), Ibuse Masuji's *Black Rain* (1965–66, tr. John Bester, 1969), Inoue Mitsuharu's *Earthly Flocks* (1963), and Sata Ineko's *Tree Shade* (1972). Hayashi Kyoko added new dimensions to the existing atomic bomb literature by introducing a fourteen-year-old's witness

---

Calligraphy in title by Shibata Kanjuro XX. The above drawing with accompanying Japanese text appears next to a written passage entitled "Atomic Desert (VI)" in Iri and Toshi Maruki, *The Hiroshima Panels* [Japanese title: *Genbaku no zu* (Paintings of the Atomic Explosions)] (Saitama, Japan: Maruki Gallery for the Hiroshima Panels Foundation, 1984). Courtesy of John Junkerman.

of the horror, by writing as a survivor with direct experience, and by providing a candid, even ironical, portrayal of the difficult subject.

In "Two Grave Markers," fourteen-year-old Wakako is someone who has seen everything. She has seen death and destruction, and she has also seen what humans are capable of doing. She herself behaved in the only way she could and feels justified, yet is tortured by guilt: she could not do otherwise than abandon her friend to die, wounded and swarming with maggots. Pressed to tell what she knows about her friend, she refuses to speak, for she knows she cannot be understood even by her mother—especially by her mother—who must believe in Wakako's innocence. Wakako has seen too much: she sees through lies and hypocrisy, and with cool indifference, remains a silent observer of people's reactions to the bomb many worlds away in the quiet village of orange groves. She is frighteningly cynical for a fourteen-year-old, as though she had bypassed youth in the few days following the bombing.

To Hayashi Kyoko, the victims are not only hurt by the bomb; they are hurt by each other, and they are hurt by their neighbors who did not directly experience the bomb. Hayashi does not hesitate to let the girl experience cruelty; nor does she spare her from retribution, for Wakako, in her delirium, becomes surrounded by imaginary maggots, each a reincarnation of the friend she abandoned.

Hayashi's later works in the seventies include a short story "Mask of Whatchamacallit" (Nanjamonja no men, *Gunzō*, February 1976) and a sequence of twelve short stories carried in *Gunzō* from March 1977 to February 1978 and published in book form in May 1978 under the title *Cut Glass and Blown Glass* (Giyaman bidoro) in May 1978. All but the fifth story, "Yellow Sand" (Kōsa, trans. Selden, *Japanese Women Writers*, 1980), which handles the author's experience in Shanghai, are related to the bombing. The first story, "The Empty Can," was translated by Margaret Mitsutani in *Atomic Aftermath, Short Stories about Hiroshima and Nagasaki*, (Oe Kenzaburo, ed., 1984).

Hayashi's first full-length novel, *As If Nothing Had Happened* (Naki ga gotoki), was carried in the January to December 1980 issues of *Gunzō* and printed in book form in 1981. It introduces a survivor who was brought up in China and who wishes to become "a chronicler of August 9." This must be how Hayashi views herself, a chronicler of the Nagasaki bombing, whose mind, in addition, was first shaped in colonial Shanghai. Her Shanghai and Nagasaki experiences, as part of the same war, are the prime sources of her writing. *The Michelle Lipstick* (Missheru no kuchibeni, Chuo Kōronsha, 1980) is a collection of short stories about Shanghai, and *Shanghai* (June 1982 to March 1983, *Umi;* Chuo Kōronsha, 1983), which received the 1984 Women Writers' Award, is a travelogue from her recent five-day trip to Shanghai, the first after forty years. The Nagasaki theme continues in her two most recent collections, the Kawabata Prize–winning *Home in the Three Worlds* (Sangai no ie, 1984) and *The Path* (Michi, 1985). The latter collects eight Nagasaki pieces published between 1976 and 1985. One titled "On a Fair Day," 1984, is a scenario which combines stage dialogues and silent motion on a screen. Hayashi convincingly employs this form in order to present the difficulty and complexity of survivors' lives in a way not possible in short-story form. At present, during her first visit to the United States, she is writing an essay entitled "The Blue Sky of Virginia."

Two Grave Markers

Clusters of pale yellow acacia flowers sway in the early summer breeze. The wisteria-like clusters call to mind flocks of butterflies.

Wakako sits in the roots of the trees. Her hair is in braids. By her side is a baby. The baby wears a rose-colored baby dress and her small hands are open; she is dead.

Just like a doll—so sweet, Tsune thought.

Ants swarm around her lips, and maggots crawl in and out of her tear ducts.

Her cheeks are still pink, and the baby smiles as if she were tickled. At a gentle touch of the finger tips, some of her skin peels off.

Grease runs from the baby who has started to melt, making just that part of the earth glisten, dark with moisture. The clusters of flowers shine lustrously, absorbing juice from the baby's flesh.

The wind blows. The baby's fine hair trembles.

Every day the baby melts and returns to the earth, emanating fragrance and nourishing the heavy clusters of acacia blossoms.

Tsune often has the same dream. She likes the tenderly plump Wakako she sees in her dream. She likes the dead face of the baby who is an exact image of Wakako.

On the outskirts of N City, there is a small mountain with a hollow on its northern slope carved out by the blast of the explosion. The southern slope, which faced the target area of the atomic bomb, is charred in dark and light stripes, which retain traces of the arrows of radiation which shot out in all directions. Turning its back on the shifting sun, the hollow is in dark shade and utters a low groan in the wind that blows upwards. In August when the atomic bomb was dropped, a few dozen girl students died on this slope.

All that remained were several brittle pieces of bone which crumbled easily like dry sugar cakes when they were picked up.

In the mountain wind which started to blow that day, the bones rolled down the slope with a dry rustling sound.

They made a little mound in the hollow.

After a month, a grave marker of unpainted, white wood appeared in the hollow. It belonged to Yoko who had died at the age of fourteen. As though to surround it, other white wooden grave markers were erected one by one. They were for the girl students rumored to have been on the mountain.

As the days pass the few dozen grave markers which crowd the narrow hollow incline slightly in the blowing wind, sighing, each with a different voice.

Wakako's tomb is there, too. She was a close friend of Yoko's.

It was in the morning four days after the bombing of Nagasaki that Wakako returned to the village of orange groves where her mother lived. She saw Wakako standing, her face expressionless and reeling in the green light of the orange mountain that rose high over the inlet. Holding an orange branch in her two hands, Wakako's mother said syllable by syllable, as if verifying something: "Wa-ka-ko, it's you."

Many faces appeared through the brush of the orange mountain. They were the faces of villagers. Looking past the faces of men with sturdy cheekbones, Wakako sought her mother's face in the thicket from which the voice had come.

"Otsune-san, quick, quick. It's the real Waka-san," Obatchan (aunt), the oldest of the villagers, pushed Tsune forward.

Wakako's village was 180 kilometers from N City. It was a small village past several tunnels on the train from N.

With its four hundred and fifty inhabitants in seventy houses, the village bordered on a small inlet connected to O Bay. Wakako's father was the village head. The orange mountain rose right up from the steep shore of the inlet, leaving this a hilly village with hardly any flat land. They say N City is full of dead bodies, it's completely destroyed, and not even a cat is alive—rumors reached the village on the evening of the day of the bombing.

That night, as her husband had fastened his gaiters tightly around his calves and set out for N City to search for Wakako, Tsune had handed him a purple crepe scarf used for special occasions and said: "Please bring her home, if just her bones. She was a slender child, so if you see slender bones, they are probably hers." Rumor after rumor arrived, and all concerned the destruction of the city which used to love merrrymaking, with the biggest or second biggest Shinto festival in Japan; due to a single strange bomb, it had become a totally soundless city.

Had Wakako alone survived?—no, this hardly seemed possible. Besides, that day while she had been supervising village workers in the orange groves, Tsune saw the huge, tornado-like column of fire from which the atomic bomb dropped on N City. In that column of fire which shot up into the vast sky, a slender girl like Wakako would burn more easily than a mayfly thrown into a gas flame.

Tsune had given up on Wakako.

Yet, without so much as a scar, Wakako was standing before her eyes. Seeing Wakako before her, part of Tsune still wondered if this was, in Obatchan's words, the real Wakako.

The news of Wakako's safety spread from thicket to thicket of the orange groves. "Waka-san has come home? Is it true?" men asked in loud voices. "It is true," Tsune answered, a smile breaking out all over her face. "She's not injured, is she? Is Yo-chan with her?" While they questioned her, Tsune scrutinized Wakako from the thicket, then answered cheerfully, her voice equally loud: "It looks like there are no injuries; Yo-chan . . . isn't with her."

Wakako was exhausted. The unrestrained voices of the villagers making a fuss over her return, the brightness of the unpretentious sun, as transparent as paraffin, the firm green of oranges—everything in the village was so healthy it disturbed her.

"I'll steam rice and red beans right away so we can celebrate with everyone. All right, Wakako?"

Her fingertips still red from crushing the insects which sucked sap from the orange trees, Tsune held Wakako's hands. They were cold.

As she had often done when Wakako was small, Tsune pressed her lips against her daughter's forehead to see if she had a fever.

She felt slow heat from Wakako's forehead, which seemed to retain heat deep within.

"Do you have any wounds?" Tsune knit her brows checking Wakako's body with both hands.

"Otsune-san," Obatchan called, and cautioned her in a suppressed voice, "the bomb this time's different: everyone died, with or without wounds. The earlier the better. Have the doctor examine her."

"I will. Wakako, let's ask the old doctor Tanaka to take a look. He can cure any wound."

Wakako shook her head like a small child. She wanted to go home as soon as possible to the house under the thick thatched roof, where a cool wind from the sea blew in. Having spent three days and three nights on the hot soil of the burnt fields, she longed for the big, grainy pillars at home which felt cool to touch.

Wakako started to walk down the mountain trail away from the doctor's place.

"You want to go home? Then let's go home quickly, Wakako," Tsune said.

When they got home, she would wipe her daughter's entire body with water from the well in the yard. With pure water pumped from the depths of the earth, she would wipe away the horrible poison of the bomb. Tsune remembered that when Wakako was born she had given her baby her first bath in the same well water.

It was an early morning in August, and when Tsune bathed Wakako on the veranda, she yelled with a robust, almost convulsive voice, eyes tightly closed from the shock of the first sunlight—Tsune recalled this as she followed Wakako, determined never to let her die. They were followed by Obatchan and the noisy train of villagers who had thrown down their work.

Shige, Obatchan's grandchild, in a Kintarō bib which she rarely wore, walked next to Wakako, asking, "Was it scary, Waka-chan, was the flash scary?" Wakako softly shook her head as Shige repeated the question with shining eyes.

"Scary? Or not scary?" Shige pursued, not knowing which Wakako had meant. When asked this way, Wakako herself was not sure which was right. Although Shige seemed to think it roughly the same kind of scare as when thunder hit, the horror was so great that it defied Wakako's comprehension.

"Not even a single wound, Waka-san is really lucky; the gods have protected her"—the villagers made as much noise as if it were a festival night as they headed for Wakako's house on the hilltop.

A few rice paddies lay between one mountain and another. The villagers walked cheerfully, single file, along a narrow footpath.

Green grass was abundant in the village. It grew everywhere along the narrow paths between the rice paddies, steaming in the summer light and giving off a damp smell. The grass smell, moist and shapeless, was the same as the faint odor of scorched bodies carried by the wind over the burnt field.

"Mother, I smell the bomb," Wakako said, covering her nose. Obatchan, who was now walking side-by-side with Wakako along the narrow path, responded: "It's the sagebrush. Don't you like its nice smell? You are too sensitive, Waka-san." She laughed as if she breathed the laughter through her toothless mouth, "Ho-h-ho."

"Waka-chan escaped her death, so she'll live long," a man holding Shige's hand called to Tsune in a loud voice from behind her. "Thanks to you all, yes. I want her to live as long as Obatchan," Tsune said, bowing; but even as she spoke, she was anxious about Wakako's bloodless face.

When Wakako finally reached home, she lay her tired body on the wooden floor near the entrance.

The floor polished with rice bran cooled her feverish body.

Although she had not a single scar, both her arms and legs felt as heavy as if she were dragging the earth; her head was like a heavy weight she could not support. Yielding the burden of her head to the floor, Wakako opened her lips lightly. That made her feel better, since it eased the tension around her jaw.

Obatchan bent to look at Wakako, saying, "You're beautiful, Waka-san. Like a wax doll." Tsune, too, watched Wakako's pale, translucent skin and had to think, even of her own child, that she was beautiful. However, this was a beauty she had not detected in the healthy-looking Wakako who had said "I'll be back" and left with Yoko four days ago. If this beauty was something she had brought home from N City, didn't it signify death, as the rumors maintained?

"Wakako, are you feeling bad? Excuse yourself and sleep a little," Tsune said.

"Yes, yes, that's best. Yo-chan will come home eventually. She survived, didn't she, Waka-san?" Obatchan turned her gummy eyes to Wakako.

Wakako's lips convulsed lightly as she looked at her mother. "Yes?" Tsune looked into Wakako's eyes which seemed to be supplicating, but Wakako looked down without answering.

The villagers who had gathered at the entrance, too, watched her mouth, waiting for her answer.

"Please let her rest; she's tired," Tsune greeted the villagers, propping Wakako up by the shoulders. Observing Wakako's expression, she wondered what could have happened to her daughter's friendship with Yoko.

"Obatchan's asking you something. Be pleasant and tell her what you know," Tsune chided Wakako, as she hung out mosquito netting in a room facing the sea. Any little detail would help. Yoko and Wakako were among the students mobilized to work at the same factory. Since they even belonged to the same work area, Wakako couldn't get away with simply saying she didn't know what happened to Yoko. However, the inexpressible horror of the "new model" bomb had already come home to the villagers. It would be all right for her to answer that she couldn't tell because she had been overwhelmed by fear. One word about Yoko would have given Obatchan and others peace of mind.

"Yo-chan . . . is dead, is that it?"

Wakako said nothing, and pulled the summer comforter all the way up over her face. She had nothing to tell Tsune or Obatchan and the others who could say such things as "Tell her what you know," or "The gods protected you."

"That's just the smell of sagebrush," the others laughed carelessly about the wild plant along the path, without any misgivings. The four days Wakako had spent in N City were worlds away from that simplicity.

"Sleep a little," Tsune stroked Wakako's hair, and Wakako closed her eyes without resisting.

The scenes of N City where she had been until several hours ago came back before her closed eyes. Wakako did not think that what she had done to Yoko in the mountain where they took refuge was wrong. However, if she faithfully described to the villagers what had happened, they would probably condemn her as heartless. How could anyone who had not been there understand? Even for those who were there, as time passed, the extraordinary ball of fire would fade away, leaving behind nothing but judgements on the results. When all the conditions that had brought about the facts grew dim, and only the facts remained, what would Wakako do?

Just a moment ago, Wakako had encountered Yoshi, Yoko's mother. She was wearing her black *monpe*,* and said she was going to look for her daughter. Wakako told her it appeared that Yo-chan had run off into the mountains.

Appeared—no, Wakako knew it for a fact. "Did she run away by herself? She is alive, isn't she?"

Seeing the tears fill Yoshi's eyes, Wakako nodded unequivocally. The tears in the eyes of many of the people she had seen in the burnt fields dripped in strands, sticky like a sea turtle's tears.

Yoshi's tears were clear and shiny. Watching her, Wakako, too, felt as though tears were welling up. Yet she lied to Yoshi. The two of them, Wakako and the wounded Yoko, had run to the mountain on the outskirts of N City. On that mountain Yoko had died.

"I've brought bleached cotton just in case she has big burns. Did she have burns?" Evading the eyes of Yoshi who asked question after question, Wakako shook her head: I don't know.

On the day the bomb fell, it was fair in N City. And it was hot. The factory where Wakako and Yoko had been mobilized was a big armory located on the outskirts of N City.

Rumor had it that the factory involved in the war industry was producing torpedoes. Yet no one had even once seen a finished torpedo. Japan had run out of materials, the workers said. They whistled unconcernedly and added, "We're going to lose."

Wakako and others who had been mobilized to work there had nothing to do but stand around and chat in a corner of the factory.

A sharp-eyed worker, who also had nothing to do, would find the girls talking and report them. The chief, who prided himself on having lost an arm in the China Incident, called out, "Polish the windows—ready, go!" Their mobilized life meant daily window polishing.

Each of the few glass windows in the factory always sparkled.

The chief, who rarely skipped a day, was absent that day. Wakako and Yoko were chatting with each other, their backs against the large, polished windows.

Yoko in her navy blue and white *monpe* slacks stood with her back to the widest window in the factory. This single piece of glass, in which their chief took great pride, was said to be three millimeters thick.

The glass window, drinking up the summer sun, shone on Wakako's cheeks. Since Wakako was very sensitive to light, she found the sun too dazzling. As she sheltered herself in the shade of the concrete pillar beside her, something white seemed to float in one corner of the window.

"A cloud?" Wakako asked. "It looks like a parachute," said a young man who passed by carrying a grease can and making a heavy rapping noise with his cedar clogs.

The factory clock, which lost exactly one minute per hour, struck eleven o'clock. The one-armed chief was a man of

* Work pants with or without a matching top.

precision: every morning on his arrival he corrected the clock. It remained slow that day.

"It's almost lunch. I'm having rice and omelette." Yoko was fond of sweet omelette.

As if too impatient to wait till noon, she picked up her lunch box from the desk and smiled, smelling it from outside the wrap.

At the same time as Wakako saw Yoko's white eyeteeth something white tilted diagonally across the glass window and shook violently back and forth, with the sun as an axis.

In that instant, a purple light seemed pasted across the whole space of the window. Up until that moment, Wakako had thought of light as something that ran with sharp, shooting needles, like those on a metal plant holder for flower arrangement, and disappeared immediately. The lightning which had struck over the orange mountain when she was five years old had a pointed shape, creating a jagged streak drawing a track of light exactly like the ones in comics. Lightning which she had seen shoot out across the sea, too, was like that. However, this light outside the window was different. It extended all over the sky so slowly, and even tenaciously, that the eyes could follow its spread. Because its mass was felt to be tangible, this light was different from the energy without thickness that Wakako, until now, had thought of as "light."

The window glass shattered and simultaneously the light outside the window broke, blowing against the shoulders and back of Yoko, who turned her face down.

As glass chips shot against the floor like arrows from a blowpipe, spiral metal fragments scattered across the floor and whirled upwards. A black crack ran through a square beam as it fell from the ceiling.

Wakako grasped with precision what transpired in that instant. Everything was fluid, like pictures in a revolving lantern rapidly flowing across the surface of the eyeball.

Was it reality which was actually assaulting Wakako, or was it an event in a dream? In a vagueness that defied comprehension, she heard a light, scratchy noise made by the glass which landed on Yoko's back and cut into her skin.

It was the same sound made by the colorful blizzard in the autumn sun at the school athletic meet, when the huge paper ball split and released small pieces of paper which danced with a dry noise.

"Last, again? You're no good, Wakako." Yoko, who always got a red ribbon for first place, reproached Wakako for being a slow runner.

The same proud face loomed up amidst the rain of glass chips. It became contorted in a way Wakako had rarely seen, and cried: help! Looking at the cave-like darkness of Yoko's mouth, Wakako echoed her cry, in exactly the same tone of voice.

Wakako lay under the debris of the crushed factory.

Fire seemed to have broken out: she saw flames at her feet. "Help me! Isn't anyone going to help me?"—a man crawled out of the debris grabbing at any pieces of concrete that his hands could touch.

In front of his hands there was a tiny space. Smoke blew in from the space, moving the air around Wakako. It was the only space through which escape was possible.

Wakako pulled the man's leg with all her might and begged him to help her. The hairy shin of the man who wore wooden clogs kicked her shoulder. Wakako did not let go even then.

The man took off his sturdy, homemade clog, and hit her slender shoulder with its supports. Her bone creaked.

The hairy shin disappeared from her eyes with the quickness of a squirrel. Realizing that no one would help her, Wakako started to pull down, as the man had done, whatever pieces of debris she could lay her hands on. When she came to, she was standing outside the building.

Around her was a sea of fire. The wind was hot, occasionally scorching her hair. Amidst wind that made a noise like the rumbling of the earth and flames that encircled clouds of smoke, a human shape appeared.

It was a girl with long hair, probably a student. Wakako started to run after her.

Wakako did not remember from what part of the crushed factory she had crawled out. However, as she had slipped free, someone had grasped her ankle. She remembered five damp fingers clinging stubbornly to her ankle as she tried to make her escape.

Like the man, Wakako too kicked that hand with the heel of one of her sneakers. Reluctantly, one by one, the long, damp-skinned fingers released Wakako's ankle, and fell into the flaming debris.

They felt like the fingers of Yoko, whose little finger Wakako had intertwined with her own in a symbolic act of friendship.

"—I heard that a missionary school student tried to help a nun who was crushed under the church. When she ran toward the building, the nun scolded the girl and said, 'Don't come, it's all right, run away quickly.' The nun's robe caught fire . . . and the girl ran away crying, they say. Pity, how she must have felt. A young girl, not too many years behind her—"

In the next room Obatchan was talking.

"Wasn't she wonderful, that nun?" Tsune sniffed. A faint smile floated on Wakako's pale cheeks.

"That story is a fake," Wakako mumbled to herself. Obatchan's story was an embellished fabrication, not the truth. As in the tales of Urashima Taro in which the young fisherman becomes an old man in a whiff of white smoke, N City was instantly transformed into a city of the dead in one flash of light that day. Those who lived had just barely managed to save their lives. Who would have deliberately run back to help others? It could not have been possible that there was time for worrying about others.

The girl student who fled home probably fabricated the story when recounting her experiences to her parents, the image of the nun *she had forsaken* haunting her eyes. It must be that she wanted to believe in her own good will. The made-up story moved Obatchan, brought tears to Tsune's eyes, and would do the same to many other well-meaning people.

As the days pass, the lie will penetrate the girl's body and she herself will begin to believe it. For the first time, then, she will be liberated from the nun.

Just as she unconsciously lied to Yoshi, some day Wakako, too, might tell Obatchan and Tsune about Yoko, conveniently coloring the truth.

She wished the day would come soon.

While rejecting Obatchan's story as a lie, part of Wakako thought that perhaps it was how it was meant to be.

When she saw the painful expression on Yoko's contorted face amidst the falling glass chips, a glint of cruel satisfaction, although just for a second, crossing her mind.

Painting by the atomic bomb survivor Michitsuji Yoshiko. Japan Broadcasting Corporation (NHK), ed., *Unforgettable Fire, Pictures Drawn by Atomic Bomb Survivors* (New York: Pantheon Books, a Division of Random House, Inc., 1977), 29.

Wakako no longer understood herself. She wondered if something that remained unaffected by any circumstance whatsoever might not lie deep in the human mind.

"Obatchan is worrying about Yo-chan's safety," Tsune said in a soft voice, opening a screen door.

"If she's really worrying, Obatchan can go find her. She's not going, is she? In that case, be quiet." At the time of the explosion, Obatchan probably just watched, sipping tea, and said, How frightening, what can that fireball be?

"Nobody is blaming you, Wakako. You look so grim." The sudden barb in Wakako's voice was incomprehensible to Tsune.

Trying not to lose sight of the longhaired student, Wakako, the slow runner, ran with all her might. From time to time, the girl reeled, engulfed in flames. Each time this happened, her back shone in colors that changed like a chameleon's shell. In red flames it turned red; in flickering blue flames that burned horses and men, it shone coldly.

As she ran, Wakako wondered vaguely why a human back shone. Again and again she fell flat, stumbling over dead bodies. The bodies, which had just breathed their last, were still soft, and the flesh had an elasticity which was resilient to Wakako's touch.

Wakako was afraid of dead bodies. The tender flesh that pressed against her chest, and its smell, turned her stomach. She burped with a foolish noise, and vomited on the spot.

After a while she was exposed to too many deaths to feel fear any more. She also became used to the tenderness of the bodies' flesh.

Her toes learned to distinguish, on the basis of the softness of the flesh, male from female, young from old bodies.

A young woman, with thick bouncy flesh between the bone and soft skin, number 16; a man, old, with hard bones and thin flesh, number 9–unconsciously she counted with her fingers as she ran. She felt no sympathy.

However, when what she had thought was a corpse woke from the impact of her stumble and looked up, his eyes narrow slits, saying, "Give me medicine," Wakako caught her breath in horror. A human being who was clearly dying, or 90 percent dead, still wanted medicine—that attachment to life frightened her. Wakako ran on, avoiding those who appeared to be still alive.

The sunlight shone on the chameleon back of the girl running ahead of her, making slight rifts in the smoke.

Wakako found herself at the foot of the mountain which had been designated a refuge.

If anything happens, be sure to assemble at the mountain.

This is a detail from the "Boys and Girls" mural in Iri and Toshi Maruki, The Hiroshima Panels *(Japanese title: Genbaku no Zu [Paintings of the atomic explosions]) (Saitama, Japan: Maruki Gallery for the Hiroshima Panels Foundation, 1984). Courtesy of John Junkerman.*

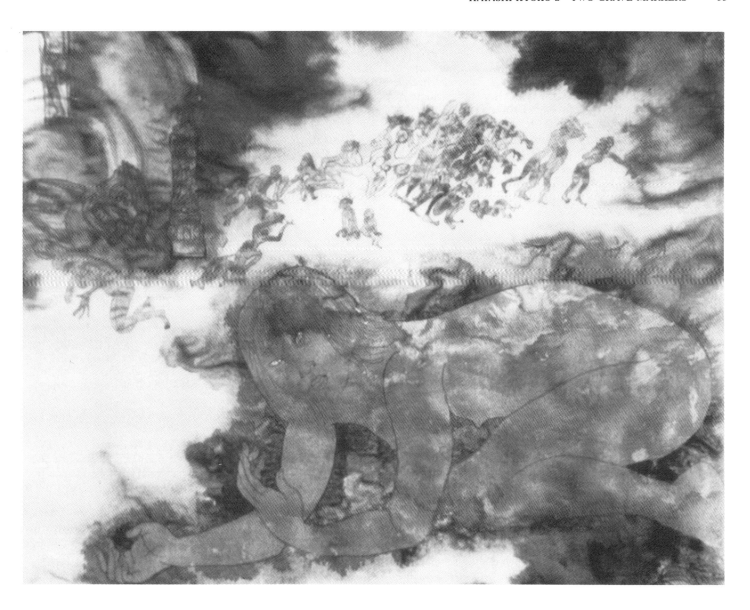

As usual, this was the instruction their teacher had given to Wakako and the others on the morning of the bombing. If only she could get to the mountain she could see her teacher and her friends. That thought had sustained Wakako as she ran desperately through the fire.

The gently sloping mountain, which had been covered with green cedars, was burning, and smoke rose everywhere. Some of Wakako's classmates were supposed to have been working on the mountain.

Since the side cave which Wakako and others had used as an air-raid shelter had simply been dug into the earth without reinforcement, mountain water had dripped from its ceiling and covered the floor to about knee-level. According to the instructions they had received, a team of girls should have been scooping up buckets of water and passing them outside the cave. Outside, students from other schools were supposed to be cutting grass.

If they were still alive, at least one would call her name.

Wakako tried skirting the foot of the mountain. When she had gone about half way around, she found a small brook about two meters wide.

A cluster of watercress still grew in the running water, creating an impression of coolness that seemed incongruous with the burnt surface of the mountain. Wakako felt like drinking water. Stripped of clothing which had burnt, and covered with blood, many people were drinking, thrusting their heads in the water of the brook. They lay on their stomachs and drank, their faces touching the surface of the water and their legs stretched apart.

There was a kind of intimacy about this scene of river and people, as if the running water were a giant centipede and the people its legs.

Wakako's throat was dry.

Finding a tiny space, she started to drink, lying on her

stomach like the others.

The water was tepid and smelled strongly of moss. The weight of the water spread throughout her empty stomach which had missed lunch. As she was absorbed in the act of drinking, she felt the finger tip of the man next to her on her cheek. When she brushed it away, the man with crew cut hair flipped upside down as simply as the shutter carrying the poisoned Oiwa in the *kabuki* story, and fell into the water.*

The man's eyes were open, and he was dead.

The river was shallow. It flowed in ripples over the man's wide open eyeballs. He seemed about forty, probably the head of a family with wife and children. He was nothing more than an object which created a slight variation to the flow of the water.

Wakako took another look at the stream.

It seemed unchanged from when she had seen it earlier that morning, and flowed calmly through a field scorched by the atomic blast. At the moment of the explosion, the water seethed as if it were boiling, and the surface, bubbling up in foam, rose twenty or thirty centimeters. But that was just for a second; the flowing water before her eyes had returned to the tranquility of the early morning.

Wakako recalled:

It was when she was in grade school. For a year or so, she lived in a city on the Chinese continent.

It was an English-style city where red brick houses stood side by side. A river flowed through the city, full, literally full, of yellow water. The amount and depth of water in that river were unfathomable.

Wakako had been fond of this river, and often walked along it with the amah who worked for them.

On early summer mornings, little boats called sampans and shaped like rabbits with ears erect floated along the river as though they were sleeping.

Putt, putt, putt came the sound of a steam boat from the upper river. It was the water police patrol boat. It made the rounds of the river every morning.

Wakako would count—one, two, three—pointing at the back of the boat with her forefinger. She was counting the number of drowned bodies tied to the stern.

Tied together in a row with a fat rope, the bodies kicked up water heroically as they were towed along.

One stretched his arms to heavens, crying for help. Another had one leg still raised, with which he had violently kicked the water trying to rise to the surface. Each body assumed a different posture as the boat tugged them behind it. They seemed to ride on the waves with their heads and swollen bellies.

Amah, which of those men do you like?—Wakako would ask. The amah always ignored her question: Miss, they aren't men, they are baggage because they're dead.

Those corpses, because they had lost the repugnant fleshiness of living human beings, were a nature poem which added colors to the yellow flow. The sight of those limbs beating the water in an effort to regain life only added a special

---

* In *Tokaido Yotsuya Kaisan* by Tsuruya Nanboku (1755–1829), Oiwa is poisoned by her husband. He ties the bodies of Oiwa and a young man on each side of a shutter and lets it float in a river. Her ghost, her face deformed from poisoning, haunts him to death.

touch to the landscape, making the river itself look that much more peaceful. It was a natural scene within which the dead were now returning to mother earth.

In comparison, the dead bodies strewn before Wakako's eyes in the burnt field suggested no peace associated with a return to nature.

"Wakako, is that you?" a girl called to her. "It's me, Yoko"—the voice approached from behind with the sound of dragging feet. Yoko's *monpe* were torn from the knees down, revealing flesh which had been scraped away in several places as though with a spoon. Her wounded legs faltering, the girl fell. Her back glistened as she lay on her side. Her blouse had burned up in the flash, and glass chips stuck in her bare back. Around the roots of each chip, powdery thin pieces, mosaic-like, formed a spiral. Each time she breathed, the tips of the fine pieces trembled. No doubt from the pain, she held her body tense, stifling her breath.

Could this be the same Yoko?—the same Yoko who, in the prime of her innocent and inviolable youth, had raised her lunch box and rather proudly announced that she had rice and omelette?

"Look what shape I'm in—" Yoko spoke in the Nagasaki dialect which was forbidden at school, showing Wakako her wounds. "I see that you didn't get any wounds," Yoko said as she rose slowly.

It looks like I didn't—as Wakako tried to give an ambiguous answer, Yoko turned just her head toward her without moving her body and said, "I wish I could give you half of my wounds."

Although they had been standing in the same place, Yoko was badly wounded, while not even a piece of glass stuck to Wakako's body. Apparently it had been a stroke of luck that Wakako had sought shelter from the light behind a large pillar a second before the explosion.

Wakako had been saved by chance, but Yoko seemed unhappy about it.

Yoko was better looking than Wakako. She was also brighter.

It was only in social status Wakako surpassed her because her father was the village head. However, Yoko's family was richer.

In the mountains, too, the sun shone longer on the oranges belonging to Yoko's family. They had a glossier, deeper color, and were sweeter than those of Wakako's family.

Yoko was superior in every respect. Yet at the moment that decided life or death, luck had favored Wakako. If ever the villagers reached an impasse or became embarrassed when they had to choose between the two, the judge's fan would be raised to the one whose family status had been higher since before the children's births. It was in the same way that chance made Wakako the winner.

The two sat silently, holding their knees, at the edge of the brook. Four or five hours had passed since the bombing. In less than an hour, the sun would sink behind the mountain, and the first night after the explosion would come to N City.

"Why don't we run to some place where there are people," Wakako stood up. "I'm tired of running," Yoko said in a low voice. "You want to run away, don't you? It's all right if you go alone."

"We'll go together," Wakako started to say, but she held the words back.

So after all those white fingers had belonged to Yoko.

The long fingers which Wakako had kicked heartlessly were Yoko's.

Yet Yoko had not even referred to this when she suggested that Wakako run away by herself. She had done so in her typically cruel, indirect manner.

Yet at the time Wakako had been unable to think of anything else to do. Yoko herself would not have had the impulse to help another.

All she could do was save herself. In fact, hadn't Yoko run ahead of Wakako—and faster than Wakako?

Yes, that chameleon back had been Yoko's. Wakako had run after her back. If this were so, Yoko had escaped from the crushed building one step ahead of Wakako.

It made sense that Wakako, sheltered behind the fat, square pillar proved lucky as far as the flash of light was concerned, but for that very reason she had been more deeply buried under rubble. Although Yoko had been burned, she must have escaped from the building more easily.

Then the white hand could not have been Yoko's. Wakako must have kicked someone else's hand. In either case, it was true that she had left a human being surrounded by flames. But

that was a separate matter.

Wakako felt the lump in her chest subside.

"If we're running at all, it's got to be both of us together," Wakako stroked Yoko's hair, which was wet with blood. Yoko had started to doze off, perhaps due to her wounds.

"Let's go near the fire," Wakako said. Yoko stood up without ado, leaning on the hand Wakako held out.

I'm cold . . . , Yoko trembled, firmly clasping Wakako's hand as tightly as if she were a little child.

The sea, the sky, and the sloping trail on the ridge of the mountains—everything glowed in the evening sun.

"Red dragonflies, so many of them," Shige's voice came from the trail.

"Do you want some?" said the voice of a village man. Shige nodded. Two days had passed since Wakako's return. She was watching red dragonflies swarming between the yard and the mountain pass.

Their diaphanous silver wings trembling, the red dragonflies flew toward the yard of Wakako's house.

The man wore only his underwear and had a wet towel around his neck. Apparently he had just taken a bath. B-29s almost never visited this village of orange groves deep in the mountains.

Even though they had heard about the disaster in N City, the villagers seemed oblivious to the war as they basked in the evening glow which dyed the sea red.

Shige, too, wore only her underwear.

"Shige, bring the throw-net."

"What are you going to do with it?" Shige, who had just turned four, ran down from the pass, her little round bottom bouncing, and returned dragging the fish net behind her.

Shige was a plucky child who would run all along the small river and the footpaths between the paddies, never wearing more than underpants.

"There," Shige handed the man the net she had been holding to her chest and nodded, sticking out her tummy and clasping her hands behind her back. "I see, you're going to catch dragonflies, right?"

"No clothes again? Girls have to wear something," the man poked her navel as he took the net.

Shige laughed, showing her white teeth, and asked, "That's really a fish net, isn't it?"

"Fish and dragonflies are all the same." The man took a step forward and struck a pose against the sky, using his left hand to hold the net closed and his right hand to pull it.

"What are you doing with the net, Uncle?"

"Just watch. There!" he drew a fan-shaped arc across the vault of the sky.

The thin threads of the net wafted toward the evening sun, opened slowly, trapped some dragonflies in its meshes, and came floating down.

The red dragonflies' silver wings danced inside the net like small fish.

"They'll get hurt if they bump against the lead weights, won't they, Uncle?" Shige asked worriedly.

"No, they won't. They won't get hurt. Now catch them quickly."

Shige sprang to the net like a grasshopper.

Catching sight of the red dragonflies trembling in the net, their thin bodies strong as piano cords, Wakako felt she could not bear watching as their lives were extinguished. She closed her eyes.

Yoko was dead—Yoshi's voice was heard, mingled with Shige's shouts.

Wakako seemed to fall asleep for several minutes. The sunset had faded, leaving both the room and the yard in gloom. Shige was still releasing red dragonflies trapped in the net.

Most had become so weak that they hovered close to the ground, lost balance in their wings, and fell.

"I would like to see the buddha and offer my prayers."* It seemed that Obatchan was still in the next room. Wakako heard her feet shuffling across the tatami.

The buddha? Wakako sat up on her mat.

Was Yoko's body in this house? Her breath hushed, Wakako listened to the sounds in the next room. Why had they carried Yoko to Wakako's house on the hilltop? Yoko's house was at the bottom of the hill.

What could Yoshi mean by this? Had she heard in N City anything about Wakako and Yoko?

"Please don't look, Obatchan. The only reason I brought her up the hill was that I thought Waka-chan must be concerned about Yoko. Yoko, too, would love to have a glimpse of Waka-chan. Besides, Yoko hasn't changed a bit. I found her dead looking exactly the same as the girl you've always known."

"Really? How fortunate. . . . She was a beautiful girl. How beautiful she must be now that she has become a buddha. Yoshi-san, please let me take one look."

"No." Yoshi paused and then said steadily: "She was dead, eaten by maggots. I wound strips of bleached cotton cloth around her and carried her home carefully so they wouldn't unwrap. So I don't want to show her to you."

"Yo-chan eaten by maggots. . . . How painful, Yoshi-san. But I'm sure it wasn't just Yo-chan. I hear all the bodies in N City were that way."

Tsune reproached Obatchan for speaking so bluntly, without regard for the feelings of whoever might be listening. Then she said to Yoko's mother, "Thank you for the trouble you've taken, Yoshi-san. I'll wake Wakako right away." Tsune quietly opened a sliding door. Wakako saw that the light was on in the adjacent room. Yoshi's face was pale under the cylindrical light, draped with black cloth as a precaution against air raids. Her hair was tightly combed with a bun in back. The front portions of her *monpe* collar were pulled tightly over one another, while the narrow strip of white kimono undergarment showing around her neck lent a sword-like focus to her expression.

Despite her day-long search for Yoko through the burnt fields, Yoshi's white collar appeared to Wakako's eyes even whiter than before.

Yoko's body lay on a shutter, under a white cloth, just beyond the circumference of the cylinder of light.

Wakako impulsively turned her face down on her bedding.

"Please, Yoshi-san, let me see the buddha just for a second. Think of it as an old woman's duty," Obatchan said to Yoshi. "I feel such pity for Yo-chan. Only Waka-san survived. I wish there was some way both of them could have lived. I wouldn't have minded taking their place, old woman that I am." As she approached the place where Yoko lay on

---

* The Japanese refer to a dead person or his soul as a buddha (*hotokesama*).

the shutter, Obatchan looked in at Wakako who was under the mosquito net.

Obatchan was so agitated by Yoko's death she was weeping. In this village, at most one or two people died every ten years. Death was not only a rare occurrence but one limited to old people. Her playmates of long ago had died one by one, leaving Obatchan alone. Now it was her turn: it was inevitable that she would die some time in the near future. Obatchan was frightened of her own death. Yet while she had been waiting for death to come, maybe today, maybe tomorrow, the fourteen-year-old Yoko had died.

Even though she was saddened by the girl's death. Obatchan appeared to derive peace of mind from this death which had upset the natural order: her own turn might, just might, come much, much later.

Perhaps even the sorrow that brought tears to her eyes was a sham. At least Wakako thought so.

As a matter of fact, Obatchan had tarried in their home ever since Wakako had run home from N City that morning. While repeating again and again that Waka-san was lucky indeed, she accurately detected that the paleness of Wakako's skin was abnormal: When will Wakako die? Wakako's death didn't seem so far off.

The villagers had welcomed Wakako's escape with festive merrymaking. The more familiar faces were around, the better her journey toward death would be as well.

"Yoko was in the hollow of the mountain, just as Waka-chan said. She was dead, all by herself, and holding her knees."

Yoko's body was stiff. The white cloth over the board bulged around it as if it were a wine keg.

"Just as Waka-san said? So she knew, after all? Some say they saw them running away to the mountain together," Obatchan said to Wakako, looking in from behind the sliding door.

"Who said so?" Tsune questioned her in a tense voice.

Could that have been yesterday, after all? Obatchan dodged Tsune's question, either because she was being evasive or because she had truly forgotten—no, it feels like it was this morning.

"Did you hear the same story, Yoshi-san?" Tsune asked. Without answering her, Yoko's mother said:

"When I held her up, a maggot on her back fell on my lap . . . and squirmed like a baby, just the way Yoko used to." She stroked Yoko's stiffened body through the white cloth. Obatchan said: "Maggots are maggots, Yoshi-san. Don't lose your senses; they say the war's going to go on for a long time."

Who could have seen them? Wakako tried to picture the day's scenes in her mind. The only live person she had encountered was the man she stumbled over when running.

He, too, was half dead. He had asked for medicine, yet, without waiting for her answer, had closed his eyes. Even if he might have been from this village, he probably died before nightfall. Besides, Wakako was alone when she passed him.

The only other person was Yoko. But Yoko was already dead by then, so she could have told neither Yoshi nor Obatchan. No one could know.

Wakako grew weaker as the days passed. Each day her skin grew paler and more transparent, until the purple capillary vessels were visible under her eyes.

Wakako, her mother would call, but Wakako would only

turn her head wearily, without speaking. Old doctor Tanaka came to examine her, but his advice was always the same: Try giving her some fresh fruit.

Stretching arms which had been reduced to nothing but bones on her summer comforter, Wakako just stared at the ceiling.

"Is there something on the ceiling?" When Tsune questioned the child who was gazing and gazing, she answered: "The ceiling—you see, its wood grain looks like Yoko."

When half a month or so passed, Tsune found a small, red spot on Wakako's arm. It was a tiny dot like a mosquito bite or a flea bite.

When Tsune scratched at it without thinking with the tip of her finger nail, it was crushed and a downy hair with a ball of pus at its root came off. When she took a careful look, she found similar red spots scattered here and there on both of Wakako's arms. Taking care not to be noticed by Wakako, Tsune scratched another dot by way of experiment.

Like a weed with a rotten root, the hair came off easily, attached to a drop of infected fat.

The new model bomb that had been dropped on N City caused the open wounds and pores of human beings who had returned alive to the village to rot, sending them to certain death.

"At this moment there is no treatment that would prevent their death," said old Doctor Tanaka. He had given up.

Tsune could only watch Wakako dying day by day. Flies gathered around, attracted by the odor of the infected skin. Tsune chased away the swarming flies.

She regretted that she could do nothing else.

Faithful to their promise to their teacher, the two girls had climbed the mountain the following morning. Although the fire had been extinguished, purple smoke rose from the charred trees and a strange heat enveloped the mountain. Yoko seemed to be suffering from the wounds on her back; every now and then she would stop and sigh, "How they hurt."

On the mountain slope which had been smooth until the day before, Wakako found a hollow of freshly exposed soil.

The hollow faced north, away from the target of the bombing, and its soil was moist. With her back against the wall of the hollow to cool her skin, Wakako sat and embraced her knees.

Yoko sat by her side, her back not touching the wall but close enough so that her skin felt the cold air of the earth. They spent the night resting in the same posture, holding their knees. It was the curled posture of the foetus in the mother's womb, floating without the least resistance in the protecting water.

The mountain was quiet. Wind blew through the hollow. They heard a sound of something tumbling down the slope.

It was a small noise, perhaps of a nut. Or could it be the teacher, or a classmate? A wounded human being only made a whimper.

Wakako strained her ears. The sound stopped when the object hit the earth with a little thump, and the mountain reverted to silence.

"I feel as if something were pecking at my back," Yoko complained of the pain, grimacing with cheeks that had turned the color of the earth.

The pieces of glass were more deeply buried in her flesh than they had been the day before. Even a splinter of wood hurts when it digs into the skin. If one single piece of glass

could be pulled out, the pain would be reduced by just that much.

A piece sticking into the middle of Yoko's back seemed at least four or five centimeters long. Trying not to touch the other pieces, Wakako swiftly pulled it out. With a scream, Yoko pushed Wakako. Knocked off balance, Wakako unintentionally grabbed the middle of Yoko's back.

Yoko gasped and hunched over even more. At that instant something fell from her back. It was a maggot.

The maggot, with blood in every section of its fat body, stretched and contracted its way up the mountain of glass, fell off, and quickly found a nearby wound, which it dug into, squeezing itself into a tight, narrow shape.

Maggots which could easily be crushed under a finger were lapping up blood and eating Yoko.

Only unclean wastes attracted maggots: a manure container beside a footpath on the farm in the village, fish bones in the trash dump, the swollen body of a cat thrown into a water pool, the intestines of a snake flushed out of a bush onto the summer road.

Only worthless things fester with maggots.

"Maggots," Wakako pointed at Yoko's back. "Maggots?" Yoko asked back. "Why me, why do they collect on me?" she queried resentfully.

"They are alive and moving, Yoko."

Even as she said this, horror at the meaning of the words she had never intended to utter made Wakako feel dizzy.

A fly which had been in the target area had survived miraculously, just as Wakako had, with even its crepe-paper wings intact. That fly must have been the first to smell out Yoko's death from among countless piles of corpses. What a clever fly! Wasting no time, it had procreated in the wastes left by the destruction.

The maggots swarming in Yoko's open wounds would soon become flies, and it would be their turn to create new lives. They were devouring Yoko's flesh at great speed as they prepared to bring forth the next generation. They would turn into flies, and then assault Wakako. The succession of life cycles had not a moment to spare. Having even eaten into Yoko's almost haughty prime of youth, they would next attack Wakako.

Just as the drowned bodies in the yellow river had returned to mother earth, the maggot might be a reincarnation of Yoko. A maggot with Yoko's eyes and eyebrows would start to eat Wakako: You're turning into a maggot, too, Wakako.

But Wakako could not grant this favor to Yoko, even if it was Yoko's right, as a best friend, to demand it. She would crush every maggot that attacked her: she was determined to defeat Yoko.

Even if Yoko disappeared from the world because of these actions, it could not be helped.

Supporting her body with her hands from underneath while maintaining a sitting posture, Wakako tried to move away from Yoko without attracting her attention.

Sensing something in the air, Yoko turned her head, her cheek still on her knee, to look at Wakako. A satiated maggot fell from her back. Disoriented by finding itself on the less slippery earth, the maggot moved its gorged belly up and down as it crawled toward Wakako.

As it moved toward her leaving a light trail in the new dirt, Wakako, still sitting, crushed it under her heel. Yoko watched in silence.

Yoko's clean eyes, whose brightness Wakako used to envy, had already lost their light.

"Maggots hatch quickly, don't they. I raise maggots, and they become me," she laughed softly.

Her slackened nerves no longer seemed to find the swarming maggots eerie. Suddenly Yoko said, staring at Wakako with dull eyes, "You mustn't kill it. It's me."

Wakako ran down the mountain as fast as she could.

"Don't leave me alone," Yoko shouted. Wakako covered her ears with both hands and raced down the slope.

Wakako did not start to walk slowly until she had reached level ground. The small river flowed brightly, reflecting clouds in the sky.

When she caught sight of the shallow water flowing in a clear streak, Wakako fell to the ground. She lay there looking up at the sky. In the blue sky was the white sun. The sun she had looked up at yesterday from beside the stream trembled like a rotting tomato with too much soft flesh to keep in shape. The sun of the midsummer noon which should have been above her head had sunk to the horizon. Now the sun was utterly calm, its sharp light like a silk needle in one corner of the vast expanse of sky. Wakako could also hear an engine.

It was the metallic sound of a B-29. But no one tried to run for shelter now. Those who were checking dead bodies, anxious about missing close relatives, as well as those wounded who were, so to speak, dressed in tattered rags, just looked languidly up at the sky.

As the noise of the approaching engine grew louder, Wakako closed her eyes. Even if the same light flashed across the sky again, I would not run; I am too tired, Wakako thought.

I'll sleep for a while—

The shadow of the low-flying airplane passed over her.

The burnt field was more crowded than it had been the day before. It was already three days after the bombing, and people from other areas who had heard about the disaster in N City had joined the crowds, looking for family members. They moved to and fro, their noses and mouths covered with towels, carrying canteens and bundles of necessities. Even in this charred field, the morning had its distinctive freshness. Some people were washing their bloodstained faces and rinsing their mouths in water gushing out of a broken water pipe. Wakako felt somewhat stronger.

Along the trail by the stream, many people were climbing toward the mountain top. Wakako, who had taken in nothing but water, joined the line of people on shaky feet.

She wondered how Yoko was doing.

"I wonder where she went to school. What a pity."

Wakako heard some women whispering and peered inside the circle of people. She was standing in front of the hollow where she and Yoko had stayed. The mothers joined their hands in prayer, while their shoulders slackened with relief at the realization that this body was not one of their daughters.

Yoko was dead. Still crouched down and holding her knees, just a few steps further away from the wall of the hollow than she had been yesterday. The stench which had accumulated in the hollow made Wakako nauseous.

"Poor child, flies are collecting on her," a woman brushed away the flies swarming on Yoko's face.

The flies' wings made a hideous noise as they flew away from the hollow.

Watching them fly toward the sun, Wakako thought: Yoko's dead.

"But that has nothing to do with me," she muttered, walking back down the mountain.

Wakako died.

She died one day after the ritual was observed marking the forty-ninth day since Yoko's death. For two or three days before death she had run a fever of approximately 104.

When she opened her eyes between long periods of sleep, the wood grain in the ceiling smiled at her. Wakako did her best to keep her eyes closed.

When she closed them, Yoko never failed to appear. Many little Yokos, smaller than the span between the joints of a finger, would appear and circle around Wakako's bed. Each wore the same long hair and navy and white *monpe* Yoko had worn that day.

The Yokos walked in step around Wakako's bed.

Yoko, Wakako would call but they didn't turn to look at her.

Each and every one of the Yokos walked with back turned to Wakako. No matter which side of the bed they were on, they never showed their faces to Wakako.

Yoko was angry.

It couldn't be helped. There was no other way at that moment, don't you see, Wakako said, but still they didn't look at her.

Walking with precise steps, the circle of Yokos gradually closed in on Wakako.

"Mother," Wakako called Tsune.

"I'm right here," Tsune held Wakako's hand in her warm hands, gently bending toward her: "What would you like?" Opening her eyes narrowly, Wakako said, "Maggots, mother." "Where?" Tsune looked around the room. Wakako pointed at her head with her finger.

"In my head." Tsune grasped Wakako's hands tightly. She was prepared for her child's death.

She had given up hope the day she found the red spots on Wakako's arms.

Tsune had heard that survivors of the bombing died insane. Was it due to the high fever or to that flash of light? The sick person would die babbling incoherently, she had heard. Moreover, almost every single one of the pores in Wakako's arms was beginning to rot, oozing pus. Now her legs had started to be affected. Even though Tsune changed her sheets every day, they immediately became soiled with blood and yellow pus.

"There are no maggots there," Tsune said, her mouth to Wakako's ear. Wakako tucked in her head and giggled as if she had been tickled. "Can't you see? The inside of my head is full of them." Gesturing as she used to as a little girl when confiding a secret, Wakako said, "I didn't help, you see. So they are rioting." "Who are you saying you didn't help?" Tsune wanted to know what had happened between Wakako and Yoko in N City. If Wakako had abandoned Yoko on the mountain as rumor had it, she wanted to somehow console her so she would feel more at peace. It must have been the sheer will to survive that led Wakako to abandon Yoko and exert her final strength to return to the orange mountain where Tsune lived.

The brief days after the bombing must have been the first time in her life that Wakako lived to the hilt, lovingly attached to her own life. If, during these most precious days of her life, she were to be blamed for not having helped Yoko, it would be too cruel, Tsune thought.

Yoshi might know the facts.

Tsune went to her house.

"Is the rumor true? Tell me if you know."

Tsune stood with her hands joined, facing the new memorial tablet in the miniature family shrine.

"True? That's something Waka-chan should know. I want to hear it from her mouth, too. The only truth I know is that Yoko was dead in the mountain all by herself. That's all," she looked at Tsune, the rosary still in her hands.

"Yoshi-san, you took the trouble to bring Yo-chan over here that day so Wakako could see her. Wakako couldn't have left Yo-chan alone on the mountain, and because you believe that, you brought her, didn't you?"

"But it was Waka-chan who told me Yoko was on the mountain."

Tsune looked steadily into the gleaming eyes of Yoshi, who so resembled Yoko.

"It's too cruel. I'm sure Wakako heard about it from someone else. The rumor is false. Wakako ran alone, all alone by herself. Think how much stronger she would have felt if she had been with Yo-chan."

"This is the truth," Tsune added.

"Then, that must be the truth. Yoko has already died. I can't ask her."

"All sympathy goes to Yo-chan anyway because only Wakako survived. Yo-chan's death has nothing to do with Wakako. All right, Yoshi-san?"

Yoshi had turned her back against Tsune. With joined palms raised toward the memorial tablet, she continued her prayers. Tsune went on, "Please make this very clear to Obatchan and the village people in your own words. She makes no excuse whatsoever, poor Wakako."

A villager came across Tsune on the road and asked her, as she was quickly passing by, "How's Waka-chan doing?" Tsune answered in a calm voice, "I won't let her die."

Tsune knew Wakako's gentleness. Even if the rumor was true, who could blame her? Even Yoshi who had lost Yoko could not blame her.

It was wrong of Yoshi to resent Wakako. If she was to resent something, let it be the huge, monster ball of fire.

Let her resent the misfortune of her child who was not able to survive.

"There are a lot of Yokos around my bed," delirious with fever, Wakako waved both hands in the air.

"There's nothing to fear, mother is watching you."

Tsune's voice did not penetrate Wakako's ears. Flies circling around inside Wakako's head buried her mother's words in the whir of their wings.

They were the flies which had lived in her head ever since she stayed in the mountain hollow.

The noise bothered her. How I long for quiet, the sooner the better, Wakako thought.

"Will you kill the flies?"

"Of course, Mother will kill everything that's nasty to you, Wakako."

A faint smile appeared on Wakako's cheeks, which were as somber and bloodless as those of a wax figure.

Taking a deep, audible breath, Wakako died with her mouth open.

Tsune kept looking long at the smile which lingered around Wakako's eyes.

The morning sun near the beginning of autumn shone into the room where Wakako lay, her pale cheeks shadowy where the flesh had sunk. The faint smile pasted on her cheeks took on a dark shade which did not become a young girl who had lived fourteen years and one month. Tsune kept fanning Wakako's body which was starting to become cold. Why Wakako had feared flies so much remained unknown to her mother. Once in her delirium she had said, "Mother, flies have teeth, so they bite me." Tsune could not begin to imagine where those words came from, but she could understand the terror Wakako had suffered from being condemned by something. She did not want to think that it was Yoko.

Obatchan, who had rushed over, said, "How frightening. Waka-san looks so grim. But everything is over now. Yoshi-san, forgive Waka-san." Her last words were addressed to Yoshi, who had arrived after her.

"Wakako has nothing to be forgiven for," Tsune said firmly, "I will have Wakako's grave dug side-by-side with Yo-chan's in that hollow. They were friends."

"Then Yoko won't be able to rest in peace," Yoshi said.

"Yoshi-san, don't spread strange rumors. If you do, then it'll be Wakako who won't be able to rest in peace. The children bear no guilt at all. I'd like you to remember that at least," Tsune said clearly.

Wakako's grave marker of fresh wood was erected beside Yoko's in the mountain hollow.

Although her husband opposed it, reminding her of the fine ancestral tomb in the village, Tsune would not hear of anything else: It's proof of Wakako's innocence.

Facing away from the burnt field of N City in the autumn wind, the grave markers of the two girls were surrounded by many grave markers. They stood side-by-side in the breeze.

Tsune carried orange branches from the village across many hills, and put one, with fruit that was still hard and green, in the flower holder at Wakako's grave. She placed another for Yoko.

Intercepted by the grave markers, the wind that blew into the hollow seemed to be speaking in a slender voice.

What's so interesting? Share it with me, Tsune asked of the two girls' graves.

She thought she was hearing the laughter of Wakako and Yoko.

The Atomic Bomb and the Citizens of Nagasaki

by Sadao Kamata and Stephen Salaff*

Introduction: A Path to Peace

Hiroshima is a universally recognized name today, but Nagasaki, the second city to suffer atomic bombing, is less well known, and in fact its destruction three days after Hiroshima seemed anticlimactic to many observers.[1] The damage to both Japanese cities would be dwarfed in scale by any future nuclear holocaust, but the joint "Hiroshima-Nagasaki" experience, which changed the world forever, still constitutes the indispensable base of knowledge for an understanding of the human and environmental decimation which would be wrought by nuclear war. The way we choose to remember these two bombings will determine whether the human community can assimilate the meaning of these weapons before they are used again, and act decisively to spare our planet from the nuclear nightmare with which it is now threatened. This article is dedicated to helping cultivate the rationality, creative imagination and commitment to human welfare necessary to ensure that Nagasaki will be the last place on earth where nuclear weapons were ever used.*

The march of events recounted in the first section of the following pages shows that the atomic bomb was not needed to end World War II, but became rather a major factor fostering disunity in the anti-fascist alliance and the opening salvo of the long nuclear arms race. Nagasaki's unique history complicated the struggle of the *Hibakusha* ("A-bomb exposed persons") to overcome the injuries they suffered in the bombing. Owing to the particular socio-economic circumstances of Nagasaki, the movement for rehabilitation and international peace organized by its citizens has been challenged by formidable local as well as national and international obstacles. The following two sections spotlight the impediments to the recovery of the *Hibakusha* and the city of Nagasaki posed by its traditions of politically passive Catholicism, direct administrative subordination to the national government under Tokugawa rule, and economic control by the giant Mitsubishi Corporation. The next two sections introduce *Hibakusha* testimonies describing the formation of the anti-A and -H bomb movement in reborn Nagasaki, while the last section views through the eyes of Nagasaki citizens the saga of Japan's nuclear-powered ship, the *Mutsu*, now berthed in nearby Sasebo against the wishes of many prefectural residents concerned about nuclear proliferation. Nagasaki's ardent nuclear disarmament effort relies strongly on the mobilization of world opinion for a ban on all nuclear explosions and for the total abolition of nuclear weapons.

The Bombing of Nagasaki: A Warning of "Others to Follow"

Directly influenced by the nuclear disarmament movement, the United Nations General Assembly declared on 24 November 1961 that the use of nuclear weapons is contrary to "the spirit, letter and aims of the United Nations" and to "the rules of international law and to the laws of humanity." Nuclear weapons are directed, not against one enemy alone, but against "mankind in general."[2] This resolution, although its sense is clearly prospective, challenges the North American contention that atomic bombs were patriotically dropped on Hiroshima and Nagasaki in August 1945 as legitimate weapons of war to compel a prompt Japanese surrender and to forestall large numbers of allied casualties. Collateral decisions of the General Assembly lend further political and moral weight to the ongoing campaign for the enactment of a "Bill for the Relief of A-bombed Survivors," based on the principles of national indemnity, which is promoted by the six opposition parties in the Japanese Diet. Hiroshima and Nagasaki were attacked with A-bombs even though the United States government knew that by early 1945 Japan had broken down economically and strategically, and that "a large element of the Japanese Cabinet was ready in the spring [of 1945] to accept substantially the same [surrender] terms as those finally agreed on."[3]

Soon after Japan's decisive military reverses at Saipan, Tinian and Guam in the Mariana island chain in July 1944, a surrender movement developed in Tokyo, which feared not defeat but domestic revolution and the demise of the imperial polity. Prince Konoe, three times premier of Japan and Emperor

* Acknowledgements. The authors appreciate the informed and skillful cooperation of Professor Seiitsu Tachibana, Nagasaki Institute of Applied Science, whose language abilities and knowledge of atomic bomb problems has materially assisted their mutual understanding. Stephen Salaff is grateful for the helpful insights on the religious, ethical and historical aspects of the Nagasaki experience shared by the following members of the Department of Religious Studies, University of Toronto: Professors Gregory Baum, Ernest Best, Heinz Guenther, Joseph O'Connell, and Cyril Powles. Salaff further thanks Professors Jerome Ch'en, York University, Edward Norbeck, Rice University, and Janet W. Salaff, University of Toronto, for reviewing earlier drafts of this manuscript. The support of Professors Hans Blumenfeld, University of Toronto, and Lee Lorch, York University, is also acknowledged.

Hirohito's favorite senior statesman, who spoke for many of the top business and government leaders, reluctantly acknowledged in his February 1945 "Memorial to the Throne" that Japan had "already lost the war," recommended its termination "as speedily as possible," and warned that if hostilities were prolonged "a Communist revolution" reinforced by "Soviet intervention" would overthrow the imperial institution.[4] The position of the war party was undermined by the fall of Okinawa in June 1945, after which the Supreme Council for the Direction of the War (the "inner cabinet" of the six chief military and government leaders) admitted defeat. On 12 July, Tokyo's ambassador to the Kremlin was instructed to enlist the Soviet Union, not yet a military combatant in the Pacific War, as a mediator between the Anglo-U.S. and Japanese governments. The Supreme Council cabled him that "unconditional surrender is the only obstacle to peace."[5] Japan's aversion to unconditional surrender was well known at the time, since U.S. intelligence, whose cryptographers earlier had broken the Japanese diplomatic codes, intercepted the 12 July cable and relayed its contents to Washington.

In the Yalta Agreement signed by Stalin, Roosevelt and Churchill on 11 February 1945, it was decided that "in two or three months" after the surrender of Germany (which occurred on 8 May 1945), "the Soviet Union shall enter into the war against Japan on the side of the Allies."[6] Before the A-bomb was tested, President Roosevelt and President Truman, who succeeded him on 12 April, had welcomed the prospect of military assistance from the USSR in routing the vaunted Japanese Kwantung Army, which possessed an independent industrial base in China. The military chiefs advised that Soviet intervention was needed to spare the lives of several hundred thousand U.S. troops which would be lost in an invasion of Japan.

With Truman's concurrence, the Kremlin rebuffed the Japanese diplomatic maneuver of 12 July. The ultimate demand for unconditional surrender was issued at the Potsdam Conference on 26 July over the signatures of Truman, Churchill and Chiang Kai-shek (in Chiang's absence). Stalin's signature, which would have strengthened the Potsdam Proclamation and might have helped occasion an earlier surrender, was never sought.[7] Nevertheless, the rapid destruction of twenty-two divisions of the million man Kwantung Army in Manchuria by the Soviets following Moscow's declaration of war as scheduled on 8 August aided the group in the Japanese government that was insisting on acceptance of the Potsdam terms.

On 9 August, the Supreme Council and all government ministers held a prearranged conference with the Emperor, during which he advocated immediate capitulation, and on 14 August Japan accepted the surrender terms of the Potsdam Proclamation (although the Kwantung Army continued its resistance for another fortnight). A small group of poorly organized, fanatical young field-grade officers on the night of 14 August tried to stage a coup d'etat to renegotiate the surrender (to "protect the future status of the Emperor and the Throne"). But the stillborn putsch did not gain the support of the troops or of the population.[8] After Japan signed the instruments of surrender on 2 September, the U.S. permitted the retention of the imperial dynasty, which it knew weeks before was the virtually sole Japanese surrender condition, even of the diehard conspirators.

An invasion of the Japanese homeland, with its expected large allied casualty toll, was not anticipated before November or December 1945, by which time Japanese resistance would surely have collapsed for other reasons. Thus the lives of few if any U.S. fighting men were saved by the atomic instrument. The chronology of atomic diplomacy shows that the idea of the demonstrative mass destruction of Japanese cities took root in the planning of the U.S. Armed Forces when they gained control of bases in the western Pacific and the skies over Japan in late 1944. A Target Committee of Army Air Force ordnance specialists and atomic scientists, guided by official instructions, decided in May 1945 that Kyoto, Hiroshima and Niigata were the best A-bomb objectives, and recommended not to try to pinpoint industrial zones but to "shoot for the center" of these cities.[9] The members of the Committee agreed, too, that the initial use of the atomic bomb should be "sufficiently spectacular for the importance of the weapon to be internationally recognized when publicity on it is released."[10]

On 31 May 1945, an Interim Committee on atomic policy was set up by presidential authority under the chairmanship of Secretary of War Stimson, with representatives from the State, War and Navy Departments and the foremost scientific circles of the Manhattan Project. The Committee advised the President that the most profound psychological impact on Japan and the world would be achieved by using two atomic bombs as rapidly as possible in sequence without prior warning on cities harboring military installations or war plants employing a large number of workers, closely surrounded by workers' homes and other buildings most susceptible to damage.[11] President Truman's 25 July Directive to the Strategic Air Force to deliver additional A-bombs after the first "as soon as made ready by the [Manhattan] project staff" was definitive, unrestrained and irrevocable.[12] Since responsibility for timing the A-bomb sorties was delegated to the bomber command on Tinian Island, Washington never scheduled a pause to monitor the Japanese response to the first assault and the entry of the USSR into the war. The atomic bombing of Nagasaki, the consequence of Washington's multiple-bombing imperative, underscores the callousness of the fixed policy resolve to cast atomic bombs upon an unwarned, conclusively beaten nation—a nation ravaged by terrible conflagrations from fire bombing of civilian targets, defenseless against further heavy air and close-range naval strikes, and whose leaders in the self-interest of their own class were desperately suing for peace.

Washington was accurately appraised in December 1944 that the U.S. Army's Manhattan Project would probably enrich sufficient uranium for a gun-type (Hiroshima) bomb by about 1 August 1945, and would produce enough plutonium and master the more complicated technology for an implosion-type (Nagasaki) bomb sometime in the latter part of July 1945.[13] The detonation of a prototype plutonium bomb at Alamagordo, New Mexico, which measured up to Washington's highest expectations, coincided with the opening of the U.S.–U.K.–U.S.S.R. summit conference at Potsdam on 16 July 1945. The Nagasaki bomb itself was ready for delivery by 6 August. (The materials for a third A-bomb, also a plutonium device, were assembled by about 24 August.[14]) The effect of the unconditional surrender doctrine was to keep Japan fighting until atomic bombs were delivered in succession.

Stimson advised Truman in April 1945 that in major military matters the Soviet government had always carried out its obligations to its allies, and in fact often exceeded its

Aerial view of Nagasaki before the atomic bombing, 7 August 1945. Courtesy of International Cultural Hall, Nagasaki City.

Aerial view of Nagasaki after the atomic bombing. Courtesy of International Cultural Hall, Nagasaki City.

promises.[15] But already in late April the deterioration in U.S.-Soviet relations had reached crisis proportions, and the new administration, troubled perhaps by what in spite of Stalin's Yalta commitment it took to be ambiguity in Moscow's policy toward Japan, never shared Stimson's firm conviction in the reliability of the Soviet Union. Paramount was the policy of utilizing the extraordinary bombs to shock Japan violently and to establish postwar world hegemony. After the technically flawless twenty-kiloton "try-out for judgment day" in the New Mexico desert, the need felt for Soviet military assistance had declined and "further diplomatic efforts to bring the Russians into the Pacific war were largely pointless."[16] What little commitment there was in the U.S. administration for the collaborative international postwar control of atomic energy all but vanished.

President Truman had already issued the A-bomb strike order, and the enriched uranium for the Hiroshima bomb had arrived at Tinian, when the Postdam Proclamation warned Japan that its alternative to unconditional surrender was "prompt and utter destruction." The prospects for terminating the war short of atomic bombings were damaged, not only by the U.S. failure to seek Stalin's signature on the Proclamation, but also by the Truman administration's failure to disclose that the U.S. had come into possession of a much more destructive weapon than the world had ever known. Use of the weapon to jolt the Soviet Union already led the U.S. agenda, and the rationale for the atomic secrecy at Potsdam included "quite possibly the fact that the American government could not reveal these matters to the Japanese without revealing them to the Russians."[17]

Washington aimed not only to destroy as many Japanese city dwellers as possible and to test the damage and after-effects of the new weapon on open cities,[18] but also to warn the Soviet Union and "all mankind" that the first A-bomb "was not an isolated weapon, but that there were others to follow."[19] As an earnest of the willingness and intention of U.S. government and military leaders to produce and use a sequence of A-bombs to establish their (ultimately unattainable) goal of nuclear supremacy, the bombing of Nagasaki presaged postwar U.S. nuclear armament and preparation for nuclear war.

The works of Stimson, Butow and Feis reveal that the shifting political configuration in spring and summer 1945, when Washington was beginning to confront the USSR as the enemy, did not permit the categorical acceptance of Stalin's Yalta commitment to open the essential second front in the Far East. These considerations foreclosed planning based, not on the exercise of atomic power, but rather upon the early, close and effective integration of U.S. and Soviet forces and policies to compel Japan's surrender. The view that tandem A-bombings were necessary to achieve victory is held primarily by those, including most recently Joseph Alsop in the *New York Review of Books,* who underestimate the strong options which would have been provided by the extension to the Pacific War of the alliance against Hitler fascism.[20]

The capriciousness of the U.S. "brink-of-surrender" atomic bomb policy is made even more evident by the roulette-like process that led to Nagasaki. Kyoto was initially favored as the largest A-bomb objective, the renowned ancient capital and center of Japanese civilization. But Stimson erased Kyoto from the target list on the grounds that the bitterness which the atomic destruction of this cultural and religious shrine would cause might turn the Japanese against the U.S. in the postwar era should trouble develop with the USSR in the Far East.[21] The prime targets then chosen in the order of their importance to the U.S. leaders became Hiroshima and Kokura (now Kita Kyushu, situated between Hiroshima and Nagasaki), followed by Niigata and Nagasaki. The pilots of the bombing planes were given leave to roam above these cities seeking the ones offering the most suitable conditions for destruction.

The exemption granted to Kyoto did not extend to Nagasaki, notwithstanding its prominence as Japan's historically most international city and despite its allied prisoner of war camps.[22] In the words of historian Martin Sherwin, "It never occured to Stimson that the destruction of any city, or two cities, might be considered 'wanton.' "[23]

The town of Niigata, on the west coast, 255 kilometers north of Tokyo, was not an important industrial center and was perhaps listed because of its proximity to the Soviet Union. The A-bomb squadron commanders on Tinian decided that Niigata was too small and too distant from their launching field, and they erased it as an objective. The Air Force bombing plane which reached the chief target Kokura on the morning of 9 August discovered that the aiming point was obscured by a pall of clouds and smoke. The aircraft circled three times, but fearing the loss of fuel, flew southwest to drop the second atomic bomb on Nagasaki. Nagasaki's citizens were thus made to substitute in death and destruction for those of Kokura, Niigata and Kyoto, and a new season of torment was decreed.

The Era of Suppression

In the wake of Japan's capitulation and occupation by the U.S. armed forces, a Civil Censorship Code was promulgated by the Counter-Intelligence Branch of General Headquarters, prohibiting all reporting on the atomic suffering. Information on the real nature and extent of the damage was regarded as detrimental to the United States, and until the peace treaty signed by Japan with the U.S.-allied combatants came into force in April 1952, it was a crime for Japanese to write or broadcast factual data on the atomic bombing.[24] Almost all early works by Japanese authors dealing with Hiroshima and Nagasaki were censored, and only after lengthy appeals and protests was publication permitted. All media were strictly forbidden to mention the censorship operation itself. While the *Hibakusha* were thus being deprived of their history, the Atomic Bomb Casualty Commission established in 1947 by the Department of Defense and the Atomic Energy Commission to investigate the long-range medical effects of radiation on the human body, but lacking a healing mission, secured a monopoly on research and study of atomic bomb casualties.[25]

The data initially collected in Hiroshima and Nagasaki were classified top secret by the occupation authorities. . . . Several Japanese medical scientists risked severe penalties to hide pathological specimens and autopsy reports, but apparently not very successfully. Most of the data were discovered and shipped to the United States with all other material collected. The United States was anxious to keep details of

the effects of the atomic bombs secret mainly because of the rapid deterioration of postwar relations with the Soviet Union.[26]

Public relief measures for the atomic victims were discouraged and in cases prohibited by the occupation authorities. "After about 1948, blood diseases, centering around acute leukemia, began to develop in the victims, and the prevalence of cataracts due to exposure to irradiation was also observed. However, these facts were known only among a limited number of physicians and it was not allowed to publicize them."[27] In Hiroshima and Nagasaki, the censorship and virtual ban on the dissemination of medical information and research results "was tantamount to regarding the existence of the survivors itself as criminal, for by the very fact that they were living witnesses to the massacre, they were forcing the nation and the world to be reminded of the unprecedented crime which the offenders wanted to hide. Under the seven-year occupation, the survivors became an untouchable subject."[28]

The Nagasaki Medical College, founded by Franciscan missionaries, and long the principal medical facility in the city, was located 700 meters from the atomic hypocenter, and was totally destroyed. Most of the teaching staff and the 530 members of the medical student body were killed. Nevertheless, emergency medical teams under Dr. Takashi Nagai and his colleagues at the College, ignoring their own injuries, undertook rudimentary treatment of victims at several temporary relief stations.

The bomb burst above a point only 500 meters from the Urakami Catholic Cathedral, located near the Medical College in the narrow Urakami Valley. The historical seat of the Roman Catholic Church in Japan, Nagasaki in 1945 was populated by about 12,000 Catholics, clustered around the Cathedral and the adjacent concentration of Mitsubishi industrial plants. Approximately 8,500 Catholics perished from direct exposure to the bomb, about 12 percent of the fatalities. After the bombing, only a few damaged stone statues of saints in the rear courtyard remained of the Urakami Cathedral.

Nagasaki was opened to European traders in 1570 and developed as the chief port for all of Japan's foreign intercourse. Catholicism, introduced by Iberian missionaires in the mid-sixteenth century, flourished for several decades. After the Tokugawa unification of Japan in 1603, all other cities except Kyoto were governed by politically decentralized feudal lords, but Nagasaki was controlled directly by the Tokugawa shogunate in Tokyo, which cruelly persecuted the city's Catholic population and expelled the missionaries from Japan in 1637.[29] Although Christianity's roots had gone deep among its converts, it ceased to exist as a public religion in Japan. The Church survived relentless persecution in Nagasaki without priests or open worship by means of crypto-Christian prayer rituals and incantations handed down by rote within Nagasaki families for over two centuries.[30]

With the forced entry of foreign traders in the 1850s, and the definitive onset of western modernization after the overthrow of the Tokugawa shogunate in the Meiji Restoration of 1868, European missionaries returned to Japan, and Nagasaki restored its trade with merchants of many nations. The doctrinally and politically passive Catholic community came into the open once again, accepting the lead of politically conservative and colonial-minded secular priests assigned from China and Indochina to Japan by the Paris Foreign Mission Society (Société des Missions Estrangères de Paris, the first religious institute of secular priests devoted exclusively to foreign missions). In order to avoid calling attention to themselves, even after religious persecution had partially abated, the Catholics refused to question state policies. The Nagasaki community of believers in 1895–1924 built the largest Catholic cathedral in the Far East as a memorial to the three-century quest for religious freedom by the Urakami parishioners.

After the war all the Nagasaki *Hibakusha* struggled to endure their severe physical handicaps and economic destitution in an atmosphere of social and political repression. The pious Catholics, who could find no other outlet for their anguish, earnestly attempted in the manner of old to seek their spiritual salvation in prayer and faith, and viewed the holocaust as a later day martyrdom faced by their creed. Many emphasized the positive value of their suffering and interpreted the A-bomb as a mysterious act of Divine Providence, provoked by the sins of mankind. They conceived the ordeal of Nagasaki as an opportunity for redemption in the mystical body of Jesus Christ and the Church as its extension, a supreme sacrifice by the elect for the sake of a new and universalist culture of peace. In the spiritual climate that fostered obedience to economic, social and administrative power since the days of the Tokugawa shogunate in Nagasaki, many Buddhist leaders, who interpreted suffering as an inevitable part of the evil of material being, also remained passive after the bombing.

Forbearance in the face of evil is evident in the eleven works written as sources of objective, humanitarian information under occupation censorship in 1945–1950 by the stricken Catholic physician Dr. Takashi Nagai.[31] In *We of Nagasaki,* Dr. Nagai described the anguish that prevented him from leaving his shelter to cross the open spaces to the ruins of his neighborhood; "I was shaking with fear. . . . Any instant now there might be another great flash overhead." Dr. Nagai also pointed to guilt, one of the lasting consequences of the flight reaction. Those who survived had abandoned their neighborhoods while friends and family died. Many of the survivors felt that they had saved their own lives without stopping to help their neighbors and they were constantly haunted by that realization. Dr. Nagai's manuscript *The Bell of Nagasaki* [*Nagasaki no Kane*], which describes his experience of the bombing, was completed in August 1946. Printing was halted by the disinformation tactics of the occupation authorities, who permitted it in April 1949 only with the incorporation of countervailing documentation—a record of

Japanese military cruelty in Manila, compiled by the intelligence division of U.S. General Headquarters.[32]

Dr. Nagai, his followers, and other Catholic faithful, standing on the ground of "unprejudiced" observers, were reluctant to question the responsibilities of either the aggressive Japanese state which caused the war, or the U.S. leaders who cast the bomb upon them. Many citizens turned their minds inward, just as the clandestine Catholics were once forced to do, but when the time and conditions ripened, they began to move creatively in their own fashion and gave expression to their activist sentiments. The principal examples (to be discussed below) are the Nagasaki Association of Young *Hibakusha* Men and Women, the Association of *Hibakusha* Teachers, and the Nagasaki Testimony Society [*Nagasaki-no Shogen-no Kai*] under Dr. Tatsuichiro Akizuki. They have become new bearers of the citizens' movement in Nagasaki against the bomb.

In 1945, one of Dr. Nagai's younger colleagues at the Nagasaki Medical College, and a member of the disaster relief team at the badly damaged Urakami First Hospital (renamed the St. Francis Hospital after the war), was Dr. Tatsuichiro Akizuki, a twenty-nine-year-old Buddhist. Akizuki was initially critical of Nagai's Catholic romanticism and did not accept his stand of fatal acquiescence to the bombing as Divine Providence. Then Akizuki contracted tuberculosis, and under the influence of Catholic believers and fathers he embraced the doctrine of the spiritual fruitfulness of suffering and converted to Catholicism in October 1948. In the wake of Nagai's death on 1 May 1951, Akizuki pledged himself to work for the complete prohibition of nuclear bombs. He published his *Documents of A-bombed Nagasaki* [*Nagasaki Genbaku ki*] in August 1966.[33] Dr. Akizuki, now the Chief Physician of the St. Francis Hospital, serves as President of the Nagasaki Testimony Society. As a Catholic peace activist representing the contemporary conscience of Nagasaki, he is one of the *Hibakusha* most closely associated with the disarmament messages issued by Pope John II in Nagasaki and Hiroshima in February 1981.

A Castle Town of the Mitsubishi Kingdom

Mitsubishi, one of the four giant corporations in modern Japan, has long held a firm economic grip upon Nagasaki and its inhabitants, and it has operated after the bombing to repress the remembrance of 1945 as a stimulus to activity against nuclear weapons.

Founded in 1870, two years after the Meiji Restoration, Mitsubishi transformed Nagasaki into its main stronghold and one of the hubs of the shipbuilding industry in Japan. In 1884, Mitsubishi leased the government-owned Nagasaki Shipyard, the first western industrial structure in Japan, which along with its engine works expanded to occupy a three-kilometer frontage along Nagasaki's well-appointed harbor. Mitsubishi became a manufacturing licensee of Duerr, Parsons, Sulzer, Vickers, Westinghouse, and other noted occidental marine builders and engineers. The Nagasaki Shipyard, along with the Mitsubishi Aircraft Company, evolved into Mitsubishi Heavy Industries, established in 1934. Mitsubishi thrived on the government's war policies, which it also helped to promote, profiting and expanding from the Sino-Japanese War (1894–1895), the Russo-Japanese War (1904–1905), and Japanese participation in World War I. During the fascist period 1931–1945, Mitsubishi, like the other zaibatsu, adapted itself easily to the new

Ohashi Factory, Mitsubishi Arms Works, after the bombing. Courtesy of International Cultural Hall, Nagasaki City.

structure, transforming itself into a partial organ of the fascist state.

The Mitsubishi arms works was opened in Nagasaki in 1917, and in the 1930s, under the patronage of the military, which was rapidly expanding the production of weapons and military equipment for aggression abroad, the concern built up three munitions factories in the Urakami Valley. Dedication of the major industries in Nagasaki to armaments production brought with it the militarization of the social and cultural life of the citizens, whose rights were suppressed and who in the prevailing war hysteria were politically silenced.

The hypocenter of the atomic bomb explosion was situated at a point approximately 1,300 meters from each one of this trio of Nagasaki plants. the arms manufacturing facilities at Ohashi (model 91 torpedo bombs for airplanes) and Morimachi (oxygen-driven torpedoes for submarines), and the Mitsubishi Steel Foundry at Morimachi. Also located along the Urakami River and 1,800 meters from the hypocenter were various buildings of the Mitsubishi Shipyards (the large battleship Musashi, and many cruisers and destroyers), the Mitsubishi Steelworks at Saiwaimachi, and the Mitsubishi Electrical Machinery and Appliances plant. Along with the rest of the Japanese industrial plant, however, Mitsubishi's armaments production was grinding to a halt by mid-1945 and the munitions industry in Nagasaki was nearly paralyzed by U.S. air raids conducted in early 1945. Nagasaki was a military bastion only in name. At the time of the bombing, more than 40,000 industrial proletarians, including a significant number of Catholic workers, were employed by Mitsubishi in Nagasaki, as well as war-mobilized students, technicians of the Imperial Navy, and foreign prisoners of war. Approximately 3,000 Koreans had been brought to toil in the Mitsubishi Shipyard, and another 4,000 in the arms manufactur-

ing plants. Scores of medium- and small-sized subcontracting factories which supplied parts to Mitsubishi were clustered in an area adjacent to the hypocenter. Thus, most of Nagasaki's working population and its families in the Urakami Valley perished.

After the war the Mitsubishi industrial base of shipbuilding, machinery and metal working was rebuilt from rubble to become the motor of the Nagasaki economy and the wielder of tremendous influence in shaping Japan's postwar economic upsurge. Nagasaki once again became a castle town of the Mitsubishi empire, and in spite of the nominal decartelization of the giant pre-1945 zaibatsu monopoly groups as the principal bearers of the spirit of Japanese militarism, Mitsubishi's military-industrial affiliations were fully reorganized and strengthened. The Mitsubishi group today is Japan's largest and strongest corporate conglomerate, whose activities have expanded to markets in every corner of the globe. Constant modernization of production facilities and technological innovation by the Mitsubishi Nagasaki Shipyard led to world records in the 1970s for the launching of oil tankers.[34]

More importantly for the *Hibakusha* of Nagasaki, Mitsubishi carries out the large-scale engineering and construction of Japanese nuclear power plants and the manufacture of other nuclear fuel cycle equipment. Mitsubishi utilizes reactor technology licensed from the Westinghouse Corporation (Mitsubishi's relationship with Westinghouse dates back to the early twentieth century), but is developing the capability of supplying standardized nuclear power plant units to electrical utilities and goverment corporations on an autonomous basis.

Furthermore, big concerns such as Mitsubishi, which follow the traditions they established as prewar and wartime arsenals, are rapidly expanding their arms output. The development of Japan's military industry was initially the result of U.S. military orders for the Korean War (1950–1953), and Mitsubishi's revival at this period was spectacular. In recent years, Japan Defense Agency contracts have constituted about one-quarter of the value of all contract items of Mitsubishi Heavy Industries,[35] and weapons manufacture is closely linked to the utilization of the latest advances in science and technology by the Mitsubishi Group. With its worldwide information network and contacts with the U.S. armaments industry, developed through years of heavy industrial and defense licensing transactions, Mitsubishi has acted as a bridge between the weapons sector in Japan and foreign military-industrial companies.

Many local citizens have strongly protested against the manufacture of the main units for the Japanese Navy in the Nagasaki Shipyard of Mitsubishi Heavy Industries: anti-submarine ships, torpedoes and missiles. (Mitsubishi's manufacture of the nuclear vessel *Mutsu* and Nagasaki's resistance to this ship is discussed below.) Along with Mitsubishi's influence on Nagasaki's industry and economy, this robust conglomerate also has a depressing effect on the consciousness of Nagasaki citizens, reinforcing the "economy-oriented" trend which has long been prevalent among the city's leaders. The movement of the *Hibakusha* for social and educational reform has to grapple with the livelihood fears of the thousands of citizens employed by corporations inherently opposed to social change or protest. The imminent threat of unemployment or ignominious demotion for political and social activism discourages many Mitsubishi workers and their families from political participation. Since the 1964 merger of its Nagasaki, Kobe and Yokohama components, Mitsubishi Heavy Industries has been successful in dividing the trade union organization of its workers and isolating militant peace activists. This has encouraged ultra-rightist groups in their attacks against the peace movement and peace education in Nagasaki.

Rebirth

Although hindered by strict occupation censorship, Catholic mystical traditions, and the repressive influence of the Mitsubishi Corporation, the *Hibakusha* movement grew up in the midst of the ruin and confusion left by the bomb and has gained in vitality over the years. The *Hibakusha* found it exceedingly difficult to regain their footing from the severe urban destruction and chaos and the obliteration of the Nagasaki civic community. To begin activities for self-help and mutual assistance, the distressed survivors organized a Victims League in December 1945. The individual and collective atomic bomb narratives written by Dr. Nagai and other creative citizens at their places of work, homes and schools, although circumscribed by the restrictions on discussion and publication imposed by the Occupation Press Code, were the product of a movement for self-expression, human dignity and rehabilitation.[36] These testimonies represent the beginning of the movement for concretizing the painful and desperate *Hibakusha* experience, both for contemporaries and as an inheritance for future generations. The literature of the *Hibakusha* who lived through the most severe years of misery, suffering and struggle marks the origin of peace education in postwar Japan. Dr. Nagai wrote that "those who have survived cry out in one voice 'no more war,' and those who left this world all had this desire at their last moment."[37]

Many readers of the *Hibakusha* testimonies from 1945 to the present have undergone the "third exposure" to the A-bomb, and have become atomic sufferers through the printed page. The victims of the first exposure are those dead or dying from the atomic explosions directly, while the second exposure sufferers are the *Hibakusha* who entered the A-bombed cities afterward and were contaminated by residual radioactivity. The third wave comprises all persons influenced by the experience of the first two groups and by the broad movement against A- and H-bombs.

In May 1949 the Japanese Diet passed laws for the construction of a peace memorial city in Hiroshima and an international cultural city in Nagasaki. The citizens of the two cities endorsed this legislation, and on 9 August 1949 the reconstruction plans for Nagasaki came into effect. A campaign of Nagasaki citizens and *Hibakusha* organizations, encouraged by Dr. Nagai, urged that the remains of the Urakami Cathedral, which symbolized the tragedy of A-bombed Nagasaki, be preserved as a monument to all *Hibakusha* and as a warning to future generations of humankind, similar to the unreconstructed and symbolically effective A-bomb dome, the frame of a building destroyed by the atomic explosion in Hiroshima. But the metropolitan Nagasaki administration in 1958 cleared the ruins and built the Cathedral anew on the same site, and has left few official reminders of the atomic bomb. Placing its emphasis on achieving a high level of industrial production and on the tourist industry, the urban administration has rebuilt with less remembrance than in Hiroshima.[38]

The Japan-U.S. Mutual Security Treaty, signed on 8 September 1951 simultaneously with the San Francisco Peace Treaty, and still in force (as amended in 1960) as Japan's military policy, promoted Japan's high growth economy in the framework of a close diplomatic, economic and military alliance with the United States. Under the early tutelage of U.S. technology and economics the postwar Japanese national and prefectural governments committed themselves to growth in gross national product and expansion of industrial scale as supreme national goods. Japan has sacrificed its social infrastructure to achieve rapid economic growth, and has to a large extent abandoned many of the humanistic values embedded in the limited democracy of earlier decades, whose development was severed for the people by the onset of fascism and World War II. Major social security programs have been left in the hands of the private sector as part of the reinforcement of corporate economic control.

The Japanese government, under Article 19 of the San Francisco Peace Treaty, surrendered the right to demand reparations for the A-bombings from the United States. "Japan therefore bears the responsibility of instituting a *Hibakusha* aid law providing for full state compensation."[39] The Diet promulgated in 1957 the Law for Health Protection and Medical Care for A-bomb Victims, creating a benefit program within the social security framework providing for biannual governmental medical examination and treatment for proximally exposed survivors. The 1968 Law for Special Measures for A-bomb Victims went somewhat beyond the primarily medical benefits of the 1957 Law and reflected the *Hibakusha* demand for livelihood security. A total of approximately 370,000 *Hibakusha* have secured a Health Notebook for A-bomb Victims issued by the Ministry of Health and Welfare, becoming eligible thereby for certain forms of medical treatment and financial compensation under these two laws. In many respects these laws provide little more than token medical care, and thousands of survivors have not yet obtained Health Notebooks, while second and third generation victims are not entitled to receive them. The Korean *Hibakusha* of Nagasaki and Hiroshima now living in South Korea, whose number exceeds at least 10,000 receive no relief or aid from either the Japanese or South Korean governments.

On 7 December 1963, the District Court of Tokyo handed down a long and complex decision on claims for compensation lodged against the Japanese government by Shimoda and Others, five residents of Hiroshima and Nagasaki (The Shimoda Case).[40] The Court concluded that the atomic attacks caused such severe and indiscriminate suffering that they violated the most basic international legal principles governing the conduct of war, but that the claimants lacked a remedy, since international law does not yet allow individuals, in the absence of an express stipulation in a treaty, to pursue claims on their own behalf against a government. The Court stated that today:

> We have the Law for Health Protection and Medical Care for A-bomb Victims. . . . but it is clear that a law of this scale cannot possibly be sufficient for the relief or rescue of the sufferers of the atomic bombs. The defendant state caused many nationals to die, injured them, and drove them to a precarious life by the war which it opened on its own authority and responsibility. Also, the seriousness of the damage cannot compare a moment with that of the general calamity. Needless to say the defendant state should take sufficient relief measures in this light. . . . It cannot possibly be understood that the above is financially impossible in Japan, which has achieved a high degree of economic growth after the war.[41]

The historically and politically compromised government of Japan, which avoids acknowledgment of Tokyo's responsibility for the aggressive war, has virtually ignored the Shimoda verdict, and, while extending palliatives for the principal grievances of the *Hibakusha*, seeks to discredit and blunt the force of their movement for restitution. As the percentage of *Hibakusha* in the population decreases and the victims gradually become older and enfeebled (the average age of the Hibakusha in February 1981 was 57.4 years), the vicious cycle entrapping them becomes more serious—atomic sickness, acute poverty and unemployment, family disintegration and social neglect. Victimization by both the U.S. and Japanese governments compounds the morbidity cycle enveloping the *Hibakusha*, but they are still determined to renew and strengthen their commitment to solidarity and peace.

In the surge of expression which began after the Peace Treaty came into force in April 1952, and following the initial period of self-help and localized *Hibakusha* relief groups, a wider institutional phase was set into motion. An exhibition of pictures by the *Hibakusha* was held in 1952, along with a display of the Hiroshima Panels, a series of paintings of bomb-stricken Hiroshima by the artists Iri and Toshi Maruki, who lost relatives and many friends there. These were the first efforts to bring home graphically the atomic horror, and made it possible for many victims to speak publicly for the first time about the bombings. The inception in 1952 of the campaign to assist the young atomic-bombed women of Hiroshima, who were branded with accumulations of scar tissue known as keloids, gave vital impulse to the national effort for *Hibakusha* medical care legis-

lation. This project sent twenty-five young women victims and two surgeons to the United States in the spring of 1955, where the young women underwent over one hundred plastic surgery operations at New York's Mt. Sinai Hospital to help overcome their disfigurement.

A profoundly tragic reminder of the atomic bomb catastrophes was the radioactive fallout from the hydrogen bomb exploded at the Bikini Atoll in the Marshall Islands on 1 March 1954, which contaminated vast areas of the Pacific Ocean, and inundated the Japanese tuna fishing trawler the *Lucky Dragon* and its 23-member crew, then fishing in nearby waters. The blast was the first in a series of six H-bomb tests over the Bikini Atoll conducted by the U.S. in an effort to recover the nuclear advantage it had lost when the USSR tested its first atomic bomb in 1949. The thermonuclear explosion showered radioactive nuclear fallout on the Marshall Islanders, and over 600 ships and their crews operating in or passing through adjoining waters, and fish caught there had to be destroyed. In response to this disaster, thirty-five million persons in Japan (one-third of the national population) signed an appeal for the prohibition of nuclear tests and nuclear weapons. The suffering and sacrifice of the *Lucky Dragon* and the Marshall Islanders recalled for all of Japan the Hiroshima and Nagasaki holocausts, which for the first time came to be considered not merely regional calamities, but subjects of utmost concern for the whole Japanese people and the human race.

The peace campaign of 1954–1955 led to the founding of the Nagasaki Association of Young *Hibakusha* Women by Chieko Watanabe and four contemporaries in June 1955. Chieko Watanabe was sixteen years old in 1945 and had been mobilized for labor in the Mitsubishi Electrical Machinery Plant, 2,500 meters from the hypocenter, when the A-bomb struck. Pinned under a steel beam, her spine and lower limbs were crushed, and she is confined to a wheelchair and has been repeatedly hospitalized. The new Association appealed to the World Mothers' Assembly held in Switzerland, 7 July 1955:

> A burst of fire wiped out Urakami and robbed 70,000 people of their lives in a single flash. Our wounds have driven us to despair, self-contempt and subterfuge. We have somehow remained alive, but we are ignored as if crouching in obscure corners of society, while our daily livelihood is always in peril. Our wounds and keloid scars make it difficult for us to find jobs and husbands. Ten years in dark disappointment, sorrow, and inhuman life! The miserable hell by A-bomb which we suffered should never again be allowed to happen again anywhere in the world.[42]

Speaking twenty-three years later, Ms. Watanabe asked:

> Just what kind of people are the Hibakusha? As I see it, the Hibakusha are those individuals who were forced to experience the first strike of the possible annihilation of humanity in the future. . . . Listen to these words, which the personal experience of the bombing compels me to utter. The next time nuclear weapons are used, the human race will not survive.[43]

The First World Conference Against A- and H-bombs was convened in Hiroshima, August 1955, where *Hibakusha* reported the actual conditions of atomic suffering for the first time to the world. Directly afterward, the Nagasaki Association of Young *Hibakusha* Men was founded by Senji Yamaguchi and other youths in October 1955. Senji Yamaguchi was burned and scarred while a 14-year-old war-mobilized student in the Nagasaki bombing, and has undergone four surgical operations for keloids. He suffers from radiation-caused hepatic lesions and leucopenia. Mr. Yamaguchi, who is now a Nagasaki architect and Vice President of the Nagasaki A-bomb Victims Council, began petitioning the Japanese Diet for relief of the *Hibakusha* at state expense in 1954, just after the Bikini disaster. Speaking at a 1980 rally in Tokyo urging the enactment of compensatory *Hibakusha* relief legislation, Mr. Yamaguchi stated the main principle of his 25-year-long fight for *Hibakusha* relief:

> *Our demand for the immediate enactment of a law for relief of all* Hibakusha *is not only a* Hibakusha *demand, but also the demand of all people in Japan, and of the whole world, for "No More* Hibakusha!"

In November 1955, the Young Women's Association and the new Young Men's group were united into the Nagasaki Association of Young *Hibakusha* Men and Women, consisting of fourteen men and thirty-one women. The Nagasaki A-bomb Victims Council was established as the unified center of the city's *Hibakusha* movements in December 1955. These organizations helped to convene the Second World Conference Against A- and H-bombs in Nagasaki in August 1956. In that year also the Japan Confederation of A-bomb Victims Organizations (Hidankyo) was created as the major unified relief organization for all *Hibakusha* in Japan.

Youth, Educators, and the Testament of Nagasaki

In the new Nagasaki people's movement, the younger generation played a central role. This same cohort of leaders, now in their fifties and sixties, has consistently campaigned to strengthen and unify the *Hibakusha* and all citizens for the enactment of comprehensive relief measures and for the abolition of nuclear weapons. A-bombed while in their critical teenage period, when they were most sensitive and impressionable, this group possessed the capacity for self-understanding and self-assertion. The iron chain of military discipline had snapped, and they experienced the constitutional renunciation of belligerency, and the democratic reforms in education, labor and trade union legislation, and the agrarian sector, as an opportunity for emancipation. Although these innovations were equivocal and inconsistently applied, they exercised a positive influence on Japan's domestic political life in the early post-war years. The atmosphere of liberal democracy and the willingness to tolerate political diversity were followed, however, by a wave of repression against the labor movement in 1947, after which the outbreak of the Korean War in 1950 resulted in further pressures and restrictions on peace activists.

Even though they despaired of recovering their health, the *Hibakusha* pledged themselves to build a democratic, anti-militarist Japan on the basis of the country's new Constitution. In contrast to the glorification of war and death in battle of the 1931–1945 emperor system, the new Constitution, although its anti-militarist clauses are increasingly under attack as Japan steadily rearms, affirms that each person has the right and duty to pursue peace and happiness. Peace and democracy are also strongly emphasized in the postwar Fundamentals of Education Act. School teachers took responsibility for describing honestly and accurately the cruel and inhuman effects of atomic bombs,

and for instilling in youth the reason and foresight necessary to prevent nuclear war. The Japan Teachers Union resolved in 1953 that peace education should be central to the entire educational process in Japan. The Association of *Hibakusha* Teachers, organized in Nagasaki in 1970, has published a four-volume text, *The Atomic Bomb Reader for Children*.[44]

In maturing from adolescence to adulthood, the Nagasaki youth leaders needed to grapple with the conservative climate of passive conformism and respectful obedience to the established authorities fostered and maintained over a long period of time under the direct rule of the Tokugawa shogunate. Nourished by the democratic, anti-war vision and by peace education, these youths undertook a revolution in their political, cultural and spiritual outlook, and contributed greatly to building a positive new spiritual culture and citizen's consciousness.

In the 1970s there occured a new invigoration in Hiroshima and Nagasaki, as Hidankyo and its supporters intensified their relief litigation campaigning. Hidankyo had by late 1981 gathered ten million signatures toward its goal of 20 million names calling for the enactment by the Diet of comprehensive *Hibakusha* relief legislation based upon the principle of state compensation. Hidankyo is now also conducting a series of "People's Tribunals" on "The A-bombings as a Violation of International Law, and the State's Responsibility for the War." The relief measures advanced by Hidankyo, to an extent now embodied in the joint opposition party *Hibakusha* assistance bill, constitute the minimum material redress owing to the *Hibakusha*, but since the human and spiritual damages to the victims can never be adequately compensated financially or legally, they stand witness on behalf of all humankind for the abolition of nuclear weapons.

Additionally, the *Hibakusha* were most likely inspired, albeit indirectly, by the gathering anti-pollution revolt of the Minamata disease victims. Beginning in the late 1940s, hundreds of fishermen, farmers and their families in the town of Minamata in Kyushu, not far from Nagasaki, were poisoned by methyl mercury wastes discharged into their bay by the nitrogen fertilizer plant of the Chisso Corporation. Today there are over 1,200 certified Minamata disease patients, and another 7,000 or more persons have applied for government certification. Medical authorities estimate that there are at least 10,000 more as yet undiscovered, perhaps latent victims of mercury poisoning in the Minamata area. In 1969, against great odds, 112 anguished claimants of twenty-nine families collectively filed a lawsuit for compensation from the Chisso Corporation, and in March 1973 secured from the court an historic $3.2 million indemnity judgment.

The revitalization of the *Hibakusha* has been possible because they have found suitable new forms of expression and solidarity, in activities involving all local citizens. These activities include the compilation of Nagasaki and Hiroshima testimonies and experiences by the Nagasaki Testimony Society, founded in March 1969 under the leadership of Dr. Tatsuichiro Akizuki to oppose nuclear weapons, aid Japanese and foreign A-bomb victims, and broadly convey the experience of the Nagasaki A-bomb tragedy, especially to the younger generation.

> *Cognition through the senses, or more correctly the shock to sensibility, through photographs, pictures and retold stories of experiences of the atomic bombing has been decisive [in]*

reaching out to human sensibility [and helping] the people of Japan and the world arrive, within the shortest possible time, at a recognition of the need to abolish nuclear weapons. . . . Those who make such an appeal should first give full play to their own creative imagination, helping others to awaken their own imaginations also. The objective, it must be stressed, is not to strike terror into people's hearts. As Japanese writer Kenzaburo Oe observed, fear is passive, while imagination is active, and leads people to action.[45]

The Nagasaki Testimony Society utilizes the main mass media of Nagasaki—radio (the broadcast of 200 typical *Hibakusha* testimonies), television (one thousand morning broadcasts of five-minute testimonies), and the daily press. The Testimony Society publishes an annual compilation of *Hibakusha* case histories and the quarterly journal *Testimonies of Nagasaki* [*Nagasaki no Shogen*], edited by Sadao Kamata. Among the more than 1,000 first-person accounts published by the Society are those from *Hibakusha* now resident in South Korea, Australia, the Netherlands, Britain, and the United States. The Nagasaki Institute of Peace Culture (NIPC), a division of the Nagasaki Institute of Applied Science, inaugurated publication in 1978 of *Studies of Peace Culture* [*Heiwa Bunka Kenkyu*] to examine the damage and after-effects of the atomic bombings, the conditions of the *Hibakusha*, and problems of the nuclear arms race, nuclear proliferation and nuclear disarmament. The NIPC seeks to cooperate in all its activities with other research workers and institutions in Japan and throughout the world.

The Odyssey of the Mutsu: A New Ordeal for Nagasaki

Hibakusha organizations, trade unions, scientists, and numerous other groups of citizens rallied vigorously in Nagasaki and skirmished in small boats against the nuclear-powered cargo ship *Mutsu,* which in October 1978 arrived in Sasebo, the second largest city of Nagasaki prefecture. Completed by the governmental Japan Nuclear Ship Development Agency in 1972, the *Mutsu* reminds many Nagasaki residents of the ordeals they underwent in World War II, the atomic bombing, and the difficult postwar years of recovery. They likewise oppose the increasing use of Sasebo as a supply and refueling base by warships of the U.S. Seventh Fleet, and the calls of the nuclear weapon-capable Seventh Fleet aircraft carrier *Midway* into the Sasebo naval base have aroused the determined opposition of Nagasaki Prefectural citizens.

The nuclear reactor of the *Mutsu* was designed and constructed by Mitsubishi Atomic Power Industries with basic Westinghouse naval propulsion technology. The antiwar and environmental protection movements in Japan argue that the *Mutsu,* apart from its potential (but speculative) uses in commercial maritime cargo transport, is one of the steps being taken by government and industry to test reactors for nuclear submarines and prepare the way for military applications of nuclear energy at sea, and later for the acquisition of nuclear weapons. Peace and ecology groups claim that the *Mutsu* was improperly inspected by the government, which failed to uncover, or concealed the basic errors in its design. But even before the *Mutsu's* initial voyage, Mitsubishi began planning for a second nuclear-powered ship with a much larger reactor, and the Ministry of Transportation formulated a construction program for a series of

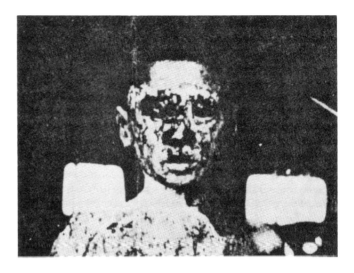

nuclear container ships.

The fishermen of Mutsu Bay in Aomori Prefecture in the north of Japan, where the ship was originally homeported, opposed the testing of the *Mutsu,* claiming that it would contaminate the sea with radioactive wastes, and they hindered its sailing for almost two years. The use of government coastguard boats and the providential intervention of a typhoon, which compelled the fishing boats blockading the ships to take shelter, finally broke the deadlock on 25 August 1975, and the *Mutsu* put out to sea on the next day. But four days later and 800 kilometers from Mutsu Bay, the reactor of the *Mutsu* sprang a radiation leak. In order to return the powerless, drifting freighter to Mutsu Bay, the government was forced to accept most of the Aomori fishermens' demands, including removal of the *Mutsu* within six months and freezing the ship's nuclear reactor. The *Mutsu* remained an idle phantom during four subsequent years of tense negotiations between these fishermen, local and regional governments, and state agencies. Finally, the Sasebo city authorities announced that they would accept the *Mutsu* in Sasebo port for repairs, since Sasebo Heavy Industries Co., the *Mutsu* repair contractor and the city's major industry, was in trouble due to the recession in the shipbuilding industry. The Nagasaki Prefectural Assembly voted in June 1978 to admit the vessel. The repair work on the radiation shielding and other defective components of the *Mutsu* being carried out at Sasebo by the Mitsubishi companies is scheduled to extend through August 1982.

The *Hibakusha* of Nagasaki champion the cause of nuclear non-proliferation and a complete ban on all nuclear explosions, as important measures against the nuclear arms buildup. They firmly oppose the possession or manufacture of nuclear weapons by Japan, and the introduction of nuclear weapons into the country. The *Hibakusha* are aware that the awesome force which killed their kinfolk and neighbors, and maimed them for life, now courses close to home through the *Mutsu,* and they know of no guarantee that this force will not be used to kill again. They know that Hiroshima was not one of a kind, and that what happened there can be repeated many times over. Their ranks constantly eroded by illness, contesting against the attrition of time on human capabilities, they persist in the struggle to spare humanity the horror they experienced. The conscience of humanity was taken by surprise in 1945, but now the *Hibakusha* bear witness that never again will it be possible to say about nuclear weapons that "We didn't know."

Notes

1. The only concerted effort undertaken thus far outside Japan to elucidate the effects of the A-bomb on Nagasaki is the non-fiction novel by journalist Frank W. Chinnock, *Nagasaki: The Forgotten Bomb* (Cleveland: World Publishing Co., 1969), which in graphic detail describes the holocaust and portrays the courage of its victims.

2. UN General Assembly Resolution 1653 (XVI), 24 November 1961, was followed by General Assembly Resolution 2936 (XXVII) of 29 November 1972, which proscribes the use or threat of force in international relations and declares for the permanent prohibition of the use of nuclear weapons.

The world's Catholic bishops addressed the dangers of nuclear warfare at the Second Vatican Council on 7 December 1967 as follows:

> *Any act of war aimed indiscriminately at the destruction of entire cities or extensive areas along with their population is a crime against God and man himself.*

The 1961 and 1972 UN resolutions and the Vatican Council II appeal were buttressed by the comprehensive recommendations for arresting and reversing the nuclear arms race issued by the Holy See on 7 May 1976. (UN Document A/AC.181/1, "Strengthening of the Role of the United Nations in the Field of Disarmament.") These universal proclamations articulate what the *Hibakusha* of Japan and non-governmental organizations for disarmament and development worldwide term the "newly aware" public opinion demanding bold action to liquidate nuclear weapons.

3. Henry L. Stimson and McGeorge Bundy, *On Active Service in Peace and War* (New York: Harper and Brothers, 1947), p. 628. As Secretary of War in 1940–1945, Stimson from the inception took full responsibility for the manufacture and use of the atomic bomb.

4. Robert J.C. Butow, *Japan's Decision to Surrender* (Stanford: Stanford University Press, 1954), pp. 47–50. Konoe argued:

> *The situation in Japan is such that every possible factor favorable to the accomplishment of a Communist revolution is on hand. There is poverty in the life of the people, a rise in the voice of labor, and an expansion of pro-Soviet feeling growing out of an increase in enmity against American and Britain . . . with defeat staring us in the face we shall simply be playing into the hands of the Communists if we elect to continue a war wherein there is no prospect of victory.*

Konoe's "Memorial," Butow, pp. 48–49. In fact, beginning in mid-August 1945, the Communist Party and other expressions of the "voice of labor" emerged from severe persecution with appreciable popular support. Konoe's logic was shared by other top leaders who regarded preservation of the emperor system and its polity as the supreme cause. Ariatsu Nishijima, *Why the Atomic Bombs Were Dropped* [*Genbaku wa Naze Toka Saretaka*] (Tokyo, 1971), p. 152. The supreme ruling circles of Japan were "extremely sensitive" to the shift in power relations between capitalism and socialism following the Soviet victory over nazi Germany. Nishijima, p. 154.

5. Butow, pp. 124 and 130.

6. Stalin had promised at the three-power Teheran Conference (November 1943 and January 1944) that the USSR would join the war against Japan as soon as the German army was beaten and destroyed.

7. According to Herbert Feis:

> *[I]f Stalin had been asked to subscribe publicly to the Potsdam Declaration . . . , it is possible that the immediate response by the Japanese government might have been quite different—and indicative of a willingness to surrender on the proferred terms if given assurances about the future of the Imperial Institution. In that case there would have been no need or occasion to use the bomb.*

Herbert Feis, *Japan Subdued: The Atomic Bomb and the End of the War in the Pacific* (Princeton: Princeton University Press, 1961), p. 96.

8. Butow, pp. 210–223.

9. Richard G. Hewlett and Oscar E. Anderson, *The New World: A History of the United States Atomic Energy Commission* (University Park, Penn.: Pennsylvania State University Press, 1972), p. 365.

10. Major J. Derry and Dr. N.F. Ramsey (both members of the Target Committee) to General Groves, 12 May 1945. The target selection process was traced by Martin Sherwin, *A World Destroyed: The Atomic Bomb and the Grand Alliance* (New York: Alfred A. Knopf, 1975), who cites the Derry-Ramsey letter on pp. 229 and 268.

11. Stimson and Bundy, p. 617.

12. Harry S. Truman, *Memoirs, Vol. 1: Year of Decisions* (Garden City, NY: Doubleday and Co., 1955), p. 420.

13. Lt. General Leslie R. Groves, Report to General George C. Marshall, 30 December 1944, in *The Conference at Malta and Yalta, 1945*, Foreign Relations of the United States, Diplomatic Papers, Publication 6199 (Washington, D.C.: U.S. Department of State, 1955), pp. 383–384. Groves was Commanding General of the Manhattan Project and Marshall was U.S. Chief of Staff.

14. Sherwin, pp. 231 and 268, citing Manhattan Project files of 23 July 1945. On 10 August 1945, however, General Groves reported that the third bomb could be ready for combat use on 18 or 19 August. Barton J. Bernstein, "The Perils and Politics of Surrender: Ending the War with Japan and Avoiding the Third Atomic Bomb," *Pacific Historical Review*, February 1977, p. 10. Bernstein cites the letter of Groves to General Marshall of 10 August 1945 in Top Secret Manhattan Project Files 5, U.S. National Archives. The pilot of the third bombing plane was scheduled to be Claude Eatherly, who from the reconnaisance aircraft on 6 August sent the all-clear weather signal to the B-29 which attacked Hiroshima. Ronnie Dugger, *Dark Star: Hiroshima Reconsidered in the Life of Claude Eatherly* (Cleveland: World Publishing Co., 1967), pp. 76–77.

15. Sherwin, p. 157, citing the entry of 23 April 1945 in the Stimson Diary.

16. Stimson and Bundy, p. 637. Winston Churchill wrote in Potsdam a few days after Alamagordo; "It is quite clear that the United States do not at the present time desire Russian participation in the war against Japan." Winston Churchill, *Triumph and Tragedy (Memoirs, Vol. 6)* (Boston: Houghton Mifflin, 1953), p. 639.

17. Feis, p. 88.

18. The target cities were embargoed against conventional air attacks in mid-July, to facilitate the planned surveys of destruction after atomic attack.

19. Karl T. Compton, "If the Atomic Bomb Had Not Been Used," *The Atlantic Monthly*, December 1946, p. 55. Physicist and science administrator Karl Compton, a leader in the Manhattan Project, served on the seven-member 1945 Interim Committee on atomic policy and then on General MacArthur's occupation staff in Japan. Stimson and Bundy endorse Compton's view that the second bomb signified a conceivably "unlimited" atomic arsenal. *On Active Service*, p. 630.

20. "Was the Hiroshima Bomb Necessary?: An Exchange," *New York Review of Books*, 23 October 1980, pp. 37–42. The participants in the exchange were Joseph Alsop and David Joravsky.

21. According to Fletcher Knebel and Charles W. Baily II, *No High Ground* (New York: Harper and Row, 1960), p. 122, Stimson considered that the A-bombing of Kyoto would have been a "wanton act."

22. The population of Nagasaki in 1945 included over 10,000 Korean workers and about 650 Chinese. Under conditions of racial chauvinism, manipulated by Japanese militarism, many Koreans were brought to Japan as laborers during the colonization of Korea, and commandeering, drafting and forced immigration increased their number to over two million as World War II neared its close. An estimated 7,000 Koreans toiled in Mitsubishi's Nagasaki industrial complex during the war, most of whom lived in makeshift temporary dwellings near the workshops. In these flimsy shacks the Koreans underwent even more serious damage than Japanese coworkers. There were delays in extending relief and first aid to them later, and few survived. Pak Su Ryong, "The Silent Ashes of the Bombed Koreans," in *Give Me Water: Testimonies of Hiroshima and Nagasaki* (Tokyo: A Citizens' Group to Convey Testimonies of Hiroshima and Nagasaki, 1972), pp. 34–35.

The Fukuoka No. 14 POW camp at the Mitsubishi Shipyard in Saiwai-machi, and the No. 12 POW camp at the Kawaname Shipyard in Koyagi, both in Nagasaki, held war prisoners from Australia, Indonesia, the Netherlands, the U.K., U.S. and other allied nations. On 2 January 1943 about 470 prisoners were sent from Singapore to Camp No. 14, of whom about 370 remained in August 1945. Jidayu Tajima, "What I Saw in War-Prisoner Camp on August 9, 1945," in *Report from Nagasaki on the Damage and After-Effects of the Atomic Bombing* (Nagasaki: Nagasaki Preparatory Committee for the International Symposium on the Damage and After-Effects of the Atomic Bombing of Hiroshima and Nagasaki, 15 February 1978), pp. 46–47. The Headquarters, U.S. Army Strategic Air Forces, Guam, communicated to the War Department on 20 July 1945 that an allied prisoner of war camp (Fukuoka No. 14) was located one mile north of the center of Nagasaki, and asked whether this intelligence had any bearing on atomic targetting. Washington replied, "Targets previously assigned for Centerboard [the mission of delivering atomic bombs on Japan] remain unchanged." General Carl Spaatz, Commander of the Strategic Air Forces, to General George Marshall, 31 July 1945, and Pasco to Spaatz, 31 July 1945. Cited by Sherwin, pp. 234, 269.

23. Sherwin, p. 231.

24. *The Truth Concealed: White Paper on Damage of Atomic Bombs* (Tokyo: Japan Council Against A- and H-bombs [Gensuikyo], December 1964), p. 6. (First published in Japanese in 1961 by the Scientists Commission of Gensuikyo.) Throughout the greater part of the occupation period, from September 1945 to November 1949, the Civil Censorship Detachment enforced strict censorship over all Japanese media—newspapers, radio, film, theater, recordings, books, magazines and pamphlets. Japanese publication of John Hersey's compassionate book *Hiroshima*, which originally appeared in *The New Yorker* in September 1946, was not permitted until March 1949.

25. *Since it placed a ban on the publication of what was discovered and studied by Japanese researchers, the United States has systematically obstructed the relief of victims in Hiroshima and Nagasaki. . . . The ABCC was set up so that the Americans responsible for the atomic bombing would be able to follow up studies on their victims after the war, in order to prepare experimental materials for a future nuclear war. . . . The Commission has never given medical treatment to victims of Hiroshima and Nagasaki.*

No More Hiroshimas!, Japan Council Against A- and H-bombs, Tokyo, August 1970, pp. 9-10. The major findings of the various studies conducted by the Commission on the delayed radiation effects of the A-bomb are reported in *Radiation Effects on Atomic Bomb Survivors*, Technical Report 6-73 (Hiroshima and Nagasaki Atomic Bomb Casualty Commission, 1973), pp. 6-10. In April 1975 the ABCC was succeeded by the Radiation Effects Research Foundation, supported equally by the governments of Japan and the United States.

26. Frank Barnaby, "The Continuous Body Count at Hiroshima and Nagasaki," *Bulletin of the Atomic Scientists*, December 1977, pp. 49-50.

27. "History of Medical Care for Atomic Bomb Victims," Working Document II-4 (English) of the International Symposium on the Damage and After-Effects of the Atomic Bombing of Hiroshima and Nagasaki, August 1977.

28. *The Truth Concealed*, p. 6.

29. "The Japanese leaders were desirous of retaining profitable trade relations with the Europeans, but they gradually came to the conclusion that for national safety and political stability, Christianity must go." Edwin O. Reischauer, *Japan: The Story of a Nation* (New York: Alfred A. Knopf, 1970), p. 93.

30. The Tokugawa shogunate suppressed the 1637–1638 Shimabara insurrection of 30,000 Catholic peasants against religious repression and collection of heavy annual tributes. This revolt was used as an added pretext to cut all but a trickle of relations with Europe and to complete the seclusion of Japan. Set in the vicinity of Nagasaki, the popular novel *Silence* by Shusaku Endo (London: Peter Owen, 1976) describes the unsuccessful attempt by European missionaries to convert seventeenth-century Japan to Christianity. It is possible that the peasants of the Shimabara Peninsula and Amakusa Island and their Catholic feudal lords who led them in tragic revolt envisaged the formation of a Catholic republic.

31. Takashi Nagai, *We of Nagasaki: The Story of Survivors in an Atomic Wasteland* (New York: Duell, Sloan and Pearce, 1951); *The Bell of Nagasaki* [*Nagasaki no Kane*], 1949; *Survivors Under the Atomic Clouds* [*Genshi-gumo no Shita ni Ikite*], 1950. In *We of Nagasaki*, written for publication in English, Dr. Nagai collected the accounts of eight relatives and neighbors who were survivors of the Nagasaki bombing. Dr. Nagai died of radiation illness in 1951.

32. The cruelty and criminality of the Japanese in Manila should, however, be examined in its own right. *Hibakusha* poetess Sadako Kurihara has written:

When we say "Hiroshima,"
Does anyone respond, with gentle sympathy,
"Ahh, Hiroshima"?
When we say "Hiroshima," we hear "Pearl Harbor."
When we say "Hiroshima," we hear "the rape of Nanking."
When we say "Hiroshima," we hear the fiery massacre of Manila,
Where women and children were driven into trenches
And burned with gasoline.
When we say "Hiroshima,"
What we hear is an echo of fire and blood.

Kurihara concludes that the peace movement of the survivors and their sup-

porters must renounce Japan's imperialist legacy in Asia, and its postwar policy of rearmament, which again threatens the Asian people ("the weapons that have been abandoned in name must be abandoned in truth"). "When We Say Hiroshima," [Hiroshima to in toki], by Sadako Kurihara (translated by Wayne Lammers, 1981).

33. Mr. Keiichi Nagata, a Nagasaki high school teacher, translated Dr. Akizuki's book, which was published as *Nagasaki 1945* (London: Quartet Books, 1981).

34. Mitsubishi's annual trading transactions approach $44 billion, equal to about one-quarter of Japan's national budget. Mitsubishi's Nagasaki Shipyard, at its crest in the late 1960s and early 1970s, registered the world's largest annual launching tonnage (five million tons deadweight) in 1974. The outlook for ocean-going shipping after the petroleum crisis and the subsequent world-wide recession is not bright, but Japan's petroleum dependence is still great and a partial recovery has been registered by some of the leading shipyards in Nagasaki Prefecture.

35. Statistics on Mitsubishi weapons contracts are from *Japan's Contribution to Military Stability in Northeast Asia*, Subcommittee on East Asian and Pacific Affairs, Senate Committee on Foreign Relations (Washington, D.C.: U.S. Government Printing Office, June 1980), p. 42.

36. These early Nagasaki *Hibakusha* accounts include: *Nagasaki: A Record of the A-bomb Experiences of Twenty-Two Survivors* [*Nagasaki: Nijuninin no Genbaku Taiken Kiroku*], 1949 (One of the accounts is by Dr. Nagai); *Survivors Under the Atomic clouds* [*Genshi-gumo no Shita ni Ikite*], 1950, edited by Dr. Nagai, a collection of compositions by *Hibakusha* children of the Yamazato Elementary and High Schools, where 1,300 pupils perished by the bomb; *The Atomic Bomb Accounts of Nagasaki Seiki Employees* [*Nagasaki Seiki Genshi Bakudan ki*], 1949. This volume contains thirty-nine personal accounts and the transcript of a round table discussion among *Hibakusha*.

37. Nagai, "The Origins of the Bell of Nagasaki" [Nagasaki no Kane no Yurai], in *The Collected Works of Takashi Nagai* [*Nagai Takashi Zenshu*] (Tokyo: Kodansha, 1971), pp. 403-404.

38. The present population of Nagasaki is about 450,000, approximately one-half that of Hiroshima, and partly for this reason the influence of Mitsubishi is concentrated more intensively than that of any single industry on the city of Hiroshima. The per capita income is less in Nagasaki, a difference which may in part be historical, but reflects also the uneven regional development of capitalism in Japan.

39. *No More Hiroshimas!*, March 1979, p. 8.

40. The plaintiff in the Shimoda group from Nagasaki, Mr. Suji Hamabe, lost his wife and four daughters to the A-bomb. Age fifty-four in 1945, he worked at the head office of Mitsubishi Heavy Industries.

41. An English translation of the Judgment was published in the Tokyo legal periodical *Hanrei Jiho*, cited as 355 *Decisions Bulletin* 17 by Richard A. Falk and Saul H. Mendlovitz, eds., *The Strategy of World Order*, Vol. 1 (New York: World Law Foundation, 1966), p. 352. Falk and Mendlovitz reprint the Judgment on their pp. 314-354.

42. This appeal is paraphrased from Chieko Watanabe, *To Live in Nagasaki* [*Nagasaki ni Ikiru*] (Tokyo: Shin Nihon Shuppansha, 1973), pp. 75-79.

43. Chieko Watanabe, speech to the 1978 International Non-Governmental Organizations Conference on Disarmament, Geneva, 27 February–2 March 1978.

44. The first of these volumes, for lower classes in primary school, was translated under the title *In the Sky Over Nagasaki: An A-bomb Reader for Children* (Wilmington, Ohio: Wilmington College Peace Resource Center, 1977). The *Hibakusha* teachers have thus far not secured the full agreement of the Nagasaki Board of Education to use their textbook series in the school curriculum.

45. Shingo Shibata, "The Role of Philosophy in the Prevention of Human Extinction," *Scientific World*, 1978, No. 4, p. 23.

"Never Again!"
Women *Hibakusha* in Osaka

by Janet Bruin and Stephen Salaff

History of the Hibakusha

In August 1945, the United States attacked the cities of Hiroshima and Nagasaki with the most catastrophic weapon in history: atomic bombs that caused more than 210,000 deaths by the end of 1945 (35 percent of the Hiroshima population and 25 percent in Nagasaki), and severe suffering for a large number of the more than 370,000 survivors.

Although the two cities contained military bases and factories, most of their residents in 1945 were women, children and old persons who were not a direct part of the Imperial war machine. Victims of the bombings, over one-half of whom are women, are known by the Japanese term "*hibakusha*," literally "A-bomb received persons." During the thirty-five years in which the war wounds of the rest of the world have gradually been healing, the *hibakusha* have been consigned to a vicious cycle of painful and terrifying disease, deep psychic wounds, social discrimination and poverty. A myriad of debilitating and deforming illnesses, often of permanent duration, followed in the wake of the bombs. Leukemia, cancer, tumors, anemia and blood degeneration, keloid scarring,[1] goiter, cataracts, embedding of glass and other solid particles deep in body tissues, "atomic bomb weakness symptoms," and sudden death from infection are still prevalent among the *hibakusha*. Invisible scars from traumatic loss of loved ones during and after the bombings even today cause constant pain. Fears for the safety and survival of humanity, intensified by the upward nuclear arms spiral, constantly beset the sufferers.[2]

Hibakusha in all of Japan's prefectures have organized A-bomb victims associations to grapple with and redress some of their medical, emotional and economic problems, but women survivors have not always been able fully to participate in these groups. A legacy of feudalistic thought, customs and social structures, with all its modern variants, has limited women to supporting roles in Japanese social, political and religious organizations.[3] In addition, the medical, emotional and social difficulties of female *hibakusha* have been difficult for men to understand. The women could not communicate freely about the diseases of the uterus and breasts common among them, or about their difficulties, as bomb victims, in deciding whether or not to marry in a country where pressure on women to marry and raise children has been severe. Nor could they speak openly about finding mates once the decision to marry was taken. Women widowed by the bombs or abandoned by their husbands after their beauty was marred could not readily discuss their solitary existence at the edge of economic survival. And perhaps most difficult to share have been their intense anxieties over the health and well-being of the "Nisei Hibakusha," the second generation of A-bomb victims.

During the decade after the bombing, when many of the victims were beginning to bear children, questions about the effects of radiation on the fetus and on the second generation were inadequately formulated. Even today, information on radiation effects is spotty, although the evidence is gradually becoming clearer.[4] Most of the *hibakusha* who were pregnant at the time of the bombings lost their babies.[5] Of the few children who survived the uterus some were born microcephalic and retarded. Many of the women who conceived within five years after the bombing had miscarriages or stillbirths. The number of twin births among women who had children later on seems to be higher than usual. Of the children born to women *hibakusha*, the incidence of leukemia, anemia, retardation, soft and fragile bones, and a number of other ailments is higher than among the rest of the population. Even those mothers whose offspring seemed to be in good health were never free from the fear that their children could be stricken with a fatal or debilitating disease as a result of their exposure to radiation.

Consequently, most of the women who survived the bombings worry about whether they made the right decision to bear life. Thirty-five years later, *hibakusha* mothers admit that they feel guilty when their children are stricken with diseases that might be attributable to radiation or other A-bomb effects.

Shizuko and Kazue's eventful meeting.

Shizuko Takagi is a native of Osaka who went to college in Hiroshima in July 1945. Kazue Miura, who was born and raised in Hiroshima, joined her two sisters in Osaka after the rest of her family perished in the bombing. Shizuko and Kazue were marginally affiliated with the largely male Osaka Association of A-bomb Victims, but the two had borne their physical and emotional troubles separately and silently until a young woman activist in the peace movement brought them together in 1967. Soon the two women poured out their long dormant emotions of loss, shame, anger, guilt and fear.

Shizuko and Kazue felt extraordinarily relieved, and long hours and many tears later they decided that it was time to put an end to the years of silent suffering. There were perhaps 1,600 women *hibakusha* in Osaka carrying the same oppressive burdens who needed help, even if it were just someone to talk with, and Shizuko and Kazue began planning how best to find them. With the aid of peace organizations and informal contacts, Shizuko and Kazue secured a list of officially registered bomb victims in Osaka. They began visiting women in hospitals and at home and successfully attracted many of them to their early gatherings, where long-suppressed sentiments flowed into "rivers of tears." After much trial and error and hard work, the Women's Section, Osaka Association of A-bomb Victims, was born in September 1967.

Help for the *Hibakusha*

News of the love, understanding, support and tangible assistance offered by the Women's Section spread, and the demand for its services increased. Recognizing the need for these services, the City of Osaka in 1969 made available a consultation room in the Municipal Social Welfare Hall, and awarded the Women's Section a modest annual grant to pay nominal wages to the consultants, all survivors themselves. The consultation room, partitioned into a business office and an inner roomlet cozily furnished in traditional style, represented a great victory for the *hibakusha*, and signified that the Osaka Municipality, the second largest in Japan, was at last willing to recognize publicly the plight of the *hibakusha* after so many years of keeping them in the shadows.

Hibakusha—male as well as female—come to the Women's Section for personal counselling and for information about the complex web of medical, social and financial benefits available to them. Governmental insensitivity has compounded the wounds of the *hibakusha,* and survivors assistance was instituted by the Ministry of Health and Welfare only after protracted mass struggles. But even now, information about *hibakusha* relief measures is often withheld and the benefits themselves frequently denied, so the Women's Section has had to wage numerous legal battles on behalf of its clients.

In addition to consultation room activities and advocacy, Women's Section members have taken on a memoir-writing project. The life histories of these women serve as historical documentation on the damages and after-effects of the atomic bombings and enable world audiences to see this solemn problem from a more personal perspective. After several dozen Osaka women had written and published their stories, they found it easier to stand on public platforms to demand their rights and give firsthand reports of the dangers the world faces if nuclear weapons are not banned.

"We hibakusha are the only living proof of the disastrous effects of nuclear weapons," declares Toyoko Fujikawa, Chairperson of the Women's Section, *"and we are not getting any younger or healthier. The Japanese government has not yet taken responsibility for fully compensating us for the pain we have suffered, and no one has guaranteed us and our children the peaceful life we believe we deserve. Our anger is focused not so much on what happened to us thirty-five years ago as it is on the continued existence and development of weapons which could make victims of the rest of humanity. So even though it is painful for us to recount our stories of misery, it is the least we can do to warn people about the grave threat to world survival which is being intensified by the arms race and the dire consequences of diverting the planet's precious resources to destructive ends. Our suffering will not have been in vain if it can help eliminate the threat of annihilation. There must never again be victims like ourselves."*

Another major activity of the Women's Section has been the collection of data on the victims of the bombings. Research on approximately 700 *hibakusha* annually has provided valuable information for the campaign in Japan to enact a comprehensive A-bomb Victims' Relief Measures Law.[6] Their findings, publicized in research reports and at local, national and international symposia, have important implications as well for people everywhere in an age threatened by the dangers of nuclear war and nuclear radiation.

An international appeal

Until the mid-1970s the work of the Osaka women was carried out for the most part locally. Section members participated strongly in the campaign against the location of a Nike missile base in Osaka Prefecture, and came to institutionalize activites for *hibakusha* rights and nuclear disarmament by collecting signatures in the streets on the 6th and 9th days of each month. The Women's Section was moved to broaden its scope by a tragic event which occurred on August 6, 1975, when Sumiko Mine lost her 17 year old son, Kenichi, from leukemia after several months of a heroic struggle for life. Sumiko had never suspected that her body was contaminated by radioactivity, even when her daughter died from leukemia in 1972. Her grief at having lost both children would probably have ended in suicide had it not been for the attention and support of other *hibakusha*. Kenichi's was the eighth leukemia death among Osaka *Nisei hibakusha* since the women had begun collecting statistics.

To Shizuko Takagi no case could be more shocking because her own son was also 17 and a soccer player like Kenichi. Shizuko and the Women's Section resolved to bring information to people all over the world about the death of this child, born in a time of peace and killed by a weapon used long before his birth in a time of war. Armed with petitions filled with signatures calling for "No More Hiroshimas! No More Nagasakis!," Shizuko, elected to represent the Women's Section on the first all-Japan delegation to the United Nations, met with UN Secretary-General Waldheim on December 8, 1975. In the name of the dead, the survivors, the world's children, and the generations yet to be born, she pleaded for a binding international agreement to prohibit nuclear weapons.

Hibakusha looked forward to the UN Special Session on Disarmament of May-June 1978 with great hopes, since it marked the beginning of a new phase of UN involvement in the disarmament process. Although the Special Session did not lead directly to concrete disarmament measures, they were heartened by UN member states' recognition that "mankind must stop the arms race or face annihilation." This time, Shizuko's son, Nobuhiko, journeyed to New York as the youngest member of the 500-strong Japanese Non-Governmental Organization delegation. He helped to deliver 20 million Japanese signatures calling for the outlawing of the use of nuclear weapons as a crime against humanity, the convening of a World Disarmament Conference, and dissemination of information about the horrors of the atomic bombing and the suffering of its victims. Women's Section members take great pride in their children's activities on behalf of peace, and it was with joy that they watched a television broadcast from New York as Nobuhiko addressed a crowd of many thousands saying: "I have come from Japan to declare that nuclear weapons must be banned."

Political, economic, military and technological developments since the Special Session, however, have dampened their hopes and caused *hibakusha* great alarm. During the International Year of the Child in 1979, they intensified their efforts by publishing more data and memoirs, holding more meetings, and reaching out to groups around the world. Meeting with representatives of the Women's International League of Peace and Freedom, Women Strike for Peace, and Voice of Women, they learned of the North American peace movement's role in bringing to an end the war in Vietnam. They are hopeful that such groups will contribute to the development of a mass mobilization to prevent a Third World War and the brutal destruction it would cause.

As bearers and protectors of life, women traditionally have been advocates for peace,[7] and Women's Section members are acting on the belief that they have a great responsibility for this advocacy. During this, the UN Decade for Women, they have appealed to women all over the world to demand an immediate end to the arms race and diversion of the more than $400 billion spent annually on armaments to the health, education and welfare of the world's people. They urge North American women in particular to exert pressure on the US government to recognize the necessity of disarmament through international negotiations and the United Nations.

NOTES

1. Caused by heat rays burned into the skin, keloid tissue leaves heavy, deforming scars.

2. "The *hibakusha* vividly remember the shocking sights and horrors of the bombing. They remember the deaths of family members and relatives, and being forced to desert their kin in trying to escape the flames. They are still tormented by the memories of those experiences, images that return at every mention of nuclear weapons and tests . . . . But an increasing number of *hibakusha* have rehabilitated themselves by finding what the external conditions were that drove them into difficulties and suffering, and they therefore seized the aim for life: a world without nuclear weapons, human solidarity for peace." Dr. Shigeru Yamate, "The Anguish of *Hibakusha*," chapter in *Proceedings of the International Symposium on the Damage and After-Effects of the Atomic Bombing of Hiroshima and Nagasaki,* July 21–August 9, 1977, Tokyo, Hiroshima and Nagasaki, p. 119.

3. Ladies Auxiliaries (*Fujin Bu*) are attached to many traditional and modern Japanese organizations. members propagate common objectives among women at large, and help within the group, but do not as a rule share leadership. When a younger woman is able to gain an executive position, she may be expected to vacate her post by around age 25 dutifully to raise a family.

4. *Proceedings of the International Symposium.* See especially "Summary Report on Medical and Genetic After-Effects of Atomic Bombing, pp. 32-34, and "Working Document on the Medical Effects of the Atomic Bombs," pp. 83-96. See also the draft report of Dr. A.M. Stewart (Regional Cancer Registry, Queen Elizabeth Medical Center, Birmingham, England), "Alternative Analysis of the Mortality Experiences of A-bomb Survivors," 23 October 1979.

5. Despite the need for more exact empirical data on the biological effects of radiation, and the efforts now being made to collect such information, it will be impossible to recover much of the past *hibakusha* childbearing experience. The information contained in the remainder of this paragraph is from Kazue Miura, *Survival at 500 Meters in Hiroshima* (Osaka: Women's Section, Osaka Association of A-bomb Victims, December 1979) p. 19.

6. "The Japanese Government, under the 1951 San Francisco Peace Treaty, surrendered the right to demand reparations for the A-bombings from the United States. Japan therefore bears the responsibility of instituting a *hibakusha* aid law providing for full state compensation." *No More Hiroshimas!,* Japan Council Against A- and H-bombs, Tokyo, March 1979, p. 8. The Diet promulgated in 1957 the Law for Health Protection and Medical Care for A-bomb Victims, which provides for biannual governmental medical examination and treatment. The 1968 Law for Special Measures for A-bomb Victims went somewhat beyond the primarily medical benefits of the 1957 law, and reflected the *hibakusha* demand for livelihood security. A total of aproximately 370,000 *hibakusha* have secured the Ministry of Health and Welfare's Health Notebook for A-bomb Victims, becoming eligible thereby for certain forms of medical treatment and financial compensation under these two laws. However, several tens of thousands of survivors have not yet obtained Health Notebooks, and second and third generation victims are not entitled to receive them.

A powerful campaign has been launched by the Japan Federation of A-bomb Survivors' Organizations to gather 20 million signatures for the enactment in the spirit of "national indemnity" by the Diet of far more comprehensive *hibakusha* relief legislation.

7. The Declaration of the Second Mothers Congress of Japan, Tokyo, August 29, 1956 affirms that "As bearers of life, mothers have the right to help bring up and protect all life." The First Mothers Congress on June 9, 1955 resolved:

Let us call the world's attention to the real conditions of the atomic bomb victims and join the forces working to protect these victims; let us further expand the movement opposing the preparations for atomic war.

A Decade of the Mothers Movement (Tokyo: Liaison Committee for the Mothers Congress of Japan, 1966) pp. 303-304.

Life Histories

The following excerpts from Women's Section life histories point to some of the difficulties which the Osaka atomic bomb victims have faced in their struggle to survive and live with dignity and purpose. The more extended case studies now becoming available further reveal the deep and terrible physical and psychic wounds of the sufferers, and provide compassionate literary documentation on the damage and after-effects of nuclear weapons. The construction of these self-portraits was in each case a significant step in overcoming the obstacles to social activism which faced the women of Osaka. The occupation given for each woman is that in August 1945, followed by her location at the time of bombing and her age.   (H.S.)

Sumiko Mine

Nagasaki, age 10

I walked with my mother from our home in a village outside Nagasaki into the ruined city on August 11 to search for my older brother, who had not returned from work there. For two days we searched the neighborhood of what proved later to be the hypocenter of the bomb explosion, until at last we found my brother, still alive. After we returned home, I developed diarrhea and began vomiting.

Although weakened by radiation sickness, I was persuaded by family and friends in 1956 to marry, and I gave birth to a son in 1958 and a daughter the next year. We moved to Osaka in 1964, where my husband took up work. But he died of a shipyard injury in 1967. Then my 12 year old daughter Junko perished of leukemia in 1972. I was left with Kenichi, in whom I was completely invested emotionally.

In November 1974 Ken developed symptoms which were diagnosed by our neighborhood doctor as rheumatic fever. It was not until Ken's teacher of English visited him in hospital in December, when he learned of my early years in Nagasaki and Junko's death from leukemia, that a closer examination was made at the teacher's urging. Ken had leukemia, and not much time was left. Despite encouragement given by his classmates, who presented him with one thousand folded paper cranes donated by his friends, and despite my constant attention to his condition and his own fierce determination to stay alive, Kenichi died on August 6, 1975. His was the eighth leukemia death among the Nisei Hibakusha of Osaka since 1967.

My lonely struggle with grief and guilt was for a time unbearable. Never suspecting that my body was contaminated by radioactivity, questions such as: "Why did I marry, and give birth to these children? Why should I continue to live?" plagued me. Fortunately, the Women's Section, as it has done with numerous sadly depressed victims, gave me a reason for living and helped pull me out of my suicidal depths.

Kazue Miura

Switchboard operator,
Hiroshima Central Telephone Exchange, age 18

When I finished school in 1941, I began to work as an operator in the Central Telephone Exchange. December eighth of that year was an especially busy day, on which Japan declared war against the Allies. As the war grew in intensity, the Telephone Exchange was staffed almost entirely by women, mobilized high school girls among them.

The Telephone Exchange was located within 500 meters of the hypocenter of the A-bomb explosion, and I was one of the few people who survived in this innermost zone. I was hurled to the floor by the fierce blast, and felt warm blood spurting from my nose and mouth. After a momentary silence, the shrill voices of my workmates rose to a mournful chorus. At one of the second floor exits, I found a girl who was thrown through a window and whose face, full of glass, was bleeding profusely. I held her in my arms, and led her out of the building.

Beautiful Hiroshima was now a wasteland of debris. I desperately wanted to make my way home, 400 meters from the hypocenter, but the heat from the burning houses was too intense. I decided instead to go with my companion to her home in the north of the city. She was in such fear that she would not part her hands from mine, even for a moment. Stunned, expressionless, monsterlike people, young and old, cried out for their mothers and begged for water. When I tried to comfort children, words would not come, only tears.

The next morning I was able to return to the place where my house had stood so sturdily. It looked as if the house had been melted and coagulated. My father, mother, little brother and sister were nowhere to be seen, and I learned later that they had all perished during or soon after the bombing. There was nothing I could do but write "Kazue, Alive!" on the wall of the water tank, now completely dry. I walked back and forth between what had been my home and my place of work, ignorant of the terrible effects of residual radioactivity, looking desperately for my family and friends.

I was suffering intensely from diarrhea. I got weaker and thinner and felt like a ghost. At the hospital the doctors were sure I would die from the terrible, mysterious symptoms which had already claimed so many lives. But through the kindness of a family friend, who took me to his quiet home by the sea and fed me fresh fish and oranges, I miraculously began to recover.

In November, although I was still weak, I went to my two sisters in Osaka, carrying the ashes of our parents in an urn wrapped in cloth hanging from my neck. My sisters nursed me back to health. They introduced me to a good man, and we married in 1948.

My first baby was stillborn, as was the case with one of my older sisters who was A-bombed in Hiroshima. I was hesitant to have another, but we wanted children very badly. In 1950 I gave birth to a boy, and in 1953 I had a girl. My daughter Maki is troubled by anemia and low blood pressure.

As she grew older, Maki noticed that newspapers in the summer featured stories of the bombings and deaths of survivors. She came to hate all reminders of the bombing because of the pain it had caused me and her fear that I, too, would succumb. When she was fourteen she looked me in the face reproachfully and asked: "Why did you give birth to me, Mom? You are a bomb victim, so you should not have brought me into the world." I had long anticipated that question, but no amount of emotional preparation could have softened the blow of those few words. I told her that I had thought a lot before giving birth to her and didn't know whether she might get a bad disease, not wanting to mention leukemia. "And what would you do if it happened to me?" she asked. What could I answer her? In painful honesty I told her that there was nothing we could do about it. That was the saddest and most heartbreaking moment of my life.

Maki is now married and has two children. She and

the Women's Section members have been a constant source of help and encouragement to me, especially since my health has deteriorated. In late 1976 I began to suffer from symptoms of anemia, and a gynecological examination revealed myoma of the uterus (a fibro-muscular tumor). Now I had joined the ranks of the seriously ill Hibakusha, many of whom had been operated on for uterine cancer, myoma or cystoma (ovarian cyst). Government benefits are often withheld and denied to Hibakusha, and it was only after this diagnosis that the government granted me "Especially Serious Case" status. To my happiness, the Women's Section published my life story Survival at 500 Meters in Hiroshima in December 1979, and I hope that it may serve to prevent any other human beings from experiencing the horrors of nuclear war.

(Kazue Miura died on 25 April 1980 of stomach cancer.)

Toshiko Nakamura

Housewife, mother of six, Nagasaki

I was cleaning our family's tiny underground air raid shelter on a hillside near our two story home in Hamaguchi-cho, when I saw a sudden flash and felt something pressed hard against my cheeks. The rest was sheer darkness. When I pushed my way out of the shelter, I saw a blaze envelop the whole neighborhood, including our home, where several of my six children were playing. The dwelling was crushed under the neighboring house, which in turn had fallen beneath the next house.

I could not even approach home, and so I fled, alongside a few other ghostlike, tottering forms which had emerged from the flames, into a sweet potato field, where I had to spend the night. The next morning, I returned to the site of my house, but whatever objects I moved only raised clouds of hot ashes. I went to the home of relatives, who told me that my face was scorched black and covered with scabs. As awful as that was, it didn't seem as important as being without my children.

On the third day, a friend of my husband came to help me salvage the debris of my home. We discovered a white, round object, An elderly passing soldier told us that it was the skull of a man in his thirties or forties. This must be my husband's, I realized. Dazed we dug up six more skulls, and my children's butterfly badges with them.

How often I thought of killing myself! Livid spots appeared all over my body, and I frequently felt very sick. My hair fell out. But I had to begin earning a living, and so I became a seamstress. In 1948, when I had still not absorbed all the effects of the atomic catastrophe, I married a man who initially promised to help me. After I realized that I could not trust him, we separated, but I was already pregnant. I decided to have the child, a baby girl who was a living image of my departed second daughter. The rest of my life will be for this girl, I resolved.

Sewing, however, became unbearable because the beautiful clothes I was making brought painful memories of my children who were no more.

I moved from city to city with my daughter, from Fukuoka to Sasebo and back to Nagasaki, working as a poorly paid hotel domestic, trying to keep her from going hungry while I was periodically hospitalized for A-bomb illness.

My first-born daughter, a high school girl in 1945, had been put to work by the Imperial Government, and this qualified me for a pension under the Relief Measures Law for the Wounded, Diseased or Bereaved in War of 1952. But neither the City of Nagasaki nor the Ministry of Health and Welfare notified me of my rights, and if it had not been for the consultation program of the Women's Section, I would have remained ignorant of this benefit.

In time, moreover, A Health Notebook for A-bomb Victims became obtainable by persons identified as Hibakusha, which qualifies for limited compensation under Hibakusha legislation. I went to the Nagasaki City Office to secure my Notebook, and the official in charge said to me sarcastically: "We envy you Hibakusha. Your Notebooks will provide you with everything you need, won't they?" That made me very angry I threw down the Notebook crying "This Book will not restore my family. Give me back my husband and my six children!"

People called me stubborn, and as such I fought my way through. My daughter completed high school and took courses in Cosmetology. She left Nagasaki to work in Osaka in late 1965. I wanted to acompany her, but had to undergo long hospitalizations after blood appeared in my phlegm. It was not until 1968 that I was well enough to come to Osaka. Here, my doctor tells me that there is a tumor in my gullet. But I won't give way to this disease so soon. How could I, after my miraculous survival through the holocaust of the bomb?

My daughter and I are managing now, but she says thoughtfully: "I feel kind of guilty when I think of my happy life with you, mother, while all my sisters and brothers were killed by the A-bomb." I am worried by her weak health, and am determined not to die until she opens a beauty shop of her own, and meets a good young man to provide for her continued happiness.

The gatherings of the Women's Section have given me the opportunity to come across my dear old Nagasaki dialect, and to give full expression to the feelings I have had ever since that fatal day. When I made up my mind to publish my life story in Unvanquished, We March, the magazine of the Women's Section, my daughter at first tried to stop me, because she was afraid that it would renew my sorrow. But when she saw my insistent look, she agreed.

My memories are inexhaustible. I am determined that the cruelty of war never be repeated. Nobody will ever cheat me into believing the the glory of war.

Fumiko Nonaka

Labor team, Hiroshima, age 24

I was working in downtown Hiroshima a little after 8

am, when a woman near me cried: "Here comes a B-29 bomber!" The instant I looked up at the sky, my face was pierced by an intense flash of light and I felt my whole body shrink. My skin was all of a sudden shredded and hanging like dried squid roasted on a fire. But at least my jacket and underwear saved my inner organs.

I lost consciousness. I don't know how much time passed before I returned to my senses. Someone must have helped me to reach a temporary first aid station. My face was swollen beyond recognition, the burnt flesh of my arms, hands and fingers was hanging out of my sleeves and drooping down my fingertips, and I was temporarily blind.

My husband searched for me in all the makeshift aid stations, and fortunately, when at last on August 9 he saw my misshapen figure, he spotted my wedding ring. To my joy he shouted in my ear "Are you Fumiko?"

I was later taken on a truck to a naval hospital in the nearby port of Kure. There, when the doctor removed the tightly sticking bandages from my face, the pain was so severe that it made my eyes water. My husband later told me that while I was in the hospital he was often tempted to kill me because he could not stand to see me suffering so much pain.

My parents, brother and sister, and several other relatives came to the hospital with two urns of firewood, prepared for my death and cremation. But instead they carried me back on a stretcher and tenderly cared for me at home. I could open my mouth only wide enough to swallow three grains of rice at a time, and my mother patiently sat at my bedside feeding me the nourishment I needed to stay alive. My brother-in-law carefully removed the darkened skin with tweezers from my face and limbs, washed my skin with salt water, and coated it with cooking oil.

When I could finally move my body, I returned to the dwelling of my husband. It was then that he found it difficult to live with such an ugly, feeble woman. Some of his friends suggested that he divorce me. He did go off with another woman, who bore him a son in 1946, but their relationship did not last, and he brought the child to me. I raised the boy with all my might, as if he were my own. However in 1950 my husband again abandoned me for another woman, taking the child with him.

Left alone, I joined a government program for the poor as a laborer for less than 400 yen ($1) per day in Niigata. There were many days when I could hardly stand up under the load, but I was at least fortunate to have the heartwarming encouragement of my fellow union members, who offered me the blood I needed for anemia transfusions. I still had to undergo scar removal, mouth widening and skin graft operations, some without anesthesia.

My husband came home again, unemployed, and my wages now had to support the child. But again my husband left me and went this time to Hiroshima. He died there in the A-bomb Hospital around 1960, a victim probably of the radiation he absorbed while searching for me in the ruins.

I moved to Osaka, originally to get away from where my husband was, and to find a more suitable climate for my convalescence. Through the Women's Section, a doctor of the Osaka Red Cross Hospital supported my application for medical compensation, and the Ministry of Health and Welfare awarded me a modest allowance. This was partly for what the doctor called "ugly looks caused by serious burn scarring." Although I am relieved by this pension, my blood boils in anger whenever untutored children gazing at me say "Hey, look at that woman's face!"

Taking part in the meetings of the Women's Section has come to be the main purpose of my life. I am glad to be alive to work for peace. How great was my joy when for the first time I spoke on the Section's behalf in public!

The Japanese Peasantry and Economic Growth Since the Land Reform of 1946–47

by Bernard Bernier[1]

The Land Reform of 1946–1947 marks a definite break in the history of Japanese rural society. It thoroughly eradicated the landlord-tenant class relation which had been a dominant feature of the Japanese countryside since the late Edo period (1600–1868). The Reform was imposed on the Japanese government by the Supreme Command of Allied Powers (SCAP). One of its basic tenets was that landlordism had been a major cause of the jingoistic and militaristic tendencies which characterized Japanese society in the 1930s and 1940s.[2] It thus had to be eliminated. But a more important goal of the Reform was to stamp out rural radicalism which had been an important aspect of agrarian Japan in the 1920s and 1930s. Rural intransigence, prompted by the misery of the peasants under the landlord system, was a major potential source of social unrest, and it was feared that the peasantry might support left-wing parties.[3] In order to eliminate all dangerous socialist tendencies in the countryside, it was necessary to return the land to the tillers, that is to transform the majority of agriculturalists into small property owners. This rural "middle class" would hopefully become a conservative political force, thus insuring that Japan remained in the anti-communist camp.[4]

The Land Reform has in fact been successful, at least until recently, in transforming the peasantry into a conservative bloc.[5] Since 1948 the countryside has voted overwhelmingly for right-of-center parties, despite mounting difficulties for peasants and growing protests against various aspects of the State's agricultural policy. But the Reform never achieved its goal of creating a "middle class" of farmers. In the first place, the Reform did not equalize land holdings. For example, in 1950, 73 percent of all farm households owned less than one hectare of arable land (see table 1).[6] Secondly, since about 1955, Japanese agriculture has had to bear up under the pressures of rapid economic growth whose prime moving force has been the heavy and chemical industries dominated by monopoly capitalism. Thus it will be necessary both to assess the various forces at work within the agricultural sector itself and to examine the national context in which these tendencies occur, taking into account the effects of Japan's "economic miracle"[7] and the State's agrarian policy. Perforce it will be useful to examine, albeit briefly, Japan's place in the international farm market.

The Agricultural Sector Since the Land Reform

Demographic Aspects

Throughout the twentieth century, the rural population has been decreasing in proportion to the total Japanese population. From a level of about 60 percent around 1900, it fell to 48 percent in 1950, 31 percent in 1965, and 19.9 percent in 1977 (see table 2). In absolute terms, the rural population had grown between 1900 and 1950 (from 26 to 37 millions, with various ups and downs), but thereafter, a sharp decline has occurred, dropping to 22.5 million in 1977. Of course, the 1950 figure is inflated because of the influx of population to the rural areas after the war, due to the destruction of homes and industrial installations in the cities and the repatriation of Japanese soldiers and former colonists. But this decline was still noticeable even after industrial production had attained its prewar level in 1953. In fact, the average annual decrease in the 22 year period between 1955 and 1977 was about 2 percent, and nearly 8 percent since 1968.[8]

The evolution of the population actively engaged in agriculture has followed a different course. The 1955 proportion was nearly equal to that of 1920: 15 million or 45 percent of the total active population in 1955; 14 million, or 52 percent in 1920 (see table 2).[9] However the farm population fell to about 12 million (30 percent) in 1960, and to 6.2 million (11.5 percent) in 1977. The annual rate of decrease stands at about 3 percent for the period from 1955 to 1977. This downward trend in the active farming population can be seen partly as a continuation of a trend—already present in the late Edo period—which intensified with industrial development in the Meiji (1868–1912) and Taisho (1912–1926) periods. This is the increase in the proportion of non-agricultural to farm labor, at least part of which is due to the exodus from overpopulated rural areas.[10] However, this postwar trend, as I will show, did not remove only *excess* farm population. It has increasingly taken *needed* labor from the farms, transforming cultivators into low-paid workers employed in factories, the construction industry and the services. Thus, the incorporation of agriculture into the capitalist economy has now entered a new phase in Japan, a process which calls for further analysis.

Table 1

NUMBER OF FARM HOUSHOLDS BY SIZE, 1940-1977
(in thousands)

Acreage categories	1940	1950	1960	1965	1970	1972	1973	1976	1977
0.0-0.3 ha	1796	2531	1283	1142	1100	1922	1922	1920	1911
0.3-0.5			992	954	899				
0.5-0.7	1768	1973	866	808	747	733	727	695	682
0.7-1.0			1041	954	851	820	805	741	734
1.0-1.5	1322	1339	1002	945	868	832	805	721	710
1.5-2.0			404	407	404	393	383	347	342
2.0-2.5	309	208	157	156	170	174	167	164	161
2.5-3.0			54	59	71	74	73	78	80
3.0 et plus	195	125	36	41	61	68	72	88	88

Source: Yujiro Hayami, *A Century of Agricultural Growth in Japan* (Tokyo, Tokyo University Press, 1975), p. 9;
Nihon Nōgyō Nenkan, (Tokyo, Ie no Hikari, 1974), p. 156.
Nihon Nōgyō Nenkan, (Tokyo, Ie no Hikari, 1978) p. 158.

Table 2

NUMBER OF FARM HOUSEHOLDS, AGRICULTURAL POPULATION AND POPULATION ACTIVE IN AGRICULTURE, 1945-1977

Year	Number of farm households (1000)	Agricultural population (1000)	Percentage of total population	Population active in agriculture (1000)	Percentage of total active population
1945	5,698			13,934	
1950	6,176	37,760	48.3	15,886	45.2
1955	6,043	36,347	40.8	15,172	37.9
1960	6,057	34,411	36.5	11,960	30.0
1965	5,655	30,083	31.0	9,810	22.8
1970	5,342	36,595	25.3	8,110	17.8
1973	5,098	24,380	22.0	6,820	13.1
1975	4,953	23.195	21.3	6,500	12.5
1976	4,891	22,900	20.5	6,429	12.1
1977	4,835	22,560	19.9	6,201	11.6

Source: Bureau of Statistics, *Statistical Handbook of Japan*, 1974, p. 29;
Oriental Economist, Nov. 1975, p. 25;
Nihon Nōgyō Nenkan, (Tokyo, Ie no Hikari, 1978) p. 155-159.
Statistical Yearbook of Ministry of Agriculture and Forestry, 1976-77, p. 22-23.

TABLE 3

AGRICULTURAL PRODUCTION AS A PERCENTAGE OF GNP 1936-7 to 1977

Year	Percentage
1934-36	16.6
1946	31.1
1950	21.3
1954	16.7
1958	13.5
1960	10.8
1970	5.5
1972	4.0
1975	3.0
1977	2.5

Source: Ogura, Ed., op. cit., p. 69; Danno, op. cit., p. 295.

TABLE 4
Rice Price Index, 1960-1978
(1965 = 100)

Year	Index
1960	63.8
1966	109.2
1968	126.1
1970	126.0
1972	137.0
1974	196.0
1976	248.0
1977	264.0
1978	274.5

Source: OCDE, op. cit., p. 27; *Japan Times*, July 7, 1976, p. 1.
Oriental Economist, *Japan Economic Yearbook*, 1976, p. 50.
Oriental Economist, *Japan Economic Yearbook*, 1977-78, p. 48.

TABLE 5
Annual Rate of Increase or Decrease in the Number of Farm Households by Acreage Categories, 1960–1977
(in percentage)

Acreage categories	1960–65	1965–70	1970–75	1976–77
0.0–0.3 ha.	−2.2	−0.8	−0.3	−0.5
0.3–0.5	−0.8	−1.2		
0.5–0.7	−1.3	−1.6	−1.7	−1.9
0.7–1.0	−1.7	−2.1	−2.9	−1.0
1.0–1.5	−1.1	−1.7	−3.6	−2.3
1.5–2.0	0.2	−0.2	−3.0	−1.7
2.0–2.5	1.1	1.8	−1.2	−1.8
2.5–3.0	1.9	3.8	0.6	2.1
3.0 plus	2.7	8.2	10.0	0.3

Source: Nihon Nōgyō Nenkin, 1974, p. 156; *Nihon Nōgyō Nenkan*, 1978, p. 158

TABLE 6

Number and Percentage of Farm Households By Source of Income, 1947–1977
(in 1000 and percentage)

Year	Full-time agricultural households	Percentage of total member of farm households	Part-time farm households category I	Percentage of total member of farm households	Part-time farm households category II	Percentage of total member of farm households
1947	3,270	55.4	1,680	28.5	951	16.1
1950	2,770	45.2	1,950	31.8	1,410	23.0
1955	2,020	34.7	2,210	37.9	1,590	24.4
1960	2,100	34.3	2,030	35.0	1,940	30.0
1965	1,200	21.5	2,080	35.5	2,360	43.0
1970	832	16.0	1,800	32.0	2,710	52.0
1973	675	12.0	1,300	23.0	3,120	65.0
1975	616	12.4	1,259	25.4	3,080	62.1
1976	659	13.5	1,002	20.5	3,231	66.1
1977	643	13.3	927	19.2	3,265	67.5

Source: Hayami, op. cit.; Bureau of Statistics, op. cit., p. 29; *Japan Times*, July 7, 1976, p. 1; *Nihon Nōgyō Nenkan*, 1974, p. 156; *Nihon Nōgyō Nenkan*, 1978, p. 155

This fact is borne out by the decrease in the number of farm households after 1960. From 1950 to 1960, the number of farm units remained relatively stable at the unprecedented high level of about 6 million. Only between 1965 and 1970 was the prewar level reached—a level that had been maintained from the late Edo period until 1945 at between 5.3 and 5.5 million families. Thereafter a sharp decrease occurred, and in 1977 the number of farm households was 4.8 million. The decline between 1960 and 1970 can be viewed as a process of elimination of the excess farm households created by the unusual conditions of the immediate postwar period, but the downward trend that has prevailed since 1970 cannot be explained in this way. In fact, in 1975, for the first time in two centuries, the number of farm families fell below 5 million.[11] This trend has continued. According to most observers,[12] the quasi-mystical attachment to the land is now breaking down among many Japanese peasants. An important feature of the feudal period when land was for many the only means of survival, this attachment has persisted because, until now, farming has been the only way for most rural inhabitants to earn a living. Now survival can be secured by non-agricultural work, and the sale of land, which until recently was thought of as disrespectful toward the family ancestors who bequeathed the land,[13] is now based on cold economic calculations. This is the case in peri-urban areas[14] but is also true of outlying regions.[15]

Agricultural Production

Agricultural production has accounted for an increasingly low percentage of the Gross National Product (see Table 3). From a level of 16.5 percent in 1934–1936, it reached 31 percent in 1946, but settled back to its prewar level in 1954. Thereafter, it has decreased constantly, falling from 13 percent in 1960, to a mere 2.5 percent in 1977. The major reason for this decline is the fantastic development of the industrial and service sectors. Overall agricultural production has increased however, at least until 1968. In fact, from 1960 to 1968, the average annual rate of increase of agricultural production in current prices has been near 4 percent.[16] But since 1969, there has been a slow decline every year, except 1972 and 1975 (good harvests, higher rice prices; see Table 4).

A main reason for the decrease in farm production is, first, a reduction in the total area of land under cultivation. For example, between 1969 and 1976, an annual average of 50,000 hectares were transferred out of cultivation.[17] While much of this is the result of urban and industrial development, it is also due to the abandonment of agriculture by many peasants, partly because of the government's policy of encouraging the curtailment of rice production.[18] Secondly, rice yields per hectare have decreased. For example, between 1967 and 1971, the yield per hectare on large farms fell from 45.4 qt. to 41 qt.[19] Finally, many farmers have abandoned winter crops, and consequently, the rate of land use has declined from 134 percent in 1960 to 100 percent in 1973. Since then, it has risen somewhat to 103 percent in 1976.[20]

The increase in production which occurred before 1969 is the result of two trends. The first is an increase in the yield per hectare which took place chiefly before 1955. This increase was prompted by the generalization of many technical innovations previously used only sporadically or regionally such as chemical fertilizers, herbicides, insecticides, high-yield varieties, etc. In this period, the emphasis was on a more intensive use of the land, and not on an increase in the productivity of labor. Labor was abundant in the countryside; there was no need to "save" it.[21] In fact, there was a 10 percent increase in the ratio of labor per hectare between 1934–36 and 1953.[22]

The second trend, which gathered momentum after 1955, is the increase in labor productivity. This increase became necessary in order to offset the heavy drain on rural labor caused by the demand for cheap labor power in the industrial and service sectors.[23] Relieved of their surplus workers, and even, later, of their required labor power, farm families have had to look for ways to save labor. Indeed, from 1955 to 1970, labor productivity in agriculture increased an average of 6.4 percent annually.[24] Between 1970 and 1976, the increase of labor productivity in agriculture has outstripped that in industry (44.2 percent compared to 30.8 percent).[25]

This second trend is the result of the massive use of small-scale agricultural machinery. In fact, peasants have tried to replace labor, which could be more gainfully employed outside agriculture, by machinery and also by the more intensive use of chemical products. To a certain extent, this shift was successful but it has not been without its cost. Once given the possibility of buying machines, many full-time farmers have also discovered the possibility of taking occasional outside jobs in order to increase family revenues, and even, in some cases, of financing the purchase of farm machinery.[26] Thus off-farm wage labor entails the closer subordination of farm households to the capitalist economy not only as a source of wage labor, but also as a profitable market for industrial farm goods. There have also been ecological effects; the use of fertilizers, herbicides and machinery cannot regenerate the soil the way hard work does. For example, the hand tractor which is widely used now does not plow the land as deeply as the old ox-drawn plows; furthermore, chemicals have changed the soil into a sticky matter that bears no resemblance to the rich organic soil which was the hallmark of Japanese wet rice agriculture.[27] The major result of this labor-saving agriculture has been a decrease in yield which I mentioned earlier. A second consequence is the weakened resistance of plants to cold temperature.

Another danger is chemical poisoning.[28] Together with industrial pollution, pollution by agricultural chemicals has hit all Japanese but especially peasants. Matsushima[29] states that 25 percent of all peasants are affected one way or another by such chemical intoxication and 4 percent are seriously poisoned. Most chemicals used in agriculture have not been tested previously (a consequence of very lax rules regarding the testing of industrial products in Japan),[30] and their side effects are not known.

Agricultural Products

Japanese agriculture is still strongly centered on cereals, particularly rice. However, since 1950 specialization in other crops has been gaining ground. In 1950 cereals accounted for more than 70 percent of total farm production. This is only slightly lower than comparable figures for the early 20th century. But since 1950 the importance of cereals has decreased. In 1960 they accounted for 55 percent of total agricultural production but this percentage had fallen to 36 percent by 1973 and to about 33 percent in 1977. The decline has been much more dramatic for cereals other than rice (wheat, barley, buckwheat, corn). In 1950 these other cereals accounted for more than 10 percent of the total farm output, but less than 1 percent in 1976. The major reason for this rapid drop in production lies in the fact that cereals cultivated in Japan are expensive. In 1969, Japanese wheat sold at more than double the international price.[31] However, this in itself is not a sufficient condition, for in the same year the price of Japanese rice was about three times that of American rice.[32] A second important factor is U.S. pressure on the Japanese government to import large quantities of American farm goods. This pressure has been applied more or less consistently since 1945. Just after the war, the Japanese government had little power to resist. The U.S. was producing large surpluses, especially of wheat and soy beans, and Japan proved to be an ideal market both because of the immediate food shortage and because of low farm productivity. Agreements were even signed in 1954 to insure the flow of certain American agricultural products into Jpan.[33] The net result was a slackening off in production of many Japanese crops, including wheat, barley and soy beans.

Conversely, the production of livestock, dairy goods, fruits, and vegetables has increased tremendously. From 35 percent of total production in 1960, these products have grown to 57 percent in 1972 and almost 60 percent in 1975.[34] The increase in the production of fruits, vegetables, meat, milk and eggs, together with the decline of cereal production, is a sign of a more diversified diet, a consequence of the higher standard of living brought about by the economic growth of the 1960s.[35] However, the sustained growth of non-cereal production has been possible only through heavy tariff protection. Since 1971 international pressure has been applied, especially by the United States, to force the easing of Japanese trade barriers on many agricultural goods. These pressures, which are analyzed in more detail below, have strained the growth of many types of products, including beef, dairy products, and citrus fruits. To offset the effects of liberalization on the peasants, the Japanese government has had to ease up on its policy of rice production control, thus putting an end to its 10-year-old farm diversification program. This policy change has led to new rice surpluses. However, by 1973, the policy of restricting rice production was again revived, resulting in a drop in Japan's overall agricultural output.

Categories of farms

Farm households in Japan, as was mentioned earlier, did not receive equal amounts of land during the Land Reform. This inequality of households based on land holdings has been a constant feature of Japanese agriculture up to the present (see table 1). In the decade from 1940 to 1950, there was an increase in the number of farms in the small holder categories (less than 2 hectares), but a decline in relative and absolute terms of large farms. This is due in large part to the unusual conditions that prevailed in the immediate postwar period. After 1950 these tendencies were reversed. From 1950 to 1960, there was an increase in the number of farms in all acreage categories except for small farms of less than one hectare. From 1960 to 1965, the decline affected the 1 to 1½ hectare category, and the 0.7 to 1 hectare group decreased at a faster rate (see table 5). From 1965 to 1970, the decline reached the 1½ to 2 hectares category and quickened for farms with 1 to 1½ hectare of land. But there was a slowdown in the rate of decline of the smallest farms. From 1970 to 1975, all small holder categories, that is farms with less than 2½ hectares, showed a decline. This process was particularly clear in the 0.7 to 2 hectare categories. Conversely the largest farms, i.e. more than 3 hectares, showed a 10 percent increase. In '76–'77, the rate of decline slackened off for the 0.7 to 2 hectare categories, but it increased for the smaller farms and for the 2 to 2½ hectare category.

In fact, what we see here is a sort of stabilization of the number of smaller farms accompanied by a rather rapid decrease in the number of larger farms, a decrease which is even more rapid now for these farms than it was for smaller ones in earlier years. Thus the downward drift which used to characterize small farms is now spreading to medium-size operations. According to Ouchi[36], this means that the lower stratum of the peasantry, i.e. farm households with insufficient land to live independently (that is, without regular off-farm work), now includes families which used to be in the middle stratum (1 to 2 hectares). The middle stratum is now confined to the 2 to 3 hectare categories, and even these seem to be dwindling at present. Only the larger farms are thriving, and they are a small minority. According to Ouchi and others [37], this is the increasingly polarized form the "decomposition of the peasantry" assumes, a form, it should be noted, that is normally found in all capitalist societies.

The determination of peasant strata, however, cannot be made solely on the basis of farm size, as the above definition of the lower stratum makes clear. It is necessary to take into account the importance of full-time or part-time farming in the different farm households. Table 6 traces the evolution of full-time and part-time farm families from 1947 to 1977. What this table shows is that the proportion of full-time or specialized farms to total farm households has dropped from 55.4 percent in 1947 to 12.4 percent in 1975. But this percentage has gone up to 13.3 percent in 1977. The fastest rate of decline was between 1960 and 1965 when the number of full-time operations decreased from 2.1 millions to 1.2 million for an average annual decline of more than 10 percent.

Part-time farms in category I (i.e. farm households whose income derives partly from non-agricultural work but which receive more than half their total income from agriculture) grew in absolute and relative number from 1947 to 1955, levelled off in the decade 1955-1965, then decreased slowly until 1970, and since then have declined rapidly. The number of part-time farm households in category II (i.e. farm households who earn less than 50 percent of their income from agriculture) has increased constantly, both in real numbers and as a percentage of total households, from 1947 to the present. From just below 1 million (16%) in 1947, these households jumped to 2.3 million (43%) in 1965, and to 3.2 million (67.5%) in 1977. It is clear from these figures that agriculture has become a secondary occupation for about two-thirds of all farming families. The net result has been a decrease in the portion of the total income all farm households derive from agriculture. This has fallen from 50 percent in 1961 to 36 percent in 1972 and finally to 31.6 percent in 1976.[38]

Table 7 gives the breakdown of full-time and part-time farm households by acreage categories between 1960 and 1973. The clearest trend is the constant decrease of full-time operations in all farm-management categories during this period. Larger farms have always fared better, starting at a much higher level of full-time farms (about 72 percent for categories over 2½ hectares, compared to less than 20 percent for small farms of less than ½ hectare), and declining less rapidly (to about 28 percent and 3.1 percent respectively for the same categories in 1973). In fact, the proportion of full-time farms increases at a

TABLE 7

Percentage of Farm Households By Source of Income According to Acreage Categories, 1960 to 1973

Acreage categories	Full-time farm households				Part-time, category I				Part-time, category II			
	1960	1965	1972	1973	1960	1965	1972	1973	1960	1965	1972	1973
Total	33.7	20.5	13.5	12.3	34.1	37.2	27.1	25.3	39.3	42.3	59.4	62.4
0.0–0.3	12.5	8.8	8.1	7.9	10.3	5.9	3.9	3.1	79.2	85.5	88.0	89.0
0.3–0.5	18.6	10.5			30.9	19.7			50.5	69.8		
0.5–0.7	27.9	14.7	9.4	8.9	45.7	39.6	16.2	13.5	26.5	45.7	74.4	77.6
0.7–1.0	39.9	21.8	12.6	11.3	48.9	55.2	33.2	29.8	11.2	23.0	54.3	58.9
1.0–1.5	64.6	31.7	18.6	17.1	42.9	60.5	52.8	49.8	3.6	7.8	28.6	33.0
1.5–2.0	63.3	40.5	25.2	22.7	35.3	56.8	63.4	63.4	1.4	2.7	11.7	13.8
2.0–2.5	68.4	45.9	28.7	24.6	30.7	52.5	64.9	67.7	1.0	1.6	6.3	8.4
2.5–3.0	71.3	50.1	29.7	26.0	27.8	48.6	66.2	68.5	0.9	1.3	1.1	1.1
3.0 plus	73.0	54.6	35.3	30.6	26.0	43.6	61.8	65.3	1.0	1.8	2.9	4.2

Source: Nihon Nōgyō Nenkan, 1974, p. 157

TABLE 8

Income of Farm Households by Size, 1976
(1000 yen and percentage)

Acreage categories	Income of farm household	Agricultural income	Non-agricultural income	Rate of dependance on agriculture
0.1–0.5 ha	3506.1	284.9	3221.2	8.1
0.5–1.0	3563.7	922.8	2640.9	25.9
1.0–1.5	3718.1	1662.1	2056.0	44.7
1.5–2.0	3847.0	2226.0	1621.0	57.9
2.0–2.5	3929.3	2717.4	1211.9	69.2
2.5–3.0	4524.1	3084.7	1439.4	68.2
3.0 plus	4781.0	3812.7	968.3	79.7

Source: Nihon Nōgyō Nenkan, 1974, p. 296; *Nihon Nōgyō Nenkan,* 1978, p. 314

TABLE 9

Income of Farm Households and Working Class Households, 1965–1976

Year	Family income of farm households (A) (1000 yen)	Family income of working-class households (B) (1000 yen)	Percentage of (A/B)	Per capita income of farm households (C) (1000 yen)	Per capita income of working-class households (D)	Percentage of (C/D)
1965	835	797	104.7	115.5	139.7	82.7
1970	1,576	1,390	114.8	236.8	248.6	95.3
1972	1,779	1,521	117.0	267.9	273.7	97.9
1973	2,150	1,713	125.5	311.5	297.9	102.5
1976	4,279	3,173	134.9	847.5	756.7	112.0

Source: Nihon Nōgyō Nenkan, 1974, p. 294; *Nihon Nōgyō Nenkan,* 1978, p. 312

whalen

constant rate as we move up in size. Conversely, the proportion of type II part-time farms has increased in all categories, especially among small holders; 89 percent of farm families owning less than ½ hectare belong to this category. And the percentage of this type of farm operation decreases constantly as we move into the larger farm categories.

The category I part-time group, which is devoted primarily to agriculture, has undergone a special evolution. In 1960, these holdings were concentrated in the medium-size categories (½ to 1½ hectare). Smaller farms had the smallest representation and larger ones occupied an intermediate position. But from 1960 to 1973, fewer smaller farms were included in the category I group while the proportion of medium-size farms increased until 1965, but decreased afterward. The percentage of farms in the 1½ to 2 hectare category increased from 1960 to 1972, but this trend seems to be reversing itself at the present time since, in 1973, it remained stable at the same level as in 1972. Finally, all categories above 2 hectares have shown a constant increase.

It is thus clear that part-time and full-time farm operations are very closely related to farm size. The link is not absolute, and we will see why below. But what is clear for the moment is that large farms tend to specialize in agriculture, although a growing proportion of even the very largest have non-agricultural sources of income.

The reasons for these trends are complex. One is that farm owners are hesitant to sell their land even when they engage in farming only as a secondary activity. As I mentioned previously, the ideological restraints on selling farm land have been weakened and peasants actually sell more than they did previously. For example, in one year, in 1971–1972, 3.5% of all cultivated land in Nagano, 4.4% in Gumma, 2.9% in Chiba and Saitama, 2.7% in Ibaragi, and 2% in Hiroshima was sold for non-agricultural purposes.[39] But despite this increase in land sales, the general tendency remains for farmers to hold on to the soil. The reasons for this "attachment" to the land are usually very concrete. Many cultivators own land whose price is rising faster than the interest they could obtain on the amount of money they would receive for their land, so, if the price is not high enough or if they do not really need to sell, they prefer to keep their land. Moreover, many farm owners prefer converting their land partly to other uses, such as apartment building, near the cities. Still others, and they are in the majority, want to keep the land as an insurance against hard times. Many farmers still remember the famine of the middle '40s and they want to be protected should the same difficulties arise again. Besides, given the inadequacy of social security programs in Japan, old people generally have a hard time of it particularly when they own nothing, and this encourages peasants to cling to their land as a form of old-age insurance.[40] Finally, prices for land or houses are so high that even should a farm owner sell at a good price, he/she is likely to spend most of it on the purchase of a new house.

Small holders thus prefer to keep their land: some cultivate it, part-time or full-time; others rent it, even if rents are very low; and still others simply allow it to lie fallow. A second reason for the trend toward part-time farming is the income differential that exists between agriculture and wage-labor.[41] The higher wage level in non-agricultural employment lures farmers, especially those with smaller farms, into outside employment. However, two facts must be noted in this regard. In the first place, given the low general wage level obtaining in Japan until 1973, non-farm income was not high enough to entice farmers entirely away from agriculture.[42] Secondly, most non-agricultural jobs for farmers are still low-paid and non-permanent and are found primarily in the construction industry. Farmers thus represent an important source of cheap labor.[43] This is particularly true of seasonal workers (dekasegi), although their working and living conditions have improved somewhat in the last few years.[44]

What is interesting, though, is that type II part-time households tend to engage in more lucrative non-agricultural pursuits, that is they are more often permanently or self-employed.[45] Thus many smaller farms, which constitute the majority of part-time category II operations, have managed to obtain a household and even per capita income higher than that of medium-size farms whose land is too small for full-time farming but too large to depend primarily on non-agricultural sources of income.[46] It is also interesting to note that the average family revenues and, since 1972, even the per capita revenues for farm households, have surpassed those of working-class families.[47] However, this is true only of type II households and has been achieved by putting to work outside of agriculture a larger number of family members whose jobs are not always stable. Furthermore, until recently, the average per capita income for workers in Japan was quite low; it was just a little under $1000 a year in 1972, at the then-prevailing exchange rate. With the later wage increases as well as the increase in the value of the yen, this average has gone up to $4000 in 1978.[48]

The consequences of these trends are complex and far-reaching. In the first place, the refusal of small holders to sell their land, coupled with high land prices resulting from urban development, have retarded farm consolidation. Thus the constitution of a substantial group of prosperous family farms has been thwarted. Secondly, the possibility of keeping the land while working outside of agriculture has led to an increase in the number of farms short of even one full-time worker (man or woman). In 1973, as well as in 1977, 50 percent of farm households were of this type.[49] Another 15 percent had only one woman as a full-time worker. In this case, it is considered "normal" for women to keep on doing household chores, a fact that cannot but diminish their effectiveness as farm workers. Moreover, if we take into account the fact that a sizeable proportion of farms with full-time employees are geared to subsistence farming and worked by old people,[50] the percentage of farm operations run on a less than adequate basis is very high, probably near 75 percent. This leads to the type of farm management that has become the trade mark of Japanese agriculture. Farming is done part-time either in the evenings or on weekends by women and old people.

A third consequence is that part-time cultivators tend to withdraw from cooperative ventures and deal with their problems individually. The net result is the breakdown of village cooooperation and the purchase of agricultural machinery at a pace much faster than is really needed. Each household requires its own machinery in order to complete the farmwork in the short periods when manpower is available.[51]

Fourthly, as has been mentioned earlier, there has been a reduction in the yield per hectare for many types of crops despite an increase in farm productivity. The replacement of labor by industrial goods does not result in as productive a use of the land. Besides, it increases the danger of toxic poisoning.

A fifth consequence is the growing strain on village and family life. Although conditions for seasonal workers have improved, it remains that, with the departure of so many villagers for the cities, the families left behind encounter serious problems and many villages have become deserted, with schools closed, etc.[52] The devastation of the countryside and urban over-population are really two sides of the same coin: the uneven regional development which characterizes all capitalist societies—Japan being, however, in this instance, an extreme case.[53]

Finally, the preservation of so many part-time farms has encouraged rice cultivation even in the period of surplus production, which began in 1966. In the last decade or so, wet rice cultivation has become highly mechanized[54] and heavily dependent on chemicals, thus making it a very suitable activity for small-scale part-time operations. In fact, in 1971, only 9 percent of full-time farms were dependent on rice production.[55] The main reason that producers keep growing rice at high levels remains the State's policy of maintaining high rice prices, as we will see below. Farmers' cooperatives, which operate as business concerns and whose profits rely heavily on the government-controlled rice market also encourage rice production.[56] But necessities of part-time farming, which has as a corollary a high degree of mechanization, and the increase in subsistence farming[57] have strengthened the tendency to support rice cultivation.

The National Context

The State's agricultural policy

An analysis of agricultural programs in Japan since the Land Reform is not easy because the policy-making process has many contradictory aspects which have forced the government to change course at different times or even to devise and implement contradictory measures. One important aspect is the fact that, since the end of World War II, the Japanese government has been structured to accommodate even more closely than before the war the interest of giant business concerns.[58] Since the economic strength of dominant *zaikai* interests is based on the export of manufactured goods, and since it is necessary to compensate for these exports by importing foreign products, the *zaikai* and its related organizations (*Keidanren*, etc.) have, since 1955, applied pressure on the government to liberalize agricultural imports, terminate government control of the rice market and consolidate farms and encourage their mechanization.[59]

A second aspect is the dependence of the ruling Liberal Democratic Party, whose relations to the *zaikai* are well known, on the rural vote.[60] In order to get the agricultural producers to vote conservative, the government has had to make concessions to them, mainly by maintaining rice prices at a high level. This points to another important aspect of agricultural policy: it must take into account the fact that agriculture is at one and the same time an economic sector and the means of livelihood for several million people.

A final aspect is the pressure exerted by foreign countries, especially the United States, to liberalize the Japanese farm market. The policy on rice prices has had the greatest importance for the peasantry since 1945. At first, the rice-price policy was geared to the regulation of foodstuffs needed for the war effort. The first government controls on the rice market were imposed in 1939, but only in 1942 were these controls explicitly applied to prices. The price of rice at that time was calculated on the costs of agricultural means of production and the price of consumer goods needed by the peasants. This policy had a double goal: to insure that agricultural production would be sufficient for the war effort, and that foodstuffs would be priced low enough to depress wages in the industrial sector.[61] This policy lasted until 1946.

In 1946, due to new economic and political circumstances, the method of determining rice prices was modified. Instead of taking as a base the cost of agricultural means of production, the price of rice was tied to a basic price-index for all products purchased by agricultural producers. This policy was devised at a time when these producers were prospering because of the food shortage and was meant to curb the inflation of food prices.[62]

Peasant affluence was short-lived. In 1949, the "Dodge plan," a package of anti-inflationary measures, was implemented, cutting deeply into peasants' gains.[63] Rural income fell rapidly in comparison to urban working-class earnings, and in 1951 peasant unrest forced the government to change its agricultural policy. The price of rice was now calculated on the basis of income parity between the country-side and the city. This new method of calculation was based not only on a comparison of prices between agricultural products and all items deemed essential to farm families, but also on a comparison of consumption levels between peasants and urban workers. The main objective of this new formula was to raise the peasants' standard of living.

However, even with this type of computation, farm household revenues were deteriorating in comparison to working-class incomes. The primary cause was wage increases linked to the heavy labor demand brought about by rapid economic growth. Under rural pressure, the government, with the implementation of the Fundamental Law on Agriculture in 1961, adopted a new way to determine rice prices by adding to the production costs of the least productive farms an amount of money intended to raise the standard of living of farm families. This method of calculating rice prices has in fact led to an increase in rural incomes, but it also resulted in a doubling of the price of rice paid to producers between 1960 and 1968 (see table 8). It is during this period that the price of Japanese rice rose far above international prices. Moreover, so as not to accelerate inflation, and to keep wages at a fairly low level while avoiding a public outcry, the government has not allowed the sales price of rice to rise at the same pace as the purchase price at the farm.

One of the most visible results of the 1961 policy was the rapid accumulation of a vast rice surplus which has been very difficult to sell. In fact, in 1970, this surplus was equivalent to the total national consumption for about one year. Secondly, by encouraging rice production, this policy has gone contrary to the government's effort to diversify agricultural production. Thirdly, the Ministry of Agriculture has had to shoulder increasing deficits.

What prompted this curiously contradictory policy is, first

of all, the necessity for the LDP to please its rural constituency. The party is elected by the rural vote. With the defection of the urban working class, the LDP has had to make some concessions to the peasants to acquire their votes. Furthermore, with a higher standard of living, rice had lost its importance as the main food item in workers' diets, and its price has been able to rise. Before 1955, it was necessary to guard against increases in the price of rice in order to keep wages low; rice was the major food item and low wages were a must for small enterprises.[64] However, it is important to note that, even though it became possible to let rice prices climb after 1960, the rate of increase was not high enough to prevent the spread of part-time farming. In fact, with the rapid progress of mechanization, the new rice policy encouraged this development by allowing small holders who normally would have been evicted from agriculture to maintain a certain level of rice production while working only part-time in agriculture, thus obtaining good secondary incomes. However, given price levels, social needs, the size of farm plots, and agricultural productivity, it was impossible for the majority of rice producers to depend mainly on agriculture for their income. Most of them have had to rely increasingly on wage labor, usually in low-paying industrial jobs. Actually, the rice policy has had to accommodate the need of many industrial sectors for a steady supply of low-paid rural labor, and the price of rice has had to satisfy rural voters while insuring a constant outflow of cheap labor to factories, shops and construction sites.[65]

There is no doubt that the maintenance of this labor force on the land has allowed for lower real wages. On the one hand, most part-time farmers are considered seasonal or temporary workers. They thus earn much less than the permanent workforce even though they work at least as much. Furthermore since they derive an income from agriculture and can live partly off of their own farms, they're prepared to accept lower wages. On the other hand, their continuing presence on the land allows their employers and the government to duck social security measures since part-time farmers are expected to live solely or mainly off the land when they are unemployed. Besides, given the fact they consider themselves peasants rather than workers even though the majority earn most of their income from wage labor, part-time farmers are often opposed to working-class organizations and labor movement activities.[66]

The government's farm policy is not limited to the price of rice. Since 1956, when the first hints of trouble in agriculture appeared, the government has tried to encourage the specialization of farms in one crop and, on a national level, the diversification of farm production.[67] The Fundamental Law of 1961 was a major plank in the government's new farm policy. Its main goal was to create through specialization and diversification independent farms, large enough to survive without off-farm wage employment and without government subsidies.[68] However, this goal was not achieved, as the increase in part-time farms between 1961 and 1977 amply demonstrates.

All through the '60s, the government attempted in various ways to speed up farm consolidation, mechanization and diversification—in short, the establishment of viable family farms. However, these efforts went contrary to the necessity, for electoral reasons, to maintain the majority of peasant families on the land. Furthermore, since diversification had to be backed up by high tariff barriers, this policy drew fire from the *zaikai* whose interests required a more open internal market for agricultural imports.[69] Criticism also came from the U.S. government which was pushing for trade liberalization. Nevertheless, the Japanese government succeeded temporarily in its efforts to protect local producers in key sectors of livestock, dairy, fruit and vegetable production. But this was done at the expense of cereal production (except rice), raw materials for fodder, and soybeans.

The entire farm program had to be changed between 1968 and 1971. In the first place, pressures from the *zaikai* and the urban working class forced the government to halt rice-price inflation for three years beginning in 1968. In fact, the new policy was only carried out for two years (1969 and 1970), for in 1971, the price of rice was hiked 3 percent, then 6.1 percent in 1972, 32.2 percent in 1974, 14.4 percent in 1975, 10.2 percent in 1976, and 4 percent in 1977. Moreover, in order to reduce rice surpluses, the government initiated its policy of subsidies for the curtailed rice production.[70] These subsidies were supposed to encourage diversification, but, in fact, as we saw, they very often resulted in the non-utilization of agricultural land. The net result, however, was to lessen the rice surplus to about 20 percent of annual consumption in 1977.

The "Nixon shock" of 1971 was the main blow to the government's diversification program. As a result of U.S. pressures, the Japanese government had to lower or abolish trade barriers on agricultural products. This led to difficulties for many agricultural producers. To compensate, the government decided to raise the price of rice, which encouraged many producers to revert to rice production. However, international pressures were not limited to the Nixon shock alone. The year 1972 saw the disappearance of the world's agricultural surpluses which had been maintained for the previous 25 years, and world food production became insufficient. Japan, whose degree of self-sufficiency in food[71] had plummeted from about 80 percent in 1960 to less than 50 percent in 1973,[72] thus faced severe problems in obtaining badly needed farm goods on the international market. The most acute problem centered on soybeans. In 1971, Japan imported 96 percent of its soybeans, 97 percent of which came from the U.S. In 1972, the U.S., for various reasons, put an embargo on soybean exports to Japan. Because of such difficulties in the international market, many groups in Japan have proposed a return to food self-sufficiency partly for security reasons. But still, in 1975, Japan depended for 97 percent on imports of soybeans, 92 percent of which came from the United States.[73]

Confronted with these many-sided problems, the government has remained indecisive since 1971. There have been tentative plans to reduce the number of farm families and industrialize the countryside, etc.[74] But most of these have been as severely criticized by the representatives of Japanese capital as by peasants and workers. However, the vacillation of the government has not prevented the uncontrolled implantation of industries in the countryside. The city continues to encroach on rural areas, and pollution is increasingly hazardous to farm villages.[75] Rural unrest has been increasing and the rural vote no longer goes automatically to the LDP. In these circumstances, it is possible that the LDP will sacrifice its rural constituency to the interest of the *zaikai*. But what would become then of this stabilizing force that is the peasantry?[76]

Big Business and Agriculture

A good share of the Japanese farm market is controlled by giant monopolies. And if we include among these the farmers'

cooperatives which are very often more concerned with capitalistic pursuits than with family farmers, monopoly capital's control of the farm market is almost complete. The case of the milk industry, which is controlled by three companies, is probably the clearest case in point.[77] All sectors of the market for agricultural means of production are also dominated by giant companies (machinery, fertilizers, feeds, herbicides, insecticides, etc.). The cooperatives are in this instance often reduced to the role of middle men; one exception is Zenkôren, associated with the co-operative movement, which is a producer of concentrated feeds, but on a much smaller scale than either Nihon Haigo Shiryô (Mitsui group) or Nihon Nôsan.[78] Furthermore, most agricultural imports are controlled by giant trading companies (Mitsui Bussan, Mitsubishi Shôji, etc.). These companies are also attempting to take over various supermarket chains.[79]

Vertical integration, a characteristic feature of agriculture in all advanced capitalist countries, has progressed very rapidly in Japan in the last decade. Vertical integration actually reduces the producer to the status of a wage laborer who works at home and is paid on a piecemeal basis. It has been gaining ground chiefly in livestock and dairy production (pigs, chickens, eggs, milk), but also in fruit and vegetable production. Even some rice producers have entered into this type of arrangement with *sake* brewers and candy manufacturers.[80]

However, vertical integration is only one step in the control of agriculture by monopoly capitalism. Since 1970, giant food combines (*Kombinats*) have been set up, especially by trading companies such as Mitsubishi Shôji, Mitsui Bussan, Itoh and Marubeni. These *Kombinats* are sometimes limited to processing only foodstuffs or feeds using local or imported products. But the trading companies have also taken over a good share of the actual production of chickens, eggs, and pigs. The four trading companies mentioned above controlled up to 71.4 percent of the total production of chicken in 1970.[81] These companies have organized production on an industrial scale, making use of automated plants with a capacity of several million chickens a year—a far cry from small-scale farming. It must be noted that most of these plants have been established in rural areas and employ local part-time farmers. They require very little land and are thus exceptions among smaller farms. They engage in agricultural production on a fulltime basis.

Finally, these trading companies have established plantation-type ventures in countries such as Indonesia and the Philippines where they produce cheap agricultural products which are then shipped to Japan for processing.[82] The effects of the increasing control of monopoly capital over agricultural production have been deeply felt by small-scale family farms. In the first place, many small cultivators have had to become vertically integrated to giant companies. Secondly, many others have decreased farm production to become workers in giant food factories. Thirdly, direct monopoly control over certain types of production, either in Japan or abroad, has weakened the position of small holders, thus forcing more family members to seek wage-employment. Fourthly, as mentioned above, this has led to a decrease in self-sufficiency in food production. Finally, the use of chemical feeds for animals in giant plants has increased the chances of poisoning consumers.

Conclusion

Since 1950, the Japanese peasantry has had to adjust to the

encroachment of monopoly capitalism on the countryside.[83] This has not been a smooth process as many peasant protest movements have clearly shown.[84] But in the long run, the peasants have obviously not had the strength to resist these pressures. Indeed, the cooperatives, which represent the strongest farmers' organization to appear in the postwar period, have been one of the agents of capitalist extension in the countryside, mainly through the sale of various means of agricultural production.

In search of profit,[85] giant companies have gained an increasingly tighter control over the entire agricultural scene: production, markets, imports, etc. Their interest is to obtain cheap agricultural products for processing and to tear various sectors of production away from small-scale farmers. They also require labor. A good portion of the cheap, young, docile and partially qualified labor force which is needed by the giant companies comes from the countryside. These are farmers' sons and daughters who, since early Meiji and up until now, have left the farm permanently to become workers.[86] But companies also need "coolie" labor, and a good portion of this is furnished by part-time farmers.

In fact, the development of postwar capitalism in Japan has had a curious impact on the rural areas. One consequence, "normal" in capitalist societies, has been the expropriation of more than 1 million farms between 1960 and 1977. Another has been the maintenance of a majority of farm owners on the land. This, as we saw, results from the dependence of the conservative parties, who represent business interests, on the rural vote. The continuing presence of so many smallholders on the land is a feature unique to Japan. It is found in no other capitalist society.

Another consequence of capitalist encroachment on the countryside has been the proletarianization of many farmers, even though these have managed to keep their land. Part-time "farm owners" who do very little farming, sometimes only for home consumption and always on a small-scale, can hardly be considered "peasants" any longer. They are really workers. To be sure, keeping the land has a certain importance. The land can be sold or used as a hedge against hard times. But for most cultivators, as long as they work for wages, it is their job which most effects and defines their life; agriculture is only a secondary occupation, a source of subsidiary income. The land actually serves to devaluate the labor force. Because part of their subsistence comes from their own farms, these cultivators accept low wages. Moreover, below a certain size (2½ hectares in 1972; see Table 8) the more land a farm household has, the lower its *per capita* income. Land is thus, paradoxically, a strain on income. Farm families with smaller holdings enjoy higher incomes than larger farms, but only where their members work outside agriculture.

With agricultural income so low (despite high prices), the trends toward the proletarianization of farmers and a decrease in agricultural output are bound to continue. The first trend is apparent in the inclusion of farms with relatively more land into the lower stratum of the "peasantry." In fact the majority of peasants owning less than 2 hectares of land are increasingly caught up in the transition to part-time farming. Not all are really workers; many still depend heavily on agriculture for a living and see farming as their primary occupation. But even here the trend toward part-time agriculture is in evidence and in fact now appears irreversible.

We arrive at the paradoxical conclusion that today more than half of all Japanese "peasants" are in reality workers. The rest can be classified into four categories: those who are vertically integrated to big companies and who are therefore in the process of becoming workers; the truly independent family farmers who live exclusively or primarily from their own production but still depend entirely on farm labor; the prosperous specialized farmers who employ a quasi-permanent labor force; and finally, capitalist agricultural entrepreneurs. The last have nothing to do with the peasantry as they are part of monopoly capital entering agriculture from the outside. Prosperous farmers, whose numbers probably do not exceed half a million, are those who have established themselves in specialized areas of production and who have gained control of most specialized cooperatives.[87] These also cannot be classified as peasants. As for the independent family farms, their number has decreased markedly with the inclusion of medium size farms in the part-time II category, and the tendency seems to be for a greater number of formerly independent farms to go this same route.

If the trends described above continue, and there is no indication that they will not, it is to be expected (1) that up to 90 percent of Japanese "farmers" will become workers owning a small plot of land; (2) that agricultural production will continue to decrease; (3) that, consequently, agricultural imports will increase; and finally (4) that big business will consolidate its grip on the entire food production process. What will be left of Japanese agriculture then?

Notes

1. I wish to thank Robert Ricketts who, together with Daniel Desmarais and Jean-Marc Fontan, is currently working with me on a research project, financed by the Canada Council, on Japanese agriculture in the Postwar period, and who read an earlier draft of this paper. His comments on the content as well as the style were very valuable I also want to thank Robert J. Smith for his suggestions on many aspects of the paper. Finally, Akio Yasue was very helpful in the choice of the Japanese literature relevant to the subject treated here.

2. See, among others, Ronald P. Dore, *Land Reform in Japan*, (Berkeley: University of California Press, 1959), pp. 115 ff; and Ronald P. Dore and Tsutomu Ouchi, "Rural Origins of Japanese Fascism," in James W. Morley (ed.), *Dilemmas of Growth in Prewar Japan* (Princeton University Press, 1971), pp. 181-209.

3. See Al McCoy, Land Reform as Counter-Revolution, *Bulletin of Concerned Asian Scholars*, vol. 3, no. 1, 1971, pp. 451-465; K. Bieda, The Structure and Operation of the Japanese Economy (Sydney: John Wiley and Sons, 1970), p. 245; Takekazu Ogura (ed.), *Agricultural Development in Modern Japan* (Tokyo: Fuji Pub., 1967), p. 69; Kiyoshi Oshima, *Nihon Keizai to Nōgyō Mondai* (Tokyo: Nōsangyoson Bunka Kyōkai, 1972), p. 215; and Makoto Hoshi, *Sengo Nihon Shihon Shugi to Nōgyō Kiki No Kōzō* (Tokyo: Ochanomizu Shobō, 1975), p. 60.

4. See Al McCoy, op. cit., p. 18; and Jon Halliday, *A Political History of Japanese Capitalism* (New York: Pantheon Books, 1975), pp. 191 ff.

5. I use the term peasant to refer not only to so-called "peasant societies" but to all types of small-holding family farming undertaken in a class society. The majority of Japanese farmers, up to the present, fit such a definition. The term has, of course, no derogatory meaning. In fact, it is intended to render the Japanese word *hyakusho*.

6. See also Yujiro Hayami, *A Century of Agricultural Growth in Japan* (Tokyo: Tokyo University Press, 1975), p. 9; Tadashi Fukutake, *Japanese Rural Society* (London: Oxford University Press, 1967), p. 21; and Dore, op. cit., p. 1.

7. Hubert Brochier, *Le miracle économique japonais* (Paris: Clamann-Levy, 1965).

8. H. Fukui, "The Japanese Farmers and Politics," in Isaiah Frank (ed.), *The Japanese Economy in International Perspective* (Baltimore: Johns Hopkins University Press, 1975, pp. 134-167) p. 136; *Nihon Nōgyō Nenkan* (Tokyo: Ie no hikari, 1978), pp. 155, 159.

9. See also Seiichi Tōhata, *Nihon Nōgyō No Henkaku Katei* (Tokyo: Iwanami Shoten, 1968), p. 9.

10. See Koji Taira, *Economic-Development and the Labor Market in Japan* (New York: Columbia University Press, 1970); Ryōshin Minami, "The Supply of Farm Labor and the 'Turning Point' in the Japanese Economy," in Kazushi Ohkawa, Bruce F. Johnston, and Hiromitsu Kaneda (eds.), *Agriculture and Economic Growth: Japan's Experience* (Princeton, N.J.: Princeton University Press, 1973), pp. 270-299; Tsutomu Ouchi, Natsuki Kanazawa and Tadashi Tukutake (eds.), *Nihon no Nōgyō* (Tokyo: Daigaku Shuppankai, 1970), chap. 1; and Mataji Umemura, "Agriculture and Labor Supply in the Meiji Era," in Ohkawa et al. (eds.), op. cit., pp. 175-197.

11. "Agricultural Households Drop Below 5 Million Level," in *Oriental Economist*, vol. 43, no. 781, Nov. 1975, p. 25.

12. See, in particular, Kahoku Shimposha Henshūkyoku, *Mura no Nihonjin* (Tokyo: Keisō Shobō, 1975), chap. 2.

13. All through the late Edo, Meiji, Taishō and early Showā periods, some peasants were forced to part with their land, very often in order to repay debts. This kind of land loss was seen as shameful, but it was inevitable. Now, many farmers sell their land for cash without a thought for the ancestors (Kahoku Shimposha Henshūkyoku, op. cit., pp. 43 ff.).

14. Akira Ebato, "Kyodai Toshi Kinkō Nōson no Henshitsu," in Daijirō Nishikawa, Yuichiro Noguchi, and Yoshio Okuda (eds.), *Nihon Rettō: Sono Genjitsu*, vol. 3, *Nōsangyoson*, (Tokyo: Keiso Shobo, 1972, pp. 261-274), p. 264.

15. Kahoku Shimposha Henshūkyoku, op. cit., chap. 2; Takumi Usui, "Kaso to Kyoka Rison," in Daijirō Nishikawa et al. (eds.), op. cit., p. 319.

16. This increase in current prices does not mean an equivalent rise in production in tonnage; a comparatively high price for agricultural products would mean an artificially high share for agriculture in the GNP.

17. Augustin Berque, "Une agriculture et une paysannerie sacrifiées aux imperatifs de la haute croissance," in *Le monde diplomatique*, Dec. 1975, p. 24; *Nihon Nōgyō Nenkan*, 1978, p. 168.

18. Augustin Berque, op. cit., p. 24; same author, "Les campagnes japonaises et l'emprise urbaine," in *Etudes Rurales*, no. 49-50, 1973, pp. 339 ff.' and OCDE, *La politique agricole du Japon* (Paris: OCDE, 1975), pp. 66 ff.

19. Augustin Berque, *Le Japon: Gestion de l'espace et changement social* (Paris: Flammarion, 1976), p. 242.

20. Ibid., p. 237; Tsutomu Umekawa, "1970 Nendai no Nihon no Nōgyō Mondai," in *Keizaigaku Zasshi*, vol. 79, no. 4, 1979, p. 1.

21. Yujirō Hayami, op. cit., pp. 28 ff. and 88 ff.

22. Ogura (ed.), op. cit., p. 75.

23. Tsutomu Ouchi, "Nihon No Nōgyō Wa Yomigaeru Ka," in *Chūō Kōron*, Sept. 1973, p. 72.

24. Hayami, op. cit., p. 30.

25. *Nihon Nōgyō Nenkan*, (Tokyo: Ie No Hikari Kyōkai, 1978), p. 119.

26. See Chūhei Kawamoto, "Dekasegi No Mura," in Nishikawa et al. (eds.), (pp. 290-304), p. 295.

27. Berque, *Le Japon . . . ,* p. 242.

28. Yoshirō Hoshino (ed.), *Kaitai Suru Nihon Rettō* (Tokyo: Gakuyō Shobō, 1975), chap. 2.

29. Shōsui Mtsushima, "Kakudai Suru Nōyakuka," in Daijirō Nishikawa et al. (eds.), op. cit., p. 390.

30. Ibid., p. 390.

31. Daijirō Nishikawa, "Ketsuron ni Kaete," in Daijirō Nishikawa et al. (eds.), op. cit., p. 476; Tsutomu Ouchi et al. (eds.), op. cit., p. 105.

32. Daijirō Nishikawa, op. cit., p. 476.

33. Ogura (ed.), op. cit., pp. 66-67.

34. OCDE, op. cit., p. 16; Tsutomu Umekawa, op. cit., p. 10.

35. Yoshiki Hanamura, "Nōsanbutsu Shijō to Kōrudochēn," in Nishikawa et al. (eds.), op. cit., p. 73; Hiromitsu Kaneda, "Long-Term Changes in Food Consumption Patterns in Japan," in Ohkawa et al. (eds.), op. cit., pp. 398-431; and Tsuneyoshi Ukita, "Hembō Suru Kinkō Sosai Seisan," in Nishikawa et al. (eds.), op. cit., p. 94.

36. Tsutomu Ouchi, *Nihon Ni Okeru Nōminsō No Bunkai* (Tokyo: Tokyo Daigaku Shuppankai, 1969, pp. 252 ff.

37. Ibid., pp. 243 ff.; and Oshima, op. cit., p. 219.

38. Tadashi Fukutake, *Japanese Society Today* (Tokyo: Tokyo University Press, 1974), p. 52; Hayami, op. cit., p. 77; *Nihon Nōgyō Nenkan*, 1978, p. 311.

39. *Nihon Nōgyō Nenkan*, 1974, j p. 116; see also Kahoku Shimposha, op. cit., 53 ff.

40. See Kahoku u . . . , op. cit., pp. 60 ff.; Berque, *Le Japon . . . ,* p. 241; Bieda, op. cit., pp. 253-54; Ouchi (eds.), op. cit., p. 41; and Ukita,

op. cit., p. 99.

41. Hayami, op. cit., p. 77; Ouchi et al. (eds.), op. cit., pp. 25-26; Taira, op. cit.; and Koji Taira, "Growth, Trends and Swings in Japanese Agriculture and Industry," in *Economic Development and Culture Change*, vol. 24, no. 2, Jan. 1976, pp. 423-36.

42. Ouchi et al. (eds.), op. cit., p. 52.

43. Berque, "Les campagnes japonaises . . . ," pp. 336 ff.; Berque, *Le Japon . . . ,* pp. 245 ff.; Fukui, op. cit., p. 164; Nishikawa, op. cit., p. 475; Ouchi et al. (eds.), op. cit., p. 47; Tōji Takase, "Mura No Senkyo," in Nishikawa et al. (eds.), op. cit., p. 410; and Tōhata, op. cit., p. 40.

44. Reiji Hayashi, "Ryōdōka No Naka No Kitakami Sanchi," in Nishikawa et al. (eds.), pp. 249 ff.; Kahoku . . . , op. cit., chap. 1; Chūhei Kawamoto, "Dekasegi No Mura," in Nishikawa et al. (eds.), op. cit., pp. 290-304; Yoshiro Kunimoto, "Rural Communities in Northeastern Japan," in *Japan Quarterly*, vol. 17, no. 4, Oct.-Dec. 1970, pp. 443-450; Brett Nee, "Japan's Internal Colony," in *Bulletin of Concerned Asian Scholars*, vol. 6, no. 3, Sept.-Oct. 1974, pp. 12-18; and Shingo Takasugi, "Shudatsu Ni Ko Suru Dekasegi Nōmin," in *Asahi Jānaru*, 22 Feb. 1974, pp. 36-40.

45. *Nihon Nōgyō Nenkan*, 1974, p. 158; Ibid., 1978, p. 157.

46. See Hoshi, op. cit., pp. 188 ff.; *Nihon Nogyo Nenkan*, 1974, p. 296; Oshima, op. cit., p. 217; and Ouchi et al. (eds.)., op. cit., pp. 28 ff.; See also Table 8.

47. *Nihon Nōgyō Nenkan*, 1974, p. 294; See Table 9.

48. See Ministry of Finance, *Main Economic Indicators of Japan* (Tokyo: Sept. 1978, p. 1; and Bureau of Statistics, Office of the Prime Minister, Japan Statistical Yearbook, 1977 (Tokyo: pp. 394 ff.; See also Tsutomu Umekawa, op. cit., p. 3.

49. Fukui, op. cit., p. 137; *Nihon Nōgyō Nenkan*, 1974, p. 125; *Nihon Nōgyō Nenkan*, 1978, p. 157.

50. Berque, "Les campagnes . . . ," p. 344.

51. Kahoku . . . , op. cit., chap. 1.

52. See, in particular, Berque, "Les campagnes . . . ," pp. 333 ff.; Nobuo Danno, "The Changing Face of Agriculture," in *Japan Quarterly*, vol. 19, no. 3, July-Sept. 1972, pp. 292-300; Anonymous, "Deserted Villages, Crammed Towns," in *Japan Quarterly*, vol. 19, no. 1, Jan.-March 1972, pp. 3-6; Kawamoto, op. cit.; Kunimoto, op. cit.; Yoshiro Kunimoto, "Deserted Mountain Villages in Western Japan" in *Japan Quarterly*, vol. 20, no. 1, Jan.-March 1973, pp. 87-96; and Usui, op. cit.

53. Berque, *Le Japon . . . ,*; Kazuyuki Hibino, "Tokyo: The Over-crowded Metropolis," in *Japan Quarterly*, vol. 20, no. 2; April-June 1973, pp. 203-211; Ken'Ichi Miyamoto, *Chiiki Kaihatsu Wa Kore De Yoi Ka* (Tokyo: Iwanami Shinsho, 1973); Nishikawa et al. (eds.), op. cit., p. 180 ff.

54. Motosuke Kaihara, *The Changing Structure of Agriculture in Japan* (Madison: Land Tenure Center, University of Wisconsin, Special Paper, 1976); and Naomi Saeki, "Nōmin," in Shōkichi Endō (ed.), *Jitsuryoku Shūdan No Shisō to Kōdō* (Tokyo: Gakuyō Shobō, 1975), pp. 137-186.

55. *Nihon Nōgyō Nenkan*, 1974, p. 125.

56. See Fukui, op. cit., pp. 154 ff.; Kōichi Nishimoto, "Nōkyō: Pressure from the Coops," in *Japan Interpreter*, vol. 7, no. 3-4, Summ.-Aut. 1972, pp. 321-331; Oshima, op. cit., chap. 2; Ouchi et al. (eds.), op. cit., chap. 4. For other financial aspects of cooperatives, see Yōtarō Hamada, "Kyodai Soshiki Nōkyō," in Nishikawa et al. (eds.), op. cit., pp. 422-454; and Kōichi Kobayashi, "Orenji beruto," in ibid., pp. 173 ff.

57. Non-commercial farms, which accounted for 14.5 percent of all farms in 1970, increased to 18.2 percent in 1973 and to 23 percent in 1977. These are prevalent mainly among smallholders. In fact, non-commercial farms account for 43 percent of the nearly 2 millions farms owning less than ½ hectare. See *Nihon Nōgyō Nenkan*, 1974, pp. 124-125; *Statistical Yearbook of Ministry of Agriculture and Forestry*, 1976-77, p. 12.

58. See H. Fukui, *Party in Power: The Japanese Liberal Democrats and Policy-Making* (Berkeley: University of California Press, 1970); Gabriel and Joyce Kolko, *The Limits of Power* (New York: Harper and Row, 1972); and Chitoshi Yanaga, *Big Business in Japanese Politics* (New Haven, Conn.: Yale University Press, 1968).

59. See Ouchi, "Nihon No Nōgyō . . ."

60. Fukui, *Party in Power . . .*; and Nathaniel Thayer, *How the Conservatives Rule Japan* (Princeton, N.J.: Princeton University Press, 1969).

61. See Hayami, op. cit., p. 75; same author, "Rice Policy in Japan's Economic Development," in *American Journal of Agricultural Economics*, vol. 54, no. 1, Feb. 1972, p. 21; and Ogura (ed.), op. cit., pp. 198-201.

62. See Ogura (ed.), op. cit., p. 208.

63. Ibid., pp. 61-67 and 81; and Kolko and Kolko, op. cit., pp. 521 ff.

64. Hayami, "Rice Policy . . . ," p. 20.

65. Ouchi, "Nihon no Nōgyō wa Yomigaeru ka," p. 72.

66. Ouchi et al. (eds.), op. cit., p. 120.

67. Hayami, *A Century* . . . , p. 72.

68. Ibid., p. 73; Bieda, op. cit. p. 250; Fukutake, *Japanese Society Today*, p. 50; and Ogura (ed.), op. cit., pp. 286 ff.

69. Jirō Iinuma, "The Curious Crisis in Japanese Agriculture," in *Japan Quarterly*, vol. 21, no. 4, Oct.-Dec. 1974, pp. 341-348; and Ouchi, "Nihon no Nōgyō . . .

70. OCDE, op. cit., pp. 67 ff.

71. The figures given here are calculated on the basis of calorie equivalence, i.e. they include not only foodstuffs *per se* but animal feeds as well. In terms of foodstuffs only, the rate of self-sufficiency was 72 percent in 1971. See *Nihon Nōgyō Nenkan*, 1974, p. 60.

72. Ibid., p. 60; Ouchi et al. (eds.), op. cit., chap. 5; Ouchi, "Nihon no Nogyō . . . ," p. 74.

73. Hayami, *A Century* . . . , p. 79; Umekawa, op. cit., pp. 5-6.

74. Miyamoto, op. cit., chap. 1, 2 and 3; Yoshiro Hoshino, "Remodeling the Archipelago," in *Japan Quarterly*, vol. 20, no. 1, Jan.-March 1973, pp. 39-45; Kakuei Tanaka, *Le pari japonais*, (Paris: Presses de la Cité, 1974).

75. See Berque, *Le Japon* . . .; Usui, op. cit., pp. 317 ff.; Michihiro Kōno, "Kōba Shinshutsu to setonaikai no Gyomin," in ibid., pp. 353-369; Yutaka Nishibe, "Kakure Minamatabyo," in ibid., pp. 370-387; and Akira Nishimura, "Tokyo No Rittō: Hachijōjima," in ibid., pp. 32-328.

76. Fukui, "The Japanese Farmers . . ."; and George O. Totten, "La crise agricole dans la politique japonaise," in *Asia Quarterly*, no. 2, 1975, pp. 175-187.

77. Berque, *Le Japon* . . . , p. 241.

78. Terutoshi Ishihara, "Rakunō to Nyūgyūshihon," in Nishikawa et al. (eds.), op. cit., p. 159.

79. Hanamura, op. cit., pp. 78 ff.

80. Berque, "Les campagnes japonaises . . . ," p. 348.

81. Ibid., p. 348; Hanamura, op. cit., pp. 79 ff.; and Masuo Ando, "Yōkei Kōjō," in Nishikawa et al. (eds.), op. cit., pp. 120-133.

82. Ouchi, "Nihon No Nōgyō . . . ," p. 78.

83. The penetration of a market economy actually dates back to the feudal period. But the encroachment of monopoly capitalism began sometime in the Meiji period. However, its expansion since the end of World War II has been much more rapid because of the elimination of landlordism and because of the high rate of economic growth which has benefitted chiefly the big companies. See Ouchi, *Nihon ni okeru* . . . . chap. 5.

84. Oshima, op. cit., chap. 10.

85. Christian Sautter in his book *Japon: le prix de la puissance* (Paris: Seuil, 1973, pp. 141 ff.) has shown that, contrary to a widespread conception, profit *is* the prime motive of Japanese capitalists; indeed it would be surprising were it otherwise. Sautter has also shown that, not only do Japanese capitalists seek profits like any others, but they also enjoy a higher rate of profit and of capital accumulation than capitalists in other countries. This high rate of accumulation is, to some, the utmost in progress and growth. What is certain, however, is that it represents the utmost in unequal income distribution. See Martin Schnitzer, *Income Distribution: A Comparative Study* (New York: Preager, 1974).

86. Robert E. Cole, *Japanese Blue-Collar* (Berkeley: University of California Press, 1971); and Joe Moore, "The Japanese Worker," in *Bulletin of Concerned Asian Scholars*, vol. 6, no. 3, Sept.-Oct. 1974, pp. 35-47.

87. Isao Kajii, "Piggu Saikuru to Yōton," in Nishikawa et al. (eds.), op. cit., pp. 134-147; Kobayashi, op. cit.; Ichirō Satō, "Sakyū Nōgyō ni Ikiru," in Nishikawa et al. (eds.), op. cit., pp. 211-224; and Ukita, op. cit.

The Japanese Working Class

by Rob Steven

The Japanese working class has the reputation, largely in the Western bourgeois press, of being notoriously hard-working, loyal to its employers, and lacking in class consciousness. Western managers envy their Japanese counterparts for the "harmony and cooperation" that is supposed to characterize industrial relations in Japan, but few of them have any idea why this supposed harmony exists. Even the Japanese bourgeoisie tends to attribute it to cultural values which are unique to Japan and which cannot be exported.

However, a truer explanation lies in the role that traditionally important attributes of persons—rankings by sex, age and education—play in channeling them into classes and into fractions within the working class. Because members of the bourgeoisie, the middle class, and the labor aristocracy are overwhelmingly middle-aged men from prestigious educational institutions, differences *between* classes take on the same form as differences *within* the working class. The power of the ruling class and the above-average conditions of the labor aristocracy seem to have the same origin: the sex, age, and education of the individuals themselves rather than the positions they occupy in the process of production. Differences between classes therefore become less visible, and Japan looks more like a stratified society than a class society.

The strong loyalty Japanese workers tend to show to their employers, as well as their overwhelming sense of rank, are direct results of the process by which people are channeled into classes. Because the same types of agents go into the same types of positions, the real determinants of class power lie concealed behind the visible attributes of persons. The dominance of the ideology of the traditional family and of one's rank in it therefore results from the fact that the personal attributes which accord rank in the traditional family are also the ones which grant access to ruling class positions. In more theoretical terms, it is only because traditional family relations function as production relations that the ideology of the traditional family can become dominant.[1] In other words, the dominance of "rank consciousness" is ensured by the ruling class positions occupied by persons of traditionally high rank. However, because such persons also occupy the upper fractions of the working class, differences between workers and managers come to look just like differences among workers and therefore lose their salience. To show why this is no more than the form assumed by class society in Japan requires examination of the real determinants of fractional divisions within the working class and of the reasons why agents are channeled into them according to age, sex, and education. I do so in some detail for each of the three main fractions: the labor aristocracy, the mass worker, and the reserve army.

Theory of the Structure and Composition of the Working Class

From the outset it must be emphasized that all three fractions of the working class are in the same fundamental relationship to the capitalist class as a whole. Together they function to produce the social surplus and promote the circulation of the total social capital under the direct domination of the capitalist class. The distinctions between them are not based on different degrees of proximity to the ruling class or on different levels of income. Rather, their different levels of income result from the different roles *capital in general* requires the working class as a whole to play in order to assist the expanded reproduction of the capitalist relation. The fundamental law of capital accumulation—that within industries, between industries, and in the economy as a whole, development is uneven and is frequently interrupted by crises and dislocations—separates workers into three groups corresponding to the three main (contradictory) things the working class must be in order to prevent uneven development from destroying the capitalist relation. This relation could not survive uneven accumulation if exactly the same agents (persons) were required to fulfill all three functions simultaneously.

To identify these functions, I examine the three main effects on the working class of capital accumulation. The first is the development of the collective worker through the concentration and centralization of capital in large corporations, that is, the growth of monopolies through the reinvestment of profits and through mergers and takeovers. Since the division of labor is greatest in large enterprises, the function of producing the whole commodity belongs to the worker as a whole, or to the collective worker. Once this happens, the contradiction between social production (the fact of a cooperative labor process) and private appropriation of the product becomes sharper and can threaten the capitalist relation. Moreover, since workers are brought together in large numbers in giant corporations, they can be more threatening if they organize. To minimize the growing threat of revolutionary working class action, capital must at the very least stabilize their standard of living to ensure their loyalty to capital.

If the first thing the working class must be is willing to accept a relationship whose contradictions are becoming sharper, the second results from the effects of uneven accumulation *within* industries. Since this process is one of constant attempts by capitalists in each industry, either to gain a productivity advantage over rivals (by introducing more efficient techniques) or to catch up to a productivity disadvantage, more concentrated and centralized capitals will continually coexist with smaller less productive capitals. I showed in a previous article how the survival of the latter depends on their paying lower wages than the former.[2] From the point of view of capital in general, this wage difference is essential, since the more threatening workers in monopoly firms are more likely to remain loyal if they have some material basis for seeing themselves as privileged. Uneven accumulation within industries, therefore, both creates some of the conditions for working class loyalty, by giving the most advanced workers the greatest material stake in capitalism, and it requires sizeable wage differentials among the working class as a whole, that is, a mass of low-paid workers in the large number of non-monopoly firms that necessarily exist side by side with the development of monopolies.

Finally, the working class must adapt to uneven accumulation of capital in general, that is, the periodic depressions in which the tendency for the rate of profit to fall manifests itself. At various times masses of workers must become unemployed for considerable periods, but they must remain available for re-employment when accumulation begins to pick up again. Marx referred to this as a reserve army role, and we discuss it in more detail when we examine the Japanese reserve army.

Clearly, it is impossible for the same persons to be all of these three things at the same time, and in Japan, as in other capitalist countries, the working class has been divided into three corresponding fractions. They are products of the dynamic laws of development of the fundamental relationship between the capitalist class and the working class. However, they can only be seen as traditional or natural divisions of rank to the extent that persons move into them according to the attributes which confer rank in the traditional family. Divisions within the working class appear to be no less natural than divisions between classes, because what are considered natural divisions

within the traditional family—sex and age—allocate family members into different classes as well as into different fractions of the working class. To what extent and why has this happened?

The Structure and Composition of the Japanese Working Class

(a) The Labor Aristocracy

Rapid accumulation and the consolidation of Japanese monopoly capital around the time of the First World War was the most important development which produced a labor aristocracy in Japan and gave it its characteristic form. Productive forces were unleashed to an unprecedented extent and led to two forms of class struggle which stood in the way of further accumulation. The first was the opportunity seized by the limited supply of workers with the skills and experience required to operate the new technologies to bid up wages by frequently changing jobs. In some cases, capital had to face an annual rate of labor turnover of 100 percent and even used gangsters either to compel workers to return or to kidnap workers from rivals. Although the situation had been serious well before the war, it became intolerable afterwards. Carefully worked out agreements by employers to prevent "piracy" of one another's workers were not adhered to, and some permanent solution was desperately sought after. The second form of class struggle which intensified after the war was an escalation of strikes by the now unionized collective worker, strikes which reached tidal proportions in 1919.

It was as a result of the intensification of these forms of class struggle that capital consciously introduced an employment system to deal with the labor aristocracy. Rather than discuss the various components of this system historically, I only outline its central present-day features, many of which were consolidated during the post-World War II period of rapid accumulation.[3] The problem it was designed to solve was how to retain a stable supply of trained workers who would not resist accumulation in the monopoly sector. Workers in this sector had to be made loyal to capital and prevented from withdrawing their labor power through strike action or through switching employers. The solution to the problem was gradually worked out in class struggles after many years of trial and error. The reason for the present system's relative success, at least during boom periods, lies in how it combines a material basis for workers' loyalty with elements of the traditional superstructure which demand the loyalty of inferiors to superiors.

The major material components of the system are various methods of deferring wage payments for workers who are loyal to capital. The most effective of these methods is the system of payment by length of service, since few workers will risk the promise of a secure living wage after some fifteen years of service by engaging in industrial action that might result in a loss of their jobs and seniority. To make these deferred wages ideologically acceptable, capital confines new recruits to school-leavers and university graduates, so that payment for length of service takes the form of payment by age. The capitalist enterprise thereby takes the form of a traditional family, which in return for loyal service also provides a secure position in the family hierarchy.

The function of the deferred wage is concealed not simply by the familial system of ranking by age, but also by the traditional roles assigned to the sexes. Since women who have children leave their jobs at least long enough to lose their seniority, most of them are separated from the labor aristocracy, and their "deferred" wages are seldom paid.

Table 1

Monthly Payment, by Age, Sex, Education and Firm Size
(1976)

Sex and Education	Age	Monthly Payments (¥)	
		Non-Monopoly Capital	Monopoly Capital
Male University Graduates	22	95,800	101,000
	25	116,400	133,300
	35	174,500	220,800
	45	229,400	328,000
	55	275,600	406,700
Male High School Graduates	18	80,200	81,400
	25	116,100	126,500
	35	165,000	193,500
	45	209,900	262,800
	55	248,100	334,500
Female High School Graduates	18	77,200	79,000
	25	101,200	104,100
	30	115,900	120,900
	35	130,700	—
Male Middle School Graduates	15	69,000	70,000
	25	111,500	119,800
	35	151,100	166,000
	45	186,400	202,500
	55	231,100	233,300
Female Middle School Graduates	15	66,800	68,600
	25	96,400	99,000
	30	107,900	111,200

Source: Chingin rōmu kanri kenkyūjo shochō [Head of the Wages and Personnel Management Research Institute], Furukawa Noboru ed., *Chingin kentō shiryō: 1977 nendokan* [1977 Research Materials on Wages] (Tokyo: Nihon Horei, 1976), p. 324.

What separates the labor aristocracy from the mass worker is the former's employment by monopoly capital, which, because of its more advanced productive forces, is both required to and can afford to provide a much more solid material basis for workers' loyalty than can non-monopoly capital. But because educational achievement (either the standing of the institution attended or the degree of success in a company entrance examination) allocates male workers into monopoly and non-monopoly firms, the different conditions of employment in the two sectors seem to result from the different educational qualifications of employees. Insofar as education also channels males into different classes, it makes divisions among workers look like divisions between workers and managers. Table 1 shows how far this is true of salary and wage differentials.

It is remarkable how divisions between classes and divisions within the working class take on the same form of strata bases on sex, age, and the "standing" of the firm employed in. For example, the salaries of middle-aged male university graduates, who by this time typically tend to enter the middle class or the bourgeoisie, are *lower* than the wages ultimately received (after many years of deferment) by elderly male workers. Both seem to be paid on the same basis of rank in the familial hierarchy, whereas in fact the former is increasingly paid out of surplus value for performing the function of capital. Also important to note is that, with the exception of women workers whose position in the reserve army makes the type of firm they are employed by irrelevant, deferred wages in monopoly firms are much greater than those in non-monopoly firms. Though men in both might have similar starting wages, the difference increases with length of employment and with education.

Education therefore serves, not merely to reproduce class agents and to legitimize class society, but to legitimize the allocation of workers into the labor aristocracy and the general mass. A worker in a non-monopoly firm is assumed to be less productive, not because he works with less advanced technology, but because he went to the wrong school or did not obtain the right grades. The educational background of a company's workers thereby seems to justify it as a first-, second-, or third-rate company, just as education seems to lie behind distinctions among members of a company. Moreover, because different levels of productive forces in monopoly and non-monopoly firms result in different pay scales between them for *all* employees, the fundamental basis of one's livelihood appears to be the type of company one works in rather than one's relationship to the means of production. Workers' loyalty to their employers therefore becomes not simply loyalty to their company, but a sense of rivalry with workers in other companies. Because of the reproduction of so many elements of the family ideology, the company assumes the form of a traditional family, and class conflict is smothered beneath the form of rivalry among companies.

The ideological effects of recruitment to the bourgeoisie, the middle class, and the labor aristocracy through competitive examination are fairly straightforward. However, it is not yet clear why, if ruling class power stems from the ownership and control of capital, and if the above-average conditions of the labor aristocracy stem from the above-average technologies of its employers, recruitment to these positions should be by educational achievement. The reason, it seems, lies in the dual function of education: to legitimize capitalist relations and to impart scientific knowledge, which is part and parcel of developing productive forces, to the only possible bearers of that knowledge, namely, labor power. Monopoly firms therefore recruit by competitive examination because the above-average techniques they employ require above-average technical knowledge. But they also do so in order to legitimize the better conditions of their workers, the majority of whom in practice require no more skill than workers in non-monopoly firms. For most workers in the monopoly sector, more advanced productive forces mean a higher division of labor and therefore a reduction in the skills actually required on the job. For them, recruitment by competitive examination has much more to do with ideology and work discipline than with the skills displayed in the examination.

The deferment of wages by age is the single most important material condition which ties workers to their companies, but it is by no means the sole condition. Another form of deferred wages is the system of twice-yearly bonuses which represent the withholding of wages for periods of up to six months. However, because the amounts increase with each of the "familial" forms assumed by fractional divisions within the working class, bonuses serve three functions in addition to securing workers' loyalty. The most important is that they are a convenient means of cutting the value of labor power without reducing regular wages. Since in monopoly firms they comprise from 20-30 percent of workers' total annual income and are presented as a type of profit-sharing for high productivity, they offer considerable scope for manipulation by capital. For example, bonuses were cut by an average of 5 percent in 1976.[4] The second additional function of bonuses is that workers tend to save out of them for old age and for the education of their children, and they thereby release cheap money to capital through the banking system. Finally, since bonuses in non-monopoly firms comprise a smaller proportion of annual income than in monopoly firms, they allow pay differentials between the two to look narrower than they actually are, as revealed by Table 2.

Apart from deferring wages, capital employs one other main material incentive, namely, the system of company welfare, which is most highly developed in monopoly firms. The discrepancy between what they and what small firms can offer is particularly significant in the provision of cheap company housing and medical facilities, since housing and medicare are among the most costly as well as most essential wage goods workers require. The historical origins of company welfare and recreation facilities reveal unambiguously that their major purpose was to bind the worker to his/her company. Capital has consistently opposed state intervention in this area, and so long as state welfare continues to lag behind company welfare, a worker who chooses or who is compelled to leave a large company loses very much more than his/her seniority wages. A lifetime's savings for old age and emergencies can be ruined in a few years at current rates of inflation, and employment in a non-monopoly firm secures at most only about half the welfare s/he previously had: on average monopoly firms spent ¥367,846 per worker on welfare in 1975, while non-monopoly firms spent only ¥157,987.[4] Table 3 provides a general picture of the facilities that have been built up in the two sectors.

The material conditions which give the Japanese labor aristocracy its specific form do not, however, exclude certain contradictory elements. Although the employment system in monopoly firms is frequently seen as one of guaranteed lifelong employment and social welfare, even in boom periods the guarantees have definite limits. These derive from the fact that capital's total wage bill depends more on the average age of its total workforce than on the absolute number employed. For example, two workers under twenty-five cost less than one over fifty. This is why new recruits are almost entirely confined to young graduates and school leavers, and why total wage costs can actually fall in a boom where the workforce expands rapidly. However, the reproduction of this happy state of affairs has required placing a relatively low upper-limit on the age, soon after fifty-five, by which workers in the labor aristocracy have to retire. To continue the seniority payments and job security beyond that age would cause two main problems: a possibly rising average-age of the workforce and insufficient flexibility in being able to adjust its absolute numbers to any unevenness in the rate of accumulation.

Monopoly capital has therefore made a rigid distinction between so-called "regular employees" (unmarried females and males under the age of about fifty-five), and various types of "temporaries." But because workers move from one group to the other when they retire, the reproduction of a sizeable proportion of the reserve army is out of the labor aristocracy, and powerful forces are generated in opposition to those which secure the loyalty of the latter to capital. When the same working class agents are made to fulfill two contradictory functions required by capital accumulation, albeit at different times in their lives, the performance of both roles might be threatened. What has held the contradictory demands on the loyalty of the labor aristocracy in balance has been the postwar boom, which has allowed capital to provide job security until, and a living wage towards the time of, retirement, and that, after this, temporary jobs have been easy to get, even if at lower wages than before.

An analysis of the composition of the labor aristocracy requires identifying those working class members of public corporations, the civil service, and monopoly firms who receive the material benefits already outlined. This requires the exclusion of two main groups of workers: (1) all the different types of temporary, part-time, and day laborers who have no seniority and therefore no overriding reason to knuckle down in order one

Table 2

Bonuses and Basic Wages by Firm Size
(1975, ¥000)

Firm Size (Operatives)	A Wages	B Bonuses	A+B	$\frac{B}{A+B}$	Indices: largest firms = 100		
					A	B	A+B
Under 30	1,495.2	274.3	1,769.5	15.5	81	35	67
30-99	1,520.6	459.8	1,980.4	23.2	82	58	75
100-499	1,571.5	533.8	2,105.3	25.4	85	68	80
500-999	1,685.1	650.1	2,335.2	27.8	91	82	89
Over 1,000	1,864.4	788.8	2,635.2	29.9	100	100	100
Average	1,575.1	455.1	2,030.2	22.4	85	74	77

Source: Kokuzeichō chōkan kanbō sōmuka [Chief Secretary of the General Affairs Section of the National Taxation Agency], *Zeimu tōkei kara mita minkan kyūyo no jittai* [Private Incomes as Revealed in Taxation Statistics] (Tokyo: Okurashō insatsukyoku, 1976), p. 13.

Table 3

Availability of Company Welfare by Firm Size

	Total of all firms	Large firms (over 5,000 employees)	Small firms (30-99 employees)
Housing			
Family	47.0%	93.9%	42.2%
Unmarried	34.9	89.9	28.8
House Buying Incentive	34.8	96.5	28.2
Homeowner Layaway	4.5	74.9	1.0
Housing Loan	18.8	93.9	10.8
Medical & Health Care			
Hospitals	3.2	31.3	2.2
Clinics	8.3	74.3	3.8
Medical Offices	24.9	85.4	18.2
Preventive Medicine	58.2	95.6	52.1
Family Medical Check-ups	2.4	37.4	1.1
Living Support			
Barber Shops, Beauty Salons	3.8	50.3	1.3
Purchasing Facilities	9.6	70.2	4.1
Nurseries	1.8	12.0	0.8
Employee Canteens	33.3	79.2	27.4
Food Provision	27.7	62.2	22.9
Mutual-aid Credit			
Marriage	94.7	98.0	93.2
Birth	87.4	90.6	85.2
Death	94.0	98.2	92.2
Disease	86.2	88.9	83.6
Accident	77.2	96.2	72.0
Private Insurance System (premiums borne by employer)	46.6	48.8	48.2
Culture, Sport, Recreation			
Libraries	22.1	75.1	14.2
Gymnasiums	3.4	54.1	2.0
Athletic Grounds	10.9	84.5	5.0
Seaside, Mountain Lodges & Ski Resorts	15.1	73.3	9.8
Rehabilitation Facilities	16.0	95.6	9.4
Tennis Courts	11.4	86.5	4.0
Swimming Pools	2.8	48.8	1.3
Cultural Clubs	31.5	94.7	19.5
Athletic Clubs	56.5	95.3	46.5
Athletic Meets	15.3	71.9	9.1
Pleasure Trips	88.4	64.3	91.5
Others			
Employee Shareholding	7.8	55.3	5.8
Supplemental Labour Compensation Insurance	31.1	93.6	23.8
Supplemental Health Insurance (Extra payment above legal minimums)	21.3	98.8	14.8

Source: Katsumi Yakabe, *Labour Relations in Japan: Fundamental Characteristics* (Tokyo: International Society for Educational Information, Inc. Japan, 1974), p. 64.

Table 4

Total Economically Active Population* by Age, Education, and Firm Size, 1974 (1,000 persons)

Firm Size	Education	Age			
		15-34	35-55	over 55	Total
1-9	School	5,884	9,309	4,649	19,841
	University	639	645	277	1,562
10-99	School	4,087	3,923	1,238	9,245
	University	729	476	173	1,378
100-299	School	1,569	1,232	309	3,091
	University	405	207	46	659
Over 1,000	School	1,058	1,397	315	2,771
	University	740	790	96	1,626
Total	School	17,519	19,056	7,011	43,585
	University	3,839	2,881	725	7,445

Source: *Shūgyō kōzō kihon chōsa hōkoku*, p. 60.

* Persons who are also studying are excluded.

day to receive deferred wage payments; (2) almost all women workers, since most of those whom the company regards as "permanent" are under thirty-five and unmarried. They will "retire" when they marry and will never receive their deferred wages. Most married women are over thirty-five and are only hired on one or another temporary basis. The only women in the labor aristocracy are the small number in monopoly firms who never marry.

If we break down the total economically active population according to the main superstructural forms that channel the Japanese into classes and class fractions, we can get a general picture of the size of the labor aristocracy. Table 4 does this by firm size, age, and education (that is, the main elements apart from sex).

Although some firms with fewer than 1,000 operatives are in the monopoly sector, the clearest cut-off point for this sector is firms larger than this and government. Since almost all persons in these sectors are employees, to get a rough estimate of the labor aristocracy we must subtract the members of the bourgeoisie, the middle class, and the reserve army. If the first two largely coincide with university graduates, and the third with men over 55 and women (of whom there were about 2.7 million in 1974), the aristocracy would be about 5.6 million. But because these include some other types of temporary worker and the members of the repressive state apparatuses (in all about a million), the aristocracy is left with approximately 4.5 million persons.

Since a precise estimate of the size of the labor aristocracy is not possible until we have a clear idea of how many workers in the monopoly sector are in the reserve army, detailed estimates are made only after we have examined the conditions of the mass worker in the massive number of non-monopoly firms scattered throughout the country.

(b) The Mass Worker

If the labor aristocracy is a product of advanced productive forces, what determines and characterizes the mass worker is employment by less concentrated and centralized capitals.

Though all workers are in identical relationships to capital in general, the fact of uneven development among the many capitals that constitute it requires a division of the working class according to the types of material conditions the different capitals are able to provide. Differences in these conditions— wages, bonuses, welfare, and so on—are not the *cause* of the divisions within the working class, but the *effects* of the fundamental cause: uneven accumulation and the continual coexistence of backward with more advanced capitals. Wages and conditions are not determined independently of the rate of accumulation, but by that rate, and differences in wages and conditions are the effects of different levels of productive forces resulting from different rates of accumulation. The more backward capitals with below-average technology can only continue to exist so long as they provide below-average working conditions to compensate for their technical disadvantages. Although uneven rates of accumulation *among* industries have also required some compensating differences in working conditions, the major differences are between monopoly and non-monopoly capitals in all industries.

Tables 2 and 3 have already shown the extent of the variations in wages, bonuses, and welfare conditions. The differences do not, however, correspond to different needs to provide a material basis to secure workers' loyalty, since the deferment of wages is practiced by both monopoly and non-monopoly capital. Rather, the differences correspond to unequal abilities to withhold wages. In order to attract young workers in the first place, non-monopoly capital must offer starting wages which are comparable to starting wages in the monopoly sector. By doing so, the proportion of the total wage which it can defer is reduced, and with it the ability to use deferred wages as a means of securing workers' loyalty. The starting wages of all workers are not very different in large and small firms, but the differentials widen with length of service.

However, non-monopoly capital's reduced ability to secure workers' loyalty by means of material incentives does not mean that it has had significantly greater problems of industrial conflict. This is partly because in most cases the more backward productive forces in small firms have not yet created a division of labor and a collective worker with the power to make larger wage deferments necessary. The greatest problems of worker indiscipline have been in medium-sized firms, which cannot compete with monopoly capital's wages, but which have considerably socialized the labor process in factories that bring together fairly large numbers of workers.[6] Elsewhere, and increasingly as firms become smaller, the familial form assumed by class relations in Japan is reproduced as much by actual personal contact between workers and bosses as through the structure of material incentives.

What the employer in a small firm cannot provide in material conditions he provides in genuine personal concern. Although he* is typically more authoritarian and reactionary than the global capitalist (or the hierarchy which performs capital's function in the monopoly sector) he is also more respected, since the loyalty he cultivates is to himself personally. Since he is personally seen as the provider of his workers' livelihood, the familial form of the capitalist relation is reproduced more purely than in the monopoly sector. Even most incorporated non-monopoly firms are largely owned by single families, and the head of this household appears as the head of an extended family which includes all his workers. Class relations therefore more thoroughly assume the form of familial relations, particularly since some of the workers will be actual relatives, either younger sons and daughters, or more distant kin. The material basis of the employer's use of extra-economic coercion (the traditional ideology demanding loyalty and obedience to him personally) is therefore a much *closer* correspondence between family relations and production relations than exists in monopoly firms. The boss is both employer and head of the household which owns the firm.

The form of class action assumed by the mass workers' difficulty in reproducing his/her labor power on non-monopoly wages and conditions is not typically strike action, which is seen and treated as a mark of gross ingratitude to the employer, but a greater propensity to change jobs in search of better conditions. Rates of labor turnover in the non-monopoly sector vary widely and have been known to reach enormous proportions. A 1972 study of small firms in Tokyo revealed that almost 60 percent of employees in commerce and services, and 42 percent in manufacturing had changed jobs twice.[7] In the 35-45 age group, the annual rates of turnover are almost three times as high in the non-monopoly as in the monopoly sector, reflecting workers' reduced incentives to stay on in small firms even after acquiring some seniority (but well before retirement age when all workers have to leave anyway). The absolute rates of turnover are higher in both sectors for the under 35's, that is, before workers receive a stake in their seniority, but large differences between the sectors remain.

One form of deferred wages which has not been mentioned yet and which reinforces the pressure on the mass worker to "vote with his feet" is his retirement pay. Some firms provide only lump sums, while others separate the total amount into a lump sum and a division of the remainder into annual payments stretched over a number of years. In either case, monopoly firms can withhold large amounts from ordinary wages to pay for what appear to be very generous handouts.[8]

Apart from these and other types of withheld wages, which together result in much wider *real* differentials between the monopoly and non-monopoly sectors, workers in the latter must endure at least two additional disadvantages: longer working hours and higher risks of industrial accidents. Table 5 indicates the extent of the difference in hours as well as the difference in the number of working days per month.

Longer working hours in small firms form a major means by which non-monopoly capital compensates for its technical backwardness, almost the entire burden of which it places on the working class. Although functionaries must put up with lower salaries than their counterparts in the monopoly sector, they are nonetheless responsible for ensuring that workers accept the conditions capital can afford, not least exposure to industrial hazards. Table 6 shows how these hazards increase as firms become smaller. In a small firm with about 40 workers, one will have an accident every year, which means that at some stage during their working lives most workers will be affected. However, in firms with over 1,000 employees the rate is only about one worker every three or four years, and few will be affected.

Since in all respects the conditions of the mass worker are vastly inferior to those of the labor aristocracy, strategies for class struggle depend greatly on the relative size of each fraction. However, because there is some mobility between small and large firms as well as from regular to temporary jobs, these estimates must await analysis of the reserve army.

(c) The Reserve Army

The function of the reserve army is to allow the usual forms of uneven development, which require reducing the value of the working class' labor power and shunting workers in and out of the labor process, to occur without threatening capitalist relations. In Japan, this role has been played more effectively than in most advanced capitalist societies and is a major reason for the relatively smooth reproduction of capitalist relations in that country. To clarify why this is so requires a detailed examination of what a reserve army is and how it works.

Since uneven development takes three main forms, the reserve army must play three corresponding roles. The first is

Table 5

Average Number of Working Days and Hours Worked per Month, by Firm Size, 1975

Firm Size (Operatives)	Days	Hours	
		Total	Of which fixed
Over 500	20.9	166.6	155.8
100-499	21.7	171.9	160.6
30-99	22.3	164.4	165.8
5-29	23.4	182.7	172

Source: Rōdō daijin kanbō tōkei jōhōbu [Statistical Information Bureau of the Secretary of the Ministry of Labour, *Maitsuki kinrō tōkei chōsa sōgo hokokusho* [Composite Report on the Monthly Survey of Employment Statistics] (Tokyo: Rōdō daijin kanbō tōkei jōhōbu, 1976), pp. 75, 93.

---

* Japanese employers are overwhelmingly male.

related to the widespread increases in accumulation that (under appropriate conditions) can follow such cases of scientific or technical progress as the invention of the steam-engine or the motor car. Accumulation in a variety of industries can be favorably affected by such momentous advances in any one of them. However, a crucial condition on which this depends is whether capital has at its disposal sufficient workers to man the expansion. To avoid drawing them from other capitalist enterprises and either bidding up wages intolerably or provoking social unrest through the rapid destruction of backward firms, a large pool of *latent* workers must be available. So that the capitalist relation is not threatened at its existing and increasingly weakest point, the bulk of the workers needed for the new developments must come from outside capitalist production. Their *departure* from their previous productive activities can only avoid a serious threat to *capital in general* if these activities are under pre- or non-capitalist relations.

However, the coexistence of rapid accumulation in some industries, with modest and often declining accumulation in others, will sooner or later lead to a social crisis unless the difference is somehow gradually reduced. Industries, or capitals within industries, that remain backward in the long-term will need to disappear. To smooth over the transition, some workers will have to float to and fro for a while, though it might be possible for most to spend their working lives where they are. Since capital will not require their reproduction, the new generations of workers can move straight into the expanding sectors and help smooth over the transition.

Apart from these epochal stages in capitalist development, it is normal in any period for all capitals to make regular, even if relatively small, adjustments to their work forces. Never sure of what lies ahead, no capital can be certain that the exact number of workers required one year will still be needed the next. For this reason as well, a pool of workers who are prepared to float from one employer to another, regardless of wages or working conditions, is necessary to the normal functioning of capitalist production.

In addition to *latent* and *floating* workers, about once each generation capital requires large numbers of workers to be shifted out of employment for extended periods corresponding to the length of these extended depressions. They will become *stagnant,* and because they have no form of subsistence, they can be the most dangerous from capital's point of view. Even outside conditions of general depression, some workers for whom no capital can find a use will be laid off and form a stagnant work force. Wherever possible, they must be somehow recycled into the latent pool, so that they have some form of subsistence to prevent their growth into a revolutionary force.

Each of the latent, floating, and stagnant groups of workers is both a product and a condition of the normal process of uneven development. Their main functions are to allow capital to adjust the *numbers* of workers needed at any time to the requirements of profitability, adjustments which involve continual movements of workers in and out of employment. However, profitability is also served by these shifts through their effects on the *value of the labor power* of the working class as a whole. The continual possibility of bringing in new workers enables capital to prevent existing ones from bidding up wages, and the reserve army as a whole ensures that the value of labor power does not rise above what profitability can tolerate.

As a cushion for uneven development in Japan, the reserve army has so far functioned close to the ideal. No large stagnant reserve has built up, and workers who are no longer needed have usually been converted into some or other latent reserve with a relatively independent subsistence. Floating workers have been available in sufficient numbers to permit fairly smooth adjustments to uneven development. Furthermore, the working class agents in the reserve army have on the whole been different from those in the other two fractions, and the danger of united working class action has been averted.

This last condition is important, because if all workers stand a more or less equal chance of sinking into the reserve, the danger that other fractions of the working class will make common cause with the reserve increases. Fortunately for the Japanese bourgeoisie, traditional familial relations have once again come to the rescue and channelled workers into the reserve army primarily according to age and sex. The insecurity of these positions thereby takes the form of the insecurity of particular persons—women and the old—in the family hierarchy.

Although because of their relative predominance in certain jobs and industries (for example, typists and the service industry) women cannot fulfill all functions of the reserve army on their own, they do so to a degree far in excess of their sisters in other capitalist societies. They are particularly useful in the ease with which they can be converted from a stagnant to a latent reserve, since even when they are laid-off and cannot find jobs they secure through their husbands a subsistence independent of their own wages. Their role in the sexual division of labor in the family also predisposes them to accept the status of latent

---

Table 6

**Rate of Industrial Accidents by Firm Size
(Manufacturing, 1975)**

	Over 1,000	500-999	300-499	100-299	50-99	30-49
	Firm Size					
Accident Rate[a]	1.64	3.23	5.14	8.27	11.91	15.81
Rate of Intensity[b]	0.29	0.34	0.43	0.48	0.74	0.91

Source: 1975 Rōdō hakusho, p. 286.
a. Numbers of persons laid off more than one day per million working hours.   b. Number of days lost per thousand working hours.

Table 7

Strength of the Ideology Supporting the Sexual Division of Labor
(1975)

Should Women Retire on Marriage or Having Children?

	Naturally	Inevitably	No	Don't Know
Men	22%	58%	12%	8%
Women	17%	61%	13%	9%

Source: Rōdōshō fujin-shōnen kyoku [Women and Youth Department of the Ministry of Labour], *Fujin rōdō no jitsujō* [Conditions of Women Workers] (Tokyo: Ōkurashō insatsukyoku, 1976), p. 75.

worker. A survey conducted in 1975 by the Office of the Prime Minister confirmed that they are both prepared and expected to sink into the latent reserve when they marry or have children. Table 7 presents their answers to the question, "What do you think of using marriage or having children as an opportunity [sic] to retire?"

Far from being an opportunity for working women, early retirement allows capital to replace older and more highly-paid workers with cheap new recruits. The widespread practice of retiring women when they marry and have children therefore simultaneously reproduces the latent reserve and uses it to keep wage costs down. The young women who retire so willingly are never paid their deferred wages, since when capital draws on this latent reserve they reenter the workforce without seniority. Neither do middle-aged mothers who have lost a few years' "experience" ever acquire any real seniority, since even if they work a full week, they receive the ambiguous status of "non-regulars" or "permanent temporaries." Table 8 shows that

middle-aged men and women who enter new jobs are treated quite differently: some of the men's previous experience is recognized, but the women are treated like young girls.

Because men who switch jobs before they reach retirement age do not lose their seniority entirely, some can often get better wages by doing so, particularly when they move from smaller to larger firms. This type of labor turnover does not concern the floating reserve, because capital cannot with impunity take the initiative when it involves men under 55. What legitimizes capital's initiative in the case of the floating reserve is that the workers have all "retired." They can then be kept on or not, but only at *reduced wages* and with the ambiguous status of "non-regular employee." Since men and women "retire" at different ages, the ages at which they enter the floating reserve are correspondingly different. Only between the ages of 15 and 29 and again after 60, when both men and women are of pre- and post-retirement age respectively, is there any comparability in their membership of different fractions of the working class. Table 8 shows that wage differentials are narrowest during these years.[9]

However, since the overwhelming majority of women under 30 are never paid their deferred wages and can be retired as soon as they marry, women are almost entirely in the reserve army. Until retirement they form a reserve of cheap floating workers; they then sink into the latent reserve for varying lengths of time, and finally some re-enter the floating reserve. Out of a total of eleven and a half million women employees in 1974, only about a half a million were in the 30-55 age group and had never married. They were unambiguously outside the reserve army.

To estimate the size of the female latent reserve, we must first subtract from the total number of employees those who are in the bourgeoisie and the middle class. Since in 1974, only 5.36 percent of persons listed in the census as managers and officials were women,[10] there were approximately 308,830 women in the bourgeoisie (this number is 5.36 percent of the

Table 8

Women's Wages as a Percentage of Men's by Age and Length of Service
(1975)

Age	Average	Length of Service (years)								
		0	1	2	3-4	5-9	10-14	15-19	20-29	30-
−17	92.7	92.6	91.9	91.7						
18-19	91.1	92.7	92.5	89.7	85.7					
20-24	85.3	84.1	85.8	86.5	87.4	83.6				
25-29	75.5	68.2	73.9	75.4	76.7	79.5	77.0			
30-34	63.9	55.1	58.2	60.0	62.9	67.1	76.5	72.1		
35-39	55.9	51.1	53.6	54.0	54.3	58.0	68.8	76.5	71.1	
40-44	54.1	50.3	52.3	53.9	53.1	55.6	62.6	69.3	81.9	85.2
45-49	56.1	52.4	54.2	55.0	55.2	57.7	62.9	66.4	82.1	96.2
50-54	53.5	50.8	62.8	55.8	53.9	57.6	63.7	64.3	73.5	90.4
55-59	58.2	60.1	58.1	56.2	57.3	59.2	66.9	67.9	71.4	85.4
60-	66.4	62.6	66.4	63.9	63.9	63.6	71.1	72.7	68.9	74.5
Average	61.4	86.6	70.7	69.7	68.3	67.0	68.1	69.4	73.8	84.5

Source: Fujin rōdō no jitsujō, p. 58.

total bourgeois employees in the private and public sectors). If we add to them the 1,154,498 females in the middle class (mainly teachers and nurses) and ignore the 521,000 full-time women in the 30-55 age group who had never married (most were probably either bourgeois or middle class), the female floating reserve would comprise about 10 million persons. If all those in the favored age group who had never married were outside the working class, the number would have been 10,119,672 in 1974.

It is impossible to attempt a similarly precise estimate of the female latent and stagnant reserves, though some survey data can provide a general idea of the numbers of women capital can draw on. According to the government's 1974 employment status survey, a full 7.7 million women, of whom only 856,000 had never married, were "wishing to work."[11]

A rough division of these people into latent and stagnant reserves can be made according to the extent of their alternative sources of subsistence. We do so by examining the employment status and annual income of the heads of their households, though other sources of subsistence are possible. Table 9 suggests that most persons wishing to work are latent rather than stagnant workers.

If under ¥0.4 million a year was too low for a family's subsistence and under ¥1 million was marginal, between one and two million women and just under one million men seem to have been in the stagnant rather than the latent reserve. Until recently, therefore, Japanese capitalism has been able to recycle unemployed married women through the sexual division of labor in the family into the less threatening of these two groups in the reserve army. We shall see below how the current crisis is beginning to interfere with this process and how the working class as a whole is affected by the changes.

Although women are overwhelmingly concentrated in and form the bulk of the reserve army, they are not the only members of it. They are joined by at least four categories of men: "non-regulars" (*shokutaku*), "part-timers" (*rinjikō*), and "day laborers" (*hiyatoi*) in the floating reserve, and the unemployed in the latent and stagnant reserves.

What distinguishes the rapid turnover of mass workers in the non-monopoly sector from the floating of reserve workers in and out of both sectors are the different reasons the two groups have for changing jobs. The former leave largely at their own initiative in search of improved conditions, while the latter typically move out of regular jobs to less secure and remunerative ones because they are of post-retirement age. This is confirmed by the reasons given by persons who changed jobs or gave up work in 1974. The overwhelming majority of the total over the age of 55 as well as women under 30 gave reasons which had little or nothing to do with any initiative of their own. In the case of men under 30, only 27.5 percent fell into this category. Table 10 reveals that, if we regard reasons for movements of workers as indicators of the class fraction to which they belong, there is a very clear distinction between the mass worker and the reserve army.

Among men over the age of 55, 71 percent of those who changed jobs and 90 percent of those who gave up work seem to be in one or other group in the reserve army. Since the male members of this fraction of the working class are overwhelmingly elderly workers, we need to examine what happens to workers after retirement. In general, they must change their places of employment as well as the type of work they do,

Table 9

Persons Wishing to Work by Sex and by Employment Status and Income of Household Head 1974 (1,000 persons)

Employment Status of Household Head	Total	Men	Women
Persons without a job	1,723	833	890
Persons with a job (annual income)	7,494	627	6,867
Under 0.4 ¥ million	158	23	135
0.4-1.0 ¥ million	1,023	121	902
Over 1.0 ¥ million	6,279	480	5,799
Not reported	35	3	32
Total Persons	9,217	1,459	7,757

Source: Shūgyō kōzō kihon chōsa hōkoku, pp. 236 and 240.

receive some form of temporary status, and accept large reductions in wages. According to a government survey of the persons (mainly men) who reached retirement age in 1967–1973, 63.3 percent had to move to jobs in different establishments, and they went overwhelmingly to smaller ones than they had been in before. Only 34.5 percent of these people did the same type of work they had done previously, revealing that they are used as mainly unskilled workers, and almost 76 percent of them received some or other form of temporary status: 66.7 percent became "non-regulars" and 9.2 percent "part-timers" or "day laborers." A full 33.7 percent had spent some time unemployed.[11] Although lower proportions of retired workers who remained on in the same establishments had to do different jobs and accept temporary status, this applied to only 36.7 percent of the people who retired during the period. Table 11 shows the average reduction in wages both groups had to accept as they changed jobs.

Since the labor aristocracy which retires out of monopoly firms must tolerate massive wage reductions when it enters the reserve army, there is an important material basis for working class unity, which as we see below, is becoming firmer as the crisis of Japanese capitalism deepens.

So far most male members of the reserve army have managed to remain in the floating category, which in addition to "non-regulars," includes what are known as "part-timers" and "day laborers." These latter are closest to sinking into the latent (insofar as they have some form of subsistence), or worse still, the stagnant reserves. Day laborers in particular are extremely insecure, since they must somehow find work each day. They tend to congregate in urban slums, such as the Sanya district in Tokyo or Kamagasaki in Osaka, and are herded onto buses employers send into the areas.

Day laborers come in all ages, though they are predominantly middle-aged men who dropped out of the normal process through which workers are fitted into the "familial" hierarchy. One study of day laborers in the Sanya district revealed that out of an average three day period, only 23.3 percent found work

Table 10

Movements of Reserve Army and Mass Workers by Age and Sex, 1974 (1,000 persons)

			Age			
	Nos.	%	Nos.	5	Nos.	5
i) Persons who changed jobs*	1,102	100.0	852	100.0	169	100.0
Mass workers[a]	365	33.1	307	36.0	27	16.0
Floating workers[b]	359	32.6	316	37.1	116	68.6
Of which Men*	633	100.0	586	100.0	143	100.0
Mass workers	251	39.7	213	36.3	21	14.7
Floating workers	174	27.5	211	36.0	102	71.3
Of which Women*	469	100.0	266	100.0	26	100.0
Mass workers	114	24.3	94	35.3	6	23.1
Floating workers	185	39.4	105	39.5	14	53.8
ii) Persons who stopped work*	1,016	100.0	678	100.0	482	100.0
Mass workers	103	10.1	94	13.9	19	3.9
Latent/Stagnant reserve[c]	720	70.9	429	63.3	415	86.1
Of which Men*	145	100.0	126	100.0	279	100.0
Mass workers	37	25.5	18	14.3	9	3.2
Latent/Stagnant reserve	52	35.9	85	67.5	251	90.0
Of which Women*	871	100.0	552	100.0	203	100.0
Mass workers	66	7.6	76	13.7	10	4.9
Latent/Stagnant reserve	668	76.7	344	62.3	164	80.8

* Totals include persons who gave reasons other than the ones included in the classification.

[a] Mass workers were regarded as those who either changed jobs or gave up work because of the wages or conditions in their former jobs.

[b] Floating workers were seen as those who changed jobs for any of the following reasons: lay-offs, bankruptcies, the job was temporary, a family member was transferred, marriage or child care, retirement, illness, and old age.

[c] Stagnant or latent workers are those who gave up work for any of the reasons in b. They are not distinguished, because whether or not they have an alternative subsistence is not relevant here.

Source: Shūgyō kōzō kihon chōsa hōkoku, pp. 258-261.

the full three days, 36.1 percent worked two days, and 13.4 percent remained on the streets.[12] Being used for mainly heavy work, such as concreting or miscellaneous factory jobs, they received about ¥2,900 a day in 1974,[13] which resulted in an annual income of less than half of what other workers receive.

The distinction between non-regulars, part-timers, and day laborers is primarily one of job security. A rough rule of thumb is the notice they receive should lay-offs be required: about a year for non-regulars, a month for part-timers, and of course no warning for day laborers. In the case of unmarried women under thirty, whom I have regarded as non-regulars even though they are accorded regular status so long as they remain single (or at least do not have children), this period is longer. The approximately four million women in this category are perhaps on the boundary between the reserve army and the other fractions of the working class.

It is not possible to make estimates of the numbers of persons in the Japanese reserve army, which turns out to be surprisingly large in view of that country's reputation for "lifelong employment." This is done in Table 12 on the basis of date

Table 11

Wage Reductions of Retired Workers, by Firm Size 1967–1973 (% Distribution of Persons)

Firm Size	% Wage Reduction			
(Operatives)	Over 100%	25-100%	0-25%	No reduction
Over 5,000	18.9	43.4	21.3	16.4
1,000-4,999	14.1	42.1	24.2	19.6
500-999	16.1	34.3	22.5	27.1
300-499	12.8	31.2	22.9	33.1
100-299	20.6	24.1	14.9	40.4
Average	16.9	41.2	22.2	19.7

Source: Teinen tōtatsusha chōsa no kekka, p. 28.

Table 12

Estimated Size of the Japanese Reserve Army
by Sex and Sector of Employment, 1974 (000 persons)

	Non-Monopoly			Monopoly			Total		
	Men	Women	Total	Men	Women	Total	Men	Women	Total
A. Floating	2,150	7,114	9,264	983	3,005	3,994	3,139	10,100	13,258
Non-regulars[a]	1,231	5,911	7,142	615	3,303	1,846	1,846	8,601	10,447
Part-timers[b]	528	925	1,453	215	242	457	743	1,178	1,910
Day labourers	391	278	669	159	73	232	550	351	901
B. Latent							604	6,733	7,337
C. Stagnant							856	1,025	1,881
TOTAL RESERVE ARMY							**4,559**	**17,877**	**22,476**

[a] The total number of women in this category is taken from the total number of women employees who are neither part-time nor day labourers (see *Shūgyō kōzō kihon chōsa hōkoku*, p. 62) and subtracting the bourgeois and middle class members. Their division into the two sectors is in the proportion in *Ibid.*, pp. 94, 100. To get the total number of male non-regulars, I have subtracted only corporation directors from the male employees over 55 who were neither part-time nor day labourers, since most capitalist functionaries are below the age of 55.

[b] The totals for both sexes come from *Ibid.*, pp. 30 and 32, and they are divided into sectors according to the same proportions as are those persons who worked less than 35 hours a week in 1974, for which see *Ibid.*, pp. 94-100.

previously provided and estimates explained in the Table.

So long as the stagnant group remains such a small proportion of the total (8.4%), the potential vulnerability of capitalist relations in Japan will remain no more than that. Some 59 percent of the total are floating workers and have been able to find jobs, while the family has taken the place of the agricultural sector as a means of ensuring that otherwise stagnant workers are safely in the latent reserve.[14] However, the large proportion of women in the reserve army is a two-edged sword, since women cannot so overwhelmingly perform both of the two main functions required of a reserve army. Although they can carry the burden of working at high rates of exploitation through their low wages, they cannot on their own enable capital to regulate the numbers of workers to the required degree in time of crisis. This is because women do not do the whole range of jobs which are affected by the crisis to the same degree as men, but are concentrated in certain industries and occupations. Table 13 shows that these are largely clerical jobs in the service and retail sectors.

Although the female reserve might be sufficient to allow capital in certain unproductive sectors[15] to tide over a prolonged crisis, other sectors will require more than women and the limited numbers of men in the floating reserve. Such a crisis would also make it extremely difficult even for this number to move from the floating to the latent(rather than to the stagnant) reserve, since the normal process through which this is done in Japan would break down in a prolonged crisis. Typically, retired male workers who cannot find temporary employment set up petty family enterprises, but these tend to yield an income per person engaged which is even less than what temporary workers receive. Even in boom times, therefore, the sinking of retired male workers into the petty bourgeoisie has been a less than ideal means of converting stagnant into latent workers.[16] In a prolonged crisis, the stagnant reserve is bound to build up, and if its sex, age, and educational composition changes significantly,

it can become the focus of wider working class struggles. I pursue this question once I have examined the organisation and ideologies with which the Japanese working class must face the crisis, and conclude this section with a summary of its structure and composition.

As a means of ensuring the reproduction of capitalist relations, channelling the members of the working class into its three main fractions on the basis of sex and education is superior to doing so on the basis of age. This is because all workers eventually become old and will sooner or later be subjected to the demands placed on retired workers, while men who have once obtained a prestige education need not otherwise experience any of what being in the reserve army implies. The price capital must pay for its ability to make class society take the form of a familial-type stratified society is that the entire working class at some time or another gets a taste of being in the bottom "strata." So long as accumulation does not falter too greatly and male members of these "strata" can at least continue to find jobs, this disadvantage of relying on age to conceal class relations is more than outweighed by its advantages. Until recently capital has used age along with sex and education background to divide the working class into fractions, which take the form of divisions within the traditional family: an aristocracy comprising middle-aged men with the "best" education, a mass of less well-educated men, also in their prime, and a reserve of women and elderly men. The correspondence between the working class *positions* in each fraction and the superstructural attributes of the *agents* who occupy the positions, although never perfect, has been close enough to guarantee the appearance of divisions within the working class as resulting from personal merits or failures, rather than from capital's demands. Women and elderly men, for example, would blame their sex and age for the conditions under which they work (or fail or work).

On the basis of the estimates made so far, Table 14 presents

Table 13

Total Employees (excluding directors) by Industry, Occupation, and Sex, 1974 (000 persons)

Industry	Men	Women	Total	Women as % of Total
Primary	415	215	630	34.1
Mining	118	20	138	14.5
Construction	2,857	426	3,283	13.0
Manufacturing	7,449	3,681	11,180	32.9
Wholesale/Retail	3,408	2,618	6,026	43.4
Finance/Insurance/Real Estate	812	684	1,496	45.7
Transport/Communications	2,693	362	3,055	11.8
Electricity/Gas/Water	275	37	312	11.9
Services	3,110	2,897	6,007	48.2
TOTAL (excluding government)	21,187	10,940	32,127	34.0
Occupation				
Professional and Technical	1,919	1,252	3,171	39.5
Clerical	4,540	3,808	8,348	45.6
Sales	2,536	1,191	3,727	32.0
Farmers, Lumbermen, Fishermen	377	208	586	35.5
Miners	76	5	81	6.2
Transport/Communications	2,118	174	2,292	7.6
Craftsmen/Production Process	8,948	2,904	11,852	24.5
Labourers	894	461	1,355	34.0
Protective Service	564	14	578	2.4
Service	713	1,456	2,169	67.1
(Regrouped)	22,685	11,473	34,158	33.6
Construction Workers	509	113	622	18.2
Total (including Government)	**22,685**	**11,473**	**34,158**	**33.6**

Source: *Shūgyō kōzō kihon chōsa hōkoku*, pp. 30-35, 44-45.

Table 14

Fractions of the Japanese Working Class

	Total Number
(A) Economically Active	25,749,083
a) Labour Aristocracy	4,626,850
b) Mass Workers	7,864,233
c) Reserve Army (Floating)	13,258,000
(B) Economically Inactive	
a) Latent Reserve	7,337,000
b) Stagnant Reserve	1,881,000
TOTAL	**34,967,083**

an overall picture of the structure and composition of the working class. The key to the survival of Japanese capitalism therefore lies not in its alleged provision of life-long employment but in the fact that over half the economically active members of the working class have been conditioned to accept the antithesis of life-long employment.

Organization and Ideology

Only when the phenomenal form assumed by class relations in fact becomes the capital-labor relation can the working class constitute itself into a revolutionary social force. This relation must not simply be determinant, it must also be *dominant*: classes must both exist and they must appear to exist. In other words, class society must take the form of class society, so that the most important *determining* influence on one's work, one's income, and one's consumption, as well as on the persons with whom one is brought together side by side in engaging in these activities, is at the same time the most *visible* influence. The essence of capitalist society, the creation and extraction of surplus value, must be laid bare so that it can dominate the minds, and not simply determine the lives, of the laboring masses.[17]

Bringing together the substance and the form of class relations is not, however, simply a matter of propaganda, but primarily of understanding the conditions on which their separation is based so as to hasten the conditions of their union. We have seen that the disjunction between the reality and the appearance of Japanese capitalism is based on the functioning of traditional familial relations as relations of production and as relations among the members of the working class. Through the traditional family's superimposition on the material forces which regulate capitalist development, the coincidence of material reality with familial relations determines the latter's dominance. It is to be expected, therefore, that the organization and ideology of the Japanese working class will reflect the familial form rather than the substance of class relations in that country.

Organization

The most striking and notorious feature of trade unions in Japan is their organization on the basis of enterprises rather than industries. Although the major enterprise unions* in any industry might form loose associations, the latter do little more than permit the exchange of information, while all negotiations take place between the employers of each particular company and its union, which is almost entirely autonomous in these matters. The sole external consideration is the tendency to confine what is negotiable to limits set by the top organizations of the bourgeoisie, such as *Keidanren,* in consultation with the state.

Since the *dominant* influences on union membership are identical to the *dominant* influences on class formation (the process by which classes assume their form), it is hardly surprising that unions function primarily to control workers and to contain class struggles rather than as vehicles of these struggles. The most important basis of union membership, which is also dominant in the formation of the labor aristocracy and the mass worker, is the status of regular employee. Union membership is limited, not simply to employees in a particular company but to its *regular* employees. Day laborers, part-timers, and persons hired temporarily after retirement—that is, the entire reserve army apart from young women (who are regulars in name only)—are excluded. Employees destined for managerial positions are included until they reach the rank of section manager, while the jobs of defeated or retired union officials are kept open at the level of seniority they would have attained had they not assumed this position. Unions are not therefore organizations of the working class, but of certain strata in the familial hierarchy, beneath which class relations are submerged in each company.

It is no accident, therefore, that organized workers are overwhelmingly in the labor aristocracy (the main exception being young women to whom we return below). Since these are potentially the most threatening workers and are in firms too large for employers to create loyalties to themselves as individuals, organizations are needed to personalize the family relations for which material incentives could only lay the foundation. The use of the company song is just one example of monopoly capital's quest for alternatives to non-monopoly capital's personal touch.

There is very little evidence that unions have had much influence on levels of wages, which vary instead with firm size and industry, that is, with variations in rates of accumulation. Rather, company unions have been essential to securing the labor aristocracy's compliance with such requirements of faltering accumulation as the recent cuts in real wages and in weekly working hours. Without company unions, wages in the monopoly sector could not be brought into line with the rate of accumulation as swiftly as they have been, particularly in the years 1972–1975. In the non-monopoly sector, this function is fulfilled by the close personal ties between workers and employers, and the former feel obliged to accept no more that what the latter can afford.

The enormous discrepancy between the degree of unionization in the monopoly and non-monopoly sectors therefore results from very much more than the greater ability of the collective worker in large factories to organize. It also has a lot to do with the fact that unions in the monopoly sector are tolerated by capital because they can be used to control workers. Monopoly capital's response to militant trade unions has rarely been an assault on unionism as such, but has almost always taken the form of encouraging the development of a rival company union, which can be used to bring workers into line. It is extremely difficult for militants to form an effective organization, because the company is the only realistic level at which this can be done, and since it will comprise only company employees, its members are always subject to the control of their employers. This means that the union can only exist on conditions which employers accept.[18] Table 15 shows that the labor aristocracy is almost completely organized in this way, since over 90% of all unions are enterprise unions, and the total employees column includes the bourgeois or middle class.

Only 3,445,776 of the total numbers of organized workers in 1975 were women, predominantly those in the monopoly sector who were of pre-retirement age.[19] Table 16 provides a breakdown of unionized workers by industry and sex.

The regular status awarded to young women, which allows them to become members of unions, does not in any way affect their position in the reserve army since unions have enforced the deferment of their wages and have excluded them when they re-enter the workforce as non-regulars. Far from assisting young female members, unions have subjected them to the political and ideological domination of the labor aristocracy, without allowing them the material advantages which this fraction of their class has been able to exact.

As will be shown below, not all unions, however, have been equally submissive to the requirements of their organizational form, although the differences must not be exaggerated. The unions affiliated with *Sōhyō (Nihon Rōdō Kumiai Sōhyōgikai,* or The General Council of Japanese Trade Unions), for example, have in general been more militant than those affiliated with *Dōmei (Zen Nihon Rōdō Sodomei Kumiai Kaigi,* or The Japan Confederation of Labour), the two major national federations which loosely bring together associations of mainly company unions in various industries.[20]

Ideology

There is little reason to doubt the general findings of a

---

* Note that the US and Japanese usages of "enterprise union" differ. In the US, the enterprise union might lie somewhere between a company union and a business union.

Table 15

Numbers of Unionized Workers and Unions
by Firm Size, 1975

Firm Size (Operatives)	Number of Unionists	Unionists as % of total Employees	Number of Unions	Average Numbers of Persons per Union
Government	3,339,681	79.9	18,799	188.3
1,000 and over	5,226,963	67.6	13,960	374.4
300-999	1,365,469	44.1	6,750	202.3
100-299	1,023,031	27.2	10,110	101.2
30-99	454,009	8.4	11,645	39.0
Under 30	69,225	0.6	5,455	12.7
Other	912,022	—	2,614	348.9
TOTAL	**12,590,400**	**34.9**	**69,333**	**181.6**

Source. Nihon rōdō nenkan, 1977, p. 181; und Chūshō kigyō to rōdō kumiai, pp. 305 ff.

number of bourgeois studies that the Japanese working class sees the world primarily in terms of rank rather than class.[21] It is widely documented that sex, age, education, and the size of firm they are employed in are the uppermost considerations in workers' minds. However, since the most perceptive studies were based on in-depth interviews or participant observation, they do not tell us much about the relative dominance of the different forms which class relations assume. Neither do they examine variations in "rank consciousness" among different types of workers. Though these gaps result partly from the questions bourgeois scholars pose, they have as much to do with the limitations of in-depth studies of small groups of workers. While this method of probing ideas and feelings produces more accurate information, its advantage turns into a shortcoming when attempts are made to generalize about different types of workers and the dominant influences on them.

Recognizing that written questionnaires can end up with either incorrect or irrelevant information, I found that my survey (of 459 employees in 53 companies of varying sizes)[22] in the summer of 1976–77 did help fill in some gaps. The sample was, however, too small to allow firm conclusions, but the results suggest some interesting tendencies on questions not raised elsewhere and on which I have been unable to locate more reliable data. Three main aspects of class awareness were probed: how far the existence of classes was recognized, how far class interests were seen as contradictory, and the extent to which struggles between classes were perceived. In each case replies were grouped into two broad categories: minimal awareness and considerable awareness (None/Little and Fair/Great in the Tables). I did not contrast consciousness of rank and class, but examined the relationship between class consciousness and the various personal attributes associated with rank to see which of these attributes is most dominant in concealing class society and which can be employed in strategies to further an understanding of that society.

Table 17 provides a general picture of the degree to which class relations are concealed. It is interesting that all employees were more prepared to recognize the dynamics of these relations, the existence of class struggle, than to accept them as class

relations or to see antagonistic interests as the cause of the struggles. In fact, the bourgeois members of the sample, perhaps not paradoxically, revealed the strongest tendency to deny that classes either exist or have conflicting interests and at the same time to realize that class struggles were a part of their lives. As far as the workers were concerned, only about a third to two-fifths could be described as having any understanding of the struggles which just under half of them acknowledged to exist.

Since about 90 percent of the female but only 40 percent of the male respondents were in the working class, one would expect the different general experiences of the two sexes even within this class to produce different degrees of class awareness. Since working men must see many of their own sex in the upper classes, they might be expected to be less class-conscious

Table 16

Organized Workers, by Industry and Sex, 1975

	Total Numbers	Of which Women (%)
Primary	114,431	11.6
Mining	65,517	7.0
Construction	676,366	15.4
Manufacturing	4,602,954	23.6
Wholesale/Retail	702,896	41.0
Finance/Insurance/Real Estate	961,382	55.2
Transportation/Communications	2,083,397	10.4
Electricity/Gas/Water	228,356	9.2
Service	1,545,389	42.2
Public Administration	1,420,047	32.8
Other	189,683	28.1
Total	**12,590,400**	**27.6**

Source: Fujin rōdō no jittai, p. 83.

Table 17

Class Consciousness, by Class Position and Sex

	None/Little				Fair/Great				Subtotal		Total
	Men		Women		Men		Women				
	Nos.	%	Nos.	%	Nos.	%	Nos.	%	Men	Women	
i Existence of Classes											
Bourgeoisie[1]	117	86.7	4	66.7	16	11.9	2	33.3	135	6	141
Middle Class[2]	47	73.4	3	50.0	15	23.4	3	50.	64	6	70
Working Class[3]	86	64.2	65	65.0	46	34.3	30	30.0	134	100	234
ii) Antagonism of Class Interests											
Bourgeoisie	112	83.0	3	50.0	22	16.3	3	50.0	135	6	141
Middle Class	40	62.5	1	16.7	21	32.8	4	66.7	64	6	70
Working Class	82	61.2	42	31.3	44	32.9	48	48.0	134	100	234
iii) Existence of Class Struggles											
Bourgeoisie	48	43.0	2	33.3	72	53.3	2	33.3	135	6	141
Middle Class	26	40.6	3	50.0	34	53.1	2	33.3	64	6	70
Working Class	59	44.0	38	38.0	64	47.8	44	44.0	134	100	234

Table 18

Workers' Class Consciousness, by Firm Size

	None/Little		Fair/Great		Total
i) Existence of Classes	Nos.	%	Nos.	%	Nos.
Under 100 workers	33	55.9	24	40.7	59
100-999	50	62.5	29	36.3	80
Over 1,000	68	71.5	23	24.2	95
ii) Antagonism of Class Interests					
Under 100	21	35.6	30	50.8	59
100-999	40	50.0	36	45.0	80
Over 1,000	63	66.3	26	27.4	95
iii) Existence of Class Struggles					
Under 100	18	30.5	28	47.5	59
100-999	35	43.8	40	50.0	80
Over 1,000	44	46.4	40	42.1	95

Table 19

**Forms of Redundancy, by Firm Size
1975 (% of firms)**

	Firm Size (Operatives)		
	Under 21	21-300	Over 300
Refrain from recruiting	52%	77%	82%
Regulate overtime	36%	47%	73%
Increase holidays	35%	18%	18%
Lay off part-timers & temporaries	9%	34%	44%
Temporary layoffs of regulars	3%	33%	35%
Invite early retirement and lay off retired workers	18%	31%	17%

Source: *Chūshō kigyō to rōdō kumiai*, p. 122.

than women. However, Table 17 suggests that this has happened only to a limited degree, possibly because gender relations obscure class relations through men's ideological and political domination of women.

Only in their perceptions of contradictory interests do female workers seem to be more class conscious than male workers, while on the other two dimensions they appear to show less awareness. This might be because of the difficulties imposed on women to express their recognition of contradictions in actual struggles. The implications of these findings, to the extent that they are representative, are explored in the final

section of the chapter on strategy.

The degree to which age (also a form of class relations and divisions within the working class) either conceals or can be used to heighten class awareness is not immediately clear, because age affects the sexes differently and together with education channels some men in to the upper classes but most women into the reserve army. Male workers are likely to exhibit diminished class consciousness as they approach the age of fifty-five, and women are considerably influenced by early retirement and non-regular employment after that. Should my small sample be representative, one could conclude that the ideological and political domination of male over female workers diminishes with age and experience, and that one way to fight sexism among workers is to emphasize the function of age in the reproduction of the reserve army. Even though they enter the reserve at different ages, the current crisis is bringing home to male and female workers that "lifelong employment" is a myth. To tackle capital on this question can provide both sexes with positive common ground from which to wage united struggles, although middle-aged male workers seem to exert a greater degree of ideological domination over young female than young male workers. This problem is also relevant to the discussion on strategy.[23]

The difficulty in trying to isolate the forms of class relations which can most effectively uncover their substance is that the processes through which class agents are produced are inseparably linked. I have shown elsewhere, on the basis of the same survey, that workers' class consciousness diminishes with education. Since education, like sex and age, channels agents into different classes as well as into different fractions within the working class, those with the highest education (or the favored age or sex qualification) are likely to have the greatest aspirations for class mobility, and they can exercise powerful ideological influences over less educated workers (as well as over younger ones, and females). Table 18 provides some confirmation that the less educated mass workers in small firms are more class-conscious than the aristocracy in the monopoly sector. The physical separation of these workers in different companies reduces the aristocracy's ideological dominance and seems to produce wide differences in class consciousness.

It is impossible to tell how far membership in a company union is an independent factor which suppresses class consciousness, since my sample included very few union members in small firms and very few non-members in large ones. Variations in class consciousness by union membership almost exactly coincided with variations by firm size. The unorganized mass workers in my sample showed a much greater recognition of the existence and antagonistic interests of classes than the labor aristocracy, though their perception of class struggles was more or less the same. Among the organized workers in the monopoly sector, about 20 percent of Sōhyō and Churitsurōren* but only 10 percent of Dōmei affiliates revealed a strong class consciousness when an overall score was computed from all the relevant questions. This suggests that Sōhyō has perhaps played a less repressive role than Dōmei and Chūritsuroren, but that it has not raised class awareness to levels which certain militant leaders might lead one to expect.

In conclusion, my survey suggests that class awareness among the Japanese working class, particularly mass workers and members of the reserve army, is greater than bourgeois studies (confined largely to the labor aristocracy) have found. Although each of the forms assumed by class relations—sex, age, education and firm size—to some extent conceals these relations by making differences between classes appear the same as differences within the working class, it also seems that they can be used to heighten class awareness, particularly since the crisis is eroding their ability to conceal. We therefore need to examine how this is happening before some general points on strategy can be made.

---

* The National Council of Independent Unions

The Crisis and the Japanese Working Class

Although during the postwar boom the attributes of class agents (sex, age, etc.) seemed to determine life chances to a degree that left the real determinant, class position, in the background, the crisis has been bringing the latter to the fore through the growing inability of agents with the favored attributes to obtain what they had been promised. The immediate effects of the crisis on the working class have been fewer jobs and falling real wages, but these have so far overwhelmingly taken the form of a crisis of an aging society, a point which even a cursory glance at the press headlines cannot fail to bring out.[24]

The reason why the crisis takes this form is that its impact falls mainly on two groups of workers: school-leavers, who find that capital refrains from hiring its normal quota of new recruits (shūshokusha), and retired persons, who cannot always get second jobs (saishūshokusha). In order to prevent the numbers of unemployed older workers from growing, pressure has been mounting to postpone retirement, but to provide jobs for young people and to avoid rising wage bills, capital is under an equal pressure to encourage early retirement. So far, the burden has been falling mainly on school-leavers and college graduates, but the consequences of this are becoming intolerable. A propaganda campaign is being mounted to elicit public support for the state to resolve the contradiction, and capital is resorting to a combination of short-term expedients, some of which are affecting even so-called regular employees. Part of the propaganda campaign is somehow to sell the idea that "lifelong employment" is a premodern institution which must be rationalized. Table 19 shows the combinations of measures firms have been employing to deal with "over-employment."

Since large firms are resorting to measures which affect even the labor aristocracy, a material basis is being laid for working class unity. In 1974–1975 the employment of regulars fell by an average of 2.0 percent, though this concealed a fall of 7.5 percent in mining (a continuation of this industry's long-term decline), 5.7 percent in construction, and 5.4 percent in manufacturing. Among manufacturing industries, the reduction was 13.4 percent in textiles, 10.4 percent in lumber, 7.3 percent in each of furniture and rubber, 8.9 percent in metal goods, 0.2 percent in electrical appliances, and 7.5 percent in precision instruments.[25] In the same period, the proportion of total employees who worked less than 35 hours a week increased by 16.3 percent (from 8.6 percent to 10.0 percent).[26] Although it is difficult to show exactly to what extent the labor aristocracy is being reduced to mass workers and the latter to the reserve army, it appears that jobs have dried up in the monopoly sector and that only the smallest firms have been able to create new ones.

It seems that all workers are being affected in one way or another, though not entirely regardless of sex, age, and education, which cannot indefinitely obscure the determining role of class position. Increasingly, even university graduates are becoming sceptical about their chances of upward mobility. The very basis of the legitimacy of Japanese capitalism is being threatened, not simply because retired workers are finding it hard to get non-regular jobs, but because of the growing scarcity of regular jobs for young workers.

In 1976 Sony Corporation introduced a new scheme which might foreshadow a more general response by capital. It recruited for a new plant *only* older workers between 50 and 60, and offered them a basic salary which was only just over half that paid to its regular employees in other factories.[27] The reasons behind this decision seem to be closely related to an important change in the role of boom-time reserve army agents.

Since reserve workers are conditioned to accept low job security and below-average wages, one might expect them to carry the main burden of layoffs and wage reductions during a crisis. However, although they must accept more of both, the emphasis falls increasingly on the latter, while workers previously outside the reserve are more and more singled out for redundancy. The reasons why this change takes place are not hard to find, because while layoffs threaten only the legitimacy of capital in general, difficulty in cutting wages threatens the survival of particular capitals. Once the very existence of the latter is brought into question, members of the capitalist class find it harder to place their common interests above their individual interests, and they tend to rely on the state to ensure that this is done.

Sony Corporation's decision to keep on persons who might otherwise have moved from the floating to the stagnant reserve, and to allow persons who would have entered the labor aristocracy to become either mass or reserve workers, is quite consistent with capital's interests, at least in the short-term: declining profitability can be arrested by *bringing in* low-paid reserve workers, rather than by replacing them with young recruits whose deferred wages will have to be paid sooner or later. Since low wages are capital's most pressing need in times of crisis, traditionally low-paid workers are more likely to be the *last* to lose their jobs as a recession deepens.[28] Unless organized workers can prevent this through effective struggles, it will also help to bring about reductions in their wages and in the value of the labor power of the working class as a whole.

Although, because large proportions of earnings comprise deferred wages, it is difficult to calculate reductions in the value of labor power, in Table 20 we can get some idea of this from the annual increases in wages, bonuses, and consumer prices in 1970–1975.

The large annual increases in real wages to which workers had become accustomed since the mid-1960s were reduced to about 2 percent in 1974, and by 1975 they had ceased altogether. Annually since then, bonuses have risen by about 3 percent and wages by 8 percent, while inflation has remained in the region of 8 percent. The role of the reserve army in making possible these cuts in real wages is revealed by a survey conducted in 1978 by the Industrial Labor Research Institute. It noted that many firms were following Sony Corporation and hiring part-time employees as a "cheap and easily replaceable" labor force, and it pointed out that part-time wages had risen by only 10 percent a year since 1973, which was only about two-thirds of the increases regular workers had received.[29] Already in the years building up to the crisis, 1970–1973, the wages of day laborers as a proportion of those of regular workers fell from 43.7 to 38.6 percent.[30]

Another recent survey, by the Ministry of International Trade and Industry, showed that capital was preparing for a second round of employment retrenchment, because the cuts that began in 1974 had proved inadequate. These had reduced the numbers of employees in the 250 major firms surveyed by 7.5 percent in the period March 1974 to March 1978.[31] The expectation that further layoffs will be required confirms that the Japanese bourgeoisie is shedding its illusions about a sudden end to the depression and is preparing for a new confrontation. It

is gradually moving towards a strategy of keeping on traditional reserve army agents, in order to raise the rate of exploitation, and of allowing the labor aristocracy to bear more of the burden of unemployment than was ever practiced during the boom.

Working Class Strategy

Our analysis of the working class suggests a number of conclusions on possible strategies for revolutionary change in Japan which need to be considered in the light of the Japanese class structure as a whole.

Since the development of a revolutionary strategy is inseparable from the development of a movement to implement it, I concentrate here on the conditions that aid the growth of appropriate working class organization and ideology.

Although the relevant conditions can be divided into infrastructural and superstructural, these do not necessarily correspond to separate processes or institutions, but to different functions of what is often one and the same process or institution. The function of the economic base is to ensure the reproduction of the capitalist relation through the production, extraction, and realization of surplus value, while the function of the superstructure is the reproduction of class agents with the required skills and willingness to do all of these things. There is no reason why both functions should not be fulfilled simultaneously by a variety of institutions or activities. For example, in the production process, particularly through its allocation of agents into jobs according to their sex, age, and education, workers produce surplus value, they acquire relevant skills, and they are socialized into familial ideology and organizations. Similarly, in the circulation process, workers both imbibe ideas through their consumption activities and they ensure the realization of surplus value.

Since the ideas workers embrace and the organizations they form are inseparable from their day-to-day activities, revolutionary strategy requires identifying those activities, and the conditions of engaging in them, which can further revolutionary organizations and ideas. However, since the same activities perform infrastructural and superstructural functions, we must look to the economic base for the ultimate determinants of revolutionary action in order to help build a revolutionary movement.

We have seen that family ideology and company unions in Japan cannot be wished away, because both are rooted in the way the familial attributes of class agents function simultaneously as infrastructure and as superstructure. It is only because age, sex, and education slot workers into the positions created (and destroyed) by the process of capital accumulation that the ideas associated with them can serve to legitimize Japanese capitalism.

However, what our analysis of the working class has shown is that to forestall a prolonged interruption of the accumulation process, capital can no longer afford to allocate agents into the different positions in the way it did during the boom. Reserve army functions are now required of men and women of all ages, and positions in the aristocracy, not to mention mobility out of the working class, cannot be guaranteed for all agents with higher education, even when this is obtained in prestige universities.

Of the main attributes of class agents which conceal production relations, our analysis suggests that only age can be

Table 20

Annual Percentage Increases in Money Wages, Bonuses, and Consumer Prices, by Firm Size, 1970–1975

Year	Money Wages		Summer Bonuses		Winter Bonuses		Consumer Prices
	Large	Small	Large	Small	Large	Small	
1970	18.5	19.9	22.2	25.2	19.2	20.8	7.3
1971	16.9	18.3	13.7	14.2	5.2	7.6	5.7
1972	15.3	16.5	5.7	9.3	16.5	18.0	5.2
1973	20.1	21.1	23.9	30.9	42.4	45.0	16.1
1974	32.9	33.3	47.0	43.0	27.4	23.5	24.5
1975	13.1	14.4	7.4	0.4	−5.0	−2.4	11.8

Source: Chingin kentō shiryō, 1977, pp. 1, 4; Chingin sōran, 1977, p. 361.

exploited to help uncover them. This is because once acquired, sex and education remain with one for life, and if they are emphasized in any way as legitimate bases for special treatment, they create contradictions among the masses which can divide them into antagonistic camps. It is therefore crucial to see in the growing insecurity of male workers with university education the emerging conditions on which these sources of division can be combated. Not until men and women with different levels of education are more equally affected by the crisis will the determining role of class assume dominance over sexism and educational elitism.

Of these two forms of working class disunity, gender is by far the less difficult to overcome, because the material factors that also make gender a form of class relations are not part and parcel of the capitalist mode of production, whereas the material factors that make education a form of class relations are much more intimately bound up with the functioning of capitalism itself. The questions raised here are important, because if essential conditions of the working class organization and unity needed for the revolutionary overthrow of capitalism include the elimination of sexism and elitism, and if both are inseparable consequences of capitalism itself, revolutionary change becomes impossible.

The reason why sexism is not peculiar to capitalism lies in certain material conditions which affect the reproduction of class agents but which are not essential to the general laws of capital accumulation, which concern the reproduction of class positions. The single most important of these conditions is women's *biological* function of *bearing* children, which so long as it is also associated with their *social* function of *rearing* children, predisposes women to serve as floating and latent agents. Since their role in the nuclear family requires them to move in and out of the workforce, they become unable to remain in the same job long enough for similar proportions as men to rise into the labor aristocracy or entirely out of the working class. The central material condition of male power in the family is therefore socially determined, because women's social role of rearing children makes them dependent on men for most of their subsistence requirements. Because most men do not leave their jobs to assume domestic responsibilities, they can remain outside the reserve army and have a more secure source of subsistence than women.

However, it is precisely because women can draw on part of their husbands' wages for their subsistence that capital is assured of women's reproduction and can pay them wages below the value of labor power. In times of crisis, therefore, other things being equal, capital will come to prefer lower-paid women to higher-paid men. Only when this happens on a wide scale, do conditions exist for child-rearing responsibilities to move either more into men's hands (if carried out privately), or (if two incomes are needed to support a family) to be socialized through the development of day nurseries as happens during wartime.

The biological function of bearing children might still, under certain conditions, place men and women in unequal social roles, but the equalization of child rearing and the associated domestic toil can reduce such inequalities to only minor questions. Making it possible for women to become regulars also makes it possible for some to enter the upper classes. Such a development, even though it is an essentially bourgeois reform, is essential if sexism among the working class is to be eliminated and class relations are to become more visible.

Unlike gender, however, technical skills are part of the forces of production which belong to labor power. To wait for a random distribution in each class of persons with different technical skills is to wait for the abolition of classes themselves. The same strategy cannot be adopted in dealing with educational divisions among workers as can be used in overcoming differences between the sexes, because the former requires a socialist revolution and not simply bourgeois democratic reforms.

Will divisions among the working class then inevitably assume the form of differences in technical skill? Not necessarily, because a period of prolonged capitalist crisis can homogenize the different working class *positions* and therefore undermine the material basis on which the dominance of educational differences rests. Once the large numbers of university-educated workers who do not move out of their class are subjected to the same job insecurities and wage reductions as other workers, the infrastructural cause of the divisions will disappear, leaving the superstructural form with nothing to ensure its reproduction. Even though the upper classes will never include anything like equal proportions of well-educated and less-educated persons, the important thing is that the Japanese working class is coming to do just that. Furthermore, the greater the proportion of workers with higher education the less will education appear as a form of class relations. The appropriate strategy is not, therefore, to support university graduates' demands for privileged jobs, but to emphasize how a sacrifice of one's youth to acquire a degree is irrelevant to the process by which classes are created. Since of all the personal attributes of workers I related to class consciousness, education emerged as the most significant, the task of uniting the labor aristocracy with the rest of the working class should not be underestimated.

The use of age in revolutionary strategy seems to be quite different, not simply because all workers sooner or later reach retirement age and are affected by capital's treatment of non-regulars, but because there are no material conditions which peculiarly suit agents of different ages to fill particular class positions. Established patterns, which were developed only in response to certain forms of class struggle, can quickly change when a crisis requires capital to adopt different solutions to problems which arose out of a solution to some earlier problem. That the current crisis so overwhelmingly takes the form of a crisis of an aging Japan only shows how easy it is for people to see divisions by age as based on "convention" rather than on "nature." The growing effects of the crisis on workers of all ages provides a unique opportunity to unite them, since all are or will be affected whichever age group capital singles out as special victims. Since even in the traditional ideology the parent-child relationship is stronger than the husband-wife relationship, there is a much firmer basis for common action between old and young in Japan than in other capitalist societies. Bringing age to the fore can therefore uncover class relations, rather than further their concealment.

Notes

1. See Maurice Godelier, "Infrastructures, Societies, and History," *Current Anthropology*, Vol. 19, No. 4 (Dec. 1978).

2. Rob Steven, "The Japanese Bourgeoisie," *Bulletin of Concerned Asian Scholars*, Vol. 11, No. 2 (April–June, 1979) pp. 12 ff.

3. For detailed historical studies, see Koji Taira, *Economic Development and the Labour Market in Japan* (New York: Columbia University Press, 1970); Ronald Dore, *British Factory-Japanese Factory* (London: George Allen and Unwin, 1973); and Sydney Crawcour, "The Japanese Employment System," *Journal of Japanese Studies*, Vol. 4, No. 3 (Summer 1978).

4. Shūkan Tōyō Keizai, *Chingin sōran*, p. 89.

5. *Zaisei kin'yū tōkei geppō*, No. 295, pp. 46–47.

6. For a discussion of industrial conflict in medium-sized firms, see Robert E. Cole, *Japanese Blue Collar: The Changing Tradition* (Berkeley: University of California Press, 1971).

7. Tokyo Metropolitan Government, *Minor Industries and Workers in Tokyo* (Tokyo Metropolitan government, 1972), p. 30.

Note 8:
Retirement Pay and Pensions, by Firm Size and Education
(1975, ¥ million)

Education and Firm Size (Operatives)	Firms with only Lump Sum Payments	Firms with Pensions and Lump Sum Payments	
		Lump Sum	Present Value of Total Pension
University			
over 1,000	13.0	10.5	4.4
300-999	9.1	8.2	4.7
100-299	7.6	7.4	4.3
30-99	7.4	7.1	3.2
High School			
over 1,000	12.2	10.1	4.3
300-999	8.6	8.5	4.6
100-299	7.6	6.9	4.2
30-99	7.0	7.5	3.4
Middle School			
over 1,000	10.0	8.2	3.4
300-999	7.8	6.8	3.7
100-299	6.6	6.3	3.9
30-99	6.2	5.6	3.4

Source: Chingin kentō shiryō: 1977 nendokan, p. 69.

Note 9
Average Years of Employment by Age and Sex, 1975

Age	Men	Women
− 17	1.2	1.4
18-19	1.4	1.4
20-24	3.3	3.1
25-29	5.8	5.0
30-36	9.2	6.2
35-39	11.7	6.4
40-44	14.1	7.7
45-49	17.4	8.8
50-54	18.6	9.6
55-59	13.7	9.3
60+	10.0	9.5
Average	10.0	5.4

Source: Fujin rōdō no jitsujō, p. 45.

10. *Shūgyō kōzō kihon chōsa hōkoku*, pp. 46 and 50.

11. *Teinen tōtatsusha chōsa no kekka*, pp. 5, 7, and 13.

Persons Wishing to Work, by Age and Sex

Age	Sex		
	Male	Female	Total
15-24	696	1,218	1,914
25-34	147	2,998	3,144
35-39	49	1,074	1,123
40-54	150	1,702	1,852
55-64	205	534	738
65 and over	213	232	445
Total	1,459	7,757	9,217

Source: Shūgyō kōzō kihon chōsa hōkoku, pp. 229 and 233.

12. Nishioka Yukiyasu et al., "Hiyatoi rōdōsha: San'ya no seikatsu to rōdō" ["Day Labourers: Life and Work in Sanya"], *Shakai Kagaku Nenpō* [Social Science Yearbook], No. 8 (1974),. 36.

13. *Maitsuki kinrō tōkei chōsa sōgō hōkokusho, 1975*, p. 108.

14. During the prewar period of uneven accumulation, unwanted workers could eke out a subsistence by returning to agriculture. However, the decline of this sector in the postwar period has made such a solution impossible for large numbers of workers.

15. These are sectors in which capital is converted from one form to another, for example, from commodity to money capital (that is, the retail sector).

16. See the chapter on the petty bourgeoisie in my forthcoming *Classes in Contemporary Japan*.

17. I am indebted to Maurice Godelier for this argument. See his "Infrastructures, Societies, and History."

18. The fact that company unions are used to control workers does not alter the fact that they remain the sole organizations workers have. Since no form of organization can transform workers into something different from what they are, it is to be expected that they will, from time to time, use even company unions to express their class interests. The ocurrence of militant strikes by company unions does not therefore contradict the general point that company unions do more to suppress than to facilitate class struggles.

19. Women union members comprised 29.0 percent of the total number of women employees, while the corresponding proportion among men was 36.4 percent. See *Fujin rōdō no jittai*, pp. 82–83.

Note 20

Affiliations of Trade Unionists, by Industry and Major National Federations, 1975

	Total	Sōhyō	Dōmei	Shinsan-betsu	Chūritsu Rōren	Other
Total Numbers (1,000)	12,590	4,573	2,266	70	1,369	4,705
Industry (%)						
Agriculture	100	21.0	19.5	—	7.4	52.2
Forestry, Hunting	100	78.6	13.6	—	—	7.8
Fisheries	100	0.3	12.9	—	17.4	69.4
Mining	100	55.4	16.9	0.1	2.6	25.0
Construction	100	19.1	4.6	—	35.1	42.0
Manufacturing	100	18.1	29.9	1.3	16.0	39.7
Wholesale/Retail	100	7.8	22.5	0.1	4.1	74.0
Finance/Ins.	100	2.3	1.1	—	32.0	65.2
Real Estate	100	26.5	6.7	0.0	0.2	87.4
Transport./Commun.	100	59.1	20.9	0.4	0.6	24.1
Elec./Gas/Water	100	26.1	62.4	—	10.1	2.7
Service	100	57.0	4.2	0.0	0.9	39.0
Public Admin.	100	89.3	1.5	—	—	9.3
Other	100	27.4	8.0	0.1	1.5	63.1

Source: 1977 Nihon rōdō nenkan, pp. 185-186. The *Chūritsurōren*, or the National Council of Independent Unions, stands somewhere between the occasional militance of *Sōhyo* and the rabid anti-communism of *Dōmei*.

21. See, for example, the works by Ronald Dore, Robert Cole, and Thomas P. Rohlen, *For Harmony and Strength* (Berkeley: University of California Press, 1974).

22. Of the 69 companies initially approached, 53 agreed to cooperate, and of the 619 questionnaires distributed, 459 (74.2 percent) were returned.

Note 23
Workers' Class Consciousness, by Age and Sex

	None/Little				Fair/Great					
	Men		Women		Men		Women		Total Nos.	
	Nos.	%	Nos.	%	Nos.	%	Nos.	%	Men	Women
i) Existence of Classes										
Under 25	8	50.0	18	39.1	8	50.0	14	30.4	16	46
25-29	36	70.6	20	76.9	15	29.4	5	19.2	51	26
30-54	40	63.5	16	59.3	21	33.3	11	40.7	63	27
Over 54	2		1		2		0		4	1
ii) Antagonism of Class Interests										
Under 25	5	31.3	23	50.0	11	68.8	18	39.1	16	46
25-29	25	49.0	11	42.3	24	47.1	13	50.0	51	26
30-54	27	42.9	10	37.0	29	46.1	9	33.3	63	27
Over 54	1		1		2		0		4	1
iii) Existence of Class Struggles										
Under 25	6	37.5	16	34.8	9	56.3	22	47.8	16	46
25-29	25	49.0	11	42.3	24	47.1	13	50.0	51	26
30-54	27	42.9	10	37.0	29	46.1	9	33.3	63	27
Over 54	1		1		2		0		4	1

Above

To interpret these data requires knowing something about the women in the different age groups. Almost all of those under 25 were unmarried and anticipated leaving their jobs by the time they turned 30, while the same applied to about 60 percent of the 25–29 age group. Those older than this comprised almost equal proportions of unmarried, married, and no-longer-married women, most of whom could either not say when they might leave (44 percent) or thought this would be between the ages of 50 and 60 (37 percent). Although the numbers of persons in the different categories are too small to generalize, a change seems to take place when women are transformed from nominally regular employees into non-regulars. They apparently become more inclined than men to recognize both the existence and the antagonistic interests of classes, but they seem to submit to their inability to engage in effective struggles and increasingly deny that class struggles take place.

24. See, for example, the series of articles on "The Graying of Japan" in *Japan Times Weekly*, 13 January to 10 February, 1979.

25. *Maitsuki kinrō tōkei chōsa sōgō hōkokusho, 1975*, pp. 6–7.

26. *Fujin rōdō no jittai*, p. 51.

27. *Japan Times Weekly*, 19 June, 1976, p. 4.

28. A recent study of the reserve army in New Zealand, to which I am indebted for a number of insights on the subject, also found that the functioning of the reserve army changes in a recession. See R.M. Hill, "Women, Capitalist Crisis, and the Reserve Army of Labour" (Unpublished masters thesis, University of Canterbury, 1979).

29. *Japan Times Weekly*, 18 November, 1978, p. 10.

30 Nihon Kyōsantō chūō iinkai kikanshi keieikyoku [Bulletin management Bureau of the Central Committee of the Japan Communist Party], *1974 Seiji Nenkan* [1974 Political Yearbook] (Tokyo: 1974), p. 264.

31. *Japan Times Weekly*, 2 December, 1978, p. 8.

Sanya: Japan's Internal Colony

by Brett de Bary

Day Laborers in Japan*

You have to get up early to know Tokyo. Take Baba as a case in point. By day, it is an ordinary, slightly run-down park beside the tracks of the city's central commuting loop, halfway between Shinjuku and Ikebukuro stations. Go at dawn and a thousand men populate the park—young men in shirts and sneakers, carpenters in their belling, knicker-like pants, the muscular *dokata,* construction workers, duffle bags thrown over their shoulders and heavy black cloth shoes on their feet, a handful of men in office suits and leather shoes, old men, hoboes—the park is a different world. At six, the action begins. Vans pull up and encircle the square, the contractors dismount, enter the crowd, and wait as clusters of men gather around them to negotiate the sale of their day's labor. Small eating carts dot the park and along the cement paths second-hand clothes vendors peddle pants and jackets piled on squares of open cloth. The bargaining reaches a climax at seven, when wages are highest, and goes on for another hour as weaker, less aggressive men take what is left. Then, one by one, the vans with their cargoes of workers drive off, the cart-owners lock up, the clothes vendors bundle their goods back into their squares of cloth, and by eight Baba is once more a drab, empty park.

But in the world of Tokyo day-laborers, Baba is only a way-station. The number of men who work out of the park, about a thousand, is comparatively small: the proportion among them of student drop-outs or temporarily unemployed who will eventually work their way back into the white-collar strata is large. Those for whom the daily morning auction and day-labor have become a way of life usually drift, instead, to the *doyagai* (flop-house town) which is Tokyo's largest community of day-laborers, Sanya.

Sanya, too, is a carefully camouflaged part of the city. When tourists from all over the world gathered in Tokyo for the 1964 Olympic Games, the city government launched a "clean-up campaign" of the possibly embarrassing eyesore, despite the fact that Sanya's human population was increasing through massive labor recruitment for the construction of super-highways, super-express railway lines, and Yoyogi Stadium. Since, needless to say, hunting for Tokyo's slums was

hardly a high-priority item on the schedules of Olympic tourist, the campaign—largely replastering of the flophouse street front entrances—achieved modest success. More recently, the JSP administration of Minobe Ryokichi again made Sanya the subject of beautification efforts, as part of its "modernization" program for Tokyo. As a result, garbage collection services in the area improved, a few more "modern" flop-houses were built, and the notorious word "Sanya" was removed from the city map. Today, only the more poetic of the area's ancient titles remain, contrasting oddly with the reality they identify: "Street of Pure Waters," "Bridge of Tears," "Jewel Princess Park."

More difficult for the zealots of cleanliness to sweep away has been the social structure of Sanya: the labor contractors and the invisible corporations which employ them, the gangster organizations which control them, the 15,000 or so men who rely on this work for their daily existence. Here, behind the garbageless streets and face-lifted entrances, the human Sanya lives on, in conditions of misery which belie current myths of prosperous Japan. Step inside a *doya*, for example, "Sanya is a place where you can live with nothing more than one *tenugui* (the small towels Japanese laborers wrap around their heads to absorb sweat) to your name," one resident said. Inside a typical Sanya flop-house, where one rents a bed by the night, the average living space is estimated at one *tatami* mat (about 3' x 6') per man. A typical *doya* room has 8 mats, and 8 men. To leave as much open space as possible in the room, two beds are placed, one on top of the other, like bunks, on each of the four walls. Set on the floor beside each bunk will be two duffel bags containing tools and work shoes, the sum of the worldly possessions of the occupants. At night, or when there is no work, men gather together on the open space left in the middle of the room talking, gambling, drinking. The crowded dark rooms, compounded by the general dampness of the Japanese climate, make them an easy breeding place for tuberculosis. This year, when statistics revealed Sanya's TB rate to be two times that of the rest of Tokyo, squeamish public officials in the local welfare office demanded ultraviolet lights over their desks to disinfect the day-laborer applicants! Alcoholism, which to an advanced degree is said to afflict over 70% of the *doya* population, is an even more serious problem than TB.

But a bed in a *doya* is not the only accommodation Sanya has to offer. This January, when a series of riots in the district made newspaper headlines, middle-class Tokyoites shuddered guiltily as their TV screens flashed shots of

* A slightly different version of this paper appeared in *Ampo* Vol. 6, Nos. 3-4 (Summer-Autumn 1974).

day-laborers in the bitter five a.m. cold, fist-fighting, crawling over each others' shoulders, even forcing their way through the windows of one of Sanya's dingy employment centers in a desperate struggle to line up for jobs. Hit first and hardest by the economic slowdown brought on by the oil "crisis," many of these men had been jobless for weeks, destitute, and facing the prospect of a night (perhaps not their first) in the cold if they went jobless that day. In fact, spending a night outdoors has always been a familiar feature of life in Sanya: in the unique slang of the slum there is even a special word for it—to "blue-can," stand under the open sky around a fire of whatever can be foraged from the street. What the TV news reports did not mention was that an average of 40 men die each year in Sanya "blue-canning." During this year's long New Year holiday, as businesses around the nation shut down to celebrate and save on fuel bills, three people froze to death in Sanya's "Jewel Princess Park."

Where Do Day-Laborers Come From?

Outcroppings of Sanya dot the city of Tokyo. The street-crews, with their picks and pneumatic drills, already hard at work when the commuters step from their doors on winter mornings, the groups of men squatting around scrapwood fires and smoke-blackened kettles, taking a noontime break at roadside construction sites, the *tobi,* or "hawks," specklike figures on the frames of skyscrapers that soar above downtown streets, the flimsy pre-fab dormitories, appearing overnight in the midst of residential areas when there is building to be done, vanishing as suddenly when the project is finished.... all these are as familiar as trains and busses on the surface of Tokyo life. But to the average citizen they are no more than disconnected fragments. He does not follow the *tobi* and the street crews home at night, does not know where the residents of the pre-fab dormitories retreat when their work is finished and the temporary shelters dismantled. A wall of prejudice prevents him from tracing them to their source in Sanya.

To inquire about Sanya among Tokyo residents at large is to discover Japanese stereotypes of the day-laborer strikingly similar to those of minority races held by dominant groups in more racially heterogeneous societies. Most prevalent is the myth of the "dangerousness" of Sanya. The majority of "respectable citizens" of Tokyo claim to know "nothing at all" about the area: "I wouldn't dare set foot in it." On the heels of this comes a refusal to admit that the plight of day-laborers is worthy of attention, no less sympathy. Sanya's residents, the citizen staunchly maintains, have "chosen to live there of their own free will." What is more, "they could leave any time they wanted to." In a logic which closely parallels that of white racism toward ghetto blacks, the entire responsibility for the existence of Sanya and the day-labor system itself is traced to the moral weakness of its victims, the individuals who live there.

Often the most heart-rending glimpses of Sanya life appear in such conversations, used as illustrations of the moral degeneracy of the residents of the slum. "You have to see it to believe it," a man who had worked briefly in an employment agency declares. "Sanya is a place where you can sell anything. You can eat rice for breakfast in the morning and sell the chopsticks and the bowl you ate out of when you're done." A prosperous doctor, who recalls with distaste doing part-time work in a bloodbank near Sanya in his student days, offers his own recollections as proof of the "good-for-nothing" character of day-laborers. "Whenever they get desperate for money, they come in and sell their blood. Most of them do it far too often. You know there are weight requirements for blood donors. Well, we'd be putting these guys on a scale and the next thing we know we'd find they'd put rocks in their pockets to get them up to standard weight." The doctor complained that collecting blood in Sanya was bad business because of the frequency with which the donors fainted and had to receive transfusions of the same amount of blood.

Who, then, becomes a day-laborer? How "freely" is the way of life chosen, and how freely can it be escaped? Sanya must first be understood in the context of the historical events and social conditions which led to its formation.

Hidden History of the *Yoseba*

To anyone familiar with the ghettoes of Europe and America, the slums of Djakarta and Hong Kong, Tokyo's Sanya will seem small and tidy by comparison. In Japan itself, conditions in Sanya are slightly better than in Osaka's day-laborer area, Kamagasaki, which has a population of 40,000. But both Sanya and Kamagasaki are only points on an extensive network of day-laborer hiring sites which runs up and down the Japanese archipelago from Sapporo to Koza, Okinawa. Every major Japanese city and port has its *yoseba,* auction site where labor is hired by the day, and surrounding slum. Supplementing these, at construction sites all over urban and rural Japan, are thousands of *hanba,* temporary dormitories for men working on a daily wage basis, although they have contracted their work for the duration of a particular project. Historically, two processes—peasant migrations during the declining period of Tokugawa feudalism and Japan's postwar industrial transformation—were decisive in the formation of the system as it exists today.

The *yoseba* first appears as a word and an institution in late 18th century Japan, where its roots overlap with a more ancient system of caste-like discrimination existing since pre-Nara times. In the mid-1700s, a series of famines and floods coupled with soaring rice prices had sent desperate peasants streaming into cities in search of food and work. A number of edicts forbidding peasant migration after 1777 failed to stem the tide and, while women were absorbed into flourishing pleasure quarters as prostitutes, men, frustrated in their search for employment, became part of a swelling, potentially explosive population of drifters. Jails and stockades filled to overflowing, and in 1790 the bakufu set up its first labor camps, known as *yoseba,* in the cities of Edo (present-day Tokyo), Nagasaki, and Osaka. The site of the Edo *yoseba* was an island called Ishikawajima, to which homeless men, rounded up at periodic intervals, were sent to perform forced labor. Initially, men sent to the *yoseba* were classified as "non-criminal homeless" people, but the island gradually became a depot for criminal offenders as well. After the breakup of Tokugawa feudalism, the area survived as the Ishikawajima Prison into the Meiji period.

While ordinary peasants were sent to the Ishikawajima labor camp, a separate *yoseba* was set up in 1848 for classes of people who had traditionally been kept separate from the rest of the society. It was this *yoseba* which existed on the site of the present-day Sanya, amidst a cluster of communities of *eta* (those working the polluted leather trades) and *hinin* (an even lower caste of "non-humans") and the Yoshiwara pleasure quarters. Forced labor for *hinin* consisted of leading prisoners to the famous Kozukahara execution site, carrying out punishments and executions, and disposing of the dead bodies.

In prewar militarist Japan and during World War II, *yoseba* persisted in camps for forced draft Korean laborers known as "octopus rooms" because, like the octopus traps used by Japanese fishermen, there was no getting out once one had gotten in. The camps were presided over by criminal gangs which used violence to coerce labor on military projects and to prevent the escape of the Korean inmates. The Kajima Gang, forerunner of today's giant Kajima Construction Company, was one of these groups.

Despite its origins in feudal Japan, the proliferation and institutionalization of the *yoseba* system has been a unique product of the postwar era. It may seem ironic that Japan's population of poverty-ridden, unskilled day-laborers was spawned and grew in numbers during precisely those decades when the nation's GNP was growing by leaps and bounds. Beneath the seeming paradox lies the stark reality of Japan's "economic miracle," with its underpinnings in a vast domestic force of sub-contract laborers of various types: day-laborers, seasonal laborers, temporary laborers, elderly and married women working in their homes, and tiny, non-union factories with five or six employees.

An increasing pace of rationalization in industry and the dramatic decline of Japan's postwar economic program have been driving forces in creating the pool of unemployed tapped by the day labor system. In the case of Sanya, the steps in the conversion of the prewar redlight, *buraku* areas into full-blown *yoseba* have paralleled almost exactly the accelerating phases in the nation's postwar industrialization. The initial influx of unemployed men to Sanya, for example, coincided with the implementation of the "Dodge Line" Occupation policy—reviving the *zaibatsu*, snuffing out small businesses, neglecting agriculture—in 1949. Between September 1949 and March 1950 the number of independent businesses in Japan dropped by 30-40%, there was widespread abandonment of small (one hectare or less) farms, and over one million people were unemployed. The establishment of the first private employment agency operating out of Sanya followed soon after, as the Korean War boom led to heavy demand for labor in teeming shipyards and construction sites.

Throughout the Fifties bankrupt farmers, handicapped war veterans, and coal miners thrown out of work by the shift to oil energy drifted into Sanya and were fed through its employment agencies into these two industries. The decade of the Sixties, famous as the era of Japan's "high-speed economic growth," witnessed a further dramatic increase in the ranks of day-laborers. Mammoth construction projects such as the Shinkansen super-express railway, the Tokyo Olympics, and the Osaka Expo coincided with such rationalization programs as the Agricultural Structural Reform, aimed at diverting farmland to industrial use. This policy brought the effective dissolution of what remained of Japan's small farmer class. Between 1962 and 1963 alone, an estimated 90,000 farmers abandoned their land. The portion of the national population involved in agriculture, 32% in 1955, had fallen to 19% by 1967. Sanya's population doubled in roughly the same period (6,000 in 1953, over 15,000 by the mid-sixties), as did that of other *yoseba* throughout the country.

While a growing pool of unemployed labor has been one half of the *yoseba* equation, the perfection and perpetuation of the system have been the work of certain sectors of big industry with close cooperation from the Japanese underworld. Prime movers in the process have been shipyard owners and the construction industry. Although a certain portion of day labor contracts is for miscellaneous distasteful or dangerous jobs (garbage collection, morgue work, hazardous aspects of steel production), the overwhelming majority of contracts come from shipyards and construction firms. At the root of the demand has been the desire of the two industries to cover their relative vulnerability to fluctuations of supply and demand by reliance on a "disposable" labor force. This has been particularly true of the construction industry, which in Japan is virtually 100% dependent on sub-contract labor. The fluid nature of construction work, in which not only the amount and type of labor used but building materials and machinery vary vastly from project to project; its vulnerability to daily weather changes; and a high accident rate caused by the prevalence of super-speed projects, all make construction capitalists loath to assume responsibility for the wage and insurance costs of a permanent labor force. The result has been the evolution of the *yoseba* system as it exists today: giant construction companies pass on the responsibility for hiring labor through a complex network of smaller and smaller companies terminating in the individual labor contractor (the often feared *tehaishi*) on the daily auction site. The *tehaishi* guarantees the firm a certain number of workers per day and receives as his salary a cut out of the wage paid to each worker. Since conditions of work are frequently illegal or involve deception in making oral contracts, the ultimate lynchpin in the system is the use or threat of physical force by the contractor on the work site. Accordingly, a majority of contractors and the small companies they represent are part of underworld organizations. (The National Police Report on Organized Crime for 1973 estimated that 2,500 construction companies were controlled by criminal gangs. Since collusion between police and underworld gangs is common, this should be seen as a low estimate.)

YOSEBA SYSTEM

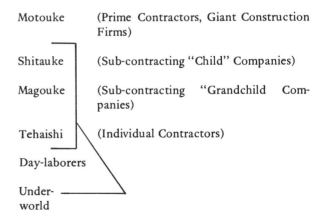

Motouke	(Prime Contractors, Giant Construction Firms)
Shitauke	(Sub-contracting "Child" Companies)
Magouke	(Sub-contracting "Grandchild" Companies)
Tehaishi	(Individual Contractors)
Day-laborers	
Underworld	

The *yoseba* system has sometimes been compared to an intricate network of nodular roots extending from the giant construction companies through the mass of day-laborers. According to conditions of the market, lengths of roots may be disconnected at any place along the nodes (the sub-contracting companies and *tehaishi*), beginning with those furthest from the parent firm. The day-laborer is thus rendered supple and pliant in the hands of capital, which passes all the brutality of the vicious cycle of supply and demand on to the *yoseba*, pitting young against old, strong against weak, in the daily struggle for survival.

Octopus Rooms in 1974?

February, 1974 ... the story of 30-year-old Mr. I., who appeared unexpectedly this February at a Soka Gakkai gathering this reporter was observing in a quiet residential area of Tokyo, illustrates vividly the forces which converge in the making of a contemporary Japanese day-laborer. Mr. I. responded to the group's questions about how he had become a "believer":

Mr. I. was one of five children born into a farming family on Sado Island off the northern coastal city of Niigata. His father, a tenant farmer at the time of the Occupation land reform, received a plot of land barely large enough to support his family. Income from raising rice was so slim that the children in the family had to gather wood and make charcoal to earn the meager amount of spending money they needed at school. I.'s only thought when he graduated from high school was to leave the difficult life on the farm and find a well-paying job in Tokyo. But with minimal social connections and no technical skills, I. was only able to land a job as a milk delivery man, rising at 3 every morning with a starting salary of 3,000 yen a month (1956). After fourteen years at this job, I. earned a modest salary of 100,000 yen per month, but in 1970 the small company where he worked fell victim to that other phenomenon of the era of "high-speed economic growth," the insolvency of small businesses. Left with no other alternatives after the milk company went bankrupt, I. kept himself alive for four years at a number of jobs which he found through newspaper ads and employment agencies—all of them extremely low paid and one requiring 24-hour work shifts twice a week. In August, 1974, I. was approached at an employment agency by a man claiming to be a representative of the Ota Steel Company, with what seemed an attractive job offer. For driving a truck transporting steel girders from the Ota factory to different construction sites, I. would receive a wage of 2,800 yen per day. The wage, the Ota man assured him, would be sheer savings, because the company would provide him with a room—bath attached!—and all his living necessities at their dormitory (*hamba*) in Saitama-ken, just beyond the northern boundaries of Tokyo. I. made an oral contract for one month's work on the spot, and left for Saitama-ken the following day.

"As soon as I got inside the dormitory I realized I was in an octopus room." I. found himself in a structure made of the thinnest plywood. Although he arrived during the last October warm spell, temperatures soon dipped, but there were no heating facilities in the building. "From the beginning of November, the tap water was frozen every day. We couldn't even get water to try to warm ourselves with tea." The "bath attached" which I. was promised turned out to be "attached" to the outside of the building: a converted oil drum heated from beneath. Far more devastating, however, was I.'s discovery that the dormitory, and all the truck drivers in the area, were controlled by an underworld organization known as the Morimoto Gang.

At the end of his first month, I. found himself with only 24,000 yen of the 84,000 yen he had been promised to clear. Two thousand yen of his daily 2,800-yen salary had been subtracted for meals, rent, and bath fee! More, he confessed frankly, was lost in nightly gambling sponsored by the gang in the dormitory. "By December I was desperate to quit. It wasn't only the loss of money and the cold, but the work itself was extremely dangerous. A little slip loading or unloading these steel girders and you're crushed. I knew there had been many accidents." But when I. announced his decision to leave, the Morimoto Gang threatened retaliation on his family and effectively forced him to work on. Finally, with the help of a boyhood friend from Sado, I. managed to escape from the dormitory during his three-day New Year's holiday, forfeiting 15-days' wages. He had temporarily found work as a painter in Tokyo and had come to the Soka Gakkai meeting because "I should practice my religion from now on. That other life must have been a punishment for my sins."

I.'s story is atypical only in its still tentative conclusion, his escape from the world of day-labor. Its basic elements are the classic ingredients in the experience of Japanese day-laborers, except that for most there is no way out. Of Sanya's peak (wintertime) population, for example, 1/3 are seasonal rural migrant workers who will return to their farms, 1/3 are permanent day-laborers who wander from *yoseba* to *yoseba*, while 1/3 are permanent residents of Sanya.

No Escape: Life Cycle of a Day-Laborer

A dissection of Sanya's social structure reveals the day-laborer trapped in a vicious cycle of economic relationships, while social prejudice bears down with equal force from outside. Caught between the two, the alienation of the day-laborer is an extreme within Japanese society. "After you live here for awhile," says Nakamori Kishin, a pastor in the ghetto for 20 years, "you realize there is absolutely no basis for community in Sanya. I can think of only two things that really bring these men together: the drinking-stand and the park bench." According to Nakamori's observation, the competition of the *yoseba*, unsteady supplies of cash which force men to drift from one inn to another, the infiltration of the *doya* by plainclothesmen hunting for fugitive criminals, all debilitate potential bonds of unity between the men. Sexual alienation reinforces their isolation. Mistrust and contempt on the part of "ordinary society" make it extremely difficult for men in Sanya to marry. At present only 200 men, about 1.5% of the population, have wives.

Underlying the day-laborer's existence in Sanya is a predatory economic network including *tehaishi*, inn-owners, restaurant-owners, underworld controlled recreational facilities, and police, which over time renders him economically, physically, and psychologically unable to leave the ghetto.

Conditions of Life in Sanya:

1. Tehaishi, Wages and Work

Daily contracts are made between 5 and 7 a.m. Seventy percent of men in Sanya seek jobs from approximately 150 blackmarket *tehaishi*, either with introductions from private employment agencies, innkeepers, or by going directly. Current blackmarket wages for day-labor range from 4,500 yen to 5,000 yen per day. While this at first glance appears high (assuming full employment, the monthly 110,000-yen income would equal that of a middle-aged male company or government worker), the impression is deceptive, for the wages are offered under conditions which in fact leave the day-laborer in the most economically weak and vulnerable position in Japanese society.

Lack of job security: Contracts negotiated on illegal terms with *tehaishi* or small sub-contracting firms offer day-laborers none of the fringe benefits and bonuses which beef up the income of ordinary salaried workers. Most damaging to the day-laborer is the failure to guarantee steady work. Completely at the mercy of supply and demand fluctuations, no day-laborer is in a position to find employment on every working day of the month. On a typical day at the Sanya *yoseba*, there is a 30% unemployment rate. Even in peak working seasons, the average day-laborer is employed only about 20 days per month.

The winter season: A city employment office set up in Sanya in the early sixties does offer a minimal dole of 1,200 yen per day to unemployed day-laborers. To qualify, however, an applicant must produce a stamped card proving that he has worked 28 days out of the preceding 60-day period. The effect of this system is to disqualify most laborers from unemployment compensation at precisely the time when they need it most. This is during the winter season, when Sanya fills to overflowing with workers from the countryside. By increasing the labor supply and accepting work at lower rates, incoming farmers drive wages down and sharply intensify competition for jobs. Since the number of jobs drops drastically after November, by late January large numbers of men in Sanya lack the qualifications even for the unemployment dole. This year, with the added impact of the oil crisis, the number of workers qualified for the dole was effectively zero—sparking the riots mentioned above. Dread of the winter season is a major factor driving men to sign up for 3- or 4-month stints at *hamba* such as the one I. went to.

Lack of accident insurance: Day-labor is by definition the most physically strenuous, distasteful, and dangerous work available. This is especially so in the construction industry, which achieves high productivity by building at the fastest speed and lowest cost possible. The hiring of inexperienced workers for hazardous work, introduction of new machinery without training sessions, failure to block traffic around worksites in congested streets, the use of flimsy scaffolding which all too frequently collapses—these and other features give the construction industry one of the highest accident rates in Japan. Despite this, firms offer virtually no accident insurance to day-laborers. While formally the giant companies sometimes provide their employees with a policy, the red-tape process involved in this all but nullifies its effect for the day-laborers.

City Employment Agencies: In the 1960s the city established two employment centers in Sanya, offering contracts on legal terms, unemployment and health insurance included. Daily wages for these jobs, however, are only 1/2 to 1/3 of the black market rates for the same work. Accordingly, only about 30% of Sanya workers, usually those whose age or weakness precludes them from effective competition on the *yoseba*, rely on these agencies.

2. Lodging, Food, Recreation

In step with Japan's spiralling inflation, inn rates in Sanya have risen exorbitantly in the last three years. The fee for one night in a bunk-bed—50 to 80 yen in the '50s—now ranges from 300 to 500 yen. Since this equals a monthly sum roughly equivalent to that paid by many Tokyo office-workers and students for small rooms in residential areas of the city, outsiders often ask "why don't they just move out of the slum?" The obstacle is the parasitic structure in which the day-laborer is caught, one which makes it literally impossible for him to accumulate the cash down-payment of three or four months' rent necessary to lease an apartment in Tokyo. Once having entered Sanya "with only one *tenugui* to his name," the day-laborer finds himself dependent for every aspect of his existence on those whose profit, in turn, derives from his daily cash wage. "Extras" like cigarettes, soap, tooth-powder, which his inn-keeper handily produces for a slight service charge, substantially inflate the cost of a night's lodging. To restaurant-owners and drinking-stand operators go payments for food and for alcohol, the fastest source of relief after an exhausting day's work. Houses of prostitution take a further cut of his daily wage. What is left sooner or later filters into the gangster-dominated gambling networks which are perhaps the cruelest form of economic and psychological oppression of the day-laborer. Race-track betting, which thrives on his pathetic hopes of the lucky break which will bring wealth, respect, and a ticket back to normal society, is so prevalent in Sanya that the *yoseba* is literally depopulated on the last day of a series of races.

No wonder that Sanya is sometimes referred to by its residents as a "great, big octopus room." A day-laborer who tries to defy these conditions of his existence finds himself confronting three tightly knit walls of resistance: the underworld gangs, the Sanya Innkeepers' Union, and the police. Sanya's twenty-odd years as a *yoseba* have been marked by an increasing degree of internal organization and cooperation between these three groups, while during most of this period day-laborers have remained a weak and divided mass.

As the first employment agency was being set up in Sanya, for example, landlord Kiyama Kinjiro allied himself with the demands of industry and the *tehaishi* by devising the "bunk-bed system" for converting the welfare barracks in the area (set up under SCAP for homeless wanderers right after the war) into lodging houses for day-laborers. The first campaign of the Sanya Innkeepers' Union, founded soon after, was to drive prostitutes out of Sanya into neighboring Asakusa, a major step in the area's conversion to a full-fledged *yoseba*. In the decade of the sixties, the Innkeepers' Union has been a driving force behind the gradual expansion of police control in the area. After the First Sanya Incident in 1959, when workers attacked the small local police box, the Inkeepers' Union backed construction of a new and greatly enlarged station in its stead, contributing chairs and funds for the building. Innkeepers and merchants, jealous guardians of the law and order which guarantee their incomes, have been firm supporters of the "candy and whip policy" (welfare measures accompanied by police repression) which the government has evolved in recent years to cope with increasing outbreaks of violence in Sanya.

Health Conditions: "A day-laborer is always shifting between three modes of life: worker, unemployed man, and sick man," says a young worker organizer in Sanya. "Usually he ends his life in the last category." The large majority of workers in Sanya, a backwater of Japanese society as far as health conditions are concerned, suffer from some kind of physical ailment. Almost all suffer from stomach, liver, and kidney diseases associated with alcoholism. Lacking health insurance policies which most Japanese receive from their companies, day-laborers are forced to rely on city hospitals, where conditions are deplorable and which are unbearably lonely for men with no family. As a result, many workers in Sanya shy away from medical treatment and put up with their ailments while they continue to work. A prevalent pattern in Sanya is for the condition to gradually worsen until a man passes out, is taken by ambulance to the hospital where he dies, perhaps never having realized to that point the extent of his illness.

There is another dimension to the problem of health in Sanya, for illness of the day-laborer provides yet another vulnerability which may be manipulated to keep him supple and pliant within the system. City hospitals and mental institutions in this sense may be seen as extensions, in slightly more subtle form, of the repressive network which maintains law and order in Sanya. This is most clearly suggested by the pattern of close cooperation between city hospitals and the police force. Sweep arrests of drunks in the Sanya area are common, particularly during economic slumps and other periods of potential unrest. Police records show the astonishingly high yearly average of 10,000 arrests for drunkenness—just short of one arrest per head of the population. Slightly over 1,200 of these arrestees, often workers who stand out for their rebellious and defiant attitudes toward authority, are turned over by the police for periods of confinement in city mental institutions, a striking commentary on the double function of these institutions. An estimated two-thirds of the patients in Tokyo's public mental hospitals are day-laborers.

Resistance and Repression

The history of organized resistance to conditions of oppression in Sanya has been a bleak one. A first labor union, formed in the early '50s by day-laborers, Koreans, and Communists released from prison under early SCAP policy, was crushed by the arrest of its leaders after the "Bloody May Day" of 1952. Sanya workers spent the rest of the decade of the '50s without any form of union organization, totally at the mercy of sub-contractors, and excluded from even the minimal welfare programs of the state.

Sanya's first outbreak of rebellion came on October 22, 1959, against the background of the escalating national struggle against the renewal of the U.S. Security Treaty. Sanya's local police-box, long an object of resentment for its role in enforcing the order of exploitation imposed by sub-contractors and merchants, was attacked by 300 men and one patrol car was set ablaze. The action provoked a wave of alarm which spread from the local power structure to the National Diet, and in the following summer the government authorized the construction of what workers have ever since referred to as "Sanya's mammoth policebox," base for a 55-man force, in Sanya. The Tamahime "Consultation Center" (its name aptly circumscribing the limits of its services) was opened in the fall, the first government welfare office to be established in Sanya. The all too obvious "candy-whip" nature of the government's policy, however, only fanned rebellion in the ghetto: the mammoth policebox was attacked a few weeks after its opening, and summer 1961 brought a chain-reaction outburst of riots in Kamagasaki. In the following year the government responded by drawing up a "Consolidated Welfare Policy" for the two ghettoes. A welfare center was opened in

Sanya in July 1962 and relocated and expanded in 1965. But so far government welfare programs, which carefully leave intact the fundamental contradictions of the *yoseba* system, have proved utterly useless in defusing worker discontentment. Riots have continued to occur with yearly regularity, gradually exposing the teeth in the policy of the government, which has simply escalated its application of police force to suppress them. Since 1970, this has included dispatching *Kidōtai,* special riot police, to quell ghetto disturbances.

The decade of the sixties brought renewed efforts by left groups to channel spontaneous worker rebellion into an organized movement, but this ended in failure, due both to the increasing severity of police repression and the lack of a viable ideology for the day-laborer struggle. Between 1964 and 1969, seven different struggle groups coalesced in Sanya, including one organized by the JCP; all but two of these collapsed within a year of their organization. Of those which have survived into the seventies, one, the Sanya Independent Consolidated Labor Union, now confines its activities largely to the operation of a small cooperative restaurant. The second, the Tokyo Day Laborers' Union, which had a substantial base among day-laborers into the early '70s, was disbanded this winter after a scandal involving misuse of funds collected from member at New Year's.

In Spring 1972 the successful action of a small band of militant workers in smashing one of Kamagasaki's notorious subcontracting groups, the Suzuki Gang, sparked the birth of a radical new form of struggle among Japanese day-laborers. Dramatically rejecting the passive, negotiating stance adopted by organizers of the '60s in favor of pitting struggle directly against the immediate agents of oppression, the sub-contractors *on the worksite,* a small group of day-laborers, disillusioned unionists, and New Left activists came together in Sanya and Kamagasaki in Autumn 1972 to form two fraternal organizations—the Worksite Struggle Group (Genba Tōsōiinkai) in Sanya, and the Joint Struggle Group (Kamakyōtō) in Kamagasaki. According to the bold vision to which these two groups have committed themselves, negotiating, which focuses on making "demands" while continuing to work within an exploitative system is an implicit acceptance of that system, and a denial of the basic right of the worker, not the capitalist, to determine the conditions under which he will work. The guiding vision of "struggle on the worksite" is a recognition of worker sovereignty, a positive endorsement of the worker's most potent weapon, spontaneous rebellion, and of the necessity, when no other means avail, of using physical force to directly counter the physical force which is the lynch-pin of day-to-day oppression. The aim is to develop a dynamic, ongoing struggle against each case of oppression, when and where it occurs: when men discover they have been deceived by contractors, made to perform excessively dangerous or dirty work, are forced to work overtime, and so forth. But since individual efforts are sure to be crushed, as they have been so many times in the past, the key to "Struggle on the worksite" is collective action: "When you come up against a problem, don't brood by yourself," advises *Notes For Workers,* a "little red book" written by and distributed among struggling Sanya workers, "call your friends and get them to help you."

The formation of the Worksite Struggle Group in Sanya was followed by a rapid series of offensive actions in Fall and Winter '72-73 which gradually elicited the support of growing numbers of day-laborers. Whenever a case of oppression was encountered in the course of a day's work, it would be reported to the group, and on the following day a workers' collective would be dispatched to the same worksite to protest. Although in many cases the *tehaishi*, numerically overwhelmed, would yield after a brief verbal debate, tactics of physical intimidation and refusal to hire were gradually adopted by Sanya gangs as they became aware of the Worksite Struggle Group and its aims. By winter a state of "near-war"—including flare-ups of violence, police interference, and worker arrests—had broken out between the struggle group and a number of Sanya's hard-core contracting companies. In July 1973 these culminated in an all-out confrontation between workers and the Arai Construction Co. (Arai, a sub-contractor for giant firms such as Mitsubishi, Kajima, and Shimizu, is notorious in *yoseba* throughout Japan for its *takobeya*—reliance on physical coercion to enforce illegal working conditions—and its affiliation with the nationwide underworld organization Kyokutō.) On July 19, a Sanya worker who had protested against working conditions on the construction site of the Mitsui Building Skyscraper in Shinjuku was threatened into submission by *tehaishi* wielding iron bars. On the following day, 50 workers filed into the Arai office on the construction site demanding an apology for the incident and redressing of the worker's complaint. Arai summoned twenty police to forcibly eject the workers from its office, but a campaign to oust Arai from all *yoseba* in Tokyo gradually gained momentum. Arai quickly found itself alienated from the majority of other sub-contracting companies in Sanya and forced to rely increasingly on bodyguards provided by the Kyokuto organization. The climax of the struggle came on September 11, when an attack by a small group of workers on a band of Arai's bodyguards flared into a small-scale riot as growing numbers of resentful workers joined in the fray. Special riot troops were brought in to suppress the riot, and 13 workers were arrested. These workers are currently involved in a court battle with Arai, but general worker resistance to the company has by now become so effective that Arai has had to completely abandon its hiring in Sanya.

Simultaneous to the development of militant struggle against sub-contractors, the Worksite Struggle Group launched a wide variety of programs designed to develop among Sanya workers the capacity to deal autonomously with their own most vital needs. Health being one of the foremost of these, worker medical cells were formed where techniques of preventive medicine, particularly acupuncture, were studied, and where procedures for receiving health and accident insurance (of which many workers were ignorant because of the bureaucratic jargon in which they are usually explained) are studied and discussed. "People's patrols" were also formed: bands of workers to patrol the streets and help men fallen through illness, hunger, or alcohol, before they are arrested. The most dramatic development on this second front-line, however, has been the yearly "Struggle to Survive the Winter," carried out during the national New Year's holiday, the most dangerous period of the year for day-laborers, since employment openings drop to zero, while dwindling supplies of cash force large numbers of men to "blue-can" in the bitter cold. In 1973-74, the Worksite Struggle Group erected huge tents in Jewel Princess Park, where food (supplied by Sanrizuka peasants), fires, and free medical attention were provided. This winter, 1974, when the heavy toll taken by the "oil crisis" in unemployment among day-laborers made the situation particularly severe, the Winter Struggle developed into a complex political struggle to demand greater attention from the city welfare structure to the acute problems of day-laborers' existence. The struggle continued into late January, when the city, attempting to avoid the high cost of paying a daily dole to the huge numbers of unemployed workers, announced a termination of the dole and herded workers into an institution where they could literally do nothing but sit on their hands all day, waiting for three sub-standard meals. On Janary 20, when worker anger over their humiliating situation welled up into a riot within the center, *kidōtai* (riot police) were again called in, 20 workers were arrested and the protest severely repressed. Two days later the center was closed and all workers sent back to Sanya. In the following month 50 other workers known to have participated in the protest movement have been arrested on various charges.

While the growth of the Worksite Struggle in Sanya clearly symbolizes a giant-step in the revolutionary consciousness of Japanese day-laborers, it has also made clearer than ever before the tenacious roots of the *yoseba* system in Japan and its vital importance to the Japanese economy. According to the struggle group members' own analysis of their experience, escalating attacks on the subcontracting system have consistently evoked greater and greater police and government intervention to unabashedly support and rescue those under attack. (Preparations for the 1974 Winter Struggle, for example, had to be carried out under surveillance of a 300-man Special Riot Force detachment.) Since May 1972, 160 members of the Worksite Struggle Group have been arrested and indicted on various charges (the figure for Kamakyōtō during the same period is 250). With the exception of the long-continuing and fierce struggle of Sanrizuka peasants to oppose the construction of an international airport at Narita, no other Japanese protest movement at the present time faces such intense state repression as the day-laborer movement.

The campaign continues to heighten at the present time. In the past few months, for example, a concentrated police campaign to label Worksite Struggle members as former Red Army members has been launched, accompanied by a wave of arrests and indictments on preposterous bombing charges which are clearly frame-ups. In the face of this repression, many members in the Tokyo and Osaka areas have been forced to disperse to *yoseba* all over the country, while those remaining in these two central cities are concentrating their energies on expanding such aspects of the movement as the medical program (which are legal and not so easily subject to repression) and waiting, as one member put it, "while the seeds of the struggle are sown in *yoseba* all over Japan."

Shimizu Ikkō's "Silver Sanctuary" (Gin no seiiki): A Japanese Business Novel

銀
の
聖
域

translated and with an introduction by Tamae K. Prindle

Introduction

"I want to describe lots of people who are directly involved in business," says Shimizu Ikkō.[1] Shimizu Ikkō (1931-   )is the pioneer of Japanese "business novels" *(kigyō shōsetsu)* and one of the most prolific and popular novelists today. Born in Tokyo, Shimizu attended Waseda University and was active as a freelance writer contributing articles to weekly magazines until he was recognized as a novelist. His *An Artery Archipelago (Dōmyaku rettō)* was awarded the 28th Japanese Detective Story Writers Association Prize in 1975.

As Shimizu notes, the business novel is "young"; they have only been in the Japanese market since the mid-1960s. The mainstay of these novels is their "immediacy to the business world." Because the novelist's artistry in fictionalizing socio-economic data makes it appealing and approachable, novels are informative and expressive at the same time, qualities which even professional economists find quite creditable. And the immense popularity of business novels also speaks for their socio-cultural significance.

Shimizu's short story "Silver Sanctuary" (Gin no seiiki) first appeared in the monthly magazine *All Reading (Ōru yomimono)* in January 1969. The story begins with the discovery of an infraction of confidentiality in the administration of three "confidential long-term savings accounts," a type of account unfamiliar to most Westerners. This is a system whereby a client opens a long-term savings account under a pseudonym. His real name and address are known by a very limited number of bank employees. Later transactions on this account will be carried out by means of a registered stamp *(inkan)*[2] bearing the client's pseudonym. It is a technical aberration Shimizu takes special interest in. The story outlines, among other things, the process of training a bank's staff, and brings to light the bank's difficult interpersonal relationships as well as its competition with other banks. We learn of the existence of two career paths: vertical and relatively horizontal. Only executives-in-training have the privilege of rising in rank. Hence, personnel rotation brings about psychological tension among employees, who, in a sense, are like machinery operated by the institution. They are requested to work under the basic principle that "A banker must be trustworthy, almost impartially serious, and at the same time, must not have any personality." Women, in particular, are underdogs. The tragic heroine's name Yōko (meaning a person who "serves," who is "constant" and even "stupid") symbolizes women's status. And in fact, Yōko becomes *persona non grata* and even a criminal, after offering everything a woman can to Tagawa, Saeki and a number of other men.

Feudalism, sexism—many such objections may be raised after a reading of "Silver Sanctuary." Nevertheless, it must be pointed out that business novels project socio-economic reality in Japan and present it in an easily graspable format.

"Silver Sanctuary" (Gin no seiiki)

1.

Exactly three months ago, Tagawa Junji was appointed to be the Manager of the Nittō Bank N Branch Office. He was the first to be nominated from his age group. The incident in question took place just when his management of the bank was beginning to run smoothly.

"Something is bothering me . . ." Assistant Manager Nishiyama Kenji looked hesitantly at Tagawa, coming out of a conference. "You must know Ikuno-shi[3] of five-chome,[4] an engineer specializing in the installation of greenhouse heating systems. He telephoned and asked me why the salesman from

Daidō Bank across the street came to visit him."

"You mean . . ., why he visited?" Tagawa repeated the question like a parrot. Tagawa had paid a courtesy visit to Ikuno's house once since becoming Manager. It was with Nishiyama. If he remembered correctly, this client lived in an old-fashioned pre-fabricated rusting steel frame house which had been expanded by annexing a brick walled shed. Seemingly, the owner of this ramshackle house without even a business sign-board has been carefully saving every penny. In the N Branch Office alone, he had a confidential long-term savings account of 25 million yen.[5] Tagawa found it difficult to put the person and the amount of his savings together.

"In other words, he is having a difficult time convincing himself that there was no purpose to the salesman's visit. He says that nobody other than our bank should know about his 25 million yen account . . . You remember his shanty, don't you? The reason why he lives in that run-down house, he says, is to get around unnecessary taxation. How did Daidō Bank find out about his savings? He is panic-stricken. He is afraid that the tax bureau may trace back his actual income, now that the Daidō Bank has learned about it."

Tagawa smiled critically. He did not disapprove of the penny-pincher mentality, but it made no sense to directly connect the salesman's visit with the problem of taxation, and to be frightened by the idea.

"It's not that Daidō demanded a transfer of his 25 million yen in our bank into theirs, is it?"

"Heaven forbid!"

"Then, there's nothing to worry about."

"The only thing is—although this may only be a coincidence—Norisaka-san on K Street, where I dropped in yesterday, had also been solicited by Daidō Bank."

Norisaka on K Street owns a small grocery store. Although the store is small, he used to be the largest landlord in the area and has been a regular customer at the Nittō Bank N Branch Office. His long-term savings account holds nearly 30 million yen.

"I wonder what they are doing at Daidō Bank, a memorial savings raising campaign, or something of that sort?"

Through the thin lace curtains, Tagawa peered into the two-storied white Daidō Bank N Branch Office kitty-corner across the narrow intersection in front of N Station.

Next-door to it was a Mutual Bank.[6] In all, there were six branches of financial institutions in the neighborhood.

"Nothing that I know of."

"Well then, did they decide to steal our regular customers?"

If only one customer had been solicited, one could say that it was just a coincidence. It would not have bothered Tagawa. But with two private account clients having been approached one after the other by the Daidō Bank salesman, a certain amount of caution was necessary.

N Station was located on a private railway network. It was only thirty minutes away from Ikebukuro Station on the National Railway Yamate Line. The daily number of passengers on this private line was approximately twenty thousand. The district had been attracting growing interest as a newly developed residential area. New banks had mushroomed at a speed comparable to that of the regional development itself. Now that the area was completely built up, as many as six branch offices of banks flanked their eaves. They competed bitterly against one another, trying to pick up more

Shimizu Ikkō

clients.

Not simply for the sake of competition, but also because no office could expect substantial savings from new home owners. Salesmen who attempted to conscript opulent savers had no choice but to take over long-committed clients from other banks.

The bank entrusted to Tagawa Junji was located in one of the most competitive zones in Tokyo. Tagawa was considered a future spearhead of the bank. He was singled out to be its Manager at the age of thirty-seven. Regardless of when or where, the bank management, by nature, demanded a steady climb in the amount of customers' deposits. Inasmuch as the survival of branch offices depended on this, the offices could not help but become sensitive to the activities of large deposit holders.

"I hope that nothing serious is going on. For now, I'll go talk with the two clients."

"That may help."

First a self-defence, next a counterattack! But the strategy for the counterattack would develop only out of a knowledge as to what the opponents knows, and what they are after.

Ikuno and Norisaka, the two clients Tagawa visited that day, reprimanded Tagawa, claiming that the financial secret of an individual should not be used as a means to promote a bank's coming out on top in the overheated competition. They demanded his assurance of the confidentiality of their accounts.

"Something is strange. The confidential deposits' list must have been leaked from within Nittō Bank." Frowning nervously, Ikuno kept after Tagawa. His expression looked unbecoming to a man of his chubby physique.

"I swear, Sir, that there was no mistake."

"But, I still can't put faith in . . ."

"It is the duty of a bank to keep the secrets of its clients." Tagawa tightened his handsome face and spoke crisply. "May I ask what the name of the salesman from Daidō Bank was?"

"I think it was Saeki, or something like that."

Tagawa had seen a calling card at Norisaka's home where he had visited before coming to see Ikuno. The name on it read Saeki Kikuo. In Norisaka's description, he was a "smooth and pale faced fellow." Tagawa decided to check up on Saeki Kikuo as soon as possible.

But upon his return to the N Branch Office, he ran into an emergency causing him to react much faster than he had planned. Another large deposit holder, Aoki Tatsuo, was waiting for his return in the Manager's office.

"What the hell is going on, Manager? This man came to see me. What does this mean?" Baldheaded Aoki tossed a calling card on a side table. As Tagawa stooped over to peer at it, he saw again Saeki's name printed on it. Tagawa was tempted to say, "Oh, he went to your house, too," but swallowed his words at the last minute.

"I see, it's Daidō Bank. Is this something new?" Tagawa sat on the sofa, facing Aoki and questioned him calmly.

"He asked me to deposit some money." Aoki's voice mirrored his disappointment that his bravado had failed to impress Tagawa. But he regained his feistiness right away; his voice grew inflated.

"I tried to get rid of him. I told him that I had no money to save. Then, what do you think? The guy with ridiculous-looking glasses had the nerve to say, 'You have some money, don't you, Sir?' He had a big grin on his face!"

"My God, he is forward!"

"He knew what he was doing, though. Listen. The man said, 'You have 50 million yen in the confidential account at Nittō Bank alone. Since it matures next month, won't you kindly take advantage of our services and deposit just half of it with us?' Can you imagine? Can you think of anything more absurd than this?"

Tagawa caught his breath at Aoki's piercing words. Aoki gained confidence to see Tagawa's reaction. He became coarse. In a sarcastic, caustic tone, he attacked Tagawa, "I don't see how my account with Nittō is known by people at Daidō."

"I assure you that there's nothing like that."

"But in fact things are getting out of hand."

Tagawa feared that this mix-up might turn into a fatal blow to his career. There couldn't be a leakage of the information about confidential long-term savings accounts unless there was inside sabotage.

"Say what you may, I can't trust you with my money. I am withdrawing all my accounts here. This bank can not be trusted," Aoki roared, banging on the armrest of the sofa, and the arteries of his boar-like neck bulged grotesquely. To the N Office, the 50 million yen was a significant amount. If the total of this sum was recalled, the achievement record of the office would suddenly go down.

"As you may know, the competition among banks is vicious. It's exactly like the saying, 'a hundred devils marching at night.' It is difficult to tell what kind of trap Daidō has set up against us. But it is, at least, unlikely that the information has leaked from within. In any event, I shall investigate the situation right away. Please kindly give us time to find out what is really going on."

Tagawa could not afford to take the case lightly. He edged forward on the sofa and tried his best to calm Aoki down. Just then, he began feeling a strange anxiety. Rather than anxiety, it may have been a gut feeling or a brainstorm that struck him. An image momentarily loomed in the back of his brain, like a shadow floating between dark waves. It disappeared and came to the surface again, and again and again.

"Please give me a week. One week will do. I can rectify the situation as soon as the cause is pinned down."

"What would you do, if you can't pin down the cause?"

"I will see to it that you will not be inconvenienced." Tagawa bowed low.

"When the Manager is young, the management is bound to fall apart." Aoki spoke spitefully, and added emphatically, "I won't wait more than a week!"

After Aoki left, Tagawa pondered over the anxiety he had just felt and thought about the shadow which had wafted through the back of his brain. It was really a crazy idea, but judging from her post, it was not totally improbable. If, moreover, her personal resentment against Tagawa still lingered, there could be a smell of revenge behind what was happening.

Tagawa lifted the inter-com receiver and asked two telephone switchboard operators, "Does the name Saeki Kikuo ring a bell to you?"

"From where, Sir?"

"What I mean is, do either of you remember anybody from our bank calling a person named Saeki, or Saeki calling somebody here?"

The two operators whispered to each other. Holding the receiver, Tagawa had the distasteful premonition that the girls would name the person whose image had just passed his brain.

"It seems that Takigami Yōko-san used to call him. She stopped calling him about two months ago."

Tagawa winced at these words. He was right . . ., exactly as the premonition had foretold. A heavy sigh escaped his mouth.

2.

It was an ironic encounter as Tagawa recalled. He couldn't help making it out as ironic to find Takigami Yōko in the N Branch Office at which he had been assigned Manager.

Tagawa had graduated from the Department of Economics of University A. After entering Nittō Bank, he worked for five years as executive-in-training. His desk was in the first section of the General Affairs Office in the main building. Subsequently, he was sent to the Ikebukuro Branch Office, which was an auxiliary branch of the bank in the Jōhoku District. This time, he was an executive-in-training in branch office management. There, for the first time, he was introduced to his co-worker Takigami Yōko. She was a clerk at the front window, in charge of the day-to-day transactions.

Yōko had graduated from high school and had worked in the office for three years already. She was twenty-one years old and was more experienced than Tagawa both as a clerk and also in terms of the ins-and-outs of life at the regional office. With the sophistication of a city woman, she covered Tagawa's blunders. Tagawa was perturbed by the monotony and uneventfulness of life in a regional office, mostly because he knew nothing outside the colorful life of the main office. Indeed, the dissatisfaction and chagrin felt by the bottom rank workers in peripheral branch offices had no outlet.

Tagawa's immediate supervisor, Konno Jun'ichi, in charge of the day-to-day transactions, for instance, had graduated from a provincial university and had been sent to a branch office from the beginning. His career had always been off the high-level executive track Tagawa was on. Konno would never be given a chance to work in the main office. It was evident that Tagawa and other future executives would pass him by soon enough. Konno would be placed under their supervision. All the more because of these circumstances, Konno would at times bicker with the inexperienced Tagawa as a mother-in-law would, but again would instantly soften up and take Tagawa to a bar. Under the influence of alcohol, he would cajole Tagawa with the words, "Please help me out in the future."

While being harassed by frustration and the need to persevere, this underling class gradually came to squeeze themselves into the "banker type" mold, a severely confining one.

The first end-of-the-year party at the Ikebukuro Office was held shortly after Tagawa was transferred there. This party fell into an unbelievable nightmare.

"Too bad Manager is going to be absent from the party this year again," Yōko remarked, giving her hands a little rest from bookkeeping. The bank's customer service was over by now.

"But he seems to be donating funds for the party. We may have a better time without him."

"Only if nothing happens . . ."

At the time, Tagawa did not catch the delicate nuances of Yōko's remark. The party was held in a neighboring restaurant and went on merrily. Suddenly, just as the fun and games started to get out of control, the lights went off. Concurrently with the female clerks' theatrical screams, Tagawa saw a number of shadows swooping toward the Deputy Manager, who was sitting kitty-corner to him. He took this movement to be a part of the entertainment and had no suspicions. But against the noise of small tables being thrown around and dishes and bowls being broken, the Deputy's pathetic cry, "Cut it out!" pierced through the darkness. Shadows swayed and muffled the shrieks. Startled by the heavy and bizarre atmosphere condensed in the darkness, Tagawa started to get up. Instantly, somebody grabbed his hand and pulled him back in his seat. He could not make head from tails in the darkness. He could not even tell who it was that had pulled his hand. There was a thud of something falling down the stairs.

"Don't move. Don't look at anything. Just sit still!"

It was Yōko who was ordering him in whispers.

The lights came back on and the party members hurrahed. But the Deputy's seat was a gaping hole. Only at the distraught screams of the restaurant workers did Tagawa realize that Yamazaki, the forty-five or forty-six-year-old Deputy Manager, had been thrown down the stairs by somebody and was groaning.

The victim took nearly a week off from work for treatment. It was an atrocious, incredible incident. It was a sinister rebellion by the bottom rank workers against the institution's forceful casting of them into a uniformity of personality. One must not stand out, must not be praised or berated. One must not become a topic of conversation. One must strive in every way possible not to commit either virtue or vice.

Overnight, the bank was back to the smiling, sophisticated work-place, just as it had always been. No one mentioned Deputy Yamazaki's injury. Those who had struck out at him in the darkness, as an outlet for their pent-up resentment, received clients with the usual smiles. They threw themselves diligently into their assigned work like a congregation of saints.

"Did you know what was going to happen?" Tagawa asked Yōko a couple of days later when they ran into each other on their way home. But Yōko shook her head with a heavy-hearted smile.

"That has nothing to do with Tagawa-san, because you don't belong here. You will return to the main office and be promoted to be a section head or an executive. It's best if you forget about it quickly and finish up your service at the branch office. Just stay away from this mess."

Tagawa momentarily felt that Yōko's age and his were reversed. Exactly a week after the party something else happened: the spotting of a forged check. Yōko, who was waiting on clients as usual, nonchalantly attached a small note to a check and sent it to Tagawa. Tagawa stretched his neck and looked at the note.

"Forged."

He re-read it in surprise. He was not mistaken.

"Please have a seat and wait." Just when Tagawa cast his glance at her Yōko was addressing with her usual calmness a pale-faced man in his forties who looked like a small factory owner. Tagawa's head throbbed with pulsating blood. He lost his composure, but Yōko, as though to divert the man's attention, took on another client.

Tagawa inserted the check along with Yōko's note in some other documents and brought them to Chief Clerk Konno. His knees trembled as he stood in front of the Chief Clerk. He was afraid he might collapse.

It was a forgery alright, but a very amateurish one. The number "6" had simply been changed to "9" with a pen.[7] Sixty-one thousand yen had been changed to ninety-one thousand yen. It was the kind of forgery to be detected sooner or later, even if the window clerk had failed to notice. Seen from another angle, it showed how hard up the forger was. The man was arrested in no time.

Assuming that the ideal image of a banker is not to be praised, not to be criticized, nor even to be talked about, Takigawa Yōko's difficulties, it may be said, started at this point.

Mostly because it happened to be the end of the year, when a crime-prevention campaign was at its peak, the incident attracted the newspapers' attention. They praised the exemplary way in which Yōko had handled the situation. The articles were entitled "An Ingenious Banker," "Skillfully Detecting a Forger," and the like. Because Tagawa was her co-worker, he was included in a picture in the papers.

Tagawa learned from the newspaper articles that the criminal's name was Hirayama Ichirō. He managed a small manufacturing business. A machine which made plastic bags was installed in the entrance of his tiny house. Both the man and his wife did everything, from delivering the products to the wholesalers, to operating the machine. They worked assiduously, even cutting down on their sleep at night, but they could not make ends meet at the end of the year. After much anguish, Hirayama made up his mind to resort to crime.

The incident precipitated an intimacy between Tagawa and Yōko. Yōko forced Tagawa to join a company skiing trip in the Jōetsu Highlands during the three day New Year's vacation. They spent the entire vacation as lovers. Yōko was in high spirits and was active as though her youth had swept her away. Her laughter and nimble movements permeated Tagawa's mind.

It was in mid-January that Yōko asked in a formal manner,

"Would you like to have tea with me on our way home?" Tagawa met her by the West Exit of the station, which was on the other side of the station from his bank building. They walked passed the insolently lined up drinking stalls in front of the station and came to a Western style delicatessen-coffee shop near North Ikebukuro.

"There's something I would like to talk over with you, Tagawa-san," Yōko began after ordering something to drink. She told Tagawa that her father was a guard at the Nippori Branch Office of the Nittō Bank. It was he who had arranged her employment at the Ikebukuro Office.

"The Deputy Manager asked me yesterday if I would be interested in moving to the General Affairs Department in the main office," Yōko announced with hardly a sign of elation.

"Sounds great!"

"I imagine that the incident has something to do with this transfer."

"Whatever the reason, it's an exceptional break for you. No matter how you look at it, the main office is the best. It makes you feel you are really working for a bank."

Apparently, the main office had been obliged to make a gesture of appreciation towards Yōko so long as the incident of the forged check had gotten so much publicity.

"But . . .," Yōko cast a glance downward as though she was thinking about something. Then quickly she looked up straight into Tagawa's handsome face. "When can Tagawa-san go back to the main office?" Yōko asked urgently without even blinking.

"I wish I knew. It's been only four months since I came to Ikebukuro. It's unlikely that I get to go back for another two or three years." Tagawa equivocated, flinching at Yōko's strangely intense stare.

"What does your father say? That's more important."

"He advises me to take the post, because it's a great honor."

"Definitely. Also, the main office has a lot of good-looking men. They won't leave you alone for long. You will be proposed to."

Tagawa talked jokingly, making himself at home. Their relationship after the forged check incident, the New Year's ski trip, and a couple of dates, one coming right after another, was close enough to permit this kind of dialogue. But the way Tagawa teased her made Yōko's eyes cloud over. Her head suddenly dropped down.

"That's why I don't want to go. If Tagawa-san talks like that, I will turn down the offer," she said in a trembling voice.

"What's wrong?" he asked in bewilderment. This change in her was something he had not expected. He did not think he had said anything wrong. The main office was better than a branch office—that was simply common knowledge. But Yōko shook her bowed head. She shook it once again after a short while, as though to shake off Tagawa's way of talking.

"Did I say something wrong?"

"You said that the handsome men there won't leave me alone."

"No kidding, though. It may really happen."

"Please. Don't talk like that. I feel rotten," Yōko interrupted Tagawa, revealing her virginal innocence. She could not tolerate the idea of a stranger proposing to her to get married.

"I have a better time at this Ikebukuro Office."

"Oh? But you won't come across another chance to go to

the main office," Tagawa admonished her, and suspected at the same time that Yōko would be transferred for certain to another office at the bank's next personnel rotation, if she lets go of this offer. Now that she had caught the forged check, had been written up in the papers, and had made herself a topic of conversation, Yōko had ceased to be the invisible clerk which all the rest were.

A bank should be a place where nothing exciting happens, a place to which clients peacefully entrust their money. Even though nothing was wrong, the sheer fact that something had happened at the front window would slow down the canvassing activities. Yōko's presence at the front window of the Ikebukuro Office would only remind customers, over and over again, of the unpleasant incident. Her presence, therefore, was undesirable. A bank usually makes an effort to wipe off the trace of such a troublesome impression quickly. Here was the merit of the personnel rotation. Tagawa meant to explain that it would be far better for her to be sent to the main office than to another nasty place, but Yōko raised her eyes as though to cut off his words.

". . . it's because, if I go to the main office, I won't be able to work with Tagawa-san."

"Work with me?" asked Tagawa, thrusting his face forward. Yōko gave a big nod. Tagawa looked back at her in surprise. Yōko's eyes, ardently looking into Tagawa's face, were filled with burning desire. Tagawa sensed a desperate affection in the sparks of her eyes which were ready to ignite. It was her suicidal proposal.

"Shall we go outside?"

"Please stay a little while longer." Yōko shook her head violently. And she pleaded in a still more precipitous tone, "I would like to work with you. But if it bothers you, I would like you to let me know clearly."

Her gasp echoed loud in Tagawa's heart.

"How can I be bothered? You taught me everything about the branch office life and work."

"No, that's not what I'm talking about. Please tell me . . ." The tone of her voice was violent and petulant. Without giving him a chance to hedge, Yōko demanded that he evaluate her feelings towards him.

"If you don't mind." Tagawa spoke looking slightly downward.

"I don't." Yōko spoke as though she clung onto Tagawa's words with her entire body.

When Tagawa raised his smiling face, rapturous jubilation spread over her blushing cheeks. Tagawa was impressed by Yōko's youthful glamor. At that instant, he wished to arrive at a deeper and more violent conviction which might satisfy his flaring passion. "Let's have a drink." Tagawa offered the initiative, being careful in the meantime not to let her know that he wanted to express his man's urgent desire and decide the issue at once.

Smiling hesitantly, Yōko nodded gently.

Outside the coffee shop, a whirling, chilly wind enveloped the two people. Yōko leaned heavily on the arm Tagawa casually thrust out. That night Tagawa got engaged to Yōko whose white flesh was stained by fresh blood.

3.

It did not take long for talk of their relationship to spread among the Ikebukuro Office employees. Yōko was in a constant rapture over the idea of marriage with Tagawa. When her colleagues teased her, she blushed happily, even appreciatively. Such scenes made Tagawa feel that he should conclude the marriage before long.

"Let's first talk to your father."

No matter how quickly he wanted to proceed, there were preparations to make. They had to be taken care of in a certain order. The happiness of having Yōko's help bolstered him through these otherwise onerous procedures.

Takigami Yūkichi, Yōko's father, who worked as a guard at the Nippori Office, met Tagawa cordially in his Takinogawa apartment.

"My daughter has been telling me about you. Please don't worry about me. I will manage by myself after she gets married. I only have this apartment of a six tatami mat[8] room to look after."

Yūkichi was courteous and calm. He showed a sensitive concern, trying to free Tagawa from any anxiety about disrupting the father-daughter bond.

"I would like to have the wedding this spring. If I wait till fall, I will be twenty-nine."

Bowing his gray-haired head low, Yūkichi cordially thanked Tagawa for suggesting that they make simple preparations to suit Yūkichi's financial condition. Tagawa decided to introduce Yōko to his parents in Yamanashi Prefecture early in February.

Very early that February, Hirayama Ichirō, the culprit who had forged the check committed family suicide.

Chief Clerk Konno, who had opened the evening paper shortly before the five o'clock closing hour, called Tagawa in a disturbed voice, "Oh, God! That son of a gun has committed suicide!"

Tagawa twisted his body to look back at Konno.

"That son of a gun?"

"Yeah, that forged check criminal."

"What! Hirayama . . ."

Tagawa kicked away his chair and rushed to Konno's desk. "Small Businessman Commits Family Suicide." The large headline jumped out at Tagawa's eyes. Tagawa bent over the caption which started with a quotation from Hirayama's will, "Once convicted of forgery, it's impossible to make a living . . ."

"It's a suicide of a family of five," Konno reported to the other clerks. All turned to look at him.

"A family suicide!" Somebody shouted.

Two or three people rushed to look at the newspaper on Konno's desk. One of them groaned, "With gas."

"I never got to see the criminal closely, but I would have never guessed that he had three such cute children. What a nightmare." Konno shook his head afflicted.

The paper reported that it appeared that Hirayama Ichirō and his wife waited till their children had fallen asleep, took sleeping pills, and turned on the gas.

The so-called check forgery was only a matter of changing the figure "sixty thousand" to "ninety thousand." It was a crime of thirty thousand yen. On the grounds that the bank incurred no real loss, it decided not to prosecute. Hirayama Ichirō had been released from jail quite awhile before.

Having read the article, and turning his face away from the picture of the family of five, Tagawa looked at Yōko.

"It was only thirty thousand yen. I don't see why he had to die," Yōko heard one of the bank clerks remark after reading the paper. She got on her feet with her pale face bent downward. Covering her mouth with her hand, she scurried out to the locker room. Tagawa hurried after her. Yōko was standing alone motionless by the end of a row of lockers. She lost control of herself at the sight of Tagawa and covered her face with both hands.

"Let's not worry about it." Tagawa held Yōko's shoulders and pulled her toward him. "It wasn't our fault, was it?"

"But, it was because I found the forgery. Yes, I drove them to family suicide." Yōko lifted her tear-filled eyes and looked up at Tagawa pleadingly.

"You are worrying too much."

"But I can't forget that man's exhausted face." Unable to control her emotions, Yōko pressed her face onto Tagawa's chest. "It was my fault. Yes, absolutely. I get to marry Junji-san because of that incident. Meanwhile, someone else was driven to commit suicide . . . how dreadful!"

"You are wrong. Pull yourself together."

There was no need to picture what kind of life the Hirayama family had led since it had been written up in the papers. But was it necessary for Yōko and Tagawa to bear the blame for it?

"Oh, I hate it. I can't stand it! He may have died cursing us. Don't you think so?"

"More serious than cursing would be the question of how Yōko and I struck him. As merciless prosecutors? As stuck-up money guards . . .?" wondered Tagawa. Yōko was not the only one to feel wretched.

"What else could we do then? You see, once a forgery is noticed, a banker is not allowed to overlook it. Even supposing that a family suicide was to follow as a consequence, we shouldn't be blamed for it, to say the least. Money. Money is the evil force."

Tagawa held Yōko tightly against his tall body, as if to chase away his delusion.

"I would like you to wait awhile before you take me to your parents," asked Yōko the next day.

It was understandable. Tagawa decided to wait till Yōko had recovered from the trauma of the Hirayama family's suicide. But as it turned out, the family suicide of the man convicted of check forgery was only an omen that the bond between Tagawa and Yōko would be disrupted. Exactly a week later, when Yōko was just pulling out of her shock and regaining mental equilibrium, Takigawa Yūkichi was embroiled in a scandal.

That morning, Tagawa was awakened by his apartment manager's call, "Telephone!"

"My father is in trouble."

The call was from Yōko, sobbing helplessly. Rubbing his sleepy eyes and gathering the collar of his night robe together, Tagawa asked clumsily, "What's going on?"

"I was right. The man who committed suicide was cursing us." Yōko's words made little sense. Only sometime later, she brought herself together to explain in a choking voice, "My father is in critical condition." Putting her choppy phrases together, Tagawa figured out that there had been a carbon monoxide poisoning caused by the imperfect combustion of a gas burner at her father's Nippori Office. Two young bankers who happened to be staying overnight in the Night Duty Room had passed away. Yūkichi alone barely survived, but had been taken to the hospital in critical condition.

"I'm calling from the hospital. My father is in the

emergency room, and . . ." Upset and distraught, Yōko lost track of what she was saying.

"Where is the hospital? Do you hear me? Which hospital are you in?"

"Right by Nippori Station, M Hospital."

"I'll be right over. Your father is safe, isn't he?"

"They are giving him oxygen."

"There's no such thing as Hirayama Ichirō's curse, so calm down. Understand? Pull yourself together."

Rushing back to his room, Tagawa changed his clothes and ran out. It was difficult to find a taxi. The one he finally caught moved cautiously and slowly. He could almost hear Yōko's desperate voice calling from the other shore of the river Styx. "Why did that gentle Takigami Yūkichi have to . . . ?" Tagawa brooded over the nature of the accident. Finally in the hospital, he found Yōko doubled up on a chair in a corridor. A chilly breeze blew through.

"How did it go?" he asked, running up to her.

Yōko raised her face vacantly. She directed her empty gaze at the emergency room. She looked like a figure drained out of the energy to cry or tears to drop.

"Does it seem as if he's going to make it?"

"I have no idea."

"I wonder if it's really bad."

". . . he may not have a chance."

"Don't be foolish." Tagawa squeezed Yōko's hand firmly.

Presently, the Deputy Manager of the Nippori Office ran over. Also, the police who had inspected the site came to check on Yūkichi's condition. The Deputy Manager explained what might have happened.

His story was that Yūkichi was on duty the night before. He must have allowed the two bank clerks to stay overnight. The two had gotten drunk in the Nippori area and had missed the last train. Judging from the appearance of the room, furthermore, it was likely that the two men started drinking what they brought. Yūkichi joined them. In drunkenness, he fell asleep on the floor without shutting off the gas burner. This was what caused the incomplete combustion.

"Please wait. Takigami-san can't drink."

"There's always such a thing as being obliged to drink."

The Nippori Deputy Manager insisted that it was improbable for Tagawa to fall asleep on the floor unless he had been drinking. Tagawa asked how it could be possible that the two young men had died and the elderly man, Yōko's father, had survived, if they had all been drinking. But the Deputy would not discuss this point. Tagawa foresaw that the finger of blame would be pointed at Yūkichi sooner or later.

Yōko's father, who pulled through by the skin of his teeth, was moved to his Takinogawa apartment after nearly ten days' hospitalization. The aftereffect of the muscular and brain paralysis, however, had turned him into a semi-vegetable. To make matters worse, the Nippori branch office dismissed Takigami Yūkichi from his post on the grounds that his fingerprints were found on a teacup.

4.

The personnel rotation at Nittō Bank usually takes place in May and November. Because Tagawa was judged to have been indirectly involved in the incident as well as the accident, his name was included in the list of the people to be transferred as part of the May rotation. He was sent back to the main building eralier than originally planned. He and Yōko stood out too conspicuously in the Ikebukuro Office.

"We could be married by now, if nothing had happened," Tagawa spoke to Yōko pensively after reporting his transfer. This was when Yōko at the Ikebukuro Office needed him more than ever, but nothing personal could countermand the periodical rotation.

"Maybe by fall my father will be better. Also, Junji-san will still be in Tokyo even after you move to the main office."

We can see each other anytime we want to—.

Yōko must have wanted to say this, but there was no time left for her now that she had to attend her father. Her father could no longer take care of his bowel movements. Three months passed without a date, to say nothing of physical relations between them. The financial burden on Yōko was tremendous. She had to scrape together, out of a twenty-one-year-old woman's salary, her father's medical expenses as well as their living costs. Yūkichi had absolutely no income. Tagawa knew the magnitude of the burden. He offered to help, but Yōko would not accept.

The last shred of hope left for Yōko to restore the hopeless invalid was mercilessly snatched away that autumn, the very autumn she had once looked forward to. Yūkichi's condition went from bad to worse. Yōko had to take off many days from work in order to look after him. Upon hearing from a clerk in the Ikebukuro Office that Yōko had missed work for over ten days, Tagawa stopped at her Takinogawa apartment. This was his first visit in months.

Yōko was sitting forlornly by Yūkichi's pillow. A sad smile appeared on her lifeless pale face when she saw Tagawa.

"The doctor came about an hour ago, and gave him a shot."

Yūkichi was asleep, his mouth agape like a child. Out of the blue, Yōko suggested taking a walk. "Once he has fallen asleep, he is alright till morning."

The red and round early October moon was almost remorselessly bright for the couple who found themselves walking side by side for the first time in some months. In silence, each craved for a place where they could embrace each other firmly. In a narrow alley leading to Asukayama Park, Tagawa saw the shabby sign-board of an inn. As he turned back, Yōko nodded pressing her body against his.

The walls and the ceiling of the somber room were filthy. The quilt, not even enclosed in a white coverlet, looked ruefully cold.

"I've done something wrong to Tagawa-san." Yōko spoke in a formal manner, facing Tagawa, but without using her usual appellation "Junji-san."

"It's not your fault," said Tagawa comfortingly.

Tagawa pulled Yōko's thin, limp hand and embraced her. Yōko lay back on the quilting and sought Tagawa's lips, trembling. It was not just her body, but the very marrow of her soul that had been craving after gentle affection. At Tagawa's first embrace in many months, her entire body instantly flared up. She kept repeating as if in a delirium, "I've done something awful to Tagawa-san."

That night, for the first time, Yōko reached climax. Tagawa also, engulfed by her frenzied and violent reaction, was bathed in a soaring intoxication.

It was right after this that Yōko broached the proposal to call off the wedding engagement. She insisted that they could not marry as long as she was taking care of her invalid father, and that there was little hope for his recovery. She pleaded desperately with Tagawa that he not let her get in his way.

"I am no longer worthy of Tagawa-san's love. I can't even offer my body when you need it." Yōko dissolved into tears, remonstrating with Tagawa—and finally even shouting at him—to forget her, because there was no hope for their future.

Never after that day did Yōko telephone Tagawa. On days when he visited the Takinogawa apartment, using Yūkichi's illness as an excuse, she would receive Tagawa only with empty formality, as if he were a stranger.

A new marriage offer came Tagawa's way in early November.

On a holiday, Business Department Manager Koyanagi Yūzō invited Tagawa to his Shiba-Takanawa home, and advised, "You are asking for misunderstanding by staying a bachelor for such a long time." The name of the woman Koyanagi brought to Tagawa's attention was Oribe Misako. She was the second daughter of Nittō Bank's leading customer, a graduate from the Department of French Literature of University A, 25 years old.

"She's by no means young, but she's good looking as you can see from this photograph. She has the perfect background for a banker's wife." Koyanagi hammered away, "You already know what kind of place a bank is. It's different from ordinary companies. One cannot marry just anyone."

"I appreciate your concern."

Tagawa was on the verge of telling Koyanagi that he was already engaged to be married to another woman when Koyanagi continued knowingly, "For example, one must not marry the daughter of a guard who, out of carelessness, got drunk and fell asleep, and as a result, took the lives of two young and promising men."

"But that accident was . . ."

"I know. I have talked with the Manager of the Ikebukuro Office. You probably want to add that the woman is the one who spotted the forged check. But even that is a problem to us now."

"Don't you see? Suppose you marry her, everytime you are reviewed for promotion, there is bound to be someone who will say that Tagawa-kun[9] is outstanding but his wife is problematic. That won't help. Think twice about what I'm saying. I mean her father's incident and the forged check case included. All of this will affect your future adversely, making you seem as problematic. You will be branded a non-desirable type of banker. This is why I transferred you out from the Ikebukuro Office. Once you are tainted it's too late. Nothing can remove the stain. A person in charge of personnel—whoever it may be—would take the less tainted one, if he had to choose between you and someone else."

"Tainted . . ."

A strange word. While it has virtually no meaning in and of itself, its connotations are endless. In the extremely limited context of bank parlance, moreover, the word has the power to take over people's personalities. Koyanagi added, "I want you to think hard about the meaning of the phrase we hear all the time, 'the image of a typical banker.'" That is, a banker must be trustworthy and almost impartially serious, and at the same time, must not have any personality. Koyanagi was asking Tagawa to fit himself into the assigned mold. One could not remain at the highly selective level of executive without coming to terms with this framework.

Tagawa refrained from making a clear-cut response. He asked Koyanagi to give him some time to make up his mind. Koyanagi patiently kept after him through the end of the year, going so far as to admonish, "This is your last chance to wipe out the stain you almost got at the Ikebukuro Office."

In January of the following year, Yōko was transferred to the Sugamo Office, as a part of an irregular rotation. The superficial reason given by the bank was that it would be easier for her to look after her father if she worked closer to her home. But in practice, the Sugamo Office was farther way from her apartment than the Ikebukuro Office. There was no telling where she might be sent next.

Tagawa finally made up his mind and told Yōko in a letter that he probably would be married in the near future.

His marriage to Oribe Misako took place just as he was offered a promotion to Chief Clerk of the Business Department, First Section. The announcement of promotion was dated May first. Ironically, it was when Tagawa returned from his honeymoon that he heard about Yūkichi's death. Yōko's father had just died after a year and several months' illness; by the time he breathed his last, he was as frightened of death as a child, because of the brain damage.

Tagawa's first son was born, and his second, two years later. In the fourth year after his marriage to Misako, Tagawa was singled out to be the Deputy Section Chief of the Business Department. At last, he had a clear sense of his future. He was definitely on the high level executive track. This turn of events could be seen as a reward for marrying someone recommended by Koyanagi, the Business Department Manager.

About a year before he was appointed as Manager of N office—that is, in the seventh year after he moved from the Ikebukuro Office back to the Main Office—Tagawa heard about Yōko, the woman he had nearly forgotten. It so happened that Aizawa Kōichi had transferred from the Sugamo Branch Office and joined Tagawa's section. Tagawa sponsored a small welcome party for him.

"Sir, have you heard of a woman named Takigami Yōko?" asked Aizawa as an afterthought, when the conversation drifted to the topic of personnel.

"Takigami Yōko!" repeated Tagawa, taken aback. It was a name he had long forgotten.

"They say she has worked with you before, in the Ikebukuro Office," Aizawa went on with a smile, probably because he was uninformed about the details.

"We used to sit next to each other at the customer window. But that's when I was twenty-eight years old. Seven years ago, wouldn't it be? How do you know her?"

"Because she is in the Sugamo Office."

"In Sugamo? Is she still single?"

"Of course. Didn't you know?"

—Oh, she hasn't married yet. Tagawa recalled his affectionate relationship with Yōko which never came to bear fruit.

"And how is she doing these days?"

"I hear she will be transferred to another office. It's because there's a problem."

"A problem?"

"Nothing serious, but we call her Miss Nymphomania in the Sugamo Office."

At Tagawa's question, "Miss Nymphomania?" Aizawa nodded with an eloquent smile.

"To make a long story short, I think she wants to get married."

"That's understandable. She must be getting on in years. But what exactly do you mean by Miss Nymphomania?" The expression was new to Tagawa.

Two or three young clerks looked at each other and giggled.

"Haven't you heard, Sir? It's a type you often see among old maids. She'll be the first one to have a date with a new comer to the office. That kind, you know. Nobody who's been in the office for awhile pays attention to her. From what I hear, women like this will even date men who approach them at the teller's window or call, sight unseen, over the phone. At least so they say."

—Yōko!

Every year around April or May, Tagawa would notice couples made up of what appeared to be experienced office women and newly employed men, in such popular dating places as Chidorigafuchi or Yoyogi Olympic Park. The thought that Yōko—now twenty-eight years old—had become expert in this role, worrying one minute whether her face powder was wearing off, yet acting quite sophisticated the next, was unbearable. It actually was not a matter of bearability. It was a scene of moral depravity.

"I wonder why she can't get married. She is a smart, polished woman."

"I'm not sure. When you talk with her, she strikes you as a nice person. She is kind and thoroughly considerate to men. It's just that she occasionally acts licentious. Maybe people are turned off by something dingy about her."

"Dingy?"

"Betrayed and tramped on by many men; that kind of impression . . ."

Tagawa found the word distasteful. It perfectly characterized the history of Yōko's relationship with men for the entire period following her separation from him. He felt guilty.

Of all places, it was in the N Office to which he moved with so much ambition that Tagawa now found Yōko. It was to the N Office that she had been transferred from Sugamo.

"How are your children?" Yōko would ask casually when they passed each other in hallways. But that was all. Tagawa invited her out once, but she smiled lightly and turned away.

5.

It was Takigami Yōko who had disclosed the confidential information which could determine the fate of the bank . . .! Tagawa fought back the idea. But Yōko had been in charge of the long-term savings accounts and was familiar with the confidential large-account holders. Once it had been proven that she had contact with Saeki Kikuo from the Daidō Bank, there was no room for further doubt.

First Tagawa thought of calling Yōko to the Branch Office Manager's office, but at the last minute he could not bring himself to make the interrogation quite so official. He told Yōko over the telephone, "I have something to ask you about Saeki Kikuo. I think you know him."

It was difficult to ascertain Yōko's reaction over the telephone, but after a moment's hesitation, Yōko returned a short reply, "I see." Tagawa told her that he wanted to meet her in front of the department store, by the west exit of Ikebukuro Station.

At 7 p.m., the appointed time, Yōko was standing, with bright lipstick on, in front of the iron grille of the closed department store.

"Shall we take a walk?"

Yōko nodded at Tagawa's proposal. Since heaven knows when, her face which used to be round and chubby had become angular and her cheek bones were protruding. Her skin looked unusually rough in the neon light at dusk.

"It's been eight years since we walked like this the last time." Tagawa spoke warmly, turning back toward her.

"Tagawa-san. Won't you be in trouble, if someone sees you walking with a woman like me?" Yōko cast her glance slightly downward.

"Don't talk to me that way. How about some food?"

". . . I'd rather drink."

"You drink?" Tagawa could only throw back the question. That evening eight years ago, when she so passionately proposed to him, Yōko had turned crimson after a glass of gin.

"Yes, that's the only way to . . ." A short petulant response was thrown back.

Bars had been cleared away from the area in front of the west exit of the station, and there sprawled a wide street. Tagawa went to the bar district near North Ikebukuro and walked down one flight to a basement Suntory Bar. Yōko ordered whiskey on the rocks. Watching her movements, Tagawa knew that he would have to maintain his detachment. Avoiding Tagawa's eyes, Yōko impatiently reached for one of the glasses that had just been brought to the table.

"Do you hate me?" Tagawa started slowly. This, in fact, was the problem tormenting him the most. Suppose it was proven that Yōko had leaked the confidential information out of her personal resentment towards him, and if she had attempted to deprive him of his professional title, there was no way he could report it to the Main Office.

"If you are disgusted with me, I won't talk any more."

As Tagawa repeated the same sentence, Yōko burst into wild laughter.

"What's the matter?"

"Don't worry. I neither hate nor have a grudge against Tagawa-san. It was I who asked you to break off the engagement."

"Then, am I right in saying that this is not revenge against me?" asked Tagawa cautiously.

Yōko took a king-size cigarette out of her pocketbook, held it in the corner of her mouth, and lit it with a lighter. Tagawa's life had changed greatly in many respects after he married Misako and got on the executive track. But he suspected that Yōko had changed even more, and possibly more than he could imagine, after he parted from her and since her father had passed away.

"Saeki-san . . .," Yōko began to talk,, but smiled, and shrugged her shoulders slightly, "looks like Tagawa-san."

"Me?"

"Especially his physique. He is tall and thin and slightly hunch-backed."

"Are you going to marry him?"

"Why?"

"Aren't you?"

"He has a wife. I can't marry him." Yōko blew a puff of cigarette at the blue lights overhead, as she spoke.

—Why does she wear such heavy makeup? Tagawa's eyes were fastened on Yōko. But Yōko lifted her eyes, with an impulse strong enough to repel Tagawa's sympathetic gaze.

"You'll never understand why a woman goes out with a

married man. But please don't look as if you feel sorry for me." Whatever may have come to her mind, Yōko abruptly placed her pocketbook on the table. "I'll show you what I always carry with me." She opened the metal clasp with a dull click.

"Four handkerchieves. Do you know what I do with them? Men often forget to bring their handkerchieves, so I let them borrow mine. I tell them just to bring them back when they are through with them. Here are needles and thread. See? Not just black and white; I have navy blue, brown; I have every kind from cotton thread to nylon thread. Three kinds of spare buttons. I mend all their lost buttons and torn clothes. I even keep an iron in my desk drawer at the office."

Poking around in her pocketbook, as a child searches in her toy box, Yōko started lining up all sorts of paraphernalia. Then, she took out from her red leather wallet about ten one thousand yen notes to show Tagawa.

"Since young men spend a lot, their salaries don't tide them over till the next payday. I can at least help out with a little. But, I never loan more than two thousand to one person. Because they'll never talk to me again, if the debt becomes more than they can pay back."

It was a strange scene: she would put down her cigarette, pick up the glass, put the cigarette back in her mouth, and ransack her pocketbook.

"Say, shall I tell you something else? You know Kaneko-san, who is getting married this fall? I introduced his fiancée to him. I used to go out with him till quite recently. Can you guess why I did that?"

"You've told me enough. Don't torture yourself any more."

"I'm used to it. It doesn't bother me. It was like this when I worked in Sugamo also. While I'm going out with young men in the office, I'm always worrying about when they refuse to have another date with me, or say, 'Let's not meet tonight.' Tagawa-san won't know what I mean. I'm lonely. So, just before anything like that turns up, I introduce them to young girls who are good matches for them. That way, I'm never totally rejected. I can avoid the pain of being abandoned. This way, they may even go on seeing me once in a while."

Yōko's words were strangely dry. After awhile, she carefully put back the thread, the needles, the handkerchieves, and the wallet which had been lying on the table.

"Laugh at me if you want to. But so much has happened. And I'm already twenty-nine years old. Nothing can change that. Saeki-san has been really nice to me. But, you see, there's nothing I can do for him. I was just wnodering what I could do for him when he asked me for the list of confidential clients."

Tagawa felt a turbulent anger churning upward in his chest, a feeling diametrically opposed to the nonchalance with which Yōko told her tale. Did she have to go that far? Just because Saeki was nice to her, did she have to ruin herself by being taken advantage of, like a toy or a tool, by a middle-aged married man? Bastard! Our enemy has taken advantage of Yōko, a woman coveting men, craving for a chance to get married, full of weaknesses and defenseless as a naked person. Tagawa could not tolerate even the idea that Saeki resembled him.

"Are you going to keep on seeing Saeki?" asked Tagawa, barely suppressing his boiling anger. The thought that he would march into the Daidō Bank as early as tomorrow had been churning in his head. He would uncover Saeki Kikuo's

cowardice, and bring back the list given by Yōko. As soon as it was made public that he had used a woman, Saeki would have to suffer the consequences—as a banker—even if it had been done for the benefit of his bank. Banks try to stay out of trouble. This case can even become a scandal.

Without answering Tagawa's question, Yōko called a waiter nearby, and ordered another drink. In coincidental togetherness, the two people let out a sigh in despair.

". . . I suppose it won't work," said Yōko in a low voice. "A man's career ends when people start to talk about him. It's the same in any bank, isn't it? No matter how hard I try to keep him, Saeki-san, in his turn, will start running away from me."

—My situation was different; I didn't run away from her. Tagawa controlled his desire to speak. He realized that a man who had chosen to project the image of a model banker had no right to defend himself in front of a woman like Yōko. He lacked even the confidence to assist Yōko who had no prospects for the future. One could even say that Saeki Kikuo, who had taken advantage of Yōko, was far more humane than Tagawa himself.

"I'll get the list back. Please don't make an issue of it. I'm sure Saeki-san will understand that a scandal would be disadvantageous to him." Yōko talked with her head gradually dropping down.

Yōko was absent from work for two days. On the third day, a special delivery envelope from her arrived in Tagawa's office. The contents were a letter of resignation and the list of the confidential long-term savings account clients. In one corner, a single line had been scribbled, "Saeki-san went along with my request."

"What shall we do, Sir? Shall we mail Takigami-kun[10] her retirement fund?"

Deputy Manager Nishiyama came to ask for Tagawa's advice. Yōko was probably still living in the Takinogawa apartment.

"Yes, please do."

"The electric iron in her drawer; we will send that back, too."

"An iron?"

"Yes, she used to press young men's shirts and things like that."

"We better not. That would be too heartless."

"Oh?"

"I'll keep it."

At Nishiyama's direction, one of the office girls brought Tagawa a rusty iron. Tagawa's hands responded to the feel of the cold iron and the peculiar weight of the lead inside. He carefully buried it deep in his bottom desk drawer.

Notes

1. My interview with Mr. Ikkō Shimizu in January 1985. This translation was made of "Gin no seiiki" as it appeared in *Chūrenpōton* [Nine Consecutive Jewel Towers] (Tokyo: Kodansha bunko, 1984), pp. 5-46. I am grateful to Mr. Shimizu, Dr. Brett de Bary, Mr. Chris Stevens and Dr. Peter Prindle for their assistance.

2. *Inkan* is a stick usually made of wood, bamboo, ivory or crystal. A name is carved on one end. By pressing onto a pad of thick ink (which is usually red), the stamp may be used any number of times. Japanese use stamps in place of the Western signature, trusting that virtually no two stamps have an identical carving on them.

3. "-shi" is a title suffix, used at more formal situations than when "-san" may be used. Its English equivalent would be "Mr."

4. *Chōme* is an area designation slightly different from a street name.

5. The historical context of this short story is not clear, but judging by the housing condition and the geographical setting in the story, the period is likely to be sometime before the international exchange rate of $1 = Y360 was altered.

6. Traditionally, a Japanese Mutual Bank used the system of mutual financing, wherein the members of the "bank" would pool in funds, and some of them as selected by drawing, for example, would have the privilege of borrowing from it. Nowadays, Mutual Banks are more like short-term financiers.

7. 六 (6), 九 (9).

8. The size of a tatami mat in the Tokyo area nowadays is 5.8 by 2.0 feet (1.76 by 0.88 meters) according to *Kodansha Encyclopedia of Japan* (Tokyo, 1983), p. 348.

9. "-kun" is a title suffix like "-san" and "-shi," but the addressee or the referent is usually a man of lower status or of younger age, unless the speaker is a child speaking to another male child.

10. Sometimes, a woman is called by a man of a higher status with the male suffix "-kun."

Shisen-dō

Japanese Corporate Zen

Inner gate at Shisen-dō

by Daizen Victoria

In the popular Western mind, contemporary Japanese Zen is characterized by austere yet beautiful Zen gardens, and monks with shaven heads seated serenely in meditation. Various television programs have also popularized the idea that monks spend a good deal of their time studying either karate or another form of the martial arts. However, contemporary Japanese Zen is also characterized by the growing number of Zen temples in the countryside which, due to a decrease in rural population, either have no permanent resident priest or only a *nichiyō-bōzu,* a priest who holds a secular job as a school teacher or clerical worker during the week and only functions as a priest on Sundays. Moreover, many urban Zen priests have utilized their temple lands to build highly profitable condominiums, supermarkets, parking lots, kindergartens, and the like.

In spite of the increasing secularization of Zen (and, for that matter, traditional Buddhism as a whole) in Japan, the close observer would notice another interesting phenomenon at those relatively few Zen temples where meditation is still practiced with some regularity. The phenomenon referred to is the increasing number of both lay men and women who are coming to Zen temples for short periods of time to participate in meditation and other forms of Zen training.

This increased lay interest might seem to indicate a revitalization of contemporary Japanese Zen. Indeed, during the past few years the popular media in Japan have often referred to a so-called *Zen-būmu* (boom). Interestingly enough, one cause given for this *Zen-būmu* is that the Japanese, particularly young people, have come to regard Zen more highly because of the attention it has received in the West. While that may be partially correct, it cannot be the complete answer. Careful investigation of these lay trainees reveals that many of them are not participating by choice. That is to say, many of these trainees have been sent to Zen temples by the companies in which they are employed. Usually these employees have just entered the company, and their Zen training is considered part of their orientation program.

Zen training is not limited to freshman employees alone, however; middle management, even top management, groups are also numerous. There are, in fact, management consultants in Japan who specialize in arranging Zen training sessions for the various strata of company employees. It is also not unknown for members of top management themselves to conduct, or at least partially conduct, these training sessions for their employees.

Unfortunately, no hard statistical data exist on the numbers of employees involved in these training programs. Observation at upwards of a dozen major Zen temples, belonging to both the Rinzai and Sōtō traditions, however, has convinced me that a significant number of individuals is involved. In the Tokyo area, for example, the Rinzai Zen-affiliated temple of Engaku-ji in Kamakura has become one of the centers of this kind of training. On any given morning, and especially on weekends, one can see anywhere from ten to over one hundred company employees filing in and out of the meditation hall. These employees are easily distinguishable from the other lay trainees because of their uniform dress, often with the company's crest emblazoned on their jackets or baseball caps. At the Sōtō Zen temple of Jōkūin in Saitama prefecture, where I trained for some time, there were approximately 5,000 lay trainees a year, between 60-70 percent of whom were in company-related groups.

What benefits do these employees, or more properly, the companies which send them, hope to derive from Zen training? Could it be that these companies wish to have a group of "enlightened beings" on their payroll? Would such enlightened beings insure greater corporate profits? As compassionate and self-sacrificing Bodhisattvas, would they perhaps be able to eliminate the cut-throat competition of the market-place? It is to the "why" of corporate Zen training that this article will address itself. At the outset, I would like to suggest that the companies involved have some very pragmatic and immediate reasons for wishing their employees, new and old, to undergo Zen training. This proposition is borne out by the fact that corporate Zen training is often conducted in tandem with, or in place of, so-called "temporary enlistment" (*Kari-nyūtai*) in the Japanese Self-Defense Forces. It seems unlikely that employees would be made to undergo military training if the company's goal were truly their enlightenment!

What, then, are these "very pragmatic and immediate reasons?" The answer to this question is closely related to what it was that made Zen training attractive to Japan's ruling elites in the past. To demonstrate the validity of this statement, however, it is necessary to investigate some relevant aspects of Zen's traditional sociopolitical role in Japanese society.

The Traditional Sociopolitical Role of Zen

Although Buddhism was first introduced to Japan in the 6th century, it was not until the Kamakura period (1185–1382) that Zen took root in Japan as an independent school.[1] The two monks primarily responsible for this were Eisai (1141–1215) and Dōgen (1200-1253), founders of the Rinzai and Sōtō Zen sects respectively. Although contemporaries, these two men had many differences. For example, the esoteric rituals of the then-predominant Shingon school played a much greater role in Eisai's Zen than they did in Dōgen's. Furthermore, Eisai taught that the goal of Zen training was the attainment of enlightenment. Dōgen, on the other hand, maintained that such training, particularly the practice of the Zen form of meditation known as zazen, was itself the manifestation of enlightenment.

There were, of course, many similarities as well. Both men had studied Zen in China and both reacted strongly against the scholastic doctrinalism and degeneracy of the Buddhist prelates of their day. In terms of this article, the most important similarity is that, to varying degrees, they both identified Zen with the welfare of the state. In his famous treatise, Kōzen-gokoku-ron (The Spread of Zen for the Protection of the Country), Eisai argued that it was through the universal adoption of the teachings of Zen that the nation could be protected. Dōgen also wrote a similar treatise entitled Gokoku-shōbō-gi (The Method of Protecting the Country by the True Dharma).

Although the contents of this latter treatise are no longer extant, its title, as well as Dōgen's other writings on the same subject, suggest a similar position to that of Eisai. In the Bendōwa section of Dōgen's masterwork, the Shōbōgenzō (lit., True Dharma Eye Treasury), for example, he states:

When the true Way is widely practiced in the nation, the various buddhas and heavenly deities will continuously protect it, and the virtue of the emperor will exert a good influence on the people, thereby bringing peace.

Eisai and Dōgen were not, of course, the first Japanese priests to identify Buddhism with the welfare of the state. Both Kūkai (774–835), the founder of the Shingon school, and Saichō (767–822), the founder of the Tendai school, had previously written tracts similar to theirs. In fact, it can be argued that this element is found in Japanese Buddhism from the very beginning. Prof. Anesaki Masaharu, for example, points this out in his book, History of Japanese Religion. In discussing the introduction of Buddhism to Japan in the 6th century, he writes that "A close alliance was established between the throne and the [Buddhist] religion, since the consolidation of the nation under the sovereignty of the ruler was greatly supported by the fidelity of the imported religion to the government."

Still, it can not be denied that by their actions Eisai and Dōgen set the stage for the later close relationship between the interests of the state and Zen. This is particularly true in the case of Eisai, who, unlike Dōgen, closely aligned himself with the feudal military government in Kamakura. It was this alignment with the Kamakura Shogunate, and its associated samurai class, that was, in the following years, to produce a uniquely Japanese development of Zen, the belief in the efficacy of Zen training in warfare.

The origin of this belief may be traced back to Shogun Hōjō Tokimune (1251-1284) and those Zen priests who surrounded him. Like his father, Hōjō Tokiyori (1227-1263), Tokimune was deeply interested in Zen. Unlike his father, however, he was faced with the first serious threat of foreign invasion in recorded Japanese history. In his book, Zen and Japanese Culture, the noted Zen scholar, D.T. Suzuki, describes how Tokimune sought strength from Zen to deal with this threat.[2] According to Suzuki, he went for guidance to his spiritual mentor, a Chinese Zen master by the name of Tsu-yüan Wu-Hsüeh (Sogen Mugaku, 1226-1286), shortly before the expected invasion.

When Tokimune said: "The greatest event of my life is here at last," the master asked: "How will you face it?" Tokimune replied by merely shouting the exclamatory word: "Katsu!," as though he were frightening all of his enemies into submission. Pleased with this show of courage, Tsu-yüan indicated his approval of Tokimune's answer by saying: "Truly, a lion's child roars like a lion." Subsequently, with the assistance of a "divine wind" (Kamikaze), which was, most likely, merely a timely typhoon, Tokimune was successful in repelling the Mongol invaders.

It should be noted that the shouting of "Katsu," a teaching method first advocated by the Chinese monk, Lin-chi I-hsüan (Rinzai Gigen, d. 867), originally had nothing to do with making one fearless in the face of an enemy. Rather it, together with the use of sharp blows, was a method of forcing the trainee to transcend discursive dualistic thinking and grasp reality immediately and directly. The purpose was to comprehend the true form of things, not to subdue an opponent who, in reality, was nothing but another manifestation of oneself.

Although dating several centuries after the preceding incident, there is a letter written by the famous Zen master, Takuan (1573-1645), which clearly shows how the mind which has transcended discursive thought, technically known in Zen as "no-mind" (mushin), came to be identified with martial prowess, particularly in the use of the sword. Addressing the famous swordsman, Yagyū Tajima no kami Munenori (1571-1646), Takuan writes:

"No mind" applies to all activities we may perform, such as dancing, as it does to swordplay. The dancer takes up the fan and begins to stamp his feet. If he has any idea at all of displaying his art well, he ceases to be a good dancer, for his mind "stops" with every movement he goes through. In all things, it is important to forget your "mind" and become one with the work at hand.

When we tie a cat, being afraid of its catching a bird, it keeps on struggling for freedom. But train the cat so that it would not mind the presence of a bird. The animal is now free and can go anywhere it likes. In a similar way, when the mind is tied up, it feels inhibited in every move it makes, and nothing will be accomplished with any sense of spontaneity. Not only that, the work itself will be of a poor quality, or it may not be finished at all.

Therefore, do not get your mind "stopped" with the sword you raise; forget what you are doing, and strike the enemy.[3]

It was during the Ashikaga Shogunate (1392-1568), when the political center of Japan was once more in Kyoto, that Zen exerted its strongest influence on almost all fields of Japanese life and culture. Zen monks were to be found in such diverse occupations as trade representatives in negotiations with China and teachers of young people in the small schools attached to temples in the countryside. Some of them also served as the spiritual and political advisers and confidants of the Ashikaga Shoguns, often, it is said, with salutary effect. Zen monk Gidō, for example, close confidant of Shogun Yoshimitsu (1358-1408), encouraged the latter to pursue religious and literary studies, with the result that Yoshimitsu became one of the greatest patrons of Zen and the arts in Japan's history.

It was, however, in the field of social philosophy that Zen, or rather Zen monks, were to have what was in many ways their most profound influence on the future development of Japanese society. It was they who had first introduced the Neo-Confucian teachings of the Song dynasty (960–1279) into Japan. While the new Buddhist-influenced metaphysics of Neo-Confucianism had only a limited appeal to the military rulers, its social philosophy was very attractive. The latter taught the need for a social order characterized by a strict hierarchical structuring of the classes. It further required the conformity of all people to the obligations imposed by the five primary human relationships: that is, the relationships between father and son, ruler and subject, husband and wife, older and younger brother, and two friends.

In medieval Japan, the obligation of a subject to his ruler came to mean, at least among the *samurai* class, complete devotion or loyalty to one's feudal lord. The emphasis that Japanese Zen came to place on such devotion can be clearly seen in the following statement of Zen monk Suzuki Shōsan (1579-1655). In a classic work on Suchido (the feudal warrior code) entitled *Hagakure*, he said: "What is there in the world purer than renouncing one's own life for the sake of one's lord?"[4] What Shōsan, and Zen Buddhism in general, did was to equate the self-renunciation of Zen, based on the Buddhist teaching of the non-substantiality of the self (*muga*), with absolute loyalty to one's lord.

Nakamura Hajime has pointed out in his book, *Ways of Thinking of Eastern Peoples*:: "The ultimate aim of Zen practice became, among the warriors, devotion to the lord."[5] How at variance this aim was with the original teachings of Buddhism can be seen in the fact that little or no esteem for the sovereign, be he/she feudal lord or king, is to be found in the early Buddhist writings of India.[6] This is not surprising, for it was Buddha Sākyamuni himself who taught the equality of all members of the Buddhist monastic community (Sanskrit, *samgha*) regardless of their prior caste affiliation. This equality was practiced in the early *samgha* by making monks' rankings dependent upon their years of service and by putting all important questions to a majority vote.

Be that as it may, Japanese Zen continued through the succeeding centuries to place heavy emphasis among the *samurai class* on loyal and faithful service to the lord. At the same time, its temple schools instilled in the common people respect for the Confucian ideal of a hierarchically structured society in which everyone had a rigidly defined place and function. In terms of social morality, at least, Confucianism, or more accurately, Neo-Confucianism, had become Zen dogma.

With the coming of the Meiji Restoration in 1868 and the elimination of the feudal system, however, devotion to one's lord became an anachronism. The temple school system, too, was abolished by the new government, and in its place a state-supported public school system was established. As a result, Zen, and the other traditional Buddhist sects which had, in general, played a similar role vis-à-vis feudal authority, were thrown into confusion. The emergence of Shinto as a state religion and the repressive governmental measures directed towards Buddhism served to worsen the situation.

Nanzen-ji

It did not, however, take traditional Japanese Buddhism, particularly Zen, long to adjust to the new environment. Though there were no longer lords, the new oligarchs of Japan needed the devotion of their subjects as much, if not more, than did the old feudal rulers. No longer was it sufficient for the military class alone to be instilled with the absolute loyalty to their superiors. Now, the whole nation must be made to respond with the same unquestioning obedience, especially as Japan had embarked on a policy of foreign conquest and expansion.

It should be pointed out that not all Zen priests supported this new sociopolitical role for themselves. A few, influenced by newly introduced socialist and anarchist ideas, objected to it quite vigorously. One of them, a Sōtō Zen monk by the name of Uchiyama Gudō (1874-1911) even dared to oppose the revitalized emperor system itself. He did this in a pamphlet entitled *Nyugoku Kinen* (In Commemoration of Those Imprisoned). The result of this publication, however, was not only his ouster from

Sanzen-in in Ōhara, near Kyoto

The photos accompanying this article are all of Kyoto-area Zen temples and were taken by David Paulson in 1968

the Sōtō sect but also his own imprisonment. Subsequently, while still imprisoned, he was charged with earlier involvement in an anarchist plot to kill the emperor, and in 1911, together with eleven other alleged co-conspirators, he was executed.

In spite of exceptions like Uchiyama, most Zen priests became adept at promoting the cause of devotion and loyalty to the new central government and its military policies. At the time of the Russo-Japanese War (1904-5), for example, Shaku Sōen (1859-1919), abbot of the Rinzai Zen-affiliated monasteries of Engaku-ji and Kenchō-ji in Kamakura, made an extended visit to the U.S. During one of his lectures given at that time and recorded in his book, *Sermons of a Buddhist Abbot,* he said: "In the present hostilities into which Japan has entered with great reluctance, she pursues no egotistic purpose, but seeks the subjugation of evils hostile to civilization, peace, and enlightenment."[8] In describing the purpose of his visit to the battlefield during this conflict, he went on to say: ". . . I also wished to inspire, if I could, our valiant soldiers with the ennobling thoughts of the Buddha, so as to enable them to die on the battlefield with the confidence that the task in which they are engaged is great and noble."[8]

Given the preceding sentiments, it is not surprising to learn that Shaku Sōen refused to sign a joint peace appeal with the famous Russian pacifist and author Leo Tolstoy. Tolstoy had appealed to the abbot on the basis of the Buddhist precept against the taking of life. Sōen replied, however, that as a loyal subject of the Japanese Empire he would never sign such a declaration. In this connection it is worthy of note that his pupil, D.T. Suzuki, was also a strong supporter of Japan's military actions on the Asian mainland. D.T. Suzuki is, as mentioned earlier, well-known for his pioneer work in introducing Zen to the West. In one of his earlier writings entitled "A Treatise on New Religion" (*Shinshūkyō-ron*), Suzuki also discussed the relationship of religion to the state. He said: "The first duty of religion is to seek to preserve the existence of the state."[9]

As Japanese militarism grew ever stronger in the 1920s and 30s, the emphasis on the efficacy of Zen training in actual combat also became more pronounced. Ichikawa Kakugen, himself a Rinzai Zen priest and professor emeritus of Kyoto's Hanazono University, has written about this development in a number of books and articles. Zen Master Iida Tōin, for example, is recorded as having said:

> *We should be well aware of how much power Zen gave to Bushido. It is truly a cause for rejoicing that, of late, the Zen sect is popular among military men. No matter how much we may do zazen, if it is of no help to present events, then it would be better not to do it.*[10]

Prof. Ichikawa also discusses one of the most famous exponents of what was to become known as *Kōdō-zen* (Imperial Way Zen), namely Rinzai Zen Master Yamazaki Ekishū, abbot of Buttsū-ji (temple). This master described the relationship of Zen to the emperor as follows:

> *With awareness of our daily actions, we investigate the "self." In the great concentrated meditative state [i.e., samādhi] of Zen, we become united with the emperor. In each of our actions we live, moment to moment, with the greatest respect [for the emperor]. When we personify [this spirit] in our daily life, we become masters of every situation in accordance with our sacrificial duty. This is living Zen.*[11]

It was in this spirit that Master Yamazaki taught the military men under his guidance. One of these, a young captain by the name of Matsumoto Goro (1900-1937), was destined to become immortalized as the very incarnation of the Japanese military spirit. It was claimed that though mortally wounded in combat in Manchuria in 1937, he not only turned toward the east and saluted in the direction of the Imperial Palace, but he actually died standing up, as if ready to give his next order.

Not only were Captain Matsumoto's utter devotion to the emperor and fearlessness in the face of death thought to be the results of his Zen training, but his ability to die while still standing was believed to be an expression of his deep spiritual attainment. This latter belief stemmed from the traditional Zen teaching that enlightened persons could choose their own posture at death.[12]

After his death Captain Matsumoto's heroism was written about and eulogized throughout Japan, particularly in the schools. His post-humous book, *Daigi* (Great Loyalty) became the object of intense study, and he became the ideal for all youth to emulate. At the same time, Zen masters occupied themselves more and more with giving military men Zen training. A large meditation hall was built in the heart of Tokyo and used exclusively to train military men to the very end of the war. What Japan lacked in material military power she hoped to make up for with spiritual military power.

Zen priests were not only busy on the home front. They served in the military itself as both soldiers and chaplains. Often they would tour the front lines to inspire the men. One of them, Zen Master Yamada Mumon, now president of Rinzai Zen-affiliated Hanazono University, is quoted by Prof. Ichikawa as having said the following during one such visit: "This is a sacred war to drive out the European and American aggressors from Asia. Please fight without any regard for your lives."[13]

In the same spirit were these words by the abbot of Hos-shin-ji (temple), Harada Sogaku (1870-1961). Prof. Ichikawa quotes him as saying:

Forgetting [the difference between] self and others in every situation, you should always become completely one with your work. [When ordered to] march—tramp, tramp; [when ordered to] fire—bang, bang; this is the clear expression of the highest Bodhi-wisdom, the unity of Zen and war . . .[14]

Needless to say, despite all the words of encouragement given by Zen masters, and the spiritual martial powers derived from Zen meditation and training, Japan lost the war. Misguided *samādha*-power was, in the end, no match for the nationalist and revolutionary resistance of the Asian peoples combined with American technological might. Seemingly, with Japan's military bankruptcy, the unity of Zen and the martial skills had come to an end, after a history of some 700 years.

Post-War Economic Development and Zen

Japan's "miraculous" emergence as a economic power less than a generation after total defeat has been described exhaustively by both Japanese and Western writers. Hence, there is no need to repeat that description here. As Japan has emerged as an ever greater economic force, however, those factors which contributed to growth have become the subject of intense study and speculation by "Japanese experts" and business analysts of every type. Each of them has attempted to unlock the secrets of "Japan, Inc.," with particular focus on those elements which make the Japanese worker into the dedicated, loyal, diligent part of the corporate machine that he/she is. In his book on Japanese business entitled *Japan: The Fragile Superpower*, Frank Gibney, for example, notes four characteristics of the modern Japanese corporation: " (1) the dedication to the group goal, (2) the sense of hierarchy, (3) the dependence on superiors, and (4) the formalism."[15]

Gibney ascribes the origin of the preceding characteristics to the social values of the Japanese village. While he may be correct to some extent, it is also equally true that, as anyone even slightly acquainted with Japanese Zen monastic life will recognize, these are exactly the same characteristics which are to be found in Zen training. Furthermore, even if these characteristics have their origins in village society of the past, the vast majority of Japanese today are born and raised in an urban environment divorced from traditional village society. Where and how, then, do they acquire these values?

It would appear that this same question has also been of concern to Japanese business leaders. In the June 1977 issue of *Focus Japan,* an English-language magazine published by the semi-governmental Japan External Trade Organization (JETRO), there is a highly revealing article entitled "Marching to the Company Tune." In describing the history of training programs for new employees, the article states:

[These programs] were developed in the late 1950's when companies realized that schools were no longer emphasizing the old virtues of obedience and conformity. Living and training together, sometimes for as long as a month, are designed to artificially recreate the old neglected virtues.

If "artificial recreation of the old neglected virtues" is the goal, what better place to accomplish it than in a Zen monastery where monk and lay trainees rise at 3:30 a.m. to meditate, eat rice gruel for breakfast, and endure the winter cold with only tiny charcoal braziers for heat! There can be no doubt that this

Ginkaku-ji

spartan life style does increase the ability to withstand adversity, and, as Prof. George A. DeVos has pointed out, endurance has long been a highly desirable virtue in Japanese business organizations.[16] In this regard, it should also be mentioned that even for the experienced meditator, let alone the novice, extended periods of sitting in the traditional cross-legged "lotus posture" can be physically quite painful. If even the slightest movement is detected, the meditator will be "encouraged" to remain immobile by repeated blows of a long wooden stick known as a *kyosaku* wielded by a senior monk-monitor.

It is, however, in the social rather than the physical, environment of a Zen monastery that the greatest emphasis on obedience and conformity is to be found. To be allowed to enter a monastery as a trainee, a monk is expected to prostrate himself in supplication before the entrance gate for hours if not days (depending on the monastery). When asked why he wishes to enter the monastery, the monk should reply: "I know nothing. Please accept my greetings!" This answer is thought to indicate that his mind is like a blank sheet of paper, ready to have his superiors inscribe on it whatever they may wish. If a monk fails to give the foregoing answer, he is struck repeatedly with the *kyosaku* until the desired state of mind is achieved.

Once given permission to enter the monastery, the monk, like his lay counterpart, finds that everyone is his superior to some degree. Even a fellow monk who was only admitted a few hours before him will automatically precede him on any formal or semiformal occasion, even at meals, and exercise some degree of authority over him. Those senior monks who have been in training for more than one or two years seem, to the new entrant, to be superior mortals; they not only wield the *kyosaku* but also determine whether or not the novice's work assignments are done satisfactorily. These senior monks wear nicer and more colorful robes than their juniors and live in more spacious quarters. They also have the official privilege of leaving the monastery for short periods of time and the unofficial privileges of surrepticiously eating meat, drinking alcohol and keeping petty monetary and in-kind gifts made to the monastery.

If the preceding description seems not unlike that of basic training in the military, I can attest, having experienced both, that the parallels are indeed striking. Senior monks act much like drill sergeants, and novice monks are their recruits. Although it is not generally well-known, the Japanese military establishment prior to W.W. II modelled itself organizationally along the lines of a Zen monastery. Even the ordinary Japanese soldier's mess kit was adapted from the monk's set of rounded eating bowls. It is little wonder, then, that Japanese corporations continue to find the military-like discipline of a Zen monastery attractive. As one new salesman who had just completed his company's training program noted: "My work has much in common with that of a soldier."[17]

If senior monks are the drill sergeants, then it is the Zen master or masters who act as the generals (or, in the contemporary context, corporate heads). They enjoy the real authority in a Zen monastery and are ultimately responsible for directing the training programs for both monks and laypersons. In the talks they give to incoming trainees, one of their most recurrent themes revolves around the Zen phrase: "*Daishu ichinyo.*"[18] This phrase means that all members of the monastic community should act as one. That is to say, when it is time to do *zazen*, everyone sits. When it is time to eat, work, sleep, etc., everyone likewise does these activities together *as if they were one body*.

To do otherwise is called *katte na kōdō*,[19] or "*self-willed* action," and condemned as the very antithesis of the Zen life. Total conformity is thus by no means an old neglected virtue in a Zen monastery.

Discipline, obedience and conformity are not the only attractive features of monastic life for corporate Japan. The traditional Buddhist teaching of the non-substantiality of the self (that is to say, the lack of any eternal and unchangeable substance in the self) has also been given a unique corporate twist. This twist is well illustrated by Ozeki Shūen, the abbot of Daisen-in (temple) and one of the best known Zen priests conducting employee training courses. In a collection of his sermons delivered during such training courses, he states:

> *Employing your vital life force, you should exert yourselves to the utmost, free of any conceptual thought . . . This is what it means to be alive. That is to say, at every time and in every place, you should work selflessly.*[20]

A further example is provided by Sakai Tokugen, another leading Zen master involved with employee training programs. Master Sakai is also a professor of Buddhist Studies at Sōtō Zen-affiliated Komazawa University in Tokyo. In the May 1974 issues of *Daihōrin*, a popular Buddhist magazine, he lamented the lack of sincerity in carrying out the orders of one's superiors on the part of post-war Japanese. He wrote:

> *Sincerity [in carrying out orders] means having feelings and actions of absolute service, giving one's all [to the task at hand]. In doing this there can be no thought of personal loss or gain . . . By carrying out our [assigned] tasks, we become part of the life of the entire universe; we realize our original True Self . . . This is the most noble thing human beings can do.*

In other words, for Master Sakai, selfless devotion to the accomplishment of one's assigned duties is none other than enlightenment itself. Little wonder that he is a popular leader of employee training courses. Here, certainly, the Protestant work ethic has met its match.

Conclusion

At the beginning of this article it was suggested that the companies which arranged for their employees to participate in Zen training programs had some very pragmatic and immediate reasons for doing so. At this point the truth of this proposition should be quite apparent. The discipline, the emphasis on group rather than individual action, the ability to endure hardship, the heightened sense of "selfless" loyalty and subordination both to one's group and to one's superiors are all aspects of Zen training which have immediate relevance to corporate life.

It should also be clear that, in essence, the same spirit pervades Suzuki Shōsan's words about "renouncing one's own life for the sake of one's lord" and Sakai Tokugen's lamentation quoted above, or for that matter, the exhortations of Harada Sogaku and the other Zen supporters of Japanese militarism. The only difference between them is on the question of to whom, or to what, one should be loyal and devoted. Originally, it was the feudal lord; later it became the central government and its policies as embodied in the person of the emperor; and now, of course, it is the corporation and its interests. It should be noted, however, that to an even greater degree than in the U.S.,

Japanese corporate interests are closely connected with those of the state.

There is one other aspect of Zen training which is very attractive from the corporate standpoint. This is none other than the practice of *zazen* itself. As Zen Master Iida pointed out earlier, the *samurai* were indeed strengthened by the concentrated state of mind achieved through the practice of *zazen*. This *samādhi*-power was originally utilized in Zen training to give the practitioner a deeper insight into his or her own nature and the nature of reality itself. Yet, it can be and, as already noted, has been applied to any work in which one may be engaged— everything from wielding a *samurai* sword with lightning swiftness, or fighting "selflessly" in battle, to assembling a color television set with flawless precision. What could be more attractive to a Japanese company than the utilization of *samādhi*-power, and thus *zazen*, for its own corporate ends?

This, however, brings up an extremely important question: "Is corporate Zen training a legitimate expression of Zen Buddhism?" The answer in the best Zen tradition, must be both yes and no. On the affirmative side it must be admitted that if one looks at corporate Zen training in terms of its historical antecedents, this training is very much a part of the popular tradition of Japanese Zen. Although historical analogies can be misleading, there is a very real sense in terms of values in which the corporate leaders of present-day Japan are actually *samurai* disguised in Western clothing. Instead of the long and short swords of the *samurai* they wield the computer and pocket calculator.

On a deeper level, however, there is reason to ask whether corporate Zen is not as alien to the true spirit of Zen as were its historical antecedents—"feudal Zen" and "militarist Zen." Although a whole article could be devoted to this topic alone, let it suffice here to quote Zen Master Dōgen's most succinct expression of the goal of Zen training. In the *Genjō-Kōan* section of the *Shōbōgenzō*, he states:

> *To study the Way is to study the self. To study the self is to forget the self. To forget the self is to be enlightened by all things. To be enlightened by all things is to remove the barriers between one's self and others.*[21]

A true student of Zen, then, would use his *samādhi*-power, first and foremost, to break through those barriers of ignorance which separate him from his own True Self and from others. Having acomplished this, he would, in accordance with the Bodhisattva ideal, use that same power to aid others in their own search for release. To use that power for his or a particular group's selfish ends, at the expense of others, would be completely alien to him. To borrow Dōgen's words again: "[Only] the foolish believe that their own interests will suffer if they put the benefit of others first."[22]

This is the true spirit of Zen. Interestingly enough, even some Zen masters who are involved in corporate training programs admit to this. How, then, do they justify their involvement in such programs? Zen Master Murase Genmyō, leader of the lay training center at Obaku Zen-affiliated Mampuku-ji, has expressed the belief that out of any large group of employee trainees there will be at least a few who will "acquire a taste" for Zen in spite of the companies' goals. This will lead to their further practice of Zen and, eventually, to an understanding of its true spirit.

While one can certainly hope this will occur, it is my experience, based on ten years of training in Japan as a Zen monk, that few if any employee participants ever do reach an understanding of Zen's true spirit. Were employees to adopt the Bodhisattva ideal they would clearly become a liability, not an asset, to their corporate bosses. Statements like those made by Master Murase are nothing more than feeble attempts to rationalize the symbiotic relationship which presently exists between Zen and corporate Japan. This relationship, as has been shown, is based on more than 700 years of Zen cooperation with, and support for, the power structure of the day. Its reform will be no easy task.

Japanese Zen is not, however, completely without hope for progressive change. As has been noted, there were Zen priests like Uchiyama Gudō who recognized the basic incompatibility of Zen and capitalism as early as the late Meiji period. He gave the following explanation of why he had become a socialist:

> *As a propagator of the Buddha's teachings, I believe that all sentient beings have Buddha-nature [i.e., the capacity to realize enlightenment]; that they are all equal, without any superiors or inferiors; and that they are all my children. These are the golden words which form the basis of my faith. I discovered that these golden words are identical with those spoken by socialists. It was for this reason that I finally became a believer in socialism.*[23]

Although priests like Uchiyama almost completely disappeared (or more accurately, were removed) from the Zen tradition during the 1920s, 30s and 40s, a few did reappear after World War II. These were priests like Ichikawa Hakugen who has already been mentioned. Included in his books condemning Zen's (and his own) collaboration with Japanese Fascism are discussions of Zen's political, economic and social thought. In

Ryōan-ji

The War Responsibility of Buddhists (*Bukkyō-sha no sensō seki-nin*), he devotes one full chapter to the direction and content of a possible "Buddhist socialism."[24] Rooted in the Buddhist concept of *sūnya* or "emptiness" (the absence of any permanent, changeless entity in the universe), he maintains that Buddhist socialism would be characterized by, among other things, a humble and open spirit cleansed of the will to power and the absolutism of self. It would, furthermore, work toward the ultimate demise of state power and the emergence of a communal society free of the capitalist mode of private property.

A generation of students of Zen at Hanazono University have grown to maturity under Ichikawa's guidance. One of them, Kashiwagi Ryūhō, has only recently written the most complete account of Uchiyama Gudō's life and thought yet available.[25] Together with a small group of Buddhist intellectuals and social activists, he has formed the "Gudō Society" (*Gudō no kai*). It already counts as one of its members, Setouchi Harumi, a Buddhist nun and one of Japan's leading woman writers.

It is, of course, still much too early to talk about the existence of a significant Zen (or Buddhist) socialist movement in Japan. The most that can be said is that the potential does exist. In the meantime, employee training programs will continue to be the main "social activity" of the majority of Japanese Zen Buddhist monasteries. In fact, in the short run these programs will undoubtedly be expanded. As the worldwide crisis of capitalism deepens, the Japanese corporate need for a disciplined *and subservient* work force will become greater than ever before. However, given the growing strength of both the external and internal forces opposed to "Japan, Inc." (and its American and European allies), there is no more reason to believe that contemporary Japanese Zen leaders will, ultimately, be any more successful in maintaining the corporate state than their predecessors were in maintaining the feudal and fascist regimes of the past.   ☆

Notes

1. The meditative aspect of Buddhism had been introduced into Japan at a relatively early date. The Japanese monk, Dōshō (628-700), in fact, built the first meditation hall in the then-capital of Japan, Nara, in the latter part of the 7th century.

2. Although there are other more "Zen-like" interpretations of this exchange, another noted Zen scholar, Heinrich Dumoulin, agrees with Suzuki that the following exchange reveals the way in which Tokimune derived courage from his Zen training to face the Mongol invaders. Thus, this incident may well be said to mark the origin of the belief in Japan that Zen training was efficacious in warfare. See Heinrich Dumoulin, *A History of Zen Buddhism*, (Boston: Beacon Press, 1963), p. 138, and D. T. Suzuki, *Zen and Japanese Culture*, (New York: Princeton University Press, 1959), pp. 66-67.

3. D. T. Suzuki, *Essentials of Zen Buddhism*, (New York: Princeton University Press, 1962), p. 458.

4. Charles A. Moore (ed.), *The Japanese Mind*, (Honolulu: University Press of Hawaii, 1967), p. 233.

5. Nakamura Hajime, *Ways of Thinking of Eastern Peoples*, edited by Philip P. Wiener, (Honolulu: East-West Center Press, 1964), p. 430.

6. Ibid., p. 429.

7. Shaku Sōen, *Sermons of a Buddhist Abbot*, (LaSalle, Illinois: Open Court Publishing Co., 1913), p. 202.

8. Ibid., p. 203.

9. Ichikawa Hakugen, 'Shūkyō-sha no sensō-seekinin o tou' in *Nihon no shūkyō*, vol. I, no. 1 (Dec. 1974), p. 38.

10. Ichikawa Hakugen, *Zen to gendai shisō*, (Tokyo: Tokuma Shoten, 1967), p. 206.

11. Op. cit., p. 45.

12. Toward the latter part of the *Fukan-zazengi* (A Universal Recommen-
dation for the Practice of *Zazen*) Dōgen wrote: "By virtue of *zazen* it is possible to transcend the difference between 'common' and 'sacred' and attain the ability to die while doing *zazen* or while standing up."

13. Maruyama Teruo, *Nihonjin no kokoro o dame ni shita meisō*, akusō, gusō, (Tokyo: Yamate Shobō, 1977), p. 49.

14. *Ichikawa Hakugen, Zen to gendai shisō*, p. 173.

15. Frank Gibney, *Japan: The Fragile Superpower*, (New York: W. W. Norton and Co., 1975); p. 204.

16. George A. De Vos, "Apprenticeship and Paternalism," in *Modern Japanese Organization and Decision-Making*, ed. Ezra F. Vogel (Berkeley: University of California Press, 1975), pp. 221-23.

17. "Marching to the Company Tune," *Focus Japan*, June 1977, p. 36.

18.

19.

20. Maruyama Teruo, Nihonjin no kokoro o dame ni shita meisō, ahusō, gusō, p. 194.

21. As quoted in Yokoi Yūhō's *Zen Master Dōpen*, (Tokyo/New York: John Weatherhill, 1976), p. 5.

22. Ibid., p. 62.

23. As quoted in Kashiwagi Ryūhō's *Taigyaku jiken to Uchiyama Gudō*, (Tokyo: JCA Shuppan-sha, 1979), p. 29.

24. Ichikawa Hakugen, *Bukkyō-sha no sensō sekinin*, (Tokyo: Shunjū-sha, 1970), pp. 150-68.

25. Kashiwagi Ryūhō, *Taigyaku jiken to Uchiyama Gudō*, (Tokyo: JCA Shuppan-shas, 1979).

Daitoku-ji

Ishimure Michiko's "The Boy Yamanaka Kuhei"

山中九平少年

courtesy of Christopher Stevens

The boy Yamanaka Kuhei.

translated by Christopher Stevens*

An abandoned boat adrift on an open sea—
this bitter sea of life and death unending

There is a village called Yudō that lines the shores of a small inlet on the Sea of Shiranui. The waves in the cove are never rough except once or twice a year when a typhoon strikes. Floating in the bay are small boats and sardine nets, riding the waves flecked with whitecaps that flutter like fretful eyelids. Children, completely naked, enjoy themselves leaping from boat to boat and plunging into the water.

In summer, the voices of these children rise up past the orange orchards and wooded groves, through the large, gnarled sumac bushes and the spaces in the stone walls, and can be heard in every house.

At the lowest spot in the village, at the foot of the first terrace from the boat mooring, is the old and large communal well and a place for washing clothes. In the shade of the moss that lines the stones of this large, square well, minnows and attractive red-colored crabs sport about. It must be that a spring bubbles up sweet-tasting water into this well that has crabs such as these living in it. In this area there are springs that bubble up even at the bottom of the sea.

Lying sunken at the bottom of the well water that no one draws anymore, the accumulated sediment assumes the forms of ship spikes and the flowers of camellias.

From the rocky slope above the well, aged camellia bushes whose years no one can determine hang in masses over the washing place and the terrace before it. Their darkened leaves and twisting branches embrace the boulders their own roots have split apart, releasing the ancient spirit of these crags; and the shadows beneath are always cool and still.

Near the inlet on which the village of Yudō is situated there used to be landfall sentinel stations of the Higo clan and a sea entry station at the border of Satsuma. Beyond lies the Sea of Shiranui. The fishermen say things like "We stopped over at Go Sho no Ura last night and then zipped right back here while it was calm in the morning." From Yudō, Go Sho no Ura is in sight in the island group of Amakusa. Facing Amakusa, if you turn to the left, you can see both the land and sea routes that link up with Satsuma. Beyond the inlet is the hamlet of Modō. On the outskirts of this village runs a river where you can wash clothes. Like a moat, it is the prefectural boundary, "The River of the Gods" by name. If you wash rice standing on the pebbled river bank, the milky water will cross over the border towards the farther shore where they speak the dialect of Kagoshima.

Beyond Modō heading south in Kagoshima Prefecture are Izumi City and Kome no Tsu. On the Kumamoto Prefecture side travelling along Route Three from Modō, one arrives at Fukuro, Yudō, Detsuki, and then enters the harbor of Hyakuken. This is the region where outbreaks of Minamata disease are prevalent. From the harbor one enters the city streets of Minamata. In Hyakuken harbor is the drainage pipe from the New Japan Chisso Factory at Minamata.

Standing on this plain dotted with wells is a public building—a young men's club—whose wooden rooms and walls are beginning to decay. This cabin, faded by the sea breezes, has long been vacant. It is as if the loneliness the older men have come to secretly feel has condensed in this building and blows about in the air. This unused clubhouse has robbed the village of its vitality to a significant degree. The days when young men would settle down in Yudō as fishermen have long since passed. Especially since Minamata disease first appeared, things have never been the same. No

---

* This translation is of the first chapter of *Ku gai jo do* (Bitter sea, pure land) by Ishimure Michiko, who has given permission for its publication here.

139

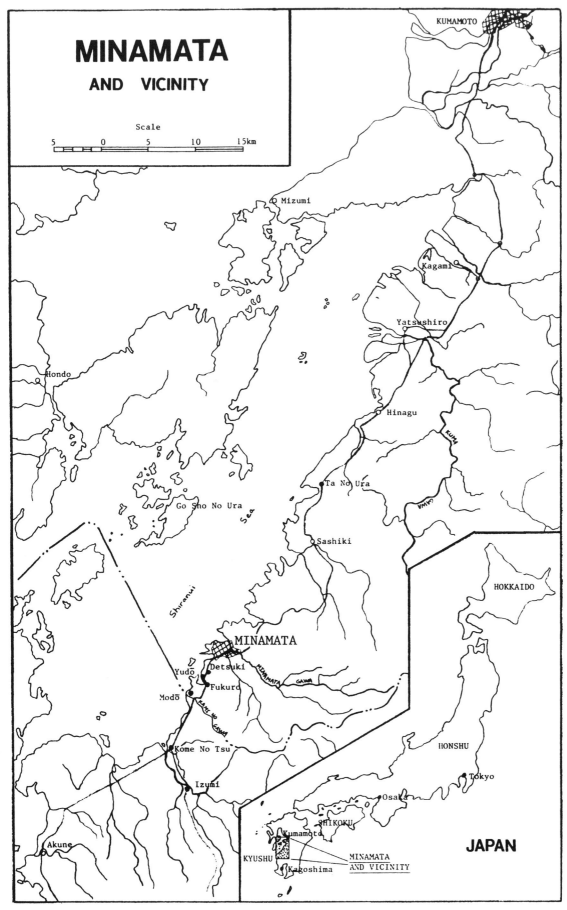

map by G.R. Frantz

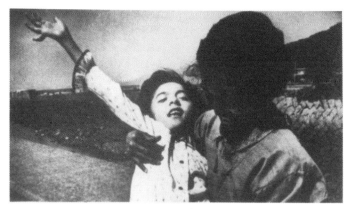

Isayama Takako, a congenital Minamata disease victim, in her mother's arms. She was born in 1961.

matter how skillful the fisherman, he can no longer hand down his knowledge to his son. The older fishermen think about this grimly. Each one considers himself the expert at catching sea bream, or the best man at spear fishing, or the cleverest with mullet traps. It is just as they say; each man is an expert, the likes of whom exist nowhere else. Their pride supports their livelihood, the city fish market, the protein source for the citizens of Minamata, and one part of the fishing industry on the coast of the Sea of Shiranui.

An old man sits on the floor of the abandoned clubhouse, its door awry, with his grandchild he has brought with him. His ear, like a conch shell, is turned towards the Shiranui Sea. Like an overcast sky, his eyes are dim. Perhaps it is because he can no longer see well enough even to repair nets that his youngest grandchild has been given to him to baby-sit.

The floorboards of this young men's clubhouse, which continue to split apart day by day, should have held memories for him of the vitality he had when he was young, but all the old fisherman shows is an uneasy and vacant expression as he looks at the sea and his grandchild. The child is crawling around on the floor, and the old fisherman knows he cannot match his grandchild in bodily strength. The old man seems half asleep, and already in another world from his descendant, who has stopped crawling around and is sucking his thumb.

This old fisherman's face has a look similar to those of the old farmers from my village. Their sons and daughters no longer know when to draw water for their rice fields, and when to drain them, and where to cut the embankment between their neighbor's fields and their own on the appointed evening in order to drain their own fields, and how to repair the bank afterwards, and so forth. At rice planting time the old farmers would hang around the tiller brought in to turn up the soil. Staring steadily at it they would suddenly raise their voices—it was impossible to tell if they were sighing or cursing—saying, "Yeah, nowadays, people who own machines have it made. In the old days, if you worked your whole life maybe you could buy a cow or a horse. If you can buy a tractor, you're spoiled." With a sigh they would pull off the leeches stuck to their calves and crush them to death on the embankment.

Like those old farmers crushing leeches to death, the old fisherman uses the end of his walking stick to try to mash a boat worm that has crawled up between his legs, but the worm in its panic is more nimble than the end of the stick the old

man lowers on it with a vague expression in his eyes. Its rear end half crushed, it rolls and falls through to the floor, leaving a smear on the planks.

The older people endure within themselves the uneasy feeling that this formless inheritance, this secret knowledge that must be handed down to their descendants, will perish with themselves. Like the clubhouse that continues to decay, their living spirit and flesh continue to weather. Even in the summertime, no matter where one walks along the beach, this feeling lurks in the air.

I remember the afternoon of a day after summer had passed, two years ago. It was the fall of 1963. The children had long since come back up to the village from their summer frolic in the sea. The autumn sun cast long shadows on the red earth of the hillside paths around Yudō. The flowers in the fields had already fallen and the smell of still-green oranges floated through the air. There was hardly a sound, either from the ocean or the houses. It was that time of day when a soothing silence visits this village of many fishermen's homes. Everyone must have gone down to the sea or into town, and even the chickens were napping in their roosts.

Breathing shallowly, I stood in the front yard of Kuhei's house, which stands halfway up the slope in the village facing the sea. Surprisingly enough, he was outdoors. He was repeating some kind of "practice" with complete determination. It apparently was some kind of baseball practice, but his movements were so awesome that I felt deterred from calling out to him. Rooted to the spot, I started to breathe with the same rhythm as the boy. Whether he tried to stand up or squat down, he gave the impression of being a hunchback or a cripple. His posture was completely inappropriate for a boy his age. If you only glanced casually at the lower half of his body from behind, you could not help but think that he was an old man. This outward appearance belies his natural constitution and his inner will. If you looked closely, you would see that the back of his neck was smooth just like any other boy his age, and that if he had not contracted Minamata disease his physique would be that of a husky boy entering his early manhood who had grown up in a fishing village like Yudō. He had a battered pair of clogs on his feet. I knew that it required a lot of effort for him to put them on.

He stretched his legs. The strain was so great that faint tremors ran up and down both legs to his waist. He squatted down and drew an arc on the ground with the stick like a compass. He inched along, leaning his head with its closely cropped hair to one side. And now with one hand on the ground, he thrust the stick he held in the other hand along in the dirt. He seemed to be searching for something with its tip. After a number of trials, it made a noise of hitting the rock he was searching for. Kuhei was blind. With great care he laid the stick on the ground and for a long time held the rock that he had been groping for in his left hand between his bent knees as though he were caressing it. He used his left hand because his right hand was half paralyzed. This rock was the size of a fist and protruded slightly from his hand. It was oval shaped rather than perfectly round and fitted the palm of his crippled left hand quite well. The moisture from the rock and the sweat from his hand mixed faintly together.

(I learned later that he had picked up this rock five years before at the time when a road was being constructed in front of his house. The boy had cherished it ever since. He would always squirrel it away in a hole he had dug in a corner of the dirt-floored room in the house so that it wouldn't roll away any great distance. With his eyes averted and half-closed in blindness he would creep forward, groping for the cavity he had dug, and would touch it with trembling fingers. The sight of this boy putting away his rock was painful to watch and I sensed a heaviness that the rock contained.)

After a while, Kuhei half rose, the way an extremely old man would get up, and with a serious expression faced the sky and threw the rock he had been grasping up in the air. Then, with the nimblest of all the movements he had made so far, he flailed the stick sideways with both hands. His body buckled, but he didn't fall down. By the time he swung his stick, the stone had come down in the wrong direction and had hit the ground, so he missed it. He quietly tilted his head in the direction where the stone had fallen and once again started to probe the ground with his bat.

The noon meal was over and everyone had gone to the fields or to fish or to the town. The entire village had become a vacuum. Although on an autumn afternoon like this you can hear from amongst the stone walls and houses and the narrow winding paths on the hillside the sound of boats chugging in the inlet below and the voices of older people calling their grandchildren and the clucking of chickens as they peck at the earth, it was as though Kuhei alone was the single driving force of human will in this afternoon village, making this vacuum move with his strenuous actions as he played "baseball" by himself. Nothing else stirred.

My breathing was attuned: it mingled with the stones and plants and trees that release their breath from the earth. It merged with his movements. The back of his neck was sopping wet with sweat. I felt that a long time had passed. I drew closer to him, and called out his name.

He was extremely startled and dropped his stick with a thud. Somehow the harmony that had come into being between the soundless village and himself collapsed at that very moment. He was unable to move. He seemed to be trying to concentrate on where the door to his house was. And then, walking backwards, as if he were making a dash for it, he diappeared behind the door.

This was the first time that Kuhei and I had ever met in person. I have a son who is about the same age as Kuhei. I became upset, and maternal feelings writhed within me.

When I talked with employees from the Minamata City Health Department about Kuhei, they abruptly flashed broad smiles at me which mixed confusion with feelings of affection for the boy. They said things like, "Yamanaka Kuhei, yes . . . well . . . that Kuhei really is something else . . ."

The Health Department had made a big stir about the boy. Of those at the Department, Mr. Yomogi, in particular, would narrow his eyes when discussing Kuhei, as though he were even keeping a personal watch over the boy. It is the officials of the City Health Department who get in touch with the patients when the Kumamoto University Medical School gives the disease victims medical examinations and performs other research at the Minamata Municipal Hospital or in the local hamlets.

The Health Department owns a private bus to transport the patients to the examination facility. The driver of this private bus, a young man by the name of Ōtsuka, squeezes the bus into the narrow lanes of the village, getting as close as he can to each patient's house. He honks his horn when he pulls up. And then, from on the bus, there leisurely comes into view groups of three or five people assembled in the village lanes, and next to the rice fields, and the cliff sides, and the cryptomeria groves, and the road that runs along the ocean.

Held in the arms of their mothers or their grandparents, or else carried on their backs as their heads loll to and fro, the children are gathered together with the adult victims who hobble despondently along. This scene, as these people stand on the side of the road next to the rice fields or the seashore, is, to say the least, different from that of an ordinary bus stop.

People walking past draw back slightly and look at the groups of deformed children. Greetings are kept to a minimum, and one can perceive both kindness and its absence in the passers-by. The rice fields and the muddy roads and the glinting crests of the sea waves somehow seem to freeze, if only because the children are there with the adults who are standing around. The grown-ups look pathetically modest and bewildered. They show feelings welling up from hearts that have been very profoundly moved. Smiles of friendliness are constantly drifting across their faces.

Ōtsuka, the driver, calls out, "Tomoko, I see you made it!" in a vigorous voice.

And then, as soon as this young man uses his strength to

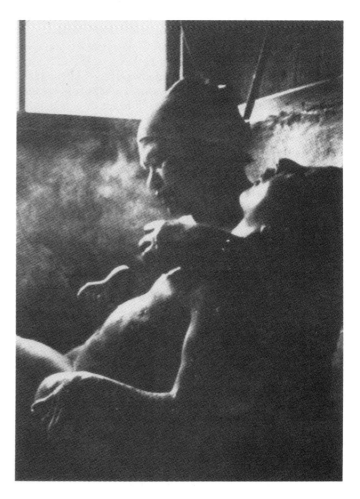

Uemura Tomoko being held in her mother's arms. She was born in 1956.

shut the bus door with a big slam, I always sense a subtle change in mood that is different from the anxiety these people felt when they were outside. The conversations of the adults unwind smoothly against the background murmuring of the speech-impaired children. The children, who are ten years old or so, are held in the arms of their mothers or grandparents. They *feel* the passing scenery outside the bus as their heads droop backwards. These children are either completely blind, or else have an extremely restricted field of vision. Judging from the voices of these speech-defective children, and what they appear to be gazing at, it seems clear that these kids, who hold their stiffened, skinny, birdlike limbs drawn close to their chests, looking for all the world like some "four legged human animal," are absolutely delighted at being given a ride on the bus. The adults compare the children with their eyes, smile at each other, and gradually slip into an intimate conversation.

The situation on a bus such as this one tells us that these people have been getting through life since Minamata disease first occurred without ever completely fitting into life when they *aren't* on the bus, that is to say, into the life of their hometown, where they were born and grew up and are making a living for themselves. The moment Ōtsuka, the driver, shuts the door with a bang, and in a booming voice calls out "Well, here we go!" as he grasps the steering wheel, everyone feels relieved, and the atmosphere of congeniality revives. They are liberated from the frozen scene outside. Their awareness of the young driver fades away, and the interior of the bus dissolves into a kind of natural scene in itself.

The young man keeps his lips firmly sealed except when he calls out greetings, such as "Hi there" and "hello," to these children who can make him no reply. After he and the Health Department officials help the children to get their exhausted and unmanageable bodies into the seats, he returns to the driver's seat and erases the smile from around his eyes. He even looks angry. This shows that he will not waste a single word in unnecessary small talk.

His manner is always like this when he comes in contact with people who have Minamata disease. His goodwill gives

Fishing.

the impression of being forced. The truth, however, is that he conceals it in the depths of an expression that is sullen, brusque, and yet somehow amiable all at once. Without him realizing it consciously, he has come to store a pool of anger within himself, and even seems irritated with the situation. This young man, who lives near the upper reaches of the Minamata River, and grew up exchanging visits with his friends from the seaside, surely has an instinctual bond with those kindred souls from the same home town. There are any number of ways that the residents reveal their reactions to the Minamata disease situation; his attitude is pragmatic. Like water that circulates at a subterranean level, he gives indications of his feelings of communion.

When Minamata disease first appeared, he was a taxi driver in the city. In the midst of that uproar he drove all over the place, giving rides to people who poured into town from all over the country—reporters, officials from the Welfare Ministry or the Ministry of Such-and Such, Congressional Representatives, and other unfamiliar and unusual people who were apparently academic types. The destinations of these personages, about whom he must have thought that they had come because of Minamata disease, were places like the Chisso factory, and the Yu no Ji Hot Springs Resort, and the Yamatoya Inn, and the Municipal Hospital, and City Hall, and so forth. Members of the Kumamoto Medical School visited their patients and the villages where they were from on a regular basis. Having gone through all of this, the young man must have had his own opinion about the whole Minamata disease situation, but he kept it to himself.

Now he is a driver for the City Health Department. When he gets on the bus and shuts the door, the disease-ridden children and the adults all feel relaxed, and they burst into gleeful laughter even at little things, even when little Miss Shinobu's flowered hat flies off of her head with a puff of wind from the bus window.

The accuracy of certain statistics has been called into question. These statistics indicate a higher rate of concentration of congenital cerebral palsy amongst the children born in fishermen's households between 1954 and 1959 in those villages where Minamata disease had already appeared. However, in January of 1962 the Minamata disease Investigation Committee reported that seventeen children were afflicted with congenital Minamata disease. At the end of March of 1964 they reported the names of six or more children, bringing the total to twenty-three in all. These children were invaded with mercury poisoning while they were still in their mothers' wombs and came into this world enduring its affliction.

Congenital Minamata disease has cropped up in the same general region where other forms of the disease have appeared. This zone extends from the villages along the downreaches of the Kami no Kawa River, Izumi City and Kome no Tsu in Kagoshima Prefecture, past Minamata City in Kumamoto Prefecture, up to Ta no Ura in the Ashikita District.

Even when they were two years old, these children could not walk, let alone crawl, talk, or use chopsticks to eat. They were seized with spasms and convulsions from time to time; the real reason why the fits occurred remained hidden. Their mothers never even suspected that those milk-suckling babies, who have never eaten fish, were suffering from Minamata disease. Until they heard that diagnosis, the parents walked around the hospital in town selling off their boats and fishing equipment in order to scrape together enough money to pay for the medical treatments.

Four or five years pass. The children have no choice but to be left lying around the house for the greater part of the day. Shuttered in houses along the village lanes, they spend their lives sensing with their entire being the activities of their parents working outdoors, and the cats and kittens and boat bugs that frisk about their bedside.

The ones who are able to crawl around and stand up weakly by themselves require more attention. In order to keep them from falling into the fireplace where the kettle and the warming blankets are, or from rolling off of the raised floor of the entrance hall, these kids are lashed onto a house pillar by means of a sash wrapped around their skinny stomachs that is long enough to permit them to stand up or crawl around with a certain amount of freedom. Even then, most of them have burns from falling into the hearth, or bruises from falling off of the porches. Most of these children cannot call for help, even if they fall into the fireplace. Some of them have lost their fathers or their older brothers or sisters to Minamata disease. They are totally unaware that they are the victims of congenital Minamata disease, to say nothing of their ignorance of the fate that has befallen their families. At any rate, even if their brothers and sisters are still alive and off at school, and their parents are out fishing or in the fields, it is not their own idea to be forced to live lashed onto a pillar in an empty house. The gaze of these children left lying around for years at a time shows more than mere wonderment; it looks clairvoyant.

It is up to the age of about ten or so that children are the most sensitive to solitude and isolation in all the aspects of their emotional life. Therefore, it is hardly surprising that their faces light up when they look at the sky outside their house and then get on the bus. They start to realize that soon they will be on the bus and on their way, as soon as their diaper and kimono are changed and they are carried in the arms of one of their parents away from the house they have been isolated in.

Even though these children are ten years old, they invariably have a look of infantile innocence about them. They express with their entire bodies their anticipation (mingled, of course, with anxiety) of getting on the bus and going to the hospital—which is to say that they are looking forward to getting in touch with the life of the community that is so different from the situation they have been experiencing inside their own house.

It certainly must be wrenching for a parent to see her child in such a state of health as this. She cannot help but wonder what will happen to him or her after she is gone. But now that they are both alive and in each other's arms, the mutual sympathy that is closer than a hand's breadth must be a consolation to them both. The interior of the bus is filled with the sad affection of family members such as these. When little Miss Shinobu's flowered hat, which she is so proud of, is wafted off of her head by a breeze from the bus window and falls onto the floor between the seats, and the little girl (who can neither see nor hear very well) stares off in some other direction, not knowing that her hat has fallen off, the passengers find it hilarious. The bus sways from side to side as the scene dissolves in laughter, and even though little Master Kazumitsu and little Miss Matsuko are getting their heads bumped around, the bus suddenly becomes a romper room.

Yamanaka Kuhei obstinately refuses to get on the bus and go to be examined. Yamanaka Kuhei is sixteen years old (born in July of 1949). His father and his ancestors were fishermen

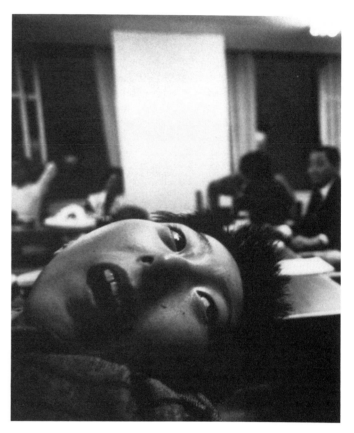

Uemura Tomoko at the Central Pollution Board.

in Yudō in the City of Minamata, but his father died unexpectedly of a cold in 1950. His older sister Satsuki (born in 1927) contracted Minamata disease in July of 1956 and died that same year on 2 September. He got sick one year before his sister did, in May of 1955. He and his sister were both admitted to the Shirahama Contagious Diseases Hospital for a period of time, but since then until now he has been treated as an outpatient. He is patient number 16. He lives with his mother Chiyo, who is getting along in years; she is fifty-seven.

From autumn, through winter and spring, the boy usually wears a black cotton school uniform, and in the wintertime he also wears a large quilted vest over it. This vest has vertical stripes and is padded with cotton. It is very thick and threadbare; it has thoroughly blended in with the life in a fisherman's household.

The Shiranui Sea where they used to go to fish looks as though it were spread out on the front yard of the Yamanaka house. In the yard, not a single one of those tools of the trade whereby fishermen earn their living is in evidence: nets, fish baskets, landing nets with handles and so forth, which in other circumstances would be arranged and hanging up to dry. Somehow the yard looks too big. A breeze blows gently through the tall trunks of an old persimmon tree, as it embraces to itself the faint rustling of the leaves of corn planted beneath its branches.

However, this oversized and thickly padded vest that the boy wears has absorbed the long history of time spent soaking up the salt breezes. It could tell the story of how they used to

Fishing.

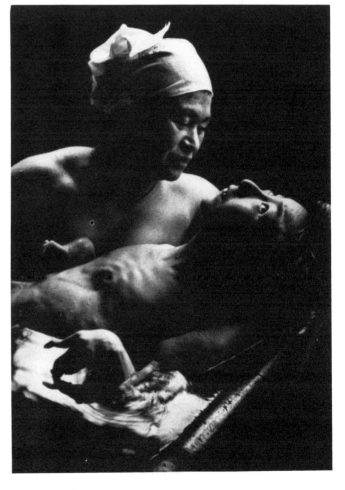

Uemora Tomoko in her mother's arms.

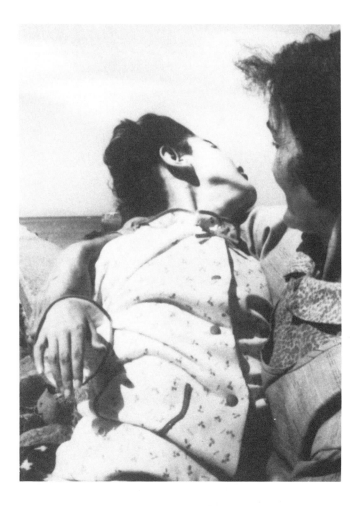

The congenital Minamata disease victim Isayama Takako.

All photos accompanying this article, with the exception of the photo of Yamanaka Kuhei supplied by Christopher Stevens, are by Aileen or W. Eugene Smith, courtesy of Aileen Smith and Christopher Stevens.

The drainage pipe into the sea.

live their lives up until ten years ago. His father wore it on the boat, and so did his sister. Now that both these workers are dead, the boy's mother has given this piece of hand-me-down work clothing to her youngest child to wear.

Interrupted during his "baseball" practice, the boy now was sitting in front of a radio placed on the wooden floor of a dimly-lighted room in the house. As usual, he was wearing his quilted vest. I had heard that when people showed up from other places at the Yamanaka house—people from the Municipal Hospital and Kumamoto University, and officials from City Hall, and people who came to observe, or should we say express sympathy for, a Minamata disease victim, and mysterious strangers like myself—Kuhei would sit in front of the radio and gruffly turn his back on them. So, I knew what to expect. He sat in front of the radio this time also, looking as though he had been in the same place since the beginning of time. His back was turned towards me, and his squared shoulders and his closely cropped hair gaven an impression of real boyishness. He was stretching his neck and leaning forward from the waist as he clicked the radio on and off.

His bent back was arched and taut like a bow, held in a posture that was filled with an extraordinary tension. But it was bowed in such a way that it also gave the painful impression that he had not been able to release it swiftly and decisively at its target, even once. His left hand quivered irritably as it groped for the on-off switch and the tuning dial of the radio. He felt for the radio and then removed his hand, again and again, as his big, black, unseeing eyes stared up obliquely into space.

Mr. Yomogi of the City Health Department called out to him.

"Kuhei."

Kuhei didn't turn around. He twisted the radio dial, very agitated. Hashi Yukio was singing a song.

"Kuhei, the distinguished doctor from Kumamoto University has come. Why don't you come along with me to see him . . ."

Kuhei's mother glanced at her son who refused to speak and replied for him.

"I'm so sorry things are like this. You've come here so many times." She looked over in her son's direction. "Listening to the radio is the only thing he enjoys in this world . . ."

"Yes, I'm sure that's true. He can't even go to school."

Kuhei's mother started to plead with him.

"Kuhei, Kuhei, your friend from the City Health Department has come for you again . . . what are we going to do?"

The boy didn't turn around, and twisted the dial violently. A baseball game was on. Mr. Yomogi, who was used to the way the boy acted, turned nonchalantly towards his mother, and talked in a loud voice. Kuhei can hear very well.

"It's better to take the medical exam today. It looks like the condolence payments from the company might go up, even though they're next to nothing. As you know, the way they decide the amount is to divide the cases between adults and children, and between serious cases and light cases . . . It seems that they are going to raise the amount according to the severity of the damage."

Chiyo laughed vaguely and then looked at her son.

"I've heard that the condolence payments might go up. Dropping her voice, she said, "It's amazing that the doctor from Kumamoto University hasn't given up. Kuhei never makes a definite decision to go. He hates going to the hospital more than anything else. We used to go there all the time. If he felt better now, or if he could see better, or if he could even move the fingers of his right hand better, he'd be glad to go and get himself examined. For the first three years we went to the hospital every day. It was the Oda Hospital. The doctors from Kumamoto University took care of him very well. But no matter what they gave him—pills, injections—nothing worked. People tell me he has a rare disease and there is no doctor who can cure it. His sister died like this, too . . ."

There was a roar from the baseball game on the radio. Kuhei muttered something but I couldn't catch what he said.

His mother spoke again.

"It seems that there's this guy named Shibata who can really run fast. He gets all excited when Shibata runs. You know baseball is the only thing he enjoys."

Mr. Yomogi picked up the thread of her conversation.

"Oh yes, Shibata. He really runs fast. They say he runs just like a deer. Kuhei, what do you think of Nagashima*?"

There was a lot of static on the radio. The boy rocked back and forth, as though the radio were the only thing he could hear, and turned the dial violently. Another popular song. The program was a singing competition. Mr. Yomogi hung in there. The song was over. And then Mr. Yomogi, the official from the Health Department, suddenly stood up and said, "Kuhei, why don't you come along with me and get on the bus."

The boy faced the radio and kept fumbling with the dial without looking around. He got the baseball game again. There was no doubt that he was paying attention to the game. Every time he heard a roar from the stadium, he flapped his thin, trouser-clad legs up and down as he sat cross-legged on the floor. In the meantime, he kept touching the radio with his quivering right hand, and his left hand over which he had some control. He was ready to turn the dial again if he needed to. His back was obviously squared towards the intruders, and he leaned forward, like a bow that is bent with the utmost effort of the body. The dial was his answer. It was the indication of his will. The radio was his weapon, and he embraced it. It looked as though he had transformed himself into a sensitive and cautious instrument that could detect lies.

His aging mother glanced at him with a glazed eye. She gave him no rebuke. As though nodding to herself, as though talking to herself, she spoke calmly.

"We won't be able to make ends meet if the condolence payment don't go up. But our Kuhei—if things were normal he'd be an adult already. Around here, as soon as a kid goes to junior high school he's a full-fledged fisherman. When it comes to the condolence money, though, he's considered a child. It's only 30,000 yen a year. I'm sorry. He likes baseball, you know. He spends the whole time listening like this because he can't do it himself. Really, radio is the only thing he enjoys in this whole world. He'll probably go when the baseball game is over. Isn't that right, Kuhei?"

Mr. Yomogi had been getting ready to leave. Now he was thinking that his performance as an official of the Health Department was developing some cracks under the stress of this strange situation, and that he was going to have to face things more philosophically. He sat down again. Singing

---

* A famous baseball player.

competitions, Shibata baseball players—he could keep Kuhei company with all of it.

Mr. Yomogi is a loyal public servant and a citizen of the City of Minamata. Like the young bus driver, Mr. Ōtsuka, he keeps his composure, but when he is with a Minamata disease victim he gives everything he has. The real reason for his philosophy is that the boy has pierced him to the bone. He even seems to feel as close to Kuhei as he does to his own blood relations.

He felt embarassed at his own sensitivity. He said, "Well, Nagashima's the best one around, isn't he. Well, it's over. Let's go, Kuhei."

And so forth; he was crying out to the boy.

Kuhei covered the dial with his hand. He finally made his answer in a heavy, mumbling voice without turning around.

"No, I don't want to. I'll be killed."

"Be killed? . . . no, there's no such thing. The distinguished doctors from Kumamoto University are here and they'll examine you. It'll be all right because I'll be with you."

"No. If I go I'll be killed."

For a while Mr. Yomogi couldn't remember what he had planned to say.

* * * * *

The Research Division of Kumamoto University has joined forces with the Rehabilitation Hospital of thc City of Minamata to fight against Minamata disease, and the hospital would make a bed available to Kuhei if only he would agree to the arrangement. When one considers the accomplishments and authority of the Research Division of Kumamoto University, and the fact that the Rehabilitation Hospital, opened in April of 1985, uses sophisticated techniques, Kuhei's remark about being killed is utterly unjust and absurd.

Nevertheless, it is obvious that the boy has been completely cut off from what should have been a promising future for him. He rejects the officials of the Health Department, which has been dealing with Minamata disease for generation after generation, and refuses to be examined or hospitalized.

That day, he glued himself to the popular songs in the singing contest, and then gained some time listening to the pro baseball game, in the same way that he had been able to befuddle his visitors on a previous occasion with a sumo wrestling program. Shrinking away as though he were about to be captured, he spit out "No, I'll be killed" under the pressure of the situation.

The physical agent of Minamata disease has been invading his brain cells for the last ten years, during the period of his active growth from age six to age sixteen. He has been living with this substance in his body and will clearly continue to do so until the end of his life. He has been fighting it—truly, every day he has fought it like a man thrown into a tiger's lair—but he has gone completely blind and can't move his hands, or his legs, or his mouth the way he wants to. People he has felt close to, such as his older sister, and his cousins who used to be his neighborhood playmates (a boy older than himself, and a girl who was younger), have been taken away to the hospital; that was where they all finally died.

The boy cannot help but think that he will be killed. What this signifies is that time is running out for Kuhei, and that he is completely trapped in the midst of this large-scale mercury poisoning scandal that goes along burying its strange and inhuman life-essence in graves as it erupts and continues to spread.

It is the trend of the times to feel that we should forget about Minamata disease, and that we should let it slip casually into a past that has never been fully explained. Kuhei has been left behind, alone, in this darkness that stealthfully continues to entomb him. It has already half succeeded.

"Yamanaka Kuhei is still alive. He doesn't know that I wrote about him in my book." Ishimure Michiko*

---

* From a letter to Christopher Stevens, December 1984.

Nuclear Power Plant Gypsies in High-Tech Society

Who permitted them to permit?

Albert Schweitzer, in pointing out that it was scientists who determined the "permissible dosage of irradiation."

by Yuki Tanaka*

Introduction

The severe overproduction crisis that struck Japan during 1974 and 1975, accompanied by sudden inflation, brought significant changes in employment policy throughout all sectors of Japanese industry. In their efforts to economize, companies reduced new recruitments, laid off workers, sought voluntary retirements, reduced overtime, retrenched seasonal and part-time workers, and cut back on the hiring of day laborers. Hardest hit were the workers at the bottom of Japanese industry, the temporary and day laborers—in 1975 roughly 14.4 percent of the Japanese work force.[1] Most of these workers were and still are in the forty-five to sixty-five-year-old age group.[2]

In the grim economic atmosphere of structural depression, the rapidly growing Japanese nuclear power industry has provided these retrenched workers with significant new job opportunities. As of October 1986 there were thirty-six nuclear reactors operating in Japan, with eleven under construction, five more planned, and a gigantic complex known as the Mutsu Ogawara Development in the initial planning stages for far northern Aomori Prefecture. Scheduled to begin operation in 1991, the Mutsu complex will include a spent-fuel reprocessing factory and two nuclear power plants. Many of the workers

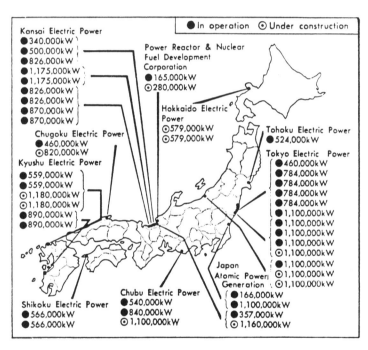

Nuclear reactors in Japan †

attracted to this growing industry have become known as *gempatsu jipushii* (nuclear power plant gypsies) because they wander from plant to plant seeking relatively highly paid jobs. They are often exploited, however, and their jobs are generally the most dangerous in the industry.

As will be explained in detail later, nuclear power companies must hire unusually large numbers of workers to keep their plants operating. The many temporary workers and day laborers needed for maintenance and repair of the plants are hired through an unusually complex recruitment system. A

* This article is based on a paper presented at the Japanese Studies Association of Australia Conference, La Trobe University, May 1985, and is an updated and shortened version of the article that was published in the *Bulletin of Concerned Asian Scholars,* Vol. 18, No. 1 (January–March 1986), 2–22. Another version of this article will be published in *Japanese Society: Modernization and Beyond,* edited by Gavan McCormack and Yoshio Sugimoto. Much of the information was made available to me by S. Saito and T. Shibano. To them I extend my most sincere appreciation; however, I accept full responsibility for the contents. I also wish to thank Kenji Higuchi for providing the photographs. (Editor's note: In this article the Japanese names are in the Western order, with the given name first and the family name second.)

† This map is from *Earth Island Journal* (San Francisco), Vol. 2, No. 2 (Spring 1987), 15.

Chart A

| Prime Contractors (Moto-Uke) | Subcontractors (Shita-Uke) | Sub-Subcontractors (Mago-Uke) | Laborer Suppliers (Nimpu-Dashi) |

Japan Atomic Power Co.
- Toshiba Plant
- Hitachi Plant —— Nishimaki Industries —— Inoue Industries —— Takeshi Umeda << —— Laborer
- Atomic Power Maintenance Co.
- Nuclear Power Industrial Group
- Kanden Industries

Diagram by Yuki Tanaka[4]

few big electric power companies, such as the Japan Atomic Power Company (JAPC), work closely with the five large nuclear power industry groups.[3] Each of the electric power companies makes a contract with several prime contractors to secure the work force needed by the power companies it is associated with. These prime contractors then require numerous subcontracting companies to recruit these workers for them. The subcontracting companies in turn employ sub-subcontracting companies to help with the recruiting, and these sub-subcontracting companies use labor suppliers who are often also workers (see chart A). In this system, as many as seven subcontractors may be involved in the hiring of one worker!

This recruitment system leads to the subcontracted workers being exploited in a number of ways. Each subcontracting company takes a percentage from the wages of the workers it has helped recruit, and workers' wages are typically reduced to one-quarter or less of what they would have been without these deductions.[5] In addition, prime contracting companies often exploit both their subcontracted and their full-time workers by withholding from them funds that have been provided for covering special expenses, such as overtime pay and housing allowances.[6] And when big businesses face bankruptcy, rather than meeting their obligations to their workers directly, they send their workers to nuclear power plants and have the subcontractors pay most of their wages.[7] Yakuza (Japanese Mafia) syndicates operate some of the subcontracting companies, and when this happens the subcontracted workers are even further exploited. Every hundred days or so nuclear power plants need thousands of extra workers for their regular inspections, and the Yakuza are especially involved in recruiting these extra workers.[8] The Yakuza syndicates sometimes use intimidation to get enough workers to fill the quotas,[9] and they finance themselves not only through the percentages they take from the workers' wages, but also through loans and drug sales to workers.

The number of subcontracted workers employed by nuclear power plants in Japan is increasing dramatically, from 1,675 in 1970 to more than 53,000 in 1986. Since 1971 subcontracted workers have made up over 80 percent of the work force of nuclear power plants in Japan, and in 1986 they made up over 90 percent of the work force. These workers are all unskilled and comparatively older, often ex-miners, day laborers, *buraku* (outcasts), farmers away from their homes during the slack season, and local retired workers. These *gempatsu jipushii* come to nuclear power plants seeking a good life for themselves through wages that are usually higher than those they can earn elsewhere, but they are being exploited in ways far more serious than the wage and benefit reductions already mentioned. They are endangering their health, and all too often risking their lives, exploited by an industry and technology that has hazards we are only beginning to understand. This article examines the difficulties and hazards these *gempatsu jipushii* face when they work at Japanese nuclear power plants, and explores the likely fate of these victims of high-tech society.[10]

Dosage of Irradiation

Why is it that nuclear power plants require such large numbers of temporary workers and day laborers? The answer is directly related to the high levels of radiation contamination inside the power plants. There is always a danger that workers will be exposed to high doses of radiation if they work beyond a certain length of time in areas of the plants where radiation levels are high. Thus electric power companies require as many laborers as possible so that jobs can be rotated in order to reduce the amount of radiation to which individual workers are exposed. The number of subcontracted workers has grown very rapidly not simply because of the increase in power plants, but also because radiation contamination at nuclear power plants worsens as time passes. Consequently it is necessary to increase both the number of subcontracted workers required during regular inspections and the number needed for everyday maintenance.

In order to understand the actual working conditions of nuclear power plant workers and the amount of radiation to which they are exposed, it is necessary to analyze the existing knowledge of radiation hazards to man. There are two units frequently used to gauge radiation levels, the rad and the rem, which are roughly equivalent. Japanese law regarding radiation hazards is based upon the advice of the International Committee for Radiation Protection. The law states that the "maximum permissible level of radiation dosage" over a period of three months is 3,000 millirems (i.e., 3 rems) for workers at nuclear power plants, and the annual *average* (not maximum) permissible level is 5,000 millirems (i.e., 5 rems). For ordinary people not engaged in work with radiation, the law stipulates a maximum of 500 millirems per year. U.S. regulations stipulate a seemingly similar 5,000 millirems (5 rems) per year for workers involved with atomic energy, but this is a *maximum* dosage, not an average dosage as in Japan. For an individual in the population at large, the U.S. regulations state that the maximum permissible level per year is 500 millirems (.5 rems), which is the same as Japan's, but then the U.S. regulations go on to recommend a maximum average of 170 millirems per person per year in any identifiable segment of the population at large, such as a particular city. This stricter regulation provides a greater degree of protection for the group as a whole because radiation is more hazardous for some people (babies and children, for example) than others; the lower maximum for the whole group will presumably give even these more vulnerable members of the group the protection they need.

These officially approved radiation hazard levels have remained the same in the U.S. even though as early as 1969 two prominent American biophysicists who worked for the Atomic Energy Commission predicted that accepting such levels could have dire results. At a meeting at the Institute for Electrical and Electronic Engineers in San Francisco, John Gofman and Arthur Tamplin presented the results of a study they had made of the expected deaths from cancer and leukemia resulting from exposure to various amounts of radiation. They predicted that:

> If the average exposure of the U.S. population were to reach the allowable 0.17 rads [170 millirems] per year average, there would, in time, be an excess of 32,000 cases of fatal cancer plus leukemia per year, and this would occur year after year.[11]

At the time these results were announced neither of these biophysicists was any longer a staff member of the U.S. Atomic Energy Commission, and they could thus be open in their criticism of the U.S. government and the nuclear industry as a whole. During the sixteen intervening years they haven't changed their views at all. In fact, both continue to claim that:

> No one has ever produced evidence that any specific amount of radiation will be without harm. Indeed, quite the opposite appears to be the case. All the evidence, both from experimental animals and from humans, leads us to expect that even the *smallest* quantities of ionizing radiation produce harm, both to this generation of humans and future generations. Furthermore, it appears that progressively greater harm accrues in direct proportion to the amount of radiation received by the various body tissues and organs.[12]

They further suggest that the present permissible level should be reduced to a maximum of 1.7 millirems. Moreover, their belief that there is no such thing as a pemissible level of radiation dosage is gaining increasing support among scientists working in this field.

To what extent are the Japanese subcontracted workers irradiated? According to my calculations, based upon official statistics published by the Bureau of Radiation Control, the annual average of 410 millirems per worker in 1978 is the highest on record. This is 241 times the permissible level that Gofman and Tamplin recommend. The annual average for the ten years between 1974 and 1986 is 292 millirems, over 170 times the level that Gofman and Tamplin suggest. Although these annual averages are very high when compared to the Gofman and Tamplin recommendations, they may seem surprisingly low when compared to the figures for irradiation dosages mentioned earlier, such as the average permissible level of 5,000 millirems per worker per year and the 300 millirems per week each worker may receive. The reason that

Table 1

Number of Nuclear Power Plant Workers

Year	A. Company Employees	B. Sub-contracted Workers	C. Total	B/C (%)
1970	823	1,675	2,498	67.1
1971	904	4,339	5,243	82.8
1972	1,056	4,753	5,809	81.8
1973	1,512	6.960	8,472	82.2
1974	2,076	10,282	12,348	83.2
1975	2,282	13,798	16,080	86.8
1976	2,555	17,241	19,796	87.1
1977	3,233	22,129	25,362	87.3
1978	3,578	30,577	34,155	89.5
1979	3,759	30,495	34,254	89
1980	3,976	31,978	35,954	88.9
1981	4,374	36,158	40,532	89.2
1982	4,688	35,941	40,629	88.5
1983	5,367	41,072	46,439	88.4
1984	5,784	45,726	51,510	88.8
1985	5,698	48,881	54,576	89.6
1986	5,735	53,131	58,866	90.3

Source: Tables 1, 2, and 3 were compiled by the author from information published in documents issued by the Bureau of Radiation Control, which is under the direction of the Ministry for Energy and Resources.

the average annual dosages are relatively low is that they are *average* dosages for *all* the subcontracted workers at Japanese nuclear power plants, and these averages thus include many unexposed subcontracted workers who are employed to do odd jobs in Areas A and B and are not engaged in the dangerous work in Area C. Even security officers are considered subcontracted workers and are included in these figures. In addition, most of the subcontracted workers working in Area C move from one nuclear power plant to another, and this means that some subcontracted workers are counted two and even three times in this official figure. Thus, although the figures for annual averages may seem relatively low, the actual irradiation dosages to which workers in Area C are exposed are much higher, and these exposed workers often exceed the Gofman and Tamplin recommended permissible levels by much more than the annual averages indicate.

It is interesting to note that although the average dosage of radiation to which an electric power company employee is exposed has decreased considerably over the years, the dosage to which subcontracted workers are exposed has remained about the same. Another important fact that can be detected from these official statistics is that prior to the worst period of the oil shock depression in 1975, the average irradiation dosage to which a company employee was exposed was much higher than that to which a subcontracted worker was exposed. However, in 1975 these levels became equal, and thereafter the situation was reversed. In 1986 the average irradiation

Table 2

Total Irradiation Dosage (rems for all workers)

Year	A. Company Employees	B. Sub-contracted Workers	C. Total	B/C (%)
1970	236	326	562	58
1971	370	896	1,266	70.7
1972	464	1,433	1,897	75.5
1973	596	2,098	2,694	77.9
1974	701	2,427	3,128	77.6
1975	716	4,283	4,999	85.7
1976	769	5,473	6,242	87.7
1977	726	7,399	8,125	91.1
1978	782	12,418	13,200	94
1979	858	10,872	11,730	92.7
1980	828	11,105	12,933	93.6
1981	785	11,933	12,718	93.8
1982	733	11,767	12,500	94.1
1983	661	11,206	11,867	94.4
1984	621	11,534	12,156	94.9
1985	572	11,933	12,505	95.4
1986	466	10,278	10,744	95.7

Table 3

Average Irradiation Dosage

Year	A. Company Employees	B. Subcontracted Workers	B/A (times)
1970	0.27	0.19	0.66
1971	0.41	0.21	0.51
1972	0.44	0.30	0.68
1973	0.39	0.30	0.77
1974	0.34	0.24	0.71
1975	0.31	0.31	1.0
1976	0.30	0.32	1.06
1977	0.22	0.33	1.5
1978	0.22	0.41	1.86
1979	0.23	0.36	1.57
1980	0.21	0.38	1.81
1981	0.18	0.33	1.83
1982	0.17	0.33	1.94
1983	0.12	0.27	2.25
1984	0.11	0.25	2.27
1985	0.10	0.24	2.40
1986	0.08	0.19	2.38

dosage to which the individual subcontracted worker was exposed was 2.38 times that of a company worker. If one considers the total irradiation dosage, it is clear that from the beginning subcontracted workers have been bearing well over 50 percent of the irradiation burden at nuclear power plants, and since 1977 well over 90 percent of the irradiation has been directed at these workers. (See tables 2 and 3, and graph 1.)

These facts indicate clearly that subcontracted workers are recruited specifically for work involving exposure to high levels of radiation, and that in such cases they act as substitutes for company employees, thereby lessening the health hazards for the latter. Thus these statistics reflect a deliberate decision by the electric power companies to foist the most dangerous jobs onto subcontracted workers and thereby avoid responsibility for problems that may arise from radioactive contamination. Because subcontracted workers constantly move from one plant to another, it would be very difficult to trace an overdose of radiation to a particular source, especially as the effects are rarely felt immediately. It should be emphasized further that when compared with first-hand information,[13] these official

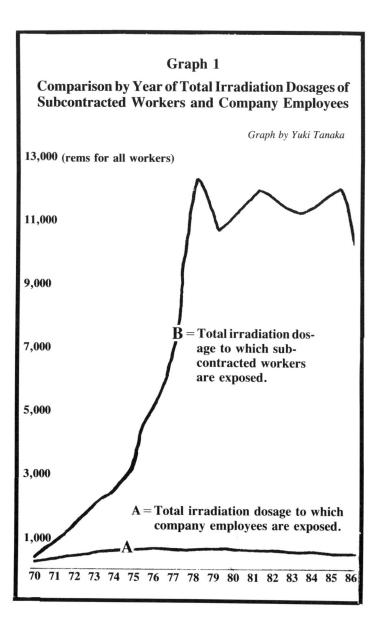

Graph 1

Comparison by Year of Total Irradiation Dosages of Subcontracted Workers and Company Employees

Graph by Yuki Tanaka

13,000 (rems for all workers)

11,000

9,000

7,000

B = Total irradiation dosage to which subcontracted workers are exposed.

5,000

3,000

A = Total irradiation dosage to which company employees are exposed.

1,000

A

70 71 72 73 74 75 76 77 78 79 80 81 82 83 84 85 86

statistics do not appear to represent accurately the actual amount of radiation to which nuclear power plant workers are exposed.

Workers' Safety Education

Legislation requires that prior to commencing actual work at a nuclear power station, subcontracted workers receive "safety education" on the work they are about to undertake. During special sessions a radiation control worker provides some information on radioactive materials and the hazards of irradiation, although this amounts to nothing more than the most basic facts. Indeed, the major content of the lectures is irrelevant to radiation and deals with such commonsense matters as the need to wear an ordinary safety helmet, which offers no protection against radiation. At some plants, subcontracted

cartoon by Gar Smith*

workers are given pamphlets on safety information to study and then are tested on their understanding of this information. There is evidence, however, that during the examination the correct answers are often dictated by a radiation control worker.[14] This so-called safety education is therefore nothing but a formality to qualify subcontracted workers officially so that they can begin work as soon as possible.

The details workers are given on radiation during these sessions is as follows. First, they are informed that their standard level of radiation dosage will be 100 millirems per day and 300 millirems per week. Most Japanese nuclear power plants take these figures as the set norm in order to keep the amount of irradiation subcontracted workers receive to within the government regulations, that is, to within 3,000 millirems (3 rems) in three months. However, the way in which "one week" is defined differs from one company to another. For example, at the Fukushima plant of the Tokyo Electric Power Company workers are officially instructed that the amount of irradiation should not exceed 300 millirems during any seven-day period. If the amount exceeds 300 millirems the worker is not allowed to work in the so-called controlled area for the following four days. At the Tsuruga plant of the JAPC, on the other hand, four days of every month—i.e., the 1st, 9th, 17th and 25th—are designated as checkup days. On each of these four days, the accumulated total irradiation of each worker is set back automatically to zero. Therefore, if, for example, a worker is exposed to 100 millirems of radiation every day for the three days between the sixth and the eighth of a particular month (i.e., a total of 300 millirems), he can still continue to work in the high radiation areas after the ninth because on that day his record reverts officially to zero.[15] Clearly, then, the safety regulations and associated education are somewhat haphazard and variable in regard to actual worker radiation exposures.

Workers' Garments and Equipment

The inside of a nuclear power plant is divided into two sections: the non-contaminated area (Area A), regarded as a radiation-free zone, and the contamination control area which is a highly irradiated zone. According to law, the so-called control areas are those registering a minimum of 30 millirems

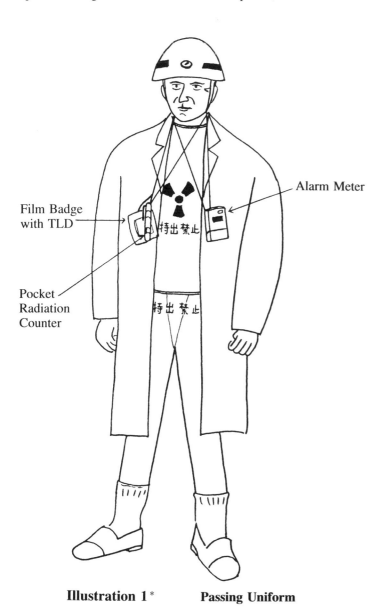

Film Badge with TLD

Pocket Radiation Counter

Alarm Meter

Illustration 1 *   **Passing Uniform**

* Illustrations 1–6 were drawn by the author based on illustrations in K. Horie, *Gempatsu Jipushii (Nuclear Power Plant Gypsies)* (Tokyo: Gendai Shokan, 1984) and in T. Shibano, *Gempatsu no Aru Fukei (A View of Nuclear Power Plants)* (Tokyo: Mirai-sha, 1983).

* This cartoon is from *Earth Island Journal* (San Francisco), Vol. 2, No. 2 (Spring 1987), 14.

during any one week. The buildings in this category are the concrete shield building (i.e., the nuclear reactor building), the buildings attached to this shield building, such as the turbine building, and the radioactive waste storage area. This control area is further divided into two sections: Area B (the secondary control area) which has a low level of contamination, and Area C (the primary control area) with high radioactive contamination. The concrete shield building and the nuclear waste storage building are classified as Area C.

When workers pass from Area B to Area C they go through a checkpoint. Before passing this checkpoint they must first use a nearby toilet, as there are no toilets inside Area C. Building of toilet facilities is prohibited in this area because of the high levels of radiation contamination. The workers then have to change into specially provided underwear (a long-sleeved singlet and longjohns), put on the socks provided, white overalls, a helmet, and special rubber shoes with steel covering over the toe area. (See illustration 1.) Having changed into this "passing uniform," they pick up an alarm meter (which beeps when the radiation reaches a certain level), a pocket radiation counter (a simple measuring instrument in the shape of a fountain pen), and a film badge with a TLD (thermo-luminescence dosimeter). The worker inserts the TLD into a reading machine which automatically records the level of radiation before entering Area C. When the worker returns to the checkpoint, the TLD is again inserted so that the difference in the level of radiation before and after working in Area C may be ascertained.[16] However, this TLD record is not usually checked unless the pocket radiation counter registers above a certain level of irradiation, usually 200 millirems.[17]

Thus equipped, the workers pass through a wooden-hinged door and walk along a corridor about 200–300 meters long to a changing room where they change into an Area C uniform. First, they take off the white overalls and put on an Area C uniform. An alarm meter, a pocket radiation counter, and a film badge with a TLD are placed in the inner pocket of the uniform. (See illustration 2.) They then put on another pair of socks, cotton gloves, rubber gloves over these, and a hood over a cloth cap. Sometimes they wear a garment made of paper called a "tie-back" over the uniform. They then put on another pair of rubber gloves and seal these tightly at the cuffs with gum tape. With the exception of the rubber gloves, none of the garments are waterproof. Finally, they put on a half-face mask in order to prevent their inhaling airborne radioactive elements. When working in highly contaminated areas such as in the pedestal directly under the nuclear reactor (see illustration 3) or in other parts of the dry well, a full mask or oxygen mask is worn. In order to enter Area C, workers then pass through an air-locked double steel door. The corridor before this door is called Matsuno Roka (Pine Corridor) by the workers. This name comes from the traditional Kabuki story *Chushingura*[18] and indicates that once you enter this corridor, you are in an area of great danger.[19] (See illustrations 4, 5, and 6.)

Working Conditions

Subcontracted workers in nuclear power plants are usually allocated the most dangerous work in the most contaminated areas. They are required to perform such tasks as pouring high-level liquid waste into drums, decontaminating nuclear waste tanks, changing waste collector filters, washing sludge from contaminated filter elements, cutting and changing pipes near

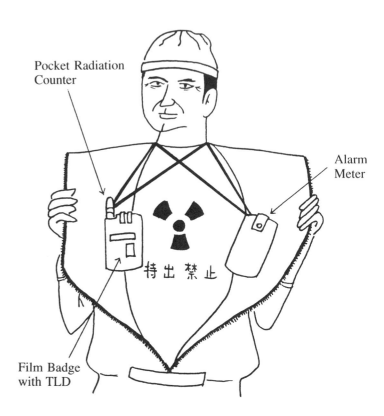

Illustration 2   **Area C Uniform**

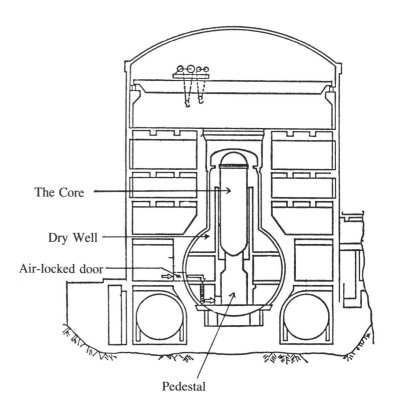

Illustration 3   **Concrete Shield Building**

the core vessel, removing radioactive dust from various parts of the pump, mopping up radioactive water, and washing work uniforms and underwear. All these jobs involve a high risk of exposure to excessive levels of radiation. Particularly during the regular inspection, the work carried out inside the dry well close to the core subjects workers to high levels of irradiation within a short time. In such cases, a worker's operation time is restricted to a few minutes or even a few seconds, so that even small jobs are done by rotating a few dozen workers. The workers refer to the teams of subcontracted workers involved in such operations as *tokko-tai* (suicide squads).

Theoretically, an alarm meter should warn workers of high levels of radiation, although in reality the system is far from perfect. There are various types of alarm meters, some with a set warning level and others with an adjustable warning level. These meters are distributed according to the danger levels at the site of each operation. When working in a

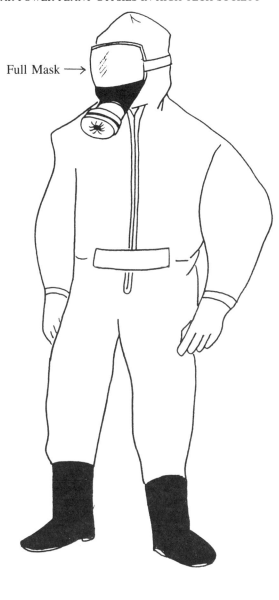

Full Mask →

Illustration 5   **Area C Uniform**

← Half-face Mask

Illustration 4   **Area C Uniform**

high-contamination area, workers are given alarm meters set with a higher warning level. However, if a worker does not specify a particular warning level when collecting the alarm meter at the checkcounter, he may be given the highest level one. A careless worker may not even be aware of the warning level on the alarm meter he is carrying.[20] But no matter what the warning level, if the meter battery is not properly charged, the alarm will not sound. Apparently inadequate charging is a frequent problem.[21]

Another problem arises when warnings sound in the middle of tasks and workers are instructed by their foremen to reset their meters so they may continue to work.[22] Similarly, when alarm meters sound it often happens that workers are unable to stop working owing to the nature of the operation in which they are engaged. The maximum warning level on alarm meters is usually 80 millirems. But in certain operations the radiation dosage is far beyond this maximum level. For

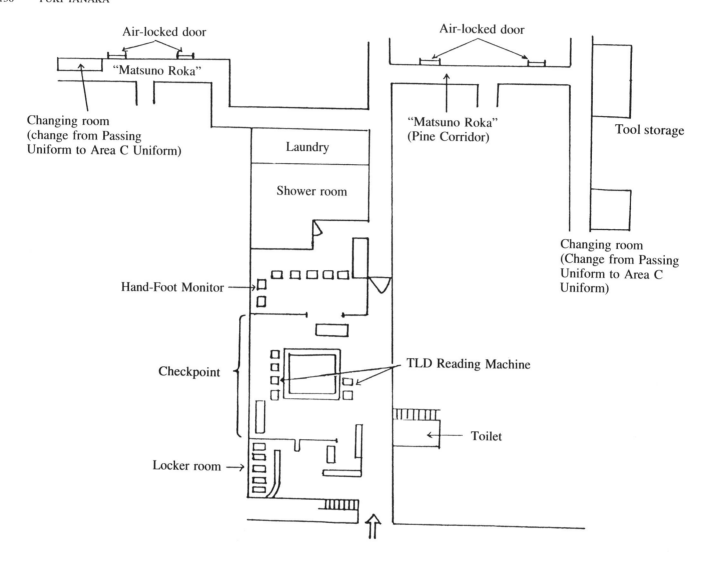

Air-locked door

"Matsuno Roka"

Changing room
(change from Passing
Uniform to Area C Uniform)

Laundry

Shower room

Hand-Foot Monitor →

Checkpoint

Locker room →

Air-locked door

"Matsuno Roka"
(Pine Corridor)

Tool storage

Changing room
(Change from Passing
Uniform to Area C
Uniform)

TLD Reading Machine

Toilet

Illustration 6

example, there is an area called the Torus sump-pit which contains highly irradiated sea water. Periodically, this area is cleaned thoroughly. First the surface fluid is removed, after which the remaining water is pumped out. Then the radioactive sludge at the bottom of the pit is scooped out and the pit itself is jet-washed. During this operation it is quite usual for workers to receive between 60–80 millirems of radiation and sometimes they are exposed to 110 millirems within a few minutes.[23] Carrying an alarm meter in such areas is no more than a formal gesture since the alarms are typically ignored.

In an attempt to maintain minimum irradiation dosages there are set levels of irradiation for each operation within the plants. It is assumed that when the total irradiation dosage to all the workers involved in a particular operation surpasses the set levels for that particular operation, the task will be temporarily stopped. However, in reality, the set levels of irradiation are often raised as the dosage to which workers are exposed increases.[24]

When workers return to the checkpoint after working in Area C, they themselves read the levels on the pocket radiation

counters and record these in notebooks. However, because electric power companies officially permit exposure amounting to only 100 millirems per worker per day, workers are often forced by their foremen to record false figures of around 70–80 millirems, even if the true reading is well over 100 millirems.[25] The main reason that workers readily obey the foremen's instructions is that if the irradiation dosage exceeds 300 millirems within one week, they will be prevented from working for the next few days. Because they are paid on a daily basis, their income diminishes according to the days they take off. Thus, although they are well aware of the danger, workers try to continue working at the nuclear power plants by forging records in this way.

As the figures recorded by the workers from the pocket radiation counters are frequently adjusted for the records, this tally naturally comes to differ considerably from the figures shown on the film badges that they wear. The latter are totalled every few weeks or monthly, and in some cases there is a difference of as much as 400 millirems in a single month.[26] In order to disguise this discrepancy so that they may continue to

Subcontracted workers busy near the core in the shield building*

work, workers often borrow film badges from others working in less dangerous areas. In extreme cases, they work in Area C without wearing their film badges.[27]

It is obvious that as far as dosages of irradiation are concerned, there is deliberate discrimination against subcontracted workers in order to protect the employees of the electric power companies and the prime contracting companies. By law, no worker may be exposed to more than 5,000 millirems (5 rems) per year, although the electric power companies and prime contracting companies stipulate that their employees (i.e., non-subcontracted workers) should not be irradiated over 1,500 millirems (1.5 rems) per year.[28] Moreover, while the irradiation dosage records of subcontractors are frequently and easily tampered with, relatively stringent checks on irradiation dosages are made on other employees. A further example of this is the routine undergone when workers leave Area C. It is standard practice for all workers to have a shower and receive an irradiation check. At the Fukushima plant of the Tokyo Electric Power Company there was, until recently, a discrepancy in the instruments used for monitoring irradiation. While subcontracted workers used only hand-foot monitors and a

simple small Geiger counter for the rest of the body, employees of the Tokyo EPC used the "gate monitor," which checks the entire body surface at once.[29]

In each nuclear power plant there are several workers called radiation control officers who are regarded as specialists on radiation. These people are usually employees of one of the prime contracting or subcontracting companies. Officially, it is their responsibility to monitor radiation levels in various areas within the plants and to control labor distribution in order to avoid irradiation of workers beyond the levels set by regulations. But this is nothing but an official policy, as the authority of these radiation control officers within labor management is virtually nonexistent. For example, these officers are never called to help plan operations within Area C. Typically, an operation in Area C is almost complete by the time they are told of it.[30] Indeed, monitoring radiation levels is often an extra task for these officers, who are normally expected to help subcontractors in various ways and to work with them.

If the radiation control officers are too strict in carrying out their radiation monitoring checks, they become disliked, not only by the electric power companies, but also by the subcontracted workers. It is the latter who suffer if officers claim that radiation levels in a particular area are excessive,

---

* All photos in this article are by Kenji Higuchi, courtesy of Yuki Tanaka.

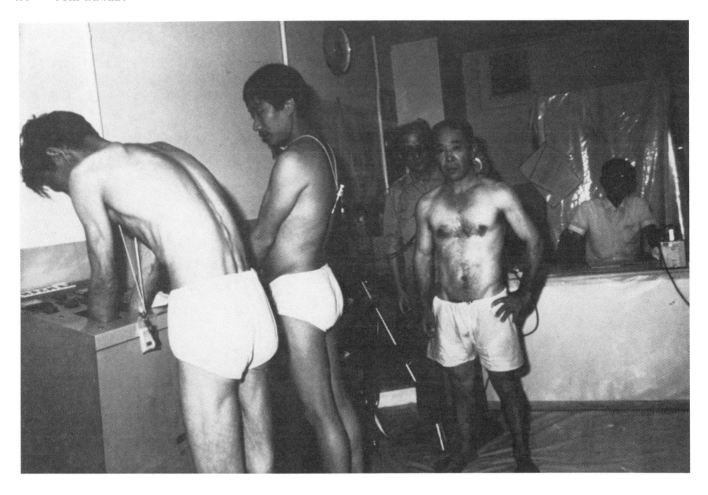

Subcontracted workers taking a routine check of radiation levels following the completion of the day's work

for they are required to carry out the decontamination work. Thus, here too, a deceptive method is often adopted. If after repeated decontamination treatment of a particular area it is impossible to reduce the level of radiation to that set by regulations, an officer generally asks subcontracted workers to clean only a small portion of the area requiring decontamination. When the radiation level of this small portion falls below the required level, decontamination work is officially declared complete.[31]

Internal Irradiation

Nuclear power plant workers face not only the physical danger of external irradiation, but also that of internal (inhaled or ingested) irradiation. Regulations demand that a half-face mask or full mask be worn in areas of high-level radiation and in dusty areas. However, those operations where masks are required are usually in areas close to the core—such as inside the dry well—where the temperature is very high. Because workers wear so much protective clothing, within a few minutes of beginning work they start to perspire profusely, have difficulty in breathing, and often experience severe headaches. In addition, steamy moisture builds up inside the full masks and makes it difficult to see one's work. Consequently, many

workers simply remove their masks, hang them around their necks, and continue their task, simultaneously inhaling radioactive gas.[32] It seems that the workers are more concerned with escaping from the immediate physical discomfort than they are worried about internal irradiation.

The danger of internal irradiation is exceedingly high among subcontracted workers who are engaged in laundry work, that is, the washing and drying of the uniforms, underwear, gloves, masks, and the like which are worn by workers assigned to dangerous areas. The workers collect the garments from special dumping bins, put them into plastic bags, and take them back to the laundry where they wash and dry them. Because uniforms are easily contaminated, workers have to change garments every time they change working areas. Each worker changes at least twice a day, once in the morning and once in the afternoon. In extreme cases, workers change four or five times a day. During regular inspections, in particular, the number of garments requiring washing increases greatly. At each barrier in Area C there are special bins designated for each item to be washed. Every time subcontracted workers from the laundry collect them (at least a few times a day) there is a danger of inhaling radioactive dust from the used garments. Normally, these workers do not wear a solid mask, but at best wear only a gauze mask to prevent

Table 4
Subcontracted Worker Deaths Related to Nuclear Power Plants
(July 1966–March 1977)

Nuclear Power Plant (Year operations began)	Accidental Deaths at Nuclear Power Plants		Deaths Resulting from Irradiation	
Japan Atomic Power Company Tokai Plant (1966)	Deaths from falls Other	2 2	Deaths from Cancer Deaths from Brain Damage Deaths from Heart Disease Other	8 6 1 3
Japan Atomic Power Company Tsuraga Plant (1970)	Deaths from falls Other	1 2	Deaths from Cancer Deaths from Brain Damage Deaths from Leukemia	4 2 1
Tokyo Electric Power Company Fukushima Plant (1971)	Deaths from falls Other	2 7	Deaths from Cancer Deaths from Brain Damage Deaths from Heart Disease Deaths from Leukemia	8 12 7 2
Chubu Electric Power Company Hamaoka Plant (1976)		0	Deaths from Cancer	3
Chugoku Electric Power Company Shimane Plant (1974)	Deaths from falls	1	Deaths from Cancer Other	2 2
Kansai Electric Power Company Mihama Plant (1970)	Deaths from falls Other	7 2	Deaths from Cancer Deaths from Brain Damage Deaths from Heart Disease	7 3 4
Kansai Electric Power Company Takahama Plant (1974)	Deaths from falls Other	2 3		0

Subtotals	Deaths from falls
	Other
		15
		16
			Deaths from:
			    Cancer
			    Brain Damage
			    Heart Disease
			    Leukemia
			    Other
				
				32
				23
				12
				3
				5

Total		31		75

Source: Based on the survey conducted by Y. Narazaki, published in *Asahi Shimbun* 17 March 1977.

inhaling dust. Of course, this does not adequately protect them from internal irradiation. Even washed garments sometimes retain radiation, so that there is still a possibility of suffering internal radiation when removing the garments from the dryer and putting them away.[33]

Internal irradiation is checked by a machine called a whole-body counter. Each worker's internal irradiation dosage is checked prior to taking up employment at a nuclear power plant, at the end of the contract, and once every three months in between. However, with this monitoring machine it is difficult to detect types of radiation from sources other than Manganese 54 and Cobalt 60. Alpha-rays and beta-rays, in particular, are impossible to monitor on this machine. Moreover, although electric power companies conduct checks with whole-body counters, they simply hand the detected *counts of radioactivity* to subcontractors and do not convert the results into *irradiation dosages*. Therefore, if no one in a subcontracting company knows how to convert the given data into irradiation dosages, the checks remain meaningless.[34]

Consequently, accurate figures of internal irradiation of nuclear power plant workers do not appear in official statistics. Once radioactive material is taken into the body, there is virtually no way to extract it. Thus it is almost impossible to estimate the quantities of irradiation to which these subcontracted workers are exposed, as they are constantly subjected to the danger of both internal and external irradiation. The only assumption one can make is that the official statistical data published by the Bureau of Radiation Control is not at all reliable. It is probably fair to assume that the true amount of irradiation subcontracted workers receive in any given period is several times greater than the amount recorded in the official statistics.

Irradiation and Cancer

It is not surprising, therefore, that the rate of cancer and leukemia occurring among subcontracted workers at nuclear power stations is extraordinarily high. In March 1977, Yanosuke Narazaki, a member of the lower house of the Japanese parliament, released the results of his own research into the causes of death of nuclear power plant workers.[35] (See table 4.) According to this survey, 106 subcontracted workers died during the ten years between July 1966 and March 1977, and seventy-five of these were due to some kind of illness. Of these seventy-five, thirty-two died from cancer or brain tumors and three deaths were due to leukemia. In other words, 46.6 percent of the workers died from diseases related to either cancer, brain tumors, or leukemia. This percentage is 2.3 times that for cancer and leukemia among the population at large. It should be noted also that this survey dealt only with already deceased workers, and that no investigation has ever been carried out into the large number of workers who are currently suffering from these types of diseases.

According to an internal report compiled in August 1984 by the nuclear power section of the Kansai Electric Power Company (which has nine nuclear reactors in Fukui Prefecture), between September 1983 and August 1984 three company employees died of cancer or leukemia, four employees are presently suffering from cancer or leukemia, and between 1978 and 1983 six subcontracted workers died of cancer. (See table 5.) According to one source, the death rate from cancer-related diseases among these subcontracted workers is six times that of the general population.[36] It should be noted that the Kansai EPC internal report does not include an investigation of how many subcontracted workers are currently suffering from this type of illness.

In 1984 Gempatsu Bunkai, the union organization for subcontracted workers at nuclear power plants, revealed the contents of this secret report to the public and criticized the abnormally high rate of cancer/leukemia patients among nuclear power plant workers.[37] In self-defense, the Kansai EPC claimed that the total irradiation dosage of an employee who died of cancer was between 200 and 1,300 millirems, and that that of a subcontracted worker who similarly died of cancer was between 20 and 4,050 millirems. The company further claimed that these figures were below the regulation permissible level of 5,000 millirems per year and 3,000 millirems for three months.[38] The company thereby denied any causal relationship between cancer-related diseases and irradiation. However, as has already been explained, the official records of irradiation dosages to which nuclear power plant workers are exposed are extremely unreliable.

It is also said that there are many cases of suicide among young workers at nuclear power plants. There is no statistical record of this problem, but most instances seem to be of unmarried or newly-married young men. It is believed that

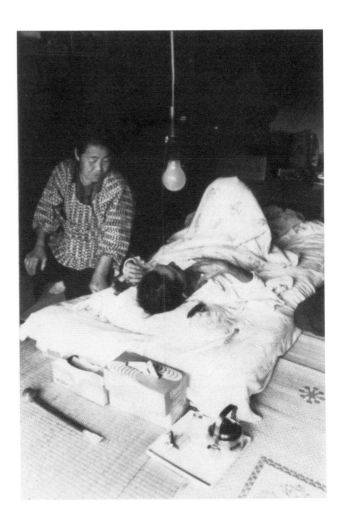

A former subcontracted worker who is currently suffering from cancer.

they are driven to this action by either the psychological pressure associated with difficulty in finding a marriage partner or the fear of producing a handicapped child because of exposure to radiation.

The wage that subcontracted workers at nuclear power plants receive is far from a reward for work, but could be called a special danger allowance. Because it is easy for subcontracted workers to gain relatively high wages for short working hours, they tend to spend their money gambling. In addition, in order to escape the psychological fears associated with irradiation, they tend to use drugs. Thus, Yakuza organizations further extend their control over subcontracted workers by lending money and selling drugs to them. In a vicious circle, the subcontracted workers are trapped into continuing to work at the nuclear power plants in order to pay back their debts. For subcontracted workers at nuclear power plants it is impossible to gain pleasure from work by learning new things and developing new skills. It is an anomaly that such premodern and unscientific modes of labor exist in the so-called high-tech industry of nuclear power. This situation vividly exposes the various contradictions of nuclear power technology.

Table 5

A. Deaths of Kansai EPC Employees (1983–1984)

Name	Age	Date of Death	Disease	Position
Mr. Shinzo Ishida	56	July 1984	Cancer of the Pancreas	Chief of the Repairs Section at Mihama Plant
Mr. A.	49	9 Dec. 1983	Acute Cardiac Insufficiency	Health Officer
Mr. Tsutomu Takagi	22	4 Dec. 1983	Leukemia	Operator at Mihama Plant
Mr. Takashi Yuhara	55	27 Sept. 1983	Leukemia	Chief of the Repairs Section in Ohi Plant
Mr. Kiyoshi Ito	40	23 Oct. 1979	Leukemia	Irradiation Control Officer at Mihama Plant

B. Kansai EPC Employees currently suffering from cancer-related diseases (August 1984)

Mr. B   (20s)   Brain tumor
Mr. C.   (50s)   Cancer of the bladder
Mr. D.   (30s)   Leukemia
Mr. E.   (20s)   Leukemia

C. Deaths of Subcontracted Workers Who Worked at Kansai EPC Power Plants (August 1978–October 1983)

Name	Age	Date of Death	Disease	Power Plant
Mr. Noboru Shimizu	54	7 Jan. 1982	Cancer of the Oesophagus	Mihama
Mr. Nobutada Kitagawa	56	Oct. 1983	Stomach Cancer	Mihama
Mr. Ryosuke Suzuki	56	1982	Liver Cancer	Mihama & other
Mr. Sakae Morimoto	58	10 Oct. 1978	Liver Cancer	Tsuruga & other
Mr. Takashi Yamazaki	38	1982	Liver Cancer	Tsuruga & other
Mr. Kenzo Nakajima	60	1 Aug. 1980	Stomach Cancer	Tsuruga & other

Source: Internal reports compiled in August 1984 by the nuclear power section of the Kansai Electric Power Company.

Notes

1. S. Nishikawa, "Sangyō Kozō no Henbō" (Changes in Industrial Structure), in *Kigyō to Rodō (Industry and Labor) (Juristo Sogō Tokushu,* No. 14, Yuhikaku, 1979), 66. "Temporary workers" are people under contract of less than one year and "day labourers" are people employed on a daily basis for the duration of several months. "Seasonal workers" are categorized, therefore, as "temporary workers."

2. Nishikawa, 69. The average age of the Japanese work force in 1985 is estimated at 41.3 years for males and 40.6 years for females.

3. H. Senda, *Enerugii Sangyōkai (The Energy Industry World)* (Tokyo: Kyoiku-sha, 1984), 202–205; K. Higuchi, *Yami ni Kesareru Gempatsu Hibakusha (Irradiated Nuclear Power Plant Workers Who Fade into Oblivion)* (Tokyo: Sanichi Shobo, 1984), 210–4.

4. This diagram is based on the case of a labor supplier, Takeshi Umeda, who in 1979 was exposed to a large dose of radiation while working at the Tsuruga Plant. The information is from T. Shibano, *Gempatsu no Aru Fūkei (A View of Nuclear Power Plants),* Vol. 1 (Tokyo: Mira-sha, 1983), 66. See also Brett de Bary's article in this volume, "Sanya: Japan's Internal Colony."

5. It is widely believed that in addition to the percentages withheld by prime contractors, subcontracting companies take percentages amounting to about 10,000 yen per worker per day. This information is from Gempatsu Bunkai, *Gempatsu Nyusu (Nuclear Power Plant News),* No. 1 (1981) and was mentioned by S. Saito, chairman of Gempatsu Bunkai, during an interview conducted by the author in 1985 in Tsuruga in Japan.

6. S. Morie, *Gempatsu Hibaku Nikki (The Diary of an Irradiated Nuclear Power Plant Worker)* (Tokyo: Gijutsu to Ningen, 1982), 158–60.

7. K. Horie, *Gempatsu Jipushii (Nuclear Power Plant Gypsies)* (Tokyo: Gendai Shokan, 1984), 107; *Shukan Posto,* 17 November 1978.

8. T. Shibano, *Gempatsu no Aru Fukei,* 160.

9. *Fukui Shimbun,* 1 February 1980.

10. For an earlier article on this same subject that includes a detailed presentation of the opinions of subcontracted workers, see Junko Yamaka, "The Hidden Foundations of Nuclear Power: Radiation and Discontent for Subcontracted Workers," *AMPO,* Vol. 13, No. 4 (1981), 46–52. See also "Voices from the Darkness: Books on Work Inside Nuclear Power Plants," *AMPO,* Vol. 12, No. 1 (1980). ED.

11. J.W. Gofman and A.R. Tamplin, *Poisoned Power: The Case Against Nuclear Power Plants Before and After Three Mile Island* (Emmaus, PA: Rodale Press, 1979), 78–9.

12. Gofman and Tamplin, 74–75. Regarding the debate about setting a permissible level of irradiation dosage, see Chap. 2 in *Nuclear Power: Both Sides—The Best Arguments For and Against the Most Controversial*

Technology, ed. by M. Kaku and J. Trainer (New York: W.N. Norton & Company, 1982), 27–79. The critical views of Japanese scientists on this issue can be found in the following works: S. Ichikawa, *Idengaku to Kakujidai (Genetics and the Nuclear Age)* (Tokyo: Shakai Shisō-sha, 1984); M. Taketani (ed.), *Genshiryoku Hatsuden (Nuclear Power)* (Tokyo: Iwanami, 1976); and S. Nakajima and I. Anzai, *Genshiryoku o Kangaeru (On Nuclear Power)* (Tokyo: Shin Nippon Shuppan, 1983).

13. Obtained during an interview conducted by the author with subcontracted workers in Tsuruga in January 1985.

14. S. Morie, *Gempatsu Hibaku Nikki,* 44 and K. Horie, *Gempatsu Jipushii,* 250–52.

15. K. Horie, 250.

16. K. Horie, 148–52.

17. S. Morie, *Gempatsu Hibaku Nikki,* 124.

25. S. Morie, *Gempatsu Hibaku Nikki,* 117, and also mentioned by S. Saito during an interview conducted by the author in Tsuruga in January 1985.

26. S. Morie, 134.

27. S. Morie, 120–1; Shibano, *Gempatsu no Aru Fūkei,* 64–65; Han Genshiryoku Hatsuden Jiten Henshu Kai, Vol. 1, 261.

28. S. Morie, *Gempatsu Hibaku Nikki,* 148.

29. K. Horie, *Gempatsu Jipushii,* 156–7 and his "Gempatsu no Uchi to Soto" (Inside and Outside Nuclear Power Plants) in *Rodosha no Sabaku (Labourers in the Desert)* ed. by E. Watanabe (Tokyo: Tsuge Shoso, 1982), 154–5.

30. S. Morie, *Gempatsu Hibaku Nikki,* 129 and 154–5.

31. S. Morie, 31, 89 and 223–4.

32. S. Morie, 183–84; K. Horie, *Gempatsu Jipushii,* 183 and 278–83; Higuchi, *Gempatsu Hibakusha,* 126–7.

Nuclear power plant looming in the background while local people enjoy a swim in Mihama Bay.

18. In this famous story, two fighting warlords met in the Pine Corridor of Edo Castle. During the ensuing encounter, one was injured. This event has brought about the association of dangerous places with the Pine Corridor.

19. K. Horie, *Gempatsu Jipushii,* 152–155.

20. K. Horie, 95.

21. S. Morie, *Gempatsu Hibaku Nikki,* 102.

22. S. Morie, 102; Shibano, *Gempatsu no Aru Fūkei,* 25–6 and also mentioned by S. Saito during an interview conducted by the author in Tsuruga in January 1985.

23. S. Morie, *Gempatsu Hibaku Nikki,* 118–120.

24. K. Horie, *Gempatsu Jipushii,* 107; Han Genshiryoku Jiten Henshu Kai, *Han Gempatsu Jiten (The Anti-Nuclear Encyclopedia), Vol. 1* (Tokyo: Gendai Shokan, 1978), 25.

33. S. Morie, *Gempatsu Hibaku Nikki,* 49 and 53–55.

34. S. Morie, 79–81, 207–9. For a more detailed scientific analysis of the effects of internal irradiation, see I. Anzai, *Karadano Nakano Hoshano (Radiation in the Human Body)* (Tokyo: Godo Shuppan, 1979).

35. *Asahi Shimbun,* 17 March 1977.

36. *Fukui Minshu Shimbun,* 25 August 1984.

37. Document obtained by the author from S. Saito in January 1985; *Fukui Shimbun,* 30 and 31 August 1984; *Asahi Shimbun,* 27 October 1984. For further details regarding subcontracted workers suffering from cancer, see Higuchi, *op. cit., Gempatsu Hibakusha* 7–143, and his *Photo Document: Japan's Nuclear Power Plant's Photo* (Tokyo: Origin Shuppan, 1979), 11–49.

38. *Fukui Shimbun,* 31 August 1984.

Contributors

Bernard Bernier received his Ph.D. in anthropology from Cornell University and is now a professor in the Department of Anthropology at Université de Montréal. He is the author of *Breaking the Cosmic Circle: Folk Religion in a Japanese Village* (1975). He has done research on various aspects of Japan's development and has published articles on religion, industrialization, labor relations, factory automation, and nationalism in Japan.

Janet Bruin is a social worker, writer, and peace activist. She edits *Pax et Libertas*, the journal for the Women's International League for Peace and Freedom, Geneva.

Brett de Bary received her Ph.D. in Japanese literature from Harvard University and is presently teaching Japanese literature at Cornell University. She has published *Three Works by Nakano Shigeharu* (1979) and other articles and translations in the area of modern Japanese literature.

John W. Dower is the Joseph Naiman Professor of History and Japanese Studies at the University of California, San Diego. His most recent book, *War Without Mercy: Race and Power in the Pacific War*, won the 1986 National Book Critics Circle prize for general nonfiction.

Hayashi Kyoko grew up in Nagasaki and Shanghai and experienced the Nagasaki bombing on August 9, 1945, while at work as a mobilized student (age fifteen). First recognized for an autobiographical story, "Matsuri no Ba" (The Ritual of Death, 1973, Akutagawa prize, translated into English by Kyoko Selden), her most important works, all related to the atomic bomb or Shanghai experiences, include *Giyaman Bidoro* (Cut Glass and Blown Glass, 1978), *Shanghai* (1983, Women Authors Award), and *Michi* (The Path, 1985).

Kamada Sadao is a professor of French literature at the Nagasaki Institute of Applied Science. He edits the annual journal *Shogen: Hiroshima-Nagasaki no koe* (Testimonies: Voice of Hiroshima and Nagasaki).

Joe Moore is currently lecturer in Japanese politics in the School of Modern Asian Studies at Griffith University in Queensland. He is co-editor of *The Japan Reader*, author of *Japanese Workers and the Struggle for Power, 1945–1947*, and former managing editor of the *Bulletin of Concerned Asian Scholars*. In 1988 he will be taking up the post of associate professor in the Department of Pacific and Asian Studies at the University of Victoria, British Columbia.

Susan Phillips has an M.A. in Japanese literature from the University of British Columbia, where her thesis was on Miyamoto Yuriko. She currently works as a Japanese-language announcer-producer for the Japanese Service of Radio Granada International (Canadian Broadcasting Corporation).

Tamae Prindle received her Ph.D. in East Asian Literature from Cornell University. She now teaches Japanese language and literature at Colby College. She is the translator/editor of the forthcoming book *Japanese Business Novels*.

Stephen Salaff is a Toronto freelance writer on science and world affairs. He is conducting long-term research on the Hiroshima, Nagasaki, and Bikini disasters and their after-effects.

Kyoko Selden is a translator working in Ithaca, New York. She received a Ph.D. in English from Yale University and has taught English, Japanese, and comparative literature in Japan and the United States. Her translations include *Stories by Contemporary Japanese Women Writers* (with Noriko Mazuta Lippit, 1982), *Geisha* (by Liza Dalby, 1985) and *Saino o Ikasu* (by Susan Grill, 1987).

Ikkō Shimizu made his debut as a business novel writer with *The Stock Market* (*Shōsetsu Shima*) in 1966. He has since written many novels on a wide variety of business activities. He is now recognized in Japan as the father of the so-called enterprise novel (*kigyō shōsetsu*).

Rob Steven is a senior lecturer in political science at the University of Canterbury, Christchurch, New Zealand. He is the author of *Classes in Contemporary Japan* (1983), and his current research is on present-day Japanese imperialism in Southeast Asia.

Christopher Stevens graduated from the College of Arts and Sciences at Cornell University and subsequently undertook Japanese language study there. He has been living in the Tokyo area since 1984 and is currently working as a professional freelance translator.

Yuki Tanaka was born in Japan and educated in Japan, England, and Australia. He previously taught at the University of Tasmania and is presently a lecturer in political economy of postwar Japan at the University of Adelaide.

E. Patricia Tsurumi is an associate professor of history at the University of Victoria, British Columbia, and is a member of the editorial board of the *Bulletin of Concerned Asian Scholars*. She is currently doing research on, among other things, Japanese colonialism in a comparative focus and the history of Japanese women.

Daizen Victoria, who was a graduate student in Oriental languages at the University of California, Los Angeles, in the early 1980s, is a Buddhist priest in the Soto Zen tradition.